"Relentlessly fascinating! Hank, the high priest of catch-it-and-cook-it, has given us his bible. A work of reverence, humility, and passion, he invites us on enviable adventures and offers culinary inspiration. From tips on using every delicious part of a fish to sermons on quality and how to handle one's catch, this is an insightful and essential kitchen guide for anglers and seafood lovers alike."

—**BARTON SEAVER**, chef and author of *American Seafood* and *The Joy of Seafood*

"Hank Shaw is the rare confluence of accomplished chef, exceptional writer, and salty fish nerd. As a result, *Hook, Line, and Supper* is a raft ride of a read, teeming with useful information and delicious, easy-to-follow recipes. I'm hooked!"

—**ANITA LO**, award-winning chef, Top Chef Masters contestant, cookbook author, culinary host, and damn good angler

"Hank Shaw has created not just a cookbook but a sort of manifesto—or to use his own word, a 'codex'—on seafood cookery. But the brilliance of this book is that it somehow miraculously offers indispensable tips and tidbits of information that will as easily assist the novice as titillate the seasoned piscivore. The crispness of the prose, the salty wisdom in the anecdotes, and the superb photographs elevate this book into something beyond the genre. If Poseidon has a cookbook, *Hook Line, and Supper* is it."

—**KIRK LOMBARD**, owner of Sea Forager and author of *The Sea Forager's Guide to the Northern California Coast*

"Where has this book been all my life!? *Hook, Line, and Supper* is a complete guide for fish lovers around the world. From sourcing and processing to pairing and delicious recipes. I've officially found my new handbook."

—**APRIL VOKEY**, founder of Anchored Outdoors

HOOK, LINE, AND SUPPER

HOOK, LINE, AND SUPPER

NEW TECHNIQUES AND MASTER RECIPES FOR EVERYTHING
CAUGHT IN LAKES, RIVERS AND STREAMS, AND AT SEA

Hank Shaw

Photographs by **HOLLY A. HEYSER**

H|H

This book is dedicated to the memory of my stepfather Frank Kilpatrick, 1932–2001.

Frank's the reason I can not only talk with anyone and everyone, but also why I enjoy it. He's the reason I love the New York Giants, hoisting one at my local bar, and—most importantly—why I love fishing so much.

Published by
H&H Books | huntgathercook.com
All H&H books may be purchased for business or promotional use or for special sales.
For information, please write to: Special Markets Dept., H&H Books, P.O. Box 2984, Orangevale, CA 95662; or email hank@huntgathercook.com, attention Special Markets.

Design and layout: Laura Shaw Design, Inc.
Food and prop styling: Hank Shaw and Holly A. Heyser
Editorial: Richard Feit Editorial
Fish icons: Allison Meierding
Photo credits: Tyson Fick, pages 6 and 33; Deirdre Meehan, page 8; Elizabeth Cornaro, page 330; Hank Shaw, pages 14–16, 25, 30, 55, 58 (top photo), 63–65, 71–72, 86, 93, 112, 152, 166, 201, 217, 219, 238, 256, 277, 288, 301, and 320.

ISBN-10: 0996944826
ISBN-13: 978-0996944823

2 3 4 5 6 7 8 9 10

Printed in the United States of America

Library of Congress Cataloging-in-Publication Data is available.

CONTENTS

Foreword 7
Preface 11

PART ONE BASICS

1. Getting to Know Fish 14
2. Getting Your Fish 21
3. Getting to Know *Your* Fish 35
4. Prepping Your Catch 39

PART TWO COOKING

5. Pairings and Freestyling 64
6. Broiling and Baking 70
7. Poaching 86
8. Searing, Sautéing, and Stir-Frying ... 93
9. The Art of Frying Fish 112
10. Steaming 140
11. Sandwiches and Other Handheld Things ... 152
12. Soups, Stews, Stocks, and Broths ... 166
13. Fritters, Cakes, and Balls 202
14. Grillin' and Chillin' 219
15. Pasta, Risotto, and Other Starches ... 238
16. Salads, Cold Dishes, and Leftovers ... 256
17. I Like it Raw 274
18. Salt, Smoke, and Time 288
19. Oddities and Fun Stuff 320

Acknowledgments 330
Index 331

FOREWORD

MOST PEOPLE WHO know me know me as a wild-game chef, not a fish and seafood cook. Truth is, long before I ever picked up a shotgun or a rifle—for twenty-five years at least—I was catching, cooking, and eating fish, both professionally and at home. I love hunting, and I spend much of my time doing it. But if I had to choose between fishing and hunting, fishing—and gathering seafoods—would win hands down. Digging clams and catching flounder are some of my earliest memories, and they remain some of the best from my childhood. Fish and seafood are just part of my DNA. This is probably why of all my cookbooks (this is my fifth), this has been the hardest to write. Where does one start with something that is so vastly familiar?

Some things about me you should know. I was born and raised in New Jersey, from a Massachusetts mother so Yankee her picture should be next to that word in the dictionary. Her upbringing in Ipswich, near the famous port of Gloucester, sealed my salty fate. She and my late stepfather, Frank Kilpatrick, were my fishing mentors. To be sure, I fished with my father a bit too, but it was less frequent when I was young.

Mom, Frank, and occasionally my brother and sisters would come fishing, often out of Manasquan or Point Pleasant. Our boat? The *Norma K III*, a venerable party boat built in 1975. She was brand new when I first sailed on her, and I am proud to say she still heads out most days, weather permitting.

Sailing on a party boat, sometimes called a head boat, is like riding on a bus where all the passengers are fishing. You pay your fare, and you're in. You can often rent rods and tackle, too, and the deckhands will fillet your fish for you afterward. The wonderful thing about these boats—and they're all over the country, wherever there are large bodies of water to fish and cities nearby—is that you meet every sort of angler. I've fished with Chinese immigrants and old-timers both black and white, with an expert retiree who fishes every week and newcomers who didn't know how to bait a line. I've fished with southerners and northerners, foreigners and locals. If you're an affable angler with a gift for gab and a willingness to trade stories, there's a world of learning available on these humble cruises, an intercultural goldmine of tips and lore about how to catch the fish you're after and how to cook them when you get home.

From my Chinese fellow anglers, I learned about steamed fish. Sounds boring—until they let you in on the part where you drizzle roaring hot chile oil over the fish at the table. A venerable

▲ Catching a triggerfish off Long Island, New York, around 1990.

Korean War vet was the first to school me in the importance of temperature when frying (if you've read my first book, *Hunt, Gather, Cook*, this is the same guy who taught me about oyster toads). I first heard about wrapping fish in banana leaves from an old Cuban who fled Castro to come work as a clerk in Newark, New Jersey. This was my real schooling. Far more than the algebra and the Latin I was forced to take, this is the education I remember.

I later took a job as a deckhand aboard the *Laura Lee*, out of Captree, near Bay Shore, Long Island. The *Laura Lee* still fishes, too. I worked just a single summer on that boat, but what I learned there has stayed with me to this day—patience (especially on those half-day trips where inexperienced fathers would tell their sons wildly incorrect information about fishing) and pain tolerance (I lost track of how many times I was accidently hooked by a customer). But I was meeting people from everywhere and of all kinds, and learning all the way.

It was as a deckhand that I developed my love for the unloved—sea robins, dogfish, mackerel, bergalls. Trash fish. These were fish the customers didn't want, but in many cases, they were going to die anyway, so I kept them and cooked them myself. I learned that not every fish is good fried. I learned that a broth made from carcasses, often with some little calico crabs tossed in—a side benefit from a day spent drinking beer and catching the larger blue crabs—can make store-bought ramen noodles worthy of serving to a guest. I've dug clams for money, worked in a restaurant where my only job was to clean fish, graduated to the fish station in another restaurant, and specialized in the fish and seafood dishes—few that they were—at an Ethiopian restaurant in Madison, Wisconsin.

As an underpaid young reporter, I lived for years off the fish and seafood I could bring back. Once, I boasted to a bartender that I could bring home something to eat every time I went out. The boast became a bet: if I succeeded, free beer for a month; if I failed, the bar tab for a night was on me. Since few things sharpen the mind quite like the prospect of financial ruin, I learned fast—about whitebait, a British name for tiny fish floured and fried; about pufferfish, eaten in the Northeast, which quickly became one of my standards; and about eel, which, as my bait for striped bass that refused to bite, was the only fish coming home with me that night. I learned how to kill them (not as easy as it might seem) and how fantastic they are as a dish—white as a blizzard, firm, and oily in a good way.

Every year and in every place I've ever lived—and I've lived in six states over the years—I've fished religiously. I even fished on my honeymoon. When my bride got seasick, we dropped her back at the dock, and I went back out to fish. (I bet you're thinking the marriage didn't last. It didn't.) But that's how driven an angler I was. And am. And probably always shall be. I live for it.

Nowadays, I follow the seasons closely, booking trips months in advance to catch California halibut and sturgeon. My late-spring calendar is anchored

▲ Miss Harlequin the cat gets an anchovy.

by the annual shad run, along with a spring trip to the Gulf of Mexico. I log all the good tides at my clamming spots six months out. I've even returned to the deck. For several summers, I helped my friend Tyson Fick, who runs the fishing vessel *Heather Anne*, a gillnetter based out of Juneau, Alaska. It's just the two of us—him the captain, me the deckhand—hauling nets for salmon. And while I am a little old to be a commercial deckhand, I've looked forward to fishing there every year.

And every year, I learn new things. Just a few years back, my friend Joe Baya, a former deckhand in Alabama who now runs the magazine *Great Days Outdoors*, showed me a better way to take collars from big bony fish like lingcod, a method he uses for red snapper. And until Tyson hammered it

into my head that first summer on his boat, I had no idea that when you pick up a large fish by the tail instead of the head, you can damage the meat.

Mastering the handling, care, and cooking of fish and seafood—to say nothing of the actual catching, which is beyond the scope of this book—is a journey. My hope is to share my own journey in these things and to help you become a better fish and seafood cook, whether you're seasoned or just starting to find your way. Fish is surprisingly easy to cook once you get your feet wet. Ready to dive in?

Hank Shaw
Orangevale, CA
March 2021

PREFACE | Simplicity

THINK OF YOUR finest fish dinners. A trout, caught minutes before, over an open fire in the woods. Porgies or sheepshead or Pacific rockfish, scaled, slashed a few times to open them up, bathed in olive oil, dusted with salt, and grilled to perfection—at the beach or in your backyard. A Friday night fish fry, or a Door County fish boil.

Keep thinking, but go higher-end: sushi, especially nigiri, its highest form—just fish and rice.

Here's the thing: with few exceptions, fish done best is done simply. A masterfully seared fillet. The perfect poach. Minimalist ceviche or crudo. Smoked salmon kissed by little more than salt, smoke, and maybe, just maybe, a little hint of something sweet. Most fish and seafood recipes are basically a piece of fish or seafood, cooked in a simple way, put next to something good to eat alongside. With fish, technique is the key that unlocks simplicity's magic. Can you add complexity? You can, especially when it comes to soups and stews. But if your technique is sound, smoked fish with twenty ingredients will never be better than smoked fish with just the right two.

What you have in your hand, then, is a different sort of cookbook. It's a book largely of techniques and methods. Sure, there are plenty of actual recipes here. But my goal is not to impress you with lots of fancy dishes. Rather, it's to help you crack the code of fish and seafood cookery. This book revels in the simple, not the easy. There is a difference. Some of these preparations require a bit of time or some equipment you might not have. But most are undemanding. Of all the books I've written, this is the one with the greatest number of recipes that can be done in thirty minutes on a work night.

You will find whole sections on techniques: frying, poaching, raw fish, cured fish, grilling, smoking and barbecuing, and soups and stews. There will be recipes in each section, but they are master recipes, designed to be applied as methods, transferrable to other fish and seafood with similar characteristics. Here, I'm far more interested in helping you master beer-battering, or smoking, or ceviche, so you can let the fish in front of you inspire its preparation. There will also be some sauces that I myself return to over and over, as well as a whole section on pairings—ingredients that work well with various types of fish and seafood.

Think of this book as a codex, a master class on fish and seafood cookery. It will enable you to develop your own recipes that suit your time, your place, your season, and your taste.

Onward!

◀ The docks at Cordova, Alaska, in 2012.

An alpine lake in the Canadian Rockies, loaded with brook trout.

PART ONE

BASICS

1
GETTING TO KNOW FISH

FISH IS HEALTHY

Fish and seafood are some of the healthiest foods you can eat. They are all high in protein and loaded with the healthiest animal fat there is. As my friend and colleague Barton Seaver says, "Bottom line is that in America, the relative lack of omega-3s in our diet contributes to an epidemic of preventable diseases. Consuming seafood, especially those rich in omega-3s, at least two times per week is so essential to our wellness that the three S's of public health should be 'Wear your seatbelt. Don't smoke. Eat seafood.'"

Ah, those fabled omega-3 fatty acids. They are abundant in the salmon and trout family and in the little silver fishes—sardines, anchovies, and mackerel. Interestingly, both oysters and swordfish are also high in these fats, as is sablefish (black cod), whose other market name, butterfish, says it all. Other fish with decent amounts of omega-3 fatty acids include pollock, seabass, walleye, tuna, tilefish, crabs, mussels, and squid.

What's the big deal? Omega-3 fatty acids improve your immune system by fighting inflammation within the body, and evidence exists that they can boost your sense of well-being. The American Psychiatric Association recommends eating fatty fish and seafood as one way to stave off depression. Seriously. It sounds crazy that regularly eating salmon or mackerel or oysters will keep you happier, but there's plenty of science to back it up.

There is also good science behind the old adage that fish and seafood are "brain food." A substance in fish called docosahexaenoic acid, which you will see as DHA, helps human brain development in a variety of ways, from memory retention to the ability to learn. And omega-3 fatty acids' ability to fight systemic inflammation means eating them will help keep you healthy, to the point where a study from the Harvard School of Public Health and the University of Washington found that older adults who had the highest blood levels of the omega-3 fatty acids found in fish lived, on average, 2.2 years longer than those with lower levels. I'm betting that those older adults who caught their own fish lived even longer. Anyone who fishes can tell you how it is at once relaxing and exciting. Not much better than that.

SUSTAINABILITY

One of the primary reasons people get all balled up about eating fish and seafood is sustainability. Most of us don't want to eat an endangered species and don't want to contribute to the destruction of the oceans. So you start looking into it, and soon you fall into the abyss. Which fish is good to eat?

Who is a fair arbiter? Some of the so-called watchdog groups shake down fisheries to gain the magic seal of approval. On the other side, some allegedly sustainable purveyors are peddling fish that are not what they say they are or are from red-listed fisheries. Are farmed fish evil or our savior? Should we really *never* eat bluefin tuna or codfish? Is it true that the red snapper in our fish markets is likely not red snapper at all? Or that there are buckets of mercury in our fish? Or worms?

It's enough to make you reach for the chicken.

RULES TO LIVE BY

But there are two simple rules to live by that will cut through most—not all—of the noise and send you on the path to righteousness.

RULE NUMBER ONE: CATCH IT YOURSELF

In general, fishing laws in the United States, Canada, Australia, New Zealand, and the United Kingdom are restrictive enough to keep a resource in decent shape. Yes, it's not perfect, and there are lots of places where things went south, but if you are an angler who follows the law, you are generally in good shape.

RULE NUMBER TWO: BUY AMERICAN

Again, in general, American commercial fisheries are among the most sustainable in the world. Europe does a good job, too, and even Canada and Mexico aren't terrible—at least compared to, say, Vietnam, Russia, and China. A great example of this is shrimp. American-caught shrimp are far more sustainable than the cheap farmed ones in Southeast Asia. Ditto for American catfish versus swai or the other Asian catfish. Same goes for my least favorite fish of all, tilapia. If you can buy American tilapia, it will be a far better product for the environment than tilapia farmed anywhere else. And with a nod to the state where I fish commercially: all of Alaska's fisheries are sustainable—by law. So if you see that it's Alaskan, buy it.

Real fish warriors will say—rightly—that this is far too simplistic. But the only real alternative is to become a student of fisheries. An example: Canadian trawl-caught codfish is wildly unsustainable. But New England hook-and-line codfish is perfectly fine. Chilean seabass is a no-go everywhere but from South Georgia Island, in the Falklands. So if you see Chilean seabass with a United Kingdom country of origin, it's OK. And all this could change by the time you read these sentences. Fisheries sustainability is a moving target in terms of species, region, gear choice, and more.

AMERICAN FISH FARMING

A side note to my buy-American recommendation is that our domestic aquaculture is some of the most tightly regulated in the world and is generally recognized as a net positive—unlike, say, the open-water salmon farms of Canada or the Southeast Asian shrimp farms. The lion's share of our aquaculture is freshwater, and the lion's share of that is catfish. I happen to like farmed catfish, although wild is more fun. The farmed are generally channel cats and are milder than many of the wild ones I catch. Coming in second place are crawfish, then trout—mostly rainbows. You will also see farmed striped bass and tilapia.

Our marine aquaculture is almost entirely dominated by shellfish. Oysters dominate, then clams, then a few farmers doing mussels; most of our farmed mussels are from Canada. It should be noted that farmed shellfish are a boon to the environment, not a hinderance. I highly recommend them when you can't dig your own. We do have a small shrimp farming industry in the Gulf. If you come across American farmed shrimp, go for it.

Everyone gets twitchy about food safety when it comes to fish and seafood. And while finfish is safer than beef or chicken, shellfish are another matter, one that you need to know a bit about. Let me walk you through it.

Before we begin, you should know that food-borne illness from fish and seafood is very rare. According to data from the Centers for Disease Control and Prevention, in 2015, only 351 Americans suffered a food-borne illness from fish or seafood. In our country of 321 million, that's a one-in-a-million chance you'll get sick. In 2016, there was a rather nasty norovirus outbreak (this is the "two exits, no waiting" illness most of us have suffered at one time or another) from shellfish that affected 529 people, but the fish and crustacean illnesses dropped to two hundred cases.

PARASITES

Most fish have some sort of parasite. The good news is that illness by parasite is rare in North America. It happens, but not very often. I know guys who have eaten raw salmon, never frozen, for decades, and as far as they know, they've never been sickened from it. Most fish parasites are in the gut cavity and need not concern us. We toss the parasite along with the guts. But there are a few that appear more often. Tops is tapeworm. There are a few species that can affect us, and they live in fresh water. Tapeworm is the only commonly found parasite of fish that can come to term in a human. All the others can make you sick for a bit, but you'll get over it. You won't get over tapeworm. How do you get it? By eating undercooked freshwater fish. Raw or undercooked trout is the single largest vector for tapeworm in the United States,

according to the Centers for Disease Control and Prevention. So trout sushi by the streamside is out, OK? You generally can't see tapeworm larvae, and chances are they're not there. But unless you want an uninvited weight-loss buddy taking up residence in your digestive tract, cook or freeze your freshwater fish before eating. If you get one, you might get some nausea, the trots, or stomach cramps. But probably not. Most tapeworms are sneaky and give you no symptoms. So how do you know? There's the weight loss, and, well, you'll see worm bits in the toilet.

The other big one is seal worm, the anisakis worm. This is the watch-spring-like worm you can see in many saltwater fishes. It's often in salmon, but I've seen it in striped bass, Pacific rockfish and lingcod, halibut, and both Atlantic and Pacific cod and haddock. I once worked at a nice restaurant cleaning fish. We had a lightbox for this—a box with a light under it that would make the fish fillets glow. You'd see the "watch springs" in there, and my job was to cut them out, as daintily as possible. Bet you didn't want to hear that.

Fortunately, even if you ate a live anisakis worm, chances are it'd only be an unpleasant gastrointestinal event, not a hospital trip. Basically, what the worm does is attach itself to your stomach or intestines. It does this because you're a mammal, and these worms want to be inside a mammal. But the mammal they really want is a marine mammal, like a seal or a whale. When the worm realizes it's made a terrible mistake, you will realize that you, too, suffered a lapse in judgment. You'll get what feels like food poisoning—crampy and nauseous. Some people get fevers; others get the trots. It's you and the worm doing battle. Luckily, you always win. For most people, symptoms fade in a day or three. The worm dies.

I hear you. You really like sushi and raw fish. So do I. The answer is to freeze your fish for a week before thawing it and eating it raw. If you have

GETTING TO KNOW FISH

▲ An anisakis worm, a parasite of saltwater fish. Not good eats.

access to a freezer that gets down to –31°F, you can eat it after a day.

Oh, and a final note: no eating live or raw crawfish, crabs, or shrimp, OK? They can carry liver flukes and flatworms that can really do a number on you. Yes, I know there's a tradition of raw spot prawns in Alaska, and you can see them in sushi. I avoid both, unless previously frozen.

WARM WATER WOES

Fish from tropical or subtropical waters can expose you to another set of potential problems: ciguatura and scombroid poisoning. In 2015, these were the top two food-borne illnesses in America, according to the CDC. Collectively, they affected just under a hundred people in thirty separate cases. And of those, only six were hospitalized. So not an epidemic, but enough to be mindful about.

Ciguatera is caused by eating fish—barracuda, sturgeon, parrot fish, and several groupers and snappers are among the main culprits—contaminated by the marine algae toxin *Gambierdiscus toxicus*, which thrive around coral reefs (herbivorous reef fish eat the algae, the big carnivorous fish eat the herbivores). Symptoms—nausea, vomiting, diarrhea, and some neurological oddities like tingling fingers and toes—can appear in a few hours or as long as a day after ingestion and can take days, weeks, or even years to go away. Fish from

the Caribbean and the Pacific and Indian Oceans have the highest risk. I've never met anyone who's gotten it.

Scombroid poisoning resembles an allergic response to eating fish in the tuna and mackerel family, often those caught in hot places. Bluefish and mahi mahi can also be affected, as can sardines, anchovies, and herring. It's caused by not refrigerating these sorts of fish fast enough, so histamine builds and builds within the flesh. Histamine survives cooking or canning, so those affected will quickly get a typical allergic reaction from eating affected fish. Fortunately, it's usually no big deal. Most people just take an antihistamine and move on.

FISH ALLERGIES

Roughly 2.5 percent of the American population has some sort of fish or seafood allergy, which, though significant, is less than those with dairy, egg, or nut allergies. Chances are if you're reading this book, you don't have such an allergy. I mention it only because many of us invite friends over for meals, and it's just a good idea to ask your guests if they have a fish or shellfish allergy. That way, you can be sure to scrub the cutting board after cleaning shrimp (which you're doing anyway, right?).

MERCURY

Mercury is in the air, water, and soil of the planet. Fish absorb methyl mercury from their food, and when you eat them, you absorb it, too. Mercury climbs up the food chain, so the flesh of apex predators like tuna and striped bass will have a far higher mercury concentration than, say, a sardine. Nearly all fish contain at least a trace amount of mercury, and the risk of mercury toxicity is real if you eat a lot of fish that have high concentrations of mercury. It's not easy to get it, but it's possible. The actor Jeremy Piven famously ate so much sushi (sometimes twice a day) that he managed to poison himself. People addicted to canned tuna can pick up unsafe levels of mercury, too.

Middle-aged men are least at risk here, so as long as we don't gorge ourselves on high-mercury fish like striped bass, tuna, sharks, and swordfish, we'll be fine. Most doctors suggest eating these fish no more than once or twice a month. On the other hand, babies, young children, and women who may become pregnant, are pregnant, or are nursing are especially at risk because mercury is toxic to a child's developing brain and nervous system. If you're in this group, you ought to avoid fish with the higher amounts of mercury.

Heavy hitters in terms of mercury include big, open-water, pelagic fish like king mackerel, swordfish, marlin, bluefin, and bigeye tuna; all sharks; and striped bass, sturgeon, tilefish, and orange roughy (a fish I've not seen in a market for years).

Fish with low levels of mercury include freshwater perch (yellow and white); walleyes and catfish; groundfish such as cod, haddock, hake, pollock, and ling; skates and rays; skipjack tuna; sardines, herring, anchovies, and small mackerel (Boston, chub, Pacific); trout and salmon; lobsters, crawfish, shrimp, squid, crab and scallops; and all flatfish except halibut, which are in the mid-range.

OTHER NASTIES

This one is mostly for the anglers. People have defiled a host of waterways, and heavy metals other than mercury, along with other pollutants, can linger in rivers, lakes, and bays long after we've stopped polluting them. Levels of pollution and contamination vary from place to place. Surf perch in the San Francisco Bay, for example, are sky-high in mercury, but those caught on California's north coast are not. Many of the Great Lakes fish have advisories for things like PCBs (polychlorinated biphenyls), as do most of the fisheries around New York City. So it's very important to check with your local and state departments of public health and/or fish and game for fish advisories.

All this is especially important when it comes to shellfish. Our fishery for clams and crabs in the Pacific Northwest is periodically closed because of domoic acid, which causes amnesiac shellfish poisoning, which, if you get it, is a really good way to meet new people every day. Or, worse, you could get paralytic shellfish poisoning. Neither is very much fun, and both can, in rare cases, be fatal. So far as I know, every state that has a coastline has a hotline that will tell you where shellfishing is open or closed. Memorize or write down this hotline. Your life could depend on it.

"Many men go fishing all of their lives without knowing that it is not fish they are after."

HENRY DAVID THOREAU

2
GETTING YOUR FISH

BUYING FISH FROM THE STORE

Not everyone reading this book will be an angler. And even anglers buy fish and seafood on occasion. Fortunately, buying fresh fish is easy if you know what to look for.

THE FISH MARKET

When it comes to the shop itself, the absolute bottom line is that a fish shop should not stink. If you walk into a fish market and it reeks, turn around and leave. Fantastic fish can be had at a farmer's market stall, a hole in the wall, or in a flashy boutique, but none should smell rotten. Ever.

Don't avoid ethnic markets. I've seen amazing octopus in Mexican markets, and Asian markets are legendary for fish and seafood—but you will always see questionable, even rotten, fish stacked alongside pristine specimens. You need to know the difference, which I'll get into in a moment.

Not everyone has access to quality fish markets. Maybe you live in the Midwest, or a small town, or in a rural area. This means most of the fish and seafood you will buy will come from a mega-mart. All is not lost, however, as there is good seafood to be had at most supermarkets—if you know where to look and what to look for.

◀ Surf casting near Bodega Bay, California.

THE SUPERMARKET

In a supermarket, go straight to the freezer section.

When I'm far from the sea, I rarely bother with the "fresh" fish displayed in the supermarket. Fish in most supermarkets will most likely stink, be days old, or worse—thawed, prefrozen seafood. Americans who live inland don't eat seafood in the quantities that coastal people do, so most supermarkets will not sell enough seafood to really get their hands on the top-quality fish. Frozen fish, on the other hand, won't be so damaged. I've seen excellent fish in small-town freezer sections. If there's no frozen-fish area at your supermarket—rare, but it happens—go to the fish counter and ask if they have frozen fish in the back. Most times, they will, because the "fresh" fish in most supermarkets is actually thawed.

BUY LOCAL

The exception to the Never Fresh Fish from Supermarkets rule is where there is a local fishery. In the northern states, walleye and yellow perch are often available; buy them whenever you can, as they are world-class fish. Smoked whitefish ("chubs") are another local favorite in some states. You can sometimes find great farmed sturgeon. Remember that American farmed catfish and trout are available nationwide, and the methods used to raise them are, for the most part, environmentally friendly.

AVOID SHELLFISH

Sorry, but unless you have access to a *really* good supermarket in a major inland city, don't buy shellfish. That means no "fresh" clams, oysters, mussels, or lobsters. Even lobsters, which will be sold live in tanks, lose a lot of quality when they languish in a tank. Again, easterners eat a lot of lobster, so the stock moves fast. A lobster in a tank in Iowa could have been sitting there for weeks. And it's tough to ship live clams, oysters, and mussels long distances without losing quality; it can be done, but you'll know that the quality is high by the price and the lack of smell. My advice? Buy frozen, or stick to fish.

LOOK FOR THE SEAL

Vacuum-sealing is a good sign of good frozen fish. *Never* buy frozen fish that has simply been placed on a Styrofoam tray, covered with plastic wrap, and tossed in the freezer—that's a recipe for freezer burn. The only exception to the vacuum-seal rule is shrimp, which are mostly blast-frozen individually and put in heavy-duty bags. Anything that says IQF ("individually quick-frozen") on the package should be fine.

BUYING FRESH WHOLE FISH

The eyes are the window to a truly fresh fish, for they fade quickly into gray dullness. Look for bright, clear eyes. Dull-eyed fish may be safe to eat, but they're past their prime. Next, look at the fish. Does it shine? Does it look metallic and clean? Or has it dulled or have discolored patches? If so, it's marginal.

Smell it. A fresh fish should smell like clean water, or a touch briny, or even like cucumbers. Under no circumstances should you buy a nasty smelling fish. Cooking won't improve it. Look at the gills, which should be a rich red or, if the fish has been bled, a clean, pale pink. Old fish turn the color of faded brick.

BUYING FISH FILLETS

Look for vibrant flesh. All fish fade as they age. If the fillet still has skin, that skin should look as pristine as the skin on an equally good whole fish—shiny and metallic. The smell test is especially important with fillets. They should have no pungent aromas.

Is there liquid on the meat? If so, that liquid should be clear, not milky. Milky liquid on a fillet is the first stage of rot. If the fishmonger lets you, press the meat with your finger. It should be resilient enough so your indentation disappears. If your fingerprint remains, move on.

BUYING LIVE FISH

The best way to choose a live fish or crab or lobster is to look for signs of life. Is it scampering around in its tank? Swimming happily? Or is it sulking in a corner or hanging motionless and panting? If so, don't buy it. Lobsters and crabs starve themselves in tanks, and when you crack open one that's been imprisoned in a tank for weeks on end, you may very well find it almost empty inside. Your best bet is to make friends with the fishmonger and find out when the new shipments arrive. Plan on being there to meet them, and buy then. You'll be rewarded for your extra effort.

BUYING SHELLFISH

Buy only at the finest fish markets. These are the places where turnover is so rapid, you can be assured of fresh mussels, clams, or oysters. You may still get a dead one, but the ratio will be far lower. How do you tell if one's dead? Shellfish are sold alive, so they should react to you. Put them on the countertop and back away for a moment. Then tap the shell; it should close tighter than it was. Another method is to tap two clams together; they should sound like rocks. If they sound hollow, one or both are dead. Oysters are a little tough to do this with, but clams and mussels will definitely react. This is important, because a few clams or mussels will never open wide, even after cooking; the old wives' tale that bad ones won't open is just that: a tale. So to check for dead and potentially toxic bivalves, you need to test them *before* cooking.

Scallops are a special case. Scallops are almost always sold shucked, so what you're looking for are "dry packed" or "untreated" scallops, meaning they are not shipped and stored in brine, or worse, in tripolyphosphate, a preservative that makes things injected with it or brined in it look glossier and firmer. Those scallops you see wallowing in milky ick? Leave them be. Better to buy frozen, vacuum-sealed scallops—which are perfectly good, by the way—than an inferior wet-packed scallop.

Shrimp are easy. Buy them shell-on and frozen, for the most part. Shell-on because the shell protects them from the rigors of being frozen without losing too much moisture, and frozen because shrimp cook (and rot) *very* rapidly. Should you be near a shrimping region or have access to truly magnificent fresh shrimp, by all means buy them fresh, with the head on if possible. Why? Because head-on shrimp stay moister. Remember: nothing says boring like a dry, overcooked shrimp.

All the information about shrimp applies to crayfish, too—unless you can get them live, in which case, follow the instructions for lobsters or crabs. I've only rarely seen cooked, unfrozen New England lobsters for sale, but it happens in places that sell a lot of lobster. I have seen precooked, fresh California lobsters fairly frequently, though. Same with Dungeness crabs. You'll see big displays of them on ice in late fall and winter in the West. Pick the ones with curled-up legs, which means they were alive when steamed or boiled. Floppy legs is not a good sign.

Blue crabs and the various walking crabs—Jonah, red and rock, peekytoe—are normally sold live or as picked meat.

Lobster tails, crayfish tails, stone crab claws, snow and king crab legs, squid, and octopus are almost always sold to the wholesaler prefrozen, so you should buy them frozen. Both squid, commonly known as calamari, and octopus, squid's more richly flavored cousin, freeze exceptionally well.

Again, if you can buy lobster tails, squid, and octopus—not to mention cuttlefish—fresh, do it! They are rare treats even at fine fish markets and should be appreciated as such. Like sizing up finfish, you should look first at their eyes, which should be clean and bright. One side note on octopus: they cook down. A lot. In many cases, two pounds of thawed or fresh octopus might only feed two hungry people. So buy more than you think you need.

CATCHING YOUR OWN
Fish Care from Water to Freezer

Enjoying a fish dinner starts long before you heat up the grease in the frying pan. Those of you who are hunters understand the importance of meat care already, but even many hunters don't fully grasp how critical field care is for fish and seafood. Fish and seafood decay *far* more rapidly than terrestrial meats—in extreme cases, damage can be done in minutes. Let that sink in a bit. You can go from wonderful to rotten in as little as thirty minutes, and certainly over the course of a day spent on the water. Which is why before you cast a lure, throw a net, or loose the lines, you must have your plan for fish care already set.

Let me walk you through the stages of field care for fish, from basic to advanced.

KEEP IT COOL

Fish, in general, live in colder environments than land animals. When they're removed from that environment, fish suffer in proportion to that thermal shock. An example. You catch a trout on a warm spring day. Maybe it's 70°F outside. Nice, right? Well, Mr. Trout lives in a stream that's closer to 40°F. Remove him from the water, and he'll soon be thirty degrees above his body temperature. Imagine that scenario with a deer—that'd be a shift from about 100°F to 130°F. Now you're talking venison cooked rare. That'd be crazy, right? Well, it's similar for your fish. This is why when you catch catfish in warm water, they don't spoil as fast. They might be living in 85°F water, and you might be catching them on a 90°F day. See the difference?

All this is to emphasize how important it is to keep your fish as cool as possible. I've been on many a party boat catching Pacific rockfish where they just toss the fish into a wet burlap sack. This is not ideal, even though the air temperature is pretty close to the water temperature, about 45°F. That equilibrium is why this method works, but it's still not what I'd prefer.

I cannot stress enough how important it is to have ice—and plenty of it—on board or in a cooler at the side of a stream or lake or beach. I know it's not always possible, especially if you're hiking to where you fish, but at least then you know it's not ideal and you can cook your fish quickly. Having ice in a cooler is the single most important thing you can do to ensure high quality fish at home. Period, end of story, no debate.

Saltwater flake ice is the best. Regular ice in seawater is good, too, as then you can create a slush that is colder than freezing, but because of the salt, neither your fish nor your water will freeze solid. This is what we do on the fishing boat in Alaska, and it serves us well.

Ice is your friend, until it's not. When is ice not your friend? When it's really cold out.

I remember ice fishing for crappies on Red Lake in Minnesota, and I noticed that whenever people would catch one, they'd simply toss it out of the ice shack onto the ice, where the fish would freeze solid in minutes. I couldn't fathom why anyone would do that, other than ignorance or laziness. Why is this bad? Well, you haven't scaled or gutted your fish yet. You will need to thaw it to do that, and then you have the inevitable moisture loss, which is particularly bad in fish. All of this is OK if you intend to eat all your fish "fresh," but most people would thaw their fish, fillet them, then refreeze those fillets. This is a terrible practice that

ON ICE

- ▶ Ice is not all the same temperature. Buy ice bags from the back of the freezer, not the front. Clear, glassy ice is close to 32°F. You want hard, opaque ice.

- ▶ Shaved or crushed ice is best for a seawater slurry.

- ▶ Block ice is best for hot-weather coolers. I like block ice in a cooler when I'm fishing in weather warmer than 90°F. It acts like a giant ice cube and keeps your cooler colder longer.

- ▶ High-tech coolers—Yeti, Orca, Pelican, Canyon—originally designed for fishing, are worth every penny. You need one for really good fish care in hot weather. On the Pacific Coast north of around Santa Barbara, you're fine with a regular cooler. Ditto for places like Maine. Fishing the Gulf? Get the high-tech cooler. (Incidentally, they make high-tech koozies for your beer, too. Also worth every penny.)

hammers the flesh (I'll go into this more in a bit). Suffice to say that you want your fish or seafood cold, but you only want it frozen solid when you're ready for it to be.

Another caveat with keeping seafood cold: thermal shock is real, and it will kill seafood. If you've ever watched the television show *Deadliest Catch*, where they fish crabs in winter, you will see them getting the crabs into the holding tank as fast as they can. They do this because crabs will die, and their legs will fall off, if they are exposed to icy air for too long.

▶ My friend Joe Navari drilling holes in the ice of Caples Lake, California.

Remember: most seafood (clams and crustaceans) must be cooked alive or at least immediately after they've died. Dump a bunch of clams dug from 65°F water into a bucket of ice, and you'll kill every one of them. As it happens, this is a really great way to get them to open up if you want to serve clams on the half shell. Shuck as they open, and have at it. You can acclimatize shellfish and crustaceans to cold environments, but you need to do it gradually.

WATER

Water, too, can be either your friend or your enemy. Remember that saltwater animals *must* remain in salt water, while freshwater animals can handle salt water—at least once they're dead. What does that mean in practice? If you want to transport seafood—clams or crabs, for instance—they need to be in the seawater they lived in. And even then, they can't be there for too long, or they will use up all the oxygen in that water and die anyway. An aquarium bubbler stone is a good thing to add to your impromptu saltwater tank if you need to transport saltwater creatures for more than about eight hours. The bubbler stone is also vital for purging crawfish in a cooler. Put your mudbugs in a cooler full of clean fresh water, and drop the bubbler stone in there so they can breathe. You can then let them hang out a day or two to purge before eating.

If you put freshwater fish into salty water, they will die. That's fine if that water is ice cold—you're basically brining them. But you can't do the opposite. Dunking saltwater animals into fresh water will also kill them, but in addition, it will degrade the meat quality. Why? Osmosis. The salt in the animal's tissues will leach into the fresh water in an attempt to equalize the salt content. This extends to rinsing off saltwater fillets or any portion of fish you intend to store. Don't do it in the sink. It's perfectly fine to rinse fish under fresh water if you intend to cook it soon, but exposing saltwater fish to fresh water for too long will degrade the flesh. You can see this if you look closely; the texture of a saltwater fish will change when rinsed heavily under freshwater.

When I want to rinse my saltwater fish before storing, I make a brine with the ratio of ¼ cup kosher salt to one quart water and put it in a big bowl that I use to rinse the fish in. Even better? Work dry. Limiting the amount of water that hits actual fish flesh (like on a fillet) will keep it in better shape. To do this, have a roll of paper towels nearby to wipe slime and blood off surfaces, the fish itself, and your knife while you're working.

TO KILL OR NOT TO KILL?

Short answer: kill.

All finfish are better killed quickly once they come over the rail. Many fish are OK when allowed to suffocate on shore or deck, but they will be inferior eating compared to those that have been killed quickly. Besides, put yourself in the position of the fish; if this were you, wouldn't you want it to be quick and clean, not a long, drawn-out suffocation in an alien environment?

So how to do it? A short, sharp shock with a wooden club that the British call a "priest" but that I like to call the "wood shampoo." I remember going to Yankee Stadium as a kid on Bat Day, and every angler within a hundred miles would show up to get the two-foot-long bats they used to give out. There's nothing better to kill an angry bluefish than a miniature Reggie Jackson slugger. But mostly, we use the wood shampoo not to kill but to stun fish. When it comes to meat quality, the best way to kill a fish is to bleed it to death in the water it lived in. It is as minimally painful for a fish as it was for the Roman nobles who, when caught in a conspiracy to overthrow the emperor, would sometimes be given the option of suicide by opening a vein in a bath of warm water (think Frankie Pentangeli in *Godfather II*). Bleeding fish also leaves the carcass almost bloodless, which is a *huge* factor in meat quality.

On the *Heather Anne* in Alaska, we bleed every single salmon that comes over the rail. A bluefish

IKEJIME

The Japanese fish-killing technique *ike-jime* ("closing the fish") has near mystic status among some chefs, and it absolutely works, resulting in firmer, cleaner-tasting fish, especially when eaten raw. It works by disrupting the fish's nervous system and destroying the swim reflex.

You perform *ikejime* by severing the fish's spine and gills with a knife cut where the two meet, right behind the eyes of most fish. Then you slice through to the spine just in front of the tail and jam a stiff wire into the spinal column. This makes the fish die almost instantly; more importantly, it relaxes it.

So it is worth it? Sorta. I have not noticed a huge difference in quality between a properly bled, gutted, and iced fish and one killed by *ikejime*. But if you aren't in a position to do all that but you can bleed your fish and stick that wire in, you'll get a better product. Where *ikejime* really shines is days later. *Ikejime*-killed fish maintain their firmness for several days longer than traditionally killed fish. Another thing to note is that *ikejime* works better on fish that are constantly swimming, especially the tuna, mackerel, jack, and bluefish family.

If you want to do this, you'll need to have on hand a few lengths of stiff wire in different diameters; a wire good for a seabass won't be thick enough for a tuna.

Bleeding tuna is an absolute must. Salmon, too. I also bleed trout and kokanee. White fish, such as walleye, bass, cod, or snapper, benefit from being bled, but it's not as critical. Halibut and other flatfish are typically bled, otherwise the blood will stain the bottom fillet. You also want to pile up your dead flatfish white-side up (on ice, of course). That's a trick I learned from the Alaskan long-liners.

How best to bleed a fish? Pop both gills with your finger or a short, sharp knife. Gills have rakers that are often sharp, so if you're not used to popping gills with your finger, use your knife. You need to make a habit of doing both gills, because some species of fish won't fully bleed if you only pop one gill. Very large fish, like tuna, shark, or swordfish, need to have both the gills and the tail cut to bleed out. Cut the gills as normal, then slice upward from just in front of the tail until the knife hits the spine.

We have a big tub of seawater on board our boat, as do many charter boats. Barring that, a regular livewell (a tank that recirculates and aerates fresh seawater) works well. Another option is to tie a line through the mouth and out the gills to secure the fish and let it ride over the side a while, like a stringer; keep a sharp eye out for seals or snapping turtles. I've also used five-gallon buckets. Stick the fish headfirst into the bucket. Not ideal, but better than nothing.

PRESSURE-BLEEDING

For the super advanced, you can pressure-bleed your fish, essentially flushing the fish with seawater to remove all traces of blood within it. We do this aboard the *Heather Anne*, and it results in the highest quality fish possible. You do this by setting up a heavy-gauge needle attached to your boat's hose line. Set the water pressure to medium-low—you don't want to blow out the fish's capillaries—and jam the needle into the primary artery just below the spine. We do this after beheading the fish, but you can partially behead the fish to

or sheepshead or cobia that's been bled out is 100 percent better in quality than one that has not been bled. The rule of thumb is that the oilier the fish, the more important it is to bleed them, and this importance increases with the size of the fish.

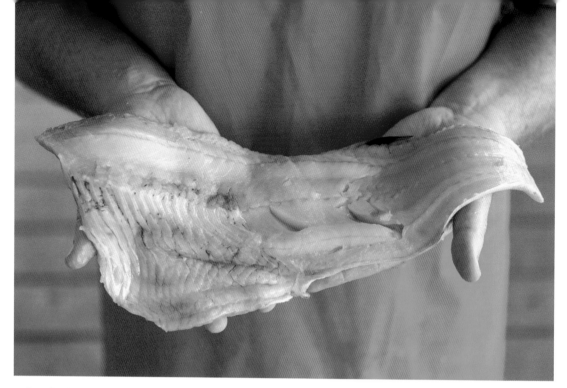

▲ Gapping in the fillet of a lingcod mishandled on the boat.

get access to the artery if you want. Flush seawater through the fish for thirty seconds or so, and you're good to go. We do this for all our fish in Alaska, but it would be useful for anyone catching tuna, lake trout, bluefish, cobia, sharks, or mahi mahi—large, oily fish.

HANDLING FINFISH

For the most part, handling your fish once they've been caught is intuitive and straightforward. But there are a few things to remember. First, many fish are spiny, and some have venom in the spines. So be careful! Second, picking up larger fish from the tail, while it may seem normal, isn't ideal. Why? Because when you do that, the weight of the fish will shear apart the flakes of meat in small but noticeable ways. Ever seen a nice salmon or cod or lake trout fillet that had big gaping areas in the grain of the meat? They can look almost like gaff holes, but there was no gaff present. This is because

someone picked that fish up from the tail, and the weight of the fish sheared the meat apart. Again, this is a trick you learn when you fish high-end salmon the way we do on the *Heather Anne*. Pick large fish up from the head end. *Always.* Another tip: lay the fish straight, belly down, in the cooler. This also helps prevent gapping of the meat, and it keeps you from having to deal with fish all curled up from rigor mortis.

Rigor Mortis

Fish get rigor the same way all other animals do. And anglers must deal with rigor in fish the same way hunters must deal with rigor in terrestrial animals. The short version is this: if you kill an aquatic animal and then cook it right away, you're good to go; but if there's a delay between catch and cook, you need to let it go through rigor, which takes anywhere from hours to days. A solid rule of thumb is to wait until a fish is floppy before filleting it. If you fillet fish that are still stiff, you run the risk of shortening, which is where the meat—still stiff—contracts violently after being freed from the skeleton. It can actually result in tough fish, which normally is never a problem. Incidentally, this happens to land animals and birds, too. An exception to this would be catching a fish, filleting it, and then freezing it—all *before* it sets into rigor. This is done on factory ships in Alaska, and some anglers manage this feat, too. But it's rare. Better to wait a bit.

HANDLING SEAFOOD

Seafood is a bit different. In a perfect world, you keep everything alive until you cook it or eat it raw. That isn't always going to happen, especially with high-strung animals like shrimp. Shrimp are generally treated like finfish, which is to say best in a seawater-ice slush.

All other seafood you can and should keep alive as best you can. Here are some tips:

▶ CLAMS OR OTHER BIVALVES are best kept in a bucket of the water they lived in. This allows you to purge them of sand.

▶ ABALONE, LIMPETS, MOON SNAILS, WHELKS, AND PERIWINKLES are pretty durable, but they do wander, so keep an eye on them. If you don't have a lid on your bucket, they'll make a slow-motion jailbreak.

▶ CRABS, LOBSTERS, AND CRAWFISH need to be kept alive. Crawfish are easy, as they can be soaked in a cooler of their native water for up to eight hours or so; see the aquarium bubbler stone trick on page 26. Lobsters and crabs can be above the water for as long as eight hours, but they will start to die within a couple of hours. Better to put them on top of ice bags than under water, unless you have a seawater tank with a bubbler stone.

Purging Sand from Shellfish

There's a library's worth of bad information out there about how to purge sand from clams, ranging from mythical to downright scary. Hopefully I can set the record straight. Here's what you need to know to get the grit out of your clams.

Let me start by saying that the vast majority of clams, mussels, and oysters you buy in the market have been purged already. You will almost never need to purge your clams if you bought them at a supermarket. The exception is if you buy from a small purveyor, and in that case, just ask. Wild clams and mussels are an entirely different story. They should always be purged, clams especially. Different clams need different purging times, too, depending on how and where they live. Hard-shell clams in clean sand, like Eastern surf clams, cockles, and quahogs, tend to be easier to purge than open-shelled clams like steamers, horseneck clams, and geoducks. The worst of them all is the western bent-nosed clam, which lives in dense mud and can take days to purge.

Adding cornmeal to the purging water does nothing. There, I said it. Think about the biology of a clam for a moment to understand why. Clams are filter feeders. The reason they have sand and grit in them is because they live buried in sand or mud. This proximity to grit naturally gets the stuff into the clams, which filter with their shells partially open—which is how the sand or mud gets in. Clams filter microscopic particles, not stones or grains of sand. Or cornmeal. Clams don't have gizzards. They don't need grit to do their jobs. Grit in your shell is just an occupational hazard of being a clam.

The myth is that cornmeal somehow causes a clam to "cough up" more grit than it normally would, or that the clam "eats" the cornmeal and spits out grit. Well, to test that, I did an experiment. First, I let fifty western littleneck clams purge themselves for eighteen hours in seawater, after which I weighed the grit after drying. I found that they had expelled about 47 grams of grit. Next, I added

▲ New England steamer clams.

exactly 150 grams of coarse cornmeal to the purging water and let another fifty western littleneck clams purge themselves for eighteen hours. After that, I carefully removed the clams, poured off the water, and spread the cornmeal on a baking sheet to dry completely. Then I weighed it again. The cornmeal plus grit weighed 196 grams. You would think that if clams had "eaten" the cornmeal, there would be a *decrease* in the dry weight of the meal after eighteen hours, no? If you were to bury clams in cornmeal, yes, some would get inside them the way sand does in the wild. But why bother?

Purging clams is mostly a function of time, with oxygen and temperature as ancillary factors. The single most important ingredient you need to purge your clams of grit is seawater. This is not so hard to obtain if you're getting your own clams. Bring a five-gallon bucket and fill it two-thirds of the way up with seawater as you leave the clamming grounds. Armed with this, you can purge virtually any clam. Oh, by the way, you cannot purge a clam

in fresh water. Fresh water kills clams. And dead clams are, with few exceptions, no good to eat.

Why is bringing home seawater so important? Because clams from different areas live at different salinity levels. The average salinity of the ocean is thirty-five parts of salt per thousand of water, but in some wide, shallow clam beds, the salinity climbs far higher through evaporation. In other beds, the salinity is lower because the clams are near an estuary where fresh water flows. If you bring seawater from where you dug the clams, you need not guess at how salty your soaking water should be.

If for some reason you forget to bring back seawater, you can recreate it decently by remembering the thirty-five parts per thousand ratio. Go buy sea salt—actual sea salt, not rock salt, not iodized salt—and dissolve thirty-five grams of it (about two tablespoons plus another teaspoon) into each liter (one thousand grams) of non-chlorinated water. You'll need enough to submerge your clams. If you want to get fancier, you can use a hydrometer, which measures water density. Where I do a lot of my clamming in Tomales Bay, California, the average salinity would read 1.024 in terms of specific gravity. This equated to one-third cup finely cut sea salt to a half gallon of non-chlorinated water. Chlorine, needless to say, is not good for living things. What's your area's normal salinity? Google it. I bet some scientist somewhere has measured and posted online the salinity of the water where you dig clams.

Temperature matters. Shock kills clams. Put clams living in 75°F water into the fridge, and they will not be happy—and open-shelled clams will die. Doing the reverse—cold to warm—is also a shock. Carry your clams home in your seawater and they'll be fine. They'll acclimate to the changing temperature as you drive home. If it's really hot or cold out, put everything in a cooler. Keep in mind that clams are capable of filter feeding at temperatures as low as 34.5°F and as high as at least 78°F, which is realistically as warm as you will get in a normal indoor room.

If you're clamming in winter where the water is cold, go ahead and do your purging in the fridge. But if it's summer, keep your clams at room temperature, or, ideally, in a place a bit colder, like a basement. How long? Even an hour will help. But you can purge your clams as long as there's oxygen in your seawater. Leave your clams too long, and they suffocate and die. Overnight is what I normally do with a fifty-clam limit of western littlenecks and four to ten horseneck or Washington clams. I submerge the clams under about 1½ to 3 inches of seawater and loosely cover the container they're in; clams spit water, so you don't want them sprinkling the inside of your fridge or basement.

To summarize:

When you're done digging, fill a large bucket full of seawater to take home. Put your clams in it for the drive. If the temperature is very different between the water and your car, put everything in a cooler.

At home, **quickly wash every clam under cold tap water to remove mud or grit on the outside of the shell.** Put the clams into a large non-reactive container (galvanized steel, for example, will kill them). I use a big Tupperware-style container.

Either let the seawater you brought home settle for about twenty minutes or filter it through a paper towel. You want it as grit-free as possible. Pour the water over the clams, covering them by one to three inches. If you're purging especially muddy clams, hold back any remaining seawater—you'll need to change it in a day.

Set the clams where the temperature is reasonably close to the water they were in—in the fridge, at room temperature, or in a cool place—and leave them for at least an hour, and up to twenty hours. Check on them once in a while; most of them should have their siphons out. You will see a lot of icky stuff all over the bottom of the container. Repeat this process for especially muddy clams.

WHY FISH STINK

Fish that are going off will stink in different ways. Saltwater fish will get worse, and this is because they contain an amine called trimethylamine oxide (TMAO), which, when the fish dies, gets broken down by both enzymes and bacteria into trimethylamine, which stinks to high heaven. Sharks, skates, and rays contain urea, which gets broken down in a similar way into ammonia. Yes, the cleanser. Not a taste treat. Interestingly, freshwater fish don't have TMAO, so they will start to smell as they go off, but so much less that I've had unusable freshwater fish that slipped past my nose.

When you're ready, rinse the clams again. Hard-shelled clams can go into the fridge. Open-shelled clams need to be eaten or shucked.

FROM STORE TO HOME

For those of you not catching your own fish, you'll want some way to keep it cold as you travel home from the store. On cool days, this isn't a problem, but buying fish or seafood in summer can be an issue. My advice is to bring a cooler with some ice in it to the market. Then, when you buy the fish, ask for some ice—any fishmonger who says no, you don't want any part of.

HOME SWEET HOME

Once you're home, you still have some work to do to keep your fish at their best. Remember what I said about the temperature difference between the water and the fish's body? Well, it holds true in the fridge, too. Most home refrigerators are set around 35°F. If you're dealing with a warm-water bass or catfish or speckled trout, then you'll be fine for up to two weeks as is. But most fish live in colder water. Think about codfish; they love water that is pretty close to 35°F. So your fridge temperatures are body temperature for this fish. It's more or less the equivalent of setting beef out at 100°F—it's gonna spoil quick.

That's why our friend ice comes back into play here. You want to set up a tub of some sort with lots of crushed ice in it to set your fish in. If they're fillets, nestle them in the crushed ice in whatever they're wrapped in. If they're fish you've caught, wrap them in something. Don't let ice touch the fillet. I like to vacuum-seal fillets and bury them in ice. Fresh fish will hold this way for a week easily. And warm-water fish, like those caught inland in the South or offshore in the Gulf of Mexico, will keep up to a couple of weeks this way.

Whole fish you want to set belly down into the crushed ice. Sometimes I put whole fish into plastic bags so they don't touch the ice directly.

Drain any melt water once or twice a day, and you can keep your fish in fine condition for a week. Longer for warm water fish.

FREEZING FISH

The single best method of freezing fish fillets is with a vacuum sealer, ideally with a medium- to heavy-gauge plastic, like 4 to 5 mm. There is nothing better than this method. But whole fish don't vacuum-seal so well, and you have to watch for broken seals. So there are other ways.

Remember that air is your enemy. Any air that touches your fish will cause freezer burn eventually, so you must prevent air from contacting the fish by vacuum-sealing it, glazing it, or wrapping it tightly. If you choose not to vacuum-seal, you can glaze fish by dipping them in cold water and putting the dipped fish on a sheet pan in the freezer. Let that water freeze, then repeat the process several more times to get a quarter-inch-thick ice glaze on the fish. You can then put your glazed

fish into a plastic bag and place it in the freezer for storage. I don't personally like this method, but it's recognized as effective.

The exception is shellfish. I do like to glaze shrimp, shucked clams, and oysters, even small fish fillets, like those from bluegills. You then put the glazed, frozen items into a heavy freezer bag. You've basically done IQF seafood at home. Not as good as the real deal, but it works.

You can also wrap your fish in plastic wrap, then put the wrapped fish into a plastic bag or wrap in waxed butcher's freezer paper. This method is not as effective as the other methods at preventing moisture loss and freezer burn, but it's cheap and will hold your fish for a couple of months.

Don't freeze your fish for longer than six months, if you can help it. After that, you'll notice a significant decline in quality. Fatty fish, such as salmon or trout, go downhill even faster. Don't freeze them longer than three months, or you'll get "salmon stink" when you cook them.

A word on freezers. Chances are your kitchen freezer isn't very cold. If you have a chest freezer, use that for your fish. Chest freezers can go down to −10°F or even lower, where a typical kitchen freezer can't get much colder than 7°F. Fortunately, new kitchen freezers are better, and they can hit that −10°F mark when on full blast.

When you freeze fish, bury them in previously frozen things so they freeze as fast as possible. The faster things freeze, the smaller the ice crystals that form inside the meat or fish—or anything else, for that matter—and the less damage freezing does to its cell structure. This is why blast-frozen fish, which is frozen at anywhere from −30°F to −100°F, is arguably better than fresh fish you buy at the store. Alas, we have no way of blast-freezing at home.

It's good to remember that some fish just aren't good frozen. These are the ones with the most fat, like bluefish, herring, mackerel, and sardines.

▶ A couple of nice coho salmon we netted aboard the *F/V Heather Anne* in Alaska.

They turn to mush when thawed, good only for bait or fish cakes. You can, however, smoke all these fish and then freeze them, preferably by vacuum-sealing. They will still soften, but they will be far better than fresh fillets thawed.

THAWING

When you thaw your frozen fish, do it gradually. Never put them in the microwave to thaw. Let the packaged fish thaw in the fridge or, if it has been vacuum-sealed, in *cold* water. Thawing at room temperature is also a bad idea. You want them to remain cold and come to temperature slowly. And don't let your fish thaw in their own juices. That leads to fishy-smelling fish. Either let them thaw on a rack over a pan or out of the package, wrapped in copious amounts of paper towels, changing the towels if they get soaked through. This really does make a difference.

3
GETTING TO KNOW YOUR FISH

ON SPECIES

One of the singular problems with most every fish cookbook ever written is their focus on specific species of fish or seafood. On the surface, this wouldn't seem like a problem. After all, you wouldn't want to use mackerel in a recipe for, say, seabass (unless you do; more on this in a moment). Consider that there are more than thirty-two thousand species of fish in the world, most of which are edible in some way, shape, or form. Even whittling it down to just the sport fish and common supermarket fish you see in North America, you're left with a list a thousand species long. I've spent my entire life cooking, catching, and eating as many different kinds of fish as I can. I will always order an odd fish on a menu, and I almost always keep bycatch—the "weird" species—when I'm fishing. And I have yet to top the four-hundred-species mark. It's just too much. So what to do about this embarrassment of riches?

First and foremost, learn the intricacies of the fish and seafood you regularly catch or buy. I eat a lot of salmon, trout, Pacific rockfish, and halibut. I have learned, over the years, of the fine differences not only between the various species of trout or salmon or rockfish, but also between individuals of the same species. Similarly, you may find that, say, crappies caught in a particular lake might be better tasting than those caught from a nearby river.

Or that carp caught in cold water are infinitely better than those caught out of a drainage ditch in August. Or that Gulf shrimp are better than Southeast Asian shrimp, or that American-raised catfish are better tasting than Vietnamese swai or basa.

There is no substitute for this learned, localized knowledge. But we can organize things a bit to make the learning more manageable. The following are the most frequently caught recreational fish in America, according to the National Ocean and Atmospheric Agency and the US Fish and Wildlife Service, in no particular order (nineteen types in two general categories, saltwater and freshwater). Get to know these fish, and you will have gone a long way toward getting that deep-level knowledge of the fish you chase.

THE BIG SORT: SALTWATER AND FRESHWATER

SALTWATER FISH

- Various drum (red, black, croaker, spot, etc.)
- Tunas and the various mackerels
- Various seabasses (black seabass, Pacific rockfish, etc.)
- Porgies, grunts, and sheepshead
- Snappers of all kinds

- ► Bluefish
- ► Various jacks (yellowtail, amberjack, etc.)
- ► Flounders (fluke, halibut, winter flounder, etc.)
- ► Mahi mahi (also known as dorado or dolphin fish)
- ► Sharks, skates, and rays

Freshwater Fish

- ► Large and smallmouth bass
- ► White bass, striped bass, and their hybrids
- ► Panfish like sunfish and crappies
- ► Catfish of various kinds
- ► Walleye, perch, and sauger
- ► Pike, pickerel, and muskies
- ► Trout and steelhead
- ► Salmon (caught in both salt and fresh water)

CATEGORIES AND CHARACTERISTICS

Next, organize your catch into categories and characteristics.

Fish or Seafood?

This is the most obvious: fish vs. seafood (walleye vs. crab, for example). Finfish generally taste different and cook differently from crustaceans and mollusks, so that's an easy pair to distinguish. Of course, even here there is no hard-and-fast rule. You can tempura-fry shrimp every bit as nicely as you can seabass. And crab is arguably better in ceviche than the traditional finfish. But having separated fish from seafood, you at least have a good sense of what to anticipate when faced with one or the other.

Fat or Lean?

A key rule is that fat equals flavor. Fatty fish and seafoods will have a more pronounced flavor than lean ones. This is why so many people like bland fish such as cod or walleye—they are blank slates.

Color

After fat, think color: white, orange, red (or pink), and gray blue. The color of the meat in a fish is an excellent clue to what it might taste like or how it might act in the kitchen. Color can often be a marker for fat, too. All white fish act similarly in the broadest sense. They are typically lean, too, with notable exceptions like black cod, Chilean seabass, eel, freshwater drum, carp, and whitefish. All orange fish range from reasonably fatty to ultra-fatty. These, without exception, are salmonids: salmon, trout, and char. They are orange because of diet, which include—and is sometimes exclusively—crustaceans. Some, like farmed rainbow trout, are golden or peach colored when raw but cook up off-white. Red-fleshed fish can be lean or fat, and all are in the tuna family. There are pink-fleshed fish, too, such as mako shark, swordfish, wahoo, Atlantic ling, and marlin; they all cook up white. All but the ling tend to be reasonably fatty, and all but the ling tend to be served and sold as steaks. All gray-blue fish are fatty. These are the jacks, bluefish, mackerels, shad, herring, anchovies, sardines, and the like.

Using color as a marker can help you get closer to what you want. With few exceptions, you can use, say, a bluefish in the same recipe as a mackerel, or a yellowfin tuna instead of a bigeye, or walleye in place of a smallmouth bass.

Flake, Density, and Firmness

Salmon, for example, which can range from a modestly sized pink salmon to a gigantic king salmon, all have a similar flake and firmness. Yes, salmon aficionados will tell you there are enormous differences among these fish—and there are, when tasted up close. But for our purposes from a slightly more distant perch, it's not a huge deal to substitute an Atlantic salmon for a coho.

Smaller fish, like all the bluegills, small bass, perch, small Pacific rockfish, porgies, grunts, spot, and smaller croakers can sub for one another.

▲ Giant fillets from a Pacific halibut in Alaska.

Will there be a difference in flavor if you do, say, a steamed whole smallmouth bass instead of a steamed whole porgy? Sure, but it won't be so dramatic that it will ruin your dinner.

Most white fish may be lean, but they are not all alike. Some are so delicate that you can't sear them in a pan. Some are so firm that you must cook them carefully or they will become dry and tasteless. Really delicate fish and seafood would include oysters, bluegills, cod and haddock, small flounder, crab, porgies, small trout, smelt, anchovies, herring, and sardines; note that these are all over the color and fattiness spectrum. Super-firm fish and seafood would include lobster, swordfish, sturgeon, shark, tuna, yellow perch, grouper, tilefish, abalone, conch, octopus, shrimp, cobia, hogfish, tautog, monkfish, amberjack, and yellowtail; these too range widely in color, fattiness, and size. Everything else falls somewhere in the middle.

Why does this matter? In some cases, it limits your cooking options. Oysters don't make the greatest kebabs, for example, and gently poached octopus will leave you chewing for days.

Size

Size matters. A fish's size makes a huge difference in how you will eventually cook it. Or at least it should. I hate seeing people on a Pacific rockfish charter get ten-inch fish filleted. "That's a taco," they'll say, ruefully. And yes, it might make a single fish taco. But you will have wasted a lot of meat by filleting that fish. Far better in that case to scale and gut the fish and serve it whole, grilled or steamed or fried.

In general, small fish are best served on the bone, ideally whole, scaled, and gutted. Why whole? Because when you chop the head off a fish, the end where the head used to be will dry out, and since that is often a spot with a lot of meat, it's a shame to damage it simply to appease the squeamish.

Larger individuals have their own issues. Really large fish, like a hundred-pound Pacific halibut or a forty-pound striped bass, will certainly be decent eating, but they are so large that the flake of the fish will be unlike that of smaller specimens, and this coarseness isn't ideal. There's also the toxin factor; really big, really old stripers or sturgeon will carry far more mercury or PCBs than younger fish. Finally, there is the question of conservation. In many species—halibut and stripers, for example—the truly giant individuals are all breeding females. And in the fish world, a giant breeding female of a species is worth exponentially more to that species' population than a smaller female; it's logarithmic, not linear. So release that two-hundred-pound halibut if you can stand it.

ANOTHER GOOD SORT

With these five basic categories in mind—fish vs. seafood; fat vs. lean; color; density and flake; and size—here's how we might group some of the more popular fish caught in North America and seen in markets (with a hat tip to the myriad species out there that we've not included):

Gray-Blue Fatty Fish

Bluefish, hickory shad, American shad, Atlantic (Boston) and Pacific mackerel, Spanish and king mackerel, all the herrings, sardines, anchovies, amberjack, yellowtail, and other jacks.

Orange and Yellowish Fish

Atlantic salmon, chinook (king) salmon, coho (silver) salmon, sockeye salmon, pink salmon, chum (keta) salmon, Arctic char, lake trout, brook trout, dolly varden, rainbow trout, brown trout, cutthroat trout.

Red and Pink Fish

Bluefin tuna, yellowfin tuna, bigeye tuna, blackfin tuna, skipjack tuna, albacore tuna, bonito, wahoo, swordfish, marlin.

Fatty White Fish

Black cod (sablefish), carp, Chilean seabass, sturgeon and most sharks, eel, whitefish, freshwater drum, white seabass. Catfish can occasionally be fatty, too.

Lean White Fish

Largemouth and smallmouth bass, all the various sunfish and crappies, walleye, pike and pickerel, freshwater and saltwater perch, codfish of all forms, flatfish in all forms, Pacific rockfish, snapper and black seabass, all porgies and grunts, striped bass, lingcod, tilapia, most catfish, all the drums except the freshwater drum.

THE BOTTOM LINE

The important thing to keep in mind here is that this is all just a guideline. You can use pretty much any fish or seafood in any of the recipes in this book. Some will be better than others, and there will be flavor and texture differences, but none, really, would be catastrophic. If you see amazing shrimp at the market and want to use them in a recipe that is normally done with, say, walleye, chances are it'll work. A fried walleye sandwich made with shrimp becomes a shrimp po'boy sandwich, and a pretty walleye baked in parchment becomes an equally pretty shrimp baked in parchment. Different? Yes. Good? Absolutely.

Follow this guideline and you will be set free. It's so liberating that instead of supplying you with suggested fish and seafoods to use with any given recipe, I will do the opposite: I'll let you know if there is a fish or group of fishes that *won't* work with it. And since I can't help myself, in some cases, I will tell you what fish I personally love to cook with said recipe, but you should keep in mind that these are just my idiosyncracies, not dogma.

4

PREPPING YOUR CATCH

EQUIPMENT

Being a good fish cook doesn't require a ton of special equipment, but there are a few items that will make your life easier. Below is a sampling of things you absolutely need, as well as some nice-to-haves.

FILLET KNIVES Ideally, you will have more than one. I use three. I mostly use a twelve-inch knife with a blade about a half-inch wide, but I also have a salmon knife that is very thin and is fifteen inches long. I also have a smaller fillet knife for smaller fish. Manufacturer doesn't really matter, so long as it makes you happy. My advice is to not spend too much money. Fillet knives are tools meant to be used, and used hard. When I'm working commercially, I'll sharpen my knives several times each day, and when I'm cutting bony fish like Pacific rockfish, several times during one filleting session. I know people who swear by electric knives, but I don't much like them. They can be effective, though.

KNIFE SHARPENER While I use Japanese water stones for my kitchen knives, I prefer an electric sharpener for my fillet knives because I need to sharpen them constantly. If you want to go with a stone, get a coarse grit and stick with it, or one with coarse and slightly finer on the other side. But if you are working dozens of fish, a few sweeps in an electric sharpener makes this work a lot easier. Stones use either water or oil as their whetting medium. Water can be used with all stones (even

so-called oil stones), but a water stone is a water stone; oil will ruin it. For stones that are designed to accept oil, once you choose oil, you cannot go back to water. I prefer water stones.

FISH SPATULA Arguably more valuable than a fillet knife, a fish spatula is an offset metal spatula with a slightly sharpened end to it. You get them either right-handed or left-handed. They are strong, thin, and light. I use mine every day, whether I'm cooking fish or not. The advantage is that you can use that beveled end to scrape along the bottom of a pan, dislodging any stray stuck-on parts.

LONG SPATULA This is the sort of spatula you see short-order cooks using, the kind with a beveled, ten-inch-long business end. Sometimes called griddle spatulas or pancake flippers, they are excellent for gently lifting fish off a grill or broiler. I have two, which allows me to slip the spatulas under a longer fish and gently carry it to a platter without the fish falling apart.

KITCHEN SHEARS Get strong, breakaway shears, ideally with a bone notch. Shears make short work of spiny fins and are very useful for cutting through strong ribs and for breaking a skeleton down into pieces for stock.

PIN-BONE PLIERS These look like giant tweezers with bent ends. They're far better for removing bones than needle-nosed pliers, although both will work. At less than $10 apiece, you can pick up a few.

FISH SCALER Not entirely necessary—a butter knife will do the job in most cases—but dedicated fish scalers are even cheaper than pin-bone pliers, and they are better at scaling fish with stubborn scales or very large scales.

CATFISH PLIERS These are super useful if you catch a lot of catfish, pufferfish, or eels. Their wide ends grab more skin to pull than other pliers and tend to rip less skin. It makes a huge difference. You can get good ones for less than $15.

LARGE CUTTING BOARD Wood is my choice in the kitchen, but outdoors, I prefer the white plastic boards that are light, cheap, and easily hosed down. You want a cutting board as long as the fish you commonly catch, within reason. Restaurant supply stores are your best bet here.

ARMORED GLOVE Again, not totally needed, but it will make your life easier when filleting lots of spiny fish. You obviously need only one—for your off hand, as the other hand has the knife. There are lots of cut-resistant gloves out there, none costing more than $20.

THERMOMETER Not for taking the temperature of the fish, but for fryer oil and poaching liquid. An actual probe thermometer—the kind you stick into the hot liquid—works better than the laser thermometers because those can sometimes give you off-readings if your pan is reflective. I prefer the quick-read digital thermometers, but anything that can accurately read temperatures up to 400°F will do.

GRUNDENS If you are a serious angler, you will want a pair. These are rubber overalls and are worth their weight in gold on a boat. They keep you dry and, when cleaning fish, prevent fish ick from embedding itself in your clothes. There are other companies that make this sort of overall, but Grundens are far and away the best.

SKILLS

This section is all about the skills you need to be a better fish cook. Starting with a whole fish, I'll walk you through gutting, scaling, shucking, picking, filleting, portioning, and skinning. You'll also pick up tips on more esoteric skills like removing collars or throats from certain fish, cutting out cheeks, and removing pin bones. To see these skills in action and in more detail, visit my YouTube channel, HuntGatherCook, where you'll find a companion video on each skill described here.

I've done most of these tasks my whole life. My methods work well, but some are idiosyncratic. There are other, equally useful ways to skin a catfish, for example. If you have another method you like better, go for it.

SCALING FISH

Scaling fish is fun to do inside—at someone else's house. Seriously, this is a messy job, but an easy one. Almost all fish can be scaled with a butter knife or one of those $1.25 fish scaler thingies. You simply anchor the fish with your off hand and scrape backward against the grain of the scales—in other words, toward the head. You can also use a very sharp knife to slice off the scales along with a thin layer of skin, again moving from the tail toward the head. Some chefs prefer this method on the theory that it damages the skin less and results in a crispier skin down the road. I myself have not noticed a difference.

You scale fish that you intend to eat whole or if you want nice crispy skin on your fillets. Always scale before you fillet. Trust me on this one.

Some fish require no scaling, as their scales are minute or non-existent, as with eels. Small trout and salmon fall into this category, as do the small mackerels. All can be scaled, and if I'm getting fancy, I'll scale them. Other fish have scales so tough that they're basically impossible to scale; big redfish and carp spring to mind. But you can turn

▲ Scaling a striped bass.

this fact to your advantage by using those scales as a shield against strong, direct heat by cooking your fish "on the half shell," as I do on page 230.

Oh, and if you absolutely positively must scale a fish indoors, do what we did at the restaurant: encase yourself in a big plastic garbage bag, preferably white, so light filters through. The scales will stay inside the bag. Not ideal, but it'll work.

GUTTING FISH

Many times, you will gut your fish before filleting and scaling. This is because many fish have enzymes and parasites in their gut cavities that, once the fish is dead, can damage the meat. Fast swimming, energetic fish like bluefish and salmon need to be gutted onboard, or the meat will suffer. And certain parasites that hang out in the guts of some fish, notably tapeworm larvae, can move to the meat after the fish is dead if given the time. Gutting a fish onboard is never really a terrible idea, because it will help chill that fish faster when you put it on ice in the cooler. And the faster a fish is chilled, the longer it will keep fresh. That said,

in some cases, you wait to gut or don't at all. Scaling a fish is easier before it's been gutted, and in many fish, especially bass-like fish, you can fillet them without ever gutting them.

If you do gut, it's easy. Run your fillet knife, blade facing up, from the vent to the collar. In most cases, you will want to slice all the way to the gills. Then reach in and pull all the guts out. In larger fish, you may need to cut the gullet up near the mouth to get everything out.

A little angler's tip: Look inside the stomach of fish you're fishing for. It can help you catch more to know what they are eating. And partially digested fish or octopus are legendarily good for catching fish like shark or lingcod.

Remember that the roe of many fish is delicious (page 318), so save it. Fish hearts and livers, in some cases, are good to eat, although I don't use them much.

Once the main guts are out, there is sometimes another step. Some fish, like cod and their cousins, have a black lining around their gut cavity that must be peeled out. You can do this simply by rubbing it off with your fingers. Salmon have a pale lining, but it too needs to go. Salmon, trout, and most other species of fish will have a dark kidney tucked under their spine, often confusingly called the bloodline, which really refers to the dark line of meat along the centerline of a fish. This kidney is bitter and must be removed. A spoon is a good tool for it. With salmon, you will need to crack the final five or six bones at the tail end of the cavity to remove all traces of the kidney.

Finally, you need to remove the gills of any fish you plan to eat whole or that you're going to use for fish stock. With small fish, you can just yank them out, but the gill rakers on larger fish will punish you for that. Better to snip them out with shears or a knife. You remove gills because like the kidney, they are bitter, and they will cloud and ruin a fish stock.

CLEANING SMALL FISH

Small fish like anchovies and smelt are cleaned a little differently (really small fish, like whitebait, are not cleaned at all; you just fry them whole—there's a reason they're called "fries with eyes"). While there are a few ways to clean these little fish, the easiest is to pinch down on the head until your fingernails meet, then yank down toward the vent. You should get the head and most of the guts in one fell swoop. Both these fish have the black lining I mentioned above, and while I rarely bother to remove it on these fish, if you want to, an old toothbrush will work. Gently rubbing smelt and anchovies in a large bowl of salty water will remove most of the scales and not damage the meat (remember, fresh water on saltwater fish can hurt meat quality).

HOW TO FILLET A FISH

I once did a cooking demo in front of a crowd of maybe 120 people, many of them avid cooks. I was demonstrating how to butterfly a fish for smoking when I casually commented that everyone there already knew how to fillet a fish, right? I could feel the fear. So I looked up and asked how many people knew this skill. Only about twenty-five people raised their hands. I should have guessed. Filleting is second nature to me—I've filleted thousands of fish, everything from bluegills to giant bluefin tuna (I once filleted 127 Pacific rockfish in about ninety minutes, a typical day for a deckhand aboard one of the party boats sailing out of San Francisco Bay)—and I simply forgot that it's a skill that most don't possess. But I'm going to break it down for you here, step by step. Do it enough times, and you, too, will be filleting like a deckhand.

Let's Start with an Easy One—A Rockfish

To begin with, you will need a fillet knife. A boning knife will do in a pinch, but in most cases, you really need a long, thin, flexible blade to do things right. Species with thick ribcages are sometimes easier with a heavy boning knife. The bigger the fish, the longer the knife.

In most cases, I prefer to fillet with the head on the fish because the head acts as an anchor. This can depend on the fish, too. Fish with giant heads, such as cobia, tuna, amberjack, and yellowtail can actually be easier to fillet if you take the head off; you outline both fillets with your knife before you take the first slab off. If you take a slab off with the head on, the second side can present you with tough angles and cause you to miss meat. But for most fish, having the head on helps. You hold it down with your off hand to steady the fish. Slice behind the head but in front of the gills down to the spine. The bones of salmon, sablefish, mackerel, and trout are relatively weak, so be careful not to whack right through the spine.

Now turn your knife toward the fish's tail and run the blade over the spine—right through the ribs—back to the tail. Once you get the hang of it, you'll be able to do this in one clean sweep of the knife.

Flip the fish over and repeat. One tip, considering that the fish's head is now bending upward because its corresponding fillet isn't there anymore, is to hang the head over the edge of the

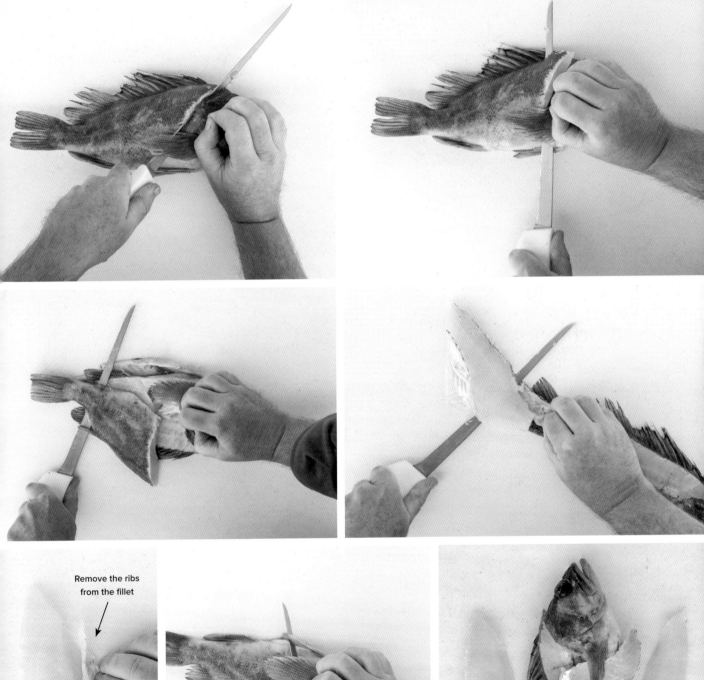

Remove the ribs from the fillet

cutting board so the fillet you are working on lies flat. Now you should have two nice fillets and the rack, or skeleton. Don't toss the rack! See the sidebar below for what to do with fish racks.

You still have ribs attached and pin bones to deal with. I like to remove the ribs by slipping the point of the blade just under the rib bones, facing up toward where the spine was, then slicing—keeping pressure on the bones—upward to free that part of the rib cage. Once you get this started, you can reverse directions and slice off the ribs with minimal meat loss. Why bother? Because the belly sections of salmon and trout have the most fat, and fat equals flavor.

Now you have two quasi-boneless fillets. Next thing to do is to remove the collars. This is the front portion of a fillet that starts at the gill arch and extends to just behind the pectoral fin (if you can picture the shape of the state of Minnesota, you've got a good idea of what it looks like). All you do is slice it off. Collars are spectacular grilled, smoked, or broiled. They're almost as fatty as bellies (page 232).

Finally—and this last step is your call—you might want to remove the pin bones. Note that this is very difficult to do with a really fresh fish. I generally wait at least one day before pulling them, and it's even easier to pull pin bones with a thawed fillet. And it's much easier to pull pin bones from a whole side as opposed to a portioned set of fillets. So do this before you portion. How? With either needle-nosed pliers or a special pin-bone puller, which looks vaguely like giant tweezers with broad nips at the end. Pin bones in all fish are set at an angle, and that angle changes with each species. In general, however, pin bones angle up and toward the head of the fish—or rather, where that head used to be. A few species of fish, notably black cod and many of the bass-like fishes, have pin bones so strongly attached they cannot be removed before cooking. If you have persnickety guests, remember to pull the bones before you serve the meal.

WHAT TO DO WITH RACKS?

Fish skeletons are not garbage. I use most of those I come home with, most often to make fish stock (page 169). But I dislike pressure-canned fish or seafood stock, and I only tolerate frozen fish stock; yeah, I am a snob, I know. So when I have lots of fresh racks, I either plan on making something like a fish or seafood risotto (page 249) or Simple Spanish Fish Soup (page 174), or I'll chop them into manageable pieces and freeze for later.

Another fun thing to do with small fish skeletons is to dust them in cornstarch and fry them whole. It sounds weird, but with small fish, it works. The bones soften and the whole thing is crunchy and nutty. See page 325 for details.

For salmon, trout, and other large fish, I will remove all the meat from the skeleton with a normal spoon, simply scraping the meat toward the tail. On a large chinook salmon, I can save more than a pound of meat. Spoon meat is excellent for Salmon Patties (page 204) or a fish salad (page 257). It's also ideal for Fish Sausages (page 326).

Got too many racks? It happens. A couple of good uses for them are as crab bait or buried in your garden for your vegetables. Just be sure to bury your skeletons at least a foot deep—preferably two—to thwart the trash pandas (some call them "raccoons") and other nighttime diggers unearthing them.

Filleting Large Bass and Similar Fish

It's not uncommon to come home with very large bass-like fish, which besides bass include walleye, perch, crappies, Pacific rockfish, snappers, and grouper. The codfish family also falls into this category. These fish have heavier bones and large ribcages, with bones so sturdy your knife won't zip through them. For these fish, the answer is to ignore those ribs. Make your fillet at an angle from the nape, right behind the head, down toward the vent. The fillet will look a bit like an odd triangle or a trapezoid.

What about all that meat over the ribs? Or the belly? In many cases, it's too thin to make it worth it; it will be overcooked by the time the main fillet is just barely done. And the bellies of most firm white fish aren't terribly great. Besides, if the fish is carrying PCBs or mercury, most will reside in the fat, and bellies are the fattest part of any fish. That said, on very large fish, like those over ten pounds, you can use kitchen shears to clip off the ribs where they meet the spine and use this cut exactly as you would pork ribs. Barbecue or smoke them, as I do on page 228.

Incidentally, the rib question is why I rarely fillet really small bass-like fish. You can get better access to that meat when the fish has been cooked whole. All is not lost, however, as the racks that have the rib and belly meat on them are fantastic for fish stock (page 169).

Filleting Pike and Similar Fish

Pike, carp, and a few other notable fish have an extra set of bones in them that can confound anglers. Small pike about fourteen inches or thereabouts can be filleted like a regular fish, removing the ribs, of course, and then slicing the fillets into little fingers perpendicular to where the backbone was. Then they're fried. This process opens up the little Y bones to the hot oil and softens them enough to where you'll barely notice them. Extra calcium, anyone? This won't work with a decent-sized pike or carp, though. For that, you really do need to deal with the Y bones. I once fished for pike at Gods Lake in Manitoba. The Cree guides who joined us on that trip filleted the northerns in the usual way, then sliced out the Y bones in a strip, leaving a normal-looking fillet (more or less). That's a perfectly good way to do the job. But the problem is that even though the pike fillet done that way might look like that of, say, a walleye, it isn't. The pike fillet will be of many different thicknesses, so cooking it whole will be a challenge. The Cree got around this by cutting the fillets into pieces and frying them up for shore lunch.

I prefer a different method, one I learned many years ago from the late, great A. J. McClane's book *Encyclopedia of Fish Cookery*. It results in not two fillets, but five. I've also improved on McClane's method by borrowing a trick from salmon anglers: using a spoon to scrape out all

▲ A pike ready to be filleted.

the extra meat from the carcass as well as from between those Y bones.

Here's how to do it. Start by slicing from behind the head all the way back to the dorsal fin. You want to make this cut so that the blade rides just over the top of the Y bones. You can often feel where this is before you cut by gently squeezing the top edges of the fish. You then fillet off the flanks of the fish, using the Y bones as your guide. You slip the point of the blade under the Y bone to the spine, then fillet over the ribs to free the flanks. Keep this fillet the same length as the top cut, which is to say no longer than where the dorsal fin is. Remove the two "tail" fillets as if the pike or carp were any other fish. Now skin as normal.

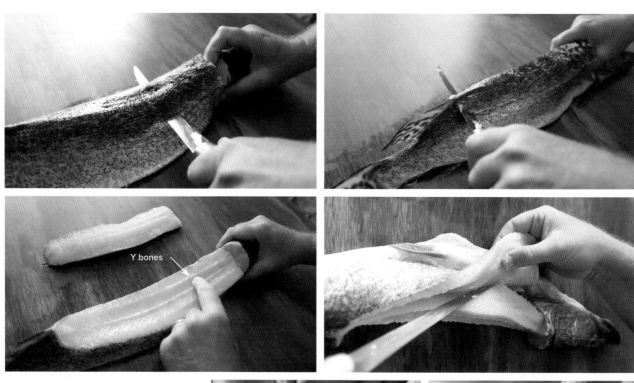

▲ Slice off top fillet first, just over the top of the Y bones. Remove fillets below Y bones above the ribs. Fillet tail sections as you would any fish. Remove the skin.

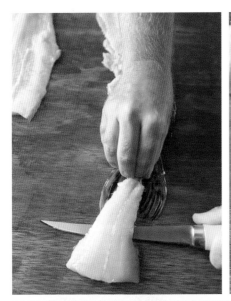
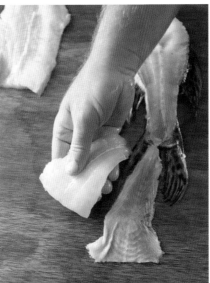
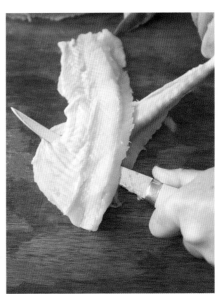

BLOODLINES

All fish have some sort of bloodline, the dark meat that runs underneath the fish's lateral line, an often visible line or stripe that runs down the center of the fish, more or less from behind the pectoral fin to the tail. This dark meat is always stronger in flavor than the white meat that surrounds it.

In very fresh white-meat saltwater fish, there is no need to remove it. But in many freshwater fish, this meat is the source of muddy flavors, especially in fish like carp or catfish. It's perfectly edible, but most people, myself included, slice it out after skinning the fillet. I also do this with large mackerel, tuna, and bluefish, as well as with most jacks. Interestingly, the bad reputations of bonito and false albacore come entirely from their unusually large bloodlines. Remove the bloodline from these small tunas, and you basically have a tiny yellowfin.

You need a sharp knife to remove the bloodline, and you need to remember that the bloodline will be thickest at the lateral line. So when you remove it, you're cutting a shallow, triangular cross section from the overall fillet.

Definitely remove the bloodlines before freezing fish. They will become unbearably fishy after thawing.

Side note: your pet cat loves bloodlines.

To Skin or Not to Skin

I love crispy fish skin—so much so that there is a recipe for fish skin "pork rinds" later in this book (page 321). Crispy fish skin, especially on lean fish, will often be the only morsel of fat and luxury in an otherwise austere fish.

Skin is fatty, and it contains a lot of collagen. It is an absolute must in making fish stock (page 169). But sometimes, this isn't such a taste treat. Take carp, for example. Skinned carp is wonderful. Skin-on carp is all too often muddy tasting. And the skin on catfish is so gelatinous, I rarely leave it on, and when I do, it is in Asian dishes where that gelatinousness is welcomed. Shark and sturgeon and swordfish have very thick skins that aren't good to eat, unless you use the pork-rinds method. I do acknowledge that this being America, most people recoil at skin-on fish, let alone whole fish. I find this frustrating, but *eso si que es*, as they say in Spanish.

So, if you want to skin your fish, with a couple of exceptions, you do it once the fillet is off the fish. Sort of. I'll explain.

The easiest and fastest way to skin a fillet is to do so before it's entirely off the skeleton. You make your fillet cut as normal, but don't go all the way through the skin at the base of the tail. Leaving that on, you flip the fillet so the fat end is facing somewhere past the tail, and then you slide your fillet knife between the meat and skin at the tail end and sweep it through to the head end—all the while keeping downward pressure on the knife. Sounds complicated, but it's really easy (see photographs on page 43).

The other way—and you do this with long fish or large fish—is to remove the fillet, then anchor the tail end with your off hand and sweep the fillet knife between skin and meat toward the head. Some people like to anchor the fillet with a beer cap nailed to a dowel. It works, but so does a reasonably strong hand, especially if you have fingernails. Pro tip: on long or large fish, you will often keep the knife almost stationary as you work the skin off with your off hand.

Here is how I fillet a flatfish. When I say "flatfish," I mean such fish as halibut, fluke, flounder, sole, plaice, and turbot. This method works with any flatfish, with the exception of really small ones like sand dabs. I generally use this procedure with flatfish larger than about a pound, up to about forty pounds. The larger the fish, the more extras, like collars or cheeks, you can collect; they're not really worth it on fish smaller than about ten pounds. Really large Pacific and Atlantic halibut are cut this way, too, more or less, but they are then steaked.

Start by getting a lightning-sharp fillet knife appropriate to your fish. I tend to use a Kershaw fillet knife with at least a nine-inch blade. You want a long blade with a larger fish so you can make long, sweeping strokes. This results in a cleaner fillet.

You fillet a flatfish with the intention of getting four boneless fillets, not two like in round fish. How to do this? Easy, as the fish itself gives you directions. First, lay it out on a work surface and look for the lateral line running down the center of the fish, which follows the fish's spine. Slice down to the spine along this line, from right behind the pectoral fin down to the tail. Then you want to make three cross cuts that will mark the ends of your fillets. First is across the tail, and the other two are from the pectoral fin to the vent and from the pectoral fin to right behind the head.

Now, starting at the tail, use your knife to free one half from the skeleton. Run the knife along the spine in long, gentle strokes. At first, you just want to get the fillet off the spine. Then, again starting at the tail end, sweep the knife against the ribs toward the line of fins at the edge of the fish. You want to have the knife touching the ribs. When you get to the tail part, run the knife all the way to the edge so you get what I call the "frill" meat; more on that in a bit.

When you have one fillet off, the second comes much easier. Take your time at first, but once you get the hang of it, you can cut even a large flatfish in a few minutes.

With both halves off the top, repeat the process on the white side of the fish. The top fillets are always thicker, and if you are nervous about filleting, you might want to start with the white side, as there is less meat there to mess up. I generally start at the top, though, as I've been doing this for many years.

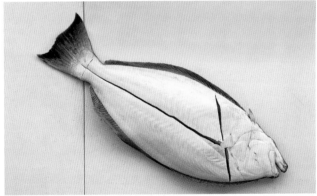

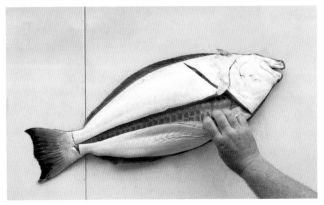

»

When you have all four fillets off, the carcass should be clean, translucent even.

If you've not been that clean, fear not. Just slice any remaining meat off the carcass and flash-freeze it overnight to kill any potential parasites. Then, eat it as sashimi with some wasabi and soy sauce.

In general, the skin on a larger flatfish isn't terribly good to eat. They have very small scales that don't come off easily, and the skin is pretty thick. I do like the skin on small flatfish, though, like sand dabs and small flounder. But for the most part, you want skinless fillets.

To do this, you again need that long knife; a short one will make skinning much harder. I start from the tail end; the tail meat, in my opinion, isn't as good as the meat behind the head. Slice down to the skin, and anchor the back of the skin with your off hand. Slide the knife between the skin and the fillet, and work the skin back to you. On a big fish, you will need to readjust your grip once or twice.

The skin comes off surprisingly easily. If you've cut too much meat off, slice it thin and add it to the sashimi pile. If you've left some skin on the fillet, carefully slice it off. This is where a truly sharp knife comes in handy.

Now, many times you will still have the "frill" meat attached to the fillet. This needs to go, as it will fall off the main fillet when you cook it. You can usually just pull it off. Save it for the sashimi pile, as this is the most sought-after cut in all of sushi, at least when it comes to flatfish. The Japanese call it *engawa*.

Again, to kill any potential parasites, be sure to flash-freeze whatever flatfish meat you intend on eating raw.

From here, you're done with smaller flatfish. For larger ones, you'll want to cut the long fillets into three kinds of meat. First is the loin, the thickest part of the fillet. Square off the head end of the fillet and use what you cut off for soups (page 169), Poke (page 280), or Thai Fish Curry (page 198) or the like. Do the same with the bottom end of the loin, where it's much thinner than the primo parts.

You then cut the loin into pretty blocks, which you'll want to sear; I especially like them brined and served with an Italian salsa verde. Finally, when you get toward the tail end, you either add it to the soup pile or keep them separate for making fish and chips.

That leaves the cheeks and the collars. Cheeks you just remove using your ingenuity; there's no particular way to get them out. Simply poke your knife through the skin, then slide it under the skin to remove. Then slice away the cheek. The only tip I can give you is that it is deeper near the eye than near the gill plate. These are best floured and fried.

Finally, on really large flatfish, you have the collars. I only bother with these when the fish is about ten pounds or larger. Halibut collars are best marinated and grilled.

To remove them, I use kitchen shears to cut them free from right behind the pectoral fin. Then I use my knife to slice down to the edge and cut the collar in half. Alternatively, you can remove halibut throats by snipping the whole collar off under the chin, then at each gill plate. You then snap it flat, and you have both collars as one piece.

Some people eat the roe and the livers, but I rarely do. Livers often harbor parasites, and I personally don't like the roes of flatfish, although they are perfectly edible.

CATFISH AND EELS

These two, along with other slimy fish, require a bit of medieval torture. You need to cut the skin behind the head of these fish and then use pliers to yank the skin off. Though you can use regular pliers for this, I highly recommend special catfish pliers, which work far better than anything you have in the house right now (page 40). With catfish, beware of the nasty spines on the pectoral and dorsal fins; on some catfish, these spines are venomous. I snip them off before getting down to business.

You skin first and fillet after, unless the catfish is huge, in which case you can fillet as you would with any other fish. One way to skin a catfish is to nail the fish to a tree, or, if you plan on doing this often, by pounding a flathead nail into a board or tree and using that to anchor the catfish or eel. Gruesome, but it works.

Gar

Garfish are unique. Their hides are so tough that they need to be removed with tin snips or stout shears. You use your knife to cut around behind the head, then use the snips or shears—one blade under the skin, the other on top—to cut the skin at the top of the gar all the way back to the tail. On really big gar, I've seen guys use a hatchet to make that first cut, and then they will anchor the fish as best they can and start from the tail. You then basically fillet off the skin. Yes, it's that tough. Once skinned, you can then fillet as normal.

Side note: garfish roe is poisonous. Don't eat it.

Bowfin

Also known as grinnel or choupique, bowfin are tricky. First, you have to fillet them alive or immediately after death, as these fish contain enzymes that turn the flesh to putty soon afterward. Fortunately, bowfin are mellow fish that, like catfish, will stay alive in your cooler for a few hours if you put them in a livewell or cooler with some water.

To clean a bowfin, stun the fish with a hammer or a club, fillet as normal, skin, and then ice down in a mixture of two parts icy water to one part vinegar, which will firm up the meat and remove any blood; bowfin are bloody fish.

Bowfin must be served absolutely fresh. It does not freeze well at all.

Mullet

Mullet can be filleted like any fish, but since it is often the roe you really want, you will want to be sure to not fillet through the ribs and risk cutting the roe. Fillet mullet like a bass, over the ribs, then crack open the ribs from the top to get at the roe. The belly meat in a mullet is strong tasting and not to everyone's liking (I myself am not a fan). Mullet bellies make excellent bait.

Mahi Mahi and Tuna

You don't strictly need to do this, but many people will peel the skin off mahi mahi, cobia, and some tuna before starting to fillet. You do this by slicing the skin as if you were outlining the fillet of the fish, then using your fingers or pliers to remove the skin. Tuna are something of a special case in that they really have top and bottom loins, not a typical side fillet. One tip on skinning is to use a standby fillet knife rather than your favorite—because this will be rough on it—to slice off the top edge of the fish, through the dorsal fins. This reveals the two sides of the fillet from the top.

Monkfish

Chances are you'll never catch a monkfish, but just in case, here's the method.

Chop off the gigantic head and remove all the innards. Some people love monkfish liver. If you're one of those people, keep the liver. Keep in mind that many monkfish livers are *loaded* with parasites.

You will be left with a rather icky, headless, slimy thing. Peel the skin off; it will come off easily. Chop off the tail section at the dorsal fin, which is far back on a monkfish. Then fillet the meat off the sturdy backbone. You'll notice some gnarly looking membrane over the fillets, a sort of second skin. This needs to go, too. Carefully remove it with your fillet knife. Portion as you will from there.

Pufferfish

First, only eat Atlantic puffers. Pacific puffers are too toxic for regular folk to mess with. Seriously, you can die; look up *fugu* and you'll see; it's the liver, which is highly poisonous. Japanese chefs who want to serve *fugu* sashimi must be specially licensed to do so. Atlantic puffers have a lot less of the poison than Pacific ones.

To clean them, cut down through the spine behind the head and fold the fish back to expose the spine. Grab the spine hard with catfish pliers or vise grips and yank the head back toward the tail, which will pull off all the skin and leave you with what on Long Island we called "fish drumsticks." Once you get the hang of it, it all takes just a second or two.

Wash thoroughly and fry.

How to Fillet a Skate or Ray

These are pretty straightforward. When you catch your skates or rays, slice off the wings and get them on ice as soon as possible. Keep in mind that rays are slimy, so you might want to segregate them from less slimy fishes in your cooler.

When you're ready to fillet them, know that there is a band of cartilage in the center of the wing. You can cook small wings with this cartilage intact, but I prefer to keep only the skates and rays that are large enough to fillet properly. Using the cartilage as a guide, you simply fillet the meat off it. The meat will look like corduroy. Then remove the skin as you would a regular fish, starting with the ends of the wings, which are the skinniest.

Butterflying, also known as splitting or kiting a fish, is a basic skill you'll want to know, especially when dealing with smaller fish such as trout, bass, or perch. It keeps the fish whole but largely debones it. The technique is ideal for smoking, salting, quick pan-frying, or for stuffing the fish.

For a butterfly cut, make sure the fish is scaled and gutted first. Start by making sure your knife is sharp—it's important; you'll mangle your fish if your knife is dull.

Remove the dorsal fin. You need to do this to let the fish lay flat when you're done; the dorsal fin also has a set of bones in it you want to remove. Do this by slicing gently on either side of the fin, all the way to the backbone. Tap the tip of your knife against the backbone when you do this. Gently pull out the fin.

Now remove the ribs. Start from the tail end of the fish, and put the tip of your knife against the backbone where the ribs begin. Slice the ribs free. Do this by slicing from the backbone toward the end of the ribs, gently pressing the knife upward against the ribs—this preserves most of the meat on the fish's flanks. Do this on both sides.

»

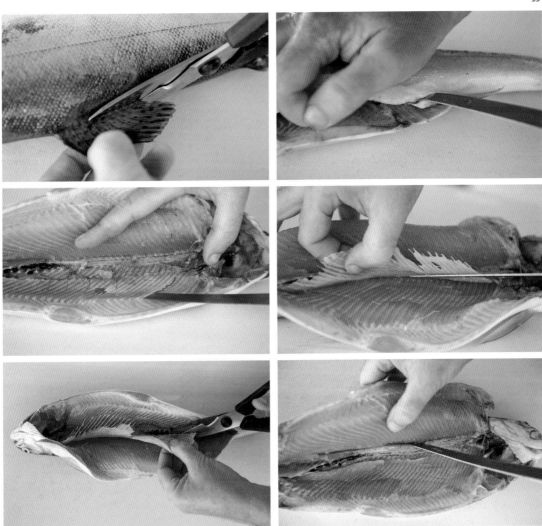

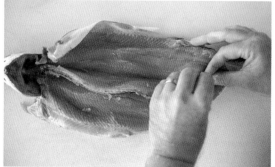

▲ A butterflied trout. You can remove the head so it lays flat if you want.

Use the knife or kitchen shears to snip off the ribs close to the backbone. Now you need to remove the backbone itself. Start by freeing the ends of the backbone from the fish's body. Use the kitchen shears to snip the backbone right behind the head and right in front of the tail. Use the knife to free the backbone from the meat. Be careful not to slice all the way up to the top of the fish and through the skin. When you get close to the fish's head, you'll feel resistance; these are the fish's pin bones. In trout, herring, sardines, and mackerel, these pin bones are small and insignificant. Leave them, as you won't even notice them once you cook

the fish. In bass, salmon, perch, and rockfish, you will want to use needle-nosed pliers or pin-bone tweezers to remove them. If you're butterflying any large fish (larger than eighteen inches or so), you'll need to remove pin bones. Do this on both sides. You'll be left with a fish lying flat and the backbone sticking up in the air.

To remove the backbone, use one hand to anchor the fish where it meets the backbone; I start at the tail end of the fish. Use the other hand to gently pull it straight up. As it comes free, use your fingers to keep the fish flat and to preserve as much meat as you can. Gently work your way up toward the head, and the backbone should come free.

You now have a fish perfect for stuffing. I like to sew stuffed fish shut, but toothpicks work just fine. If you want to pan-fry the fish instead, remove the rest of the backbone near the tail as well as the head so the fish lies perfectly flat. It takes a little practice, but once you get the hang of it, you can do this whole process in about three to five minutes.

Kiting is the opposite. You start from the top of an ungutted fish and work your way toward the belly, leaving the belly intact. Kiting is generally done when you're salting fish, like cod.

PREPARING SEAFOOD

So much to know here! There are arguably more skills to know with seafood than with finfish. Below are some bedrock skills, along with some fun tips for more obscure creatures.

CLEANING SHRIMP

Cleaning shrimp is easy, a good place to start your career cleaning fish and seafood. It's as easy as peeling the shells off, but there are a couple of variations and extra steps you can take to make things nicer.

First, pop their heads off. Most commercial shrimp are sold headless, because the enzymes in the shrimp's body will rot the meat in a hurry. So when you see head-on shrimp, you know they're ultra-fresh. Keeping the heads on shrimp keeps the meat moist, and the cooked innards are delicious, like a fatty shrimpy butter (it's the same with crawfish). Don't want to suck heads? Put your shrimp heads in stock.

Now, about the shells. Like the heads, the shells are loaded with flavor. I never toss mine until after they've been used to make shrimp stock. But you might not want to peel your shrimp at all, especially if you're grilling them. Shells help keep the

▲ Beautiful spot prawns caught near Vancouver, Canada.

meat of the shrimp moister, and they take smoke better than the meat. Don't be afraid to offer your friends and family peel-and-eat shrimp. Just have plenty of napkins around.

What about the tails? Everyone seems to love to keep the tails on shrimp. I think this is a holdover from the 1970s shrimp-cocktail era, when the tails were your handle. And yes, they are aesthetically pleasing. But leaving tails on robs you of meat or, if you know how to get at the meat in that last tail section, makes you peel an already peeled shrimp. My advice? Either keep the shrimp totally in the shell or peel the whole thing.

Oh, and if you happen to have shrimp with eggs on their tails? If it's legal to keep where you are, keep them on and serve these shrimp shell-on. Shrimp roe is amazing! Suck it off the tail before peeling.

Finally, you have the "vein," which is really a poop chute. I'm ambivalent about removing it, however. If you look at the shrimp and there's no dark line on its back, it's OK to just eat it. But no one is going to get sick eating a shrimp with even a full vein; removing it is mostly about decorum.

Spot prawns and other cold-water shrimp rarely seem to need deveining. You remove the vein with either a dedicated "shrimp deveiner," which I've used because someone gave me one once, or a paring knife. The deveiner is a plastic pointy thing that looks vaguely medical. You jam it into the space where the vein starts and run it along toward the shrimp's tail. Works fine.

Normally, however, you use a paring knife to slice right over the vein down to its level, usually about an eighth of an inch on a typical shrimp. You then use the tip of the knife to lift up the vein and remove it. It will stick a bit at the tail end. You'll want a paper towel nearby to stick the veins on, as they are sticky and get everywhere if you don't have a home for them.

CLEANING CRABS AND LOBSTERS

Lobsters and crabs can be sold alive or cooked. Maine lobsters are typically sold live, and the tails of spiny lobsters are generally sold frozen. Crabs are often sold live, but you will see pre-steamed crabs, too, especially Dungeness crabs. Neither generally needs any cleaning before cooking or removing the meat from the shells.

CLEANING SQUID AND OCTOPUS

It's fair to say that these are for the more hardcore folks out there. We tend to buy squid and octopus, and they'll almost always be cleaned. But you *can* catch them. It's not easy, especially when it comes to octopus, which are world-champion escape artists. Let's start with squid, which are more commonly caught, especially off the docks along the Pacific Coast and New England.

So you have a bucket of squid. Now what? Start by pulling them in half, mantle and tentacles. Use a small knife to slice off the eyes, and if you didn't get the little beak, cut that out, too. Inside the mantle

will be some weird, gooey stuff. Fish it out and toss it, or use as fertilizer or crab bait. The small black sac that you see contains the squid ink. If you want to save the ink, gently cut the sac away and put it in a separate bowl. Chances are you will break it, but that's OK if you get most of it in the bowl. There will also be a stiff, glassy "pen" that you need to pull out. On small squid, the pen might be hard to find, but it's in there. That's it, unless you want to skin your squid, which you can do by rubbing the thin skin off. I do this only when I want the end result to be white or if I have squeamish guests.

Octopus is another matter; they don't die easily, as squid do. Hawaiians say the best way to dispatch an octopus is to bite it right between the eyes. I prefer stabbing it with a fillet knife. Once you have a dead octopus, you use a knife to cut out the beak, as with squid, and then you can either separate it the same way as a squid, or you can slice the head open, turn it inside out, and clean out the innards. Gnarly but effective.

SHUCKING CLAMS AND OYSTERS

By clams, I mean hard-shell clams, like cherry-stones or Manila clams. And by oysters, I mean oysters you can actually pick up; a lot of wild oysters are cemented to rocks or other oyster shells, meaning you need to shuck them into a container right on the beach.

There are two ways to shuck these tasty bivalves: from the hinge or through the lips. I do both, depending on my mood, but I'm generally a hinge man. To do this, you use a short, reasonably dull clam knife or oyster knife. These knives are different. Clam knives are thin and are primarily used to slice between the two shells from the front. Oyster knives are pointier and are used to jam into the base of the hinge of an oyster, twist, and pop it off.

Here's the trick: I use an oyster knife for both, because I open them the same way. With an oyster, you hold the heavier shell in your palm—most oysters have a heavy, cupped side and a thinner, flat side—find the point where the top shell hinges onto the bottom one, jam the point of the knife in there, twist, and it should pop. You then slice right underneath the top shell to free it; you'll need to scoop under the thicker shell to totally free the oyster.

With a clam, you use the side of the knife. Holding the clam firmly in your off hand, jam the base of the knife between the shells at the hinge and twist. It should pop. Slide the knife above and below the clam to free it, as you would with an oyster.

Another way to open either clams or oysters is the finesse way, using a stiff paring knife. With this method, you use the blade of the knife to slip in between the shells. Once inside, turn the knife, and you'll pry open the shells. I generally don't use this method if I have a clam or oyster knife handy, because I've cut myself more often using the paring knife.

Once you've practiced some, shucking clams and oysters really is as easy as it sounds. Only the first thousand or so are difficult. And there are a few tricks. One is to put your clams in a 350°F oven for six minutes, then take them out and shuck them as soon as you can hold them. Makes it a lot easier, and they'll still be alive when you shuck them, although you'll need to chill them down again if you're serving your clams on the half shell (hat tip to the great chef Jacques Pepin for this one). Another trick is to set your clams or oysters in the freezer for three hours or so. When you take them out, they'll be groggy, and they won't tighten their shells as much when you try to shuck them. Or just steam your clams open, or toss your oysters on the grill—thin side up, remember!

RAZOR CLAMS

Razor clams are easy to shuck and clean, although they have brittle shells. Slide a thin knife alongside one side of the shell to free it from the clam. Now you'll see, right by the hinge, a little section of darkish stuff; that's the guts. Scrape this away with the tip of your knife. Now slide the knife under the shell to completely free the clam, and you're good

to go—unless you want to roast or sauté your razor clams, which I love to do. In this case, leave one side of the clam attached and free it after they're all cooked. One pro tip: always shuck the same side, so when you line them up for everyone to eat, the hinges are all on one side. It's a good look.

PREPPING MUSSELS

If you buy mussels, they will come already cleaned. But if you gather them, you'll want to scrub their shells well to remove random ick and many of the barnacles, and you'll also need to remove their beards, the strong little fibers that hold a mussel to a rock. You can kill a mussel by doing this, so only debeard mussels when you're planning to cook them right away. I do this with a paring knife. Anchor the beard on the flat of the knife and just twist it off, generally toward the hinge, although either way works. Another option is to leave them on and slice them off with a paring knife after the mussels are open; I do this only when I'm not serving mussels in the shell.

Here's a seldom-revealed tip: when you're removing mussels from their shells, use a paring knife to slice off the teeny "scallops" that hold a mussel's shell closed. They're delicious. The same holds true for all clams.

PREPPING SMALL SNAILS

For those of you who want to gather East Coast periwinkles or West Coast turban snails, prepping them for cooking couldn't be easier. Gather what you plan to eat—usually state limits amount to a nice meal or two, so no need to store them long—put them in an escape-proof container like a bucket with a lid, and bring them home. I like to do this in a bucket with some seawater and some clams I just dug; I rarely venture to the beach solely for snails. Scrub the shells well with a dish-cleaning brush, and you're basically done. You will need to steam or boil the snails to get them out of their shells. Once boiled for ten to twenty minutes or so, depending on how large your snails are, you can use a toothpick to corkscrew them out of the shell. Remember that they have a hard "door" to their house called an operculum that you will discard; it looks like a little black disk.

The front of the snail is all meat, the inner portions are the rest of the animal. I don't eat the innards of large snails, but I do for little periwinkles.

HOW TO CLEAN A GAPER CLAM OR GEODUCK

Clammers on the Pacific Coast have heftier bivalves to contend with than the familiar quahogs, steamers, and surf clams of the Atlantic. We have an entire family of what are collectively called "gaper" clams, so called because there is so much clam to them that their shells cannot fully close. The king of them all is the Pacific Northwest's geoduck, *Panopea generosa* (and its New Zealand cousin, *Panopea zelandica*), but more common are the Washington clam (*Saxidomus gigantea*) and the horseneck clams, *Tresus capax* and *T. nuttallii*. All can be daunting when you wrangle them out of the mud and sand. They're big, they're heavy, and they're gooey. And there's that well-endowed siphon of theirs. The very idea of eating one on the half shell makes me go pale. And frying them is out of the question—at least whole. So what to do?

Here's how to clean gaper clams to get them ready to eat. First, you need to purge your clams (see page 30 for that). When you're ready to do the cleaning, find a short, sharp knife like a paring knife or pocketknife. Get a big bowl to work over, because you want to capture all that wonderful clam juice. Be near a sink and running water.

Understand that a gaper's shell is held tight by the same two "scallop" muscles all tasty bivalves use. You want to slip your knife into the shell above the siphon and run it along the inside of the top shell, slicing free the first "scallop" muscle and all the various bits. You can now open the shell completely.

Yummy, eh? We'll get to the anatomy of a clam in a bit. Now run your knife the same way, underneath the clam this time, to free it from the bottom shell. Drop it into the bowl with all the clam juice. Repeat until you have all the clams out of their shells. I discard most horseneck clam shells, but I clean and keep the shells from large Washington clams; they're excellent for Stuffed Clams (page 82) or Baja Grilled Clams (page 236).

With a bowl of gooey clam bits floating in salty clam juice staring at you, now what? First, remove all the horseneck (or geoduck) siphons from the rest of the clams. Cut just the siphon off, leaving the rest in one piece. Set the siphons aside. The siphons of Washington clams can be left on, as they don't have the same tough skin on them.

Separate the clam juice from the clam meats. I do this by pouring the juice into another bowl through a strainer that has a paper towel set inside. The paper towel is vital because whatever grit is left after purging will settle in the bottom of your bowl. Grit is the enemy. Keep this juice (it freezes well) for seafood soups and other recipes. I also freeze my clam meats submerged in the clam juice.

The last thing you must do with the clam meats is clean the bellies. Doing this is the nastiest part of cleaning clams, so nasty that some people discard the bellies altogether. I think this is a shame. To clean the bellies, find the muscular foot and look opposite to it; you'll see a dark splotch on a soft, bag-like thing. Squeeze the belly to extrude the black ick from within the belly. When you do this, you'll see a hideous, glass-like "pen" shoot out of the belly—it's alarming until you get used to it. Discard this. Run the opened belly under clean running water, and use your fingernail to scrape out most of the black stuff.

Some people separate the "scallop" muscles from their clams to eat like scallops. Others will remove the foot and eat that separately. It's tough, but if you pound it between two pieces of plastic wrap until it's thin and tender, you can eat it like abalone. Very good in tempura or stir-fries.

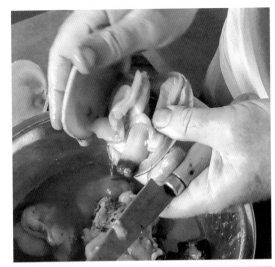
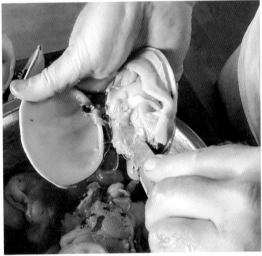

▲ Clockwise from top left: foot, "scallop" muscle, siphon, and the other scallop muscle.

Your clams are ready now to chop or grind. You can't really eat gaper clams whole like littlenecks—they're just too chewy. I grind mine for clam cakes, Chinese dumplings, or clam chowder, but many people chop them by hand. Either is fine.

As for the siphons, you need to blanch them in boiling water. I boil for thirty to sixty seconds, then plunge the siphons into a bowl of ice water. Slice off the horny end of the siphon and discard. The skin should peel off pretty easily, revealing light-colored clam meat with a pretty magenta tip.

You can chop or grind the siphons with the rest of the clam, or you can pound them thin between pieces of plastic wrap and slice for sushi, ceviche, or stir-fries. Keep in mind that all but the youngest of horseneck clams will have very tough meat, so don't skip the pounding step unless you're able to slice it so thin it's translucent.

Once cleaned, I keep my clam bits in the clam juice, which is salty and will help keep everything fresh. They'll keep in the fridge for a few days, but you should freeze them after that. When you freeze, leave at least one inch of head space in the jars because the water will expand when it freezes. Frozen like this, the clams will keep a year.

CANNING FISH

Home-canned fish and seafood can be a wonderful thing. Utilitarian, yes—nice to have a jar of home-canned tuna in the pantry for a late-night tunafish sandwich—but also uniquely delicious. This may not sound right to those of you for whom canned fish and seafood are lesser things, even poverty food. As the late, great rapper Biggie Smalls notes, he remembered when he used to eat sardines for dinner . . . before he hit it big. On a more personal note, I too once ate canned sardines on cheap bread for dinners, back in my early twenties as a cub reporter. It is not a culinary memory I cherish.

Then, later, I discovered Spanish and Italian canned fish and seafood, and it changed my opinion of this process once and for all. When well made, cared for, and properly preserved, canned fish and seafood can, in its own way, be better even than fresh. The keys are simple: use good ingredients, and keep it simple.

Here's how to go about it. First, you must pressure-can fish. Period. End of story. You cannot safely can fish and seafood using the water bath method, even if you're talking about pickled fish. This is a significant vector for botulism poisoning in North America, especially in Alaska and Canada. Use a pressure canner.

I follow the University of Georgia guidelines generally when canning anything, but carefully and to the letter when canning fish and seafood especially (there are a few exceptions that I'll get into in a moment). Those guidelines are as follows:

- Cold pack your fish into pint or half-pint jars. Not quarts.

- Add a teaspoon of sea salt, and maybe a spoonful of oil, maybe a pinch of an herb. Remember, keep it simple. I will generally toss the fish pieces with whatever I'm adding first, then pack the jars.

- Leave one inch of headspace in the jars. Keep that space, as well as the rims, scrupulously clean. If any oil gets on them, wipe it off with a paper towel dipped in a little vinegar.

- Close the lids, put the jars in the canner, and follow its directions for venting and such. You'll want to can your fish at 10 psi for ninety to one hundred minutes, unless you're 1,000 feet above sea level or more, in which case you'll want to bring it to 15 psi. I use a weighted gauge canner, so my choices are just 10 and 15 psi. If you have a dial gauge canner, you are good at 11 psi from 0 to 2,000 feet, 12 psi from 2,001 to 4,000 feet, and so on, up to 14 psi above 6,000 feet.

- Always take your time when the canning is done. Let the canner return to normal pressure on its own, then remove the lid, then let the jars all pop before you remove them. I let them sit on a wooden cutting board overnight before storing them. Always, always check the lids to make sure they've sealed. If they haven't, put the jar in the fridge and eat it within a week or so.

Some Variations

First, tuna, in my opinion, should always be packed in oil. Even inexpensive olive oil makes a huge difference, and I've canned in all sorts of other oils, with good effect. You want something flavorful. Obviously, there's nothing wrong with packing tuna in a little water, enough to keep that one inch of headspace. Keep in mind that sturgeon, swordfish, marlin, shark, and similarly textured fish can all work as "tuna" in this method.

I also can my tuna for only ninety minutes, which is ten minutes below the official standard. Why? Because that's how they do it in Oregon and Washington with albacore. It's been proven safe, and it results in a slightly less hammered product. Feel free to go the entire hundred minutes if you want.

On the other hand, I will can smoked fish for a solid 110 minutes—almost two hours—as the official guideline recommends. Why the extra time? Because smoking fish in an anaerobic environment can, in very rare cases, foster the growth of botulism toxins. You don't want that, and the extra time is thought to kill them.

What about seafood? Well, you can do it, but pressure-canned seafood, with the exception of smoked oysters and mussels, is simply not as good as frozen. That said, pints of precooked seafood of any kind should be canned for about seventy-five minutes, give or take five minutes. The exception to this is shrimp, which only need forty-five minutes.

If you pressure-can crabmeat, it will darken and look weird. You can mitigate this somewhat by adding lemon juice or citric acid. You'll taste it in the final product, but it will result in a lighter colored meat. That said, I don't pressure-can crab or lobster.

And this is another place I stray from official guidelines, in an effort to follow the Spanish example. In the guidelines, they say to not add liquid to the pints. I do—specifically, good olive oil. I will toss raw or smoked clams or mussels or oysters with extra virgin olive oil, pack them into jars with a half teaspoon of fine sea salt, and can them that way. They come out lovely. Note that this method has not been cleared by official sources as safe for smoked shellfish. I'm offering it to you because it has worked for me over the years.

PART TWO

COOKING

WHAT FOLLOWS IS an admittedly idiosyncratic compendium of methods and recipes for cooking fish and seafood. They reflect my more than forty years' worth of experience cooking and eating creatures from our oceans, lakes, and rivers in practically every state, as well as in Mexico and many Canadian provinces.

You'll see emphasis on some methods over others, and for this I make no apologies. There are a few common ways to cook fish—steaming in parchment is one—that I find drab, fussy, and boring. You might have a different opinion, and that's fine, but I decided not to include a recipe or method here simply because "it ought to be in the book." The topic of fish and seafood cooking is too vast to try to include absolutely everything.

Very few of these recipes are designed for just a single species of animal. Feel free to plug and play with whatever fish or seafood you have on hand. I'd much rather see you cook a snapper recipe with, say, freshly caught walleye than see you searching from market to market until you find a decent

slab of snapper. To get you started on this, part 2 opens with a chapter that will help you go it on your own—some general principles for pairings and freestyling. Get this section down, and you'll be well on your way to grabbing the pots and pans first and the cookbooks as an afterthought.

Beyond the species variability, you will often see a section called "Variations" under any given recipe. These are suggestions to play with the recipe itself, often adjusting it not only to what you might have in your kitchen, but also to slide from one cuisine to the next. A great many master recipes for fish or seafood exist, at least in structure, all over the world; only minor details change.

This section is organized by cooking method, the most sensible approach to preparing fish and seafood. Undoubtedly, you will find yourself gravitating to one chapter over another, and that's OK. Just know that when you finally get tired of eating, say, Chinese Sweet and Sour Fish (page 106), a galaxy of other options awaits you in the rest of the book.

◄ Pacific rock crabs, steaming in the sink.

5
PAIRINGS
AND FREESTYLING

GENERAL PAIRINGS

As a child, I ate an awful lot of chicken noodle soup, usually out of a can. But even back then I wanted something a bit more entertaining, so I would look up at the spice rack above where I sat in the kitchen and pluck a little jar of whatever caught my eye. Each day it would be something different. Monday's soup might go with a few shakes of dried thyme. Wednesday I'd discover that cayenne is spicy! My approach was far from systematic, just a haphazard "herb of the day" I often knew nothing about until the moment it began playing with my chicken noodle soup.

Very quickly I learned that some flavors work well together, while some do not. I grew to love that hit of cayenne, which is why you see chiles used liberally throughout this book. But I can say definitively and from experience that apple pie spice is not so good in a bowl of chicken soup. The most fascinating thing I learned in this makeshift childhood experiment was that *most* of the herbs and spices did go well with the soup, but they would radically alter the experience of eating it. Think about a chicken soup with cardamom versus one with winter savory.

I bring all this up to tell you that the same is true for fish and seafood, which are often as amenable to outside flavors as that bowl of soup. What follows is a guide through the proverbial spice cabinet, and more.

Use the following as a resource for foods that go well with particular fish and seafood. The structure is inspired by Karen Page and Andrew Dornenburg's *The Flavor Bible*, an excellent book that I recommend highly for this sort of thing. These pairings will help you develop your own recipes or to freestyle when cooking.

◀ Casting for walleye on God's Lake in Manitoba, Canada.

PAIRINGS BASED ON FLAVORS AND ACCOMPANIMENTS

FENNEL, ANISE SEED, AND STAR ANISE These anise-like flavors and the liqueurs infused with them, like ouzo, Pernod, raki, and certain *aguardientes* in South America, can be used with all varieties of fish or seafood.

BACON Although bacon runs the risk of overpowering some fish, it's a fine addition to preparations featuring lean white fish, especially freshwater fish, which tend to be bland. Clams like bacon, too, as does salmon.

BUTTER Whether fresh or clarified (sold in many stores under its Indian name, ghee), butter is an excellent fat to cook fish in. Scallops like it, too.

COCONUT Most fish and seafood work well with either shaved coconut or coconut milk. Even the dark, oily fish work well with it. Salmon and trout are only so-so with coconut, though.

HERBS Think soft herbs like basil, chervil, dill, parsley, cilantro, tarragon, chives, mint, lemon verbena, fresh oregano. Parsley and anchovies are especially good together.

ONIONS AND GARLIC They go with everything.

CITRUS All citrus goes well with fish—lemon for a European or Middle Eastern flair, limes for Central American, South American, and Southeast Asian preparations. Preserved lemons are especially good, as their salty, funky nature boosts lean, white fish and can stand up to full-flavored fish like salmon or mackerel.

CREAM Think of cream specifically for white fish. Most white fish are very lean, so cream adds needed fat.

CURRIES Most fish and seafood are good in curry, whether it's Indian, Southeast Asian, or African. Thai curries are especially fine with fish and seafood.

GINGER Use ginger, or its Thai-leaning cousin galangal, especially when going Asian, West African, or Caribbean.

CHILE PEPPERS In general, use the lighter, brighter chiles for fish. All fresh chiles will work with fish and seafood. When using dried chiles, avoid the dark and smoky ones like anchos, pasillas, and chipotle—except with octopus, which can take it. Guajillo is an excellent choice, as is chile puya or habanero. I also like Basque Espelette pepper. All the little hot dried ones are good, too—Thai, arbol, chiltepin, cayenne. The South American ajis are excellent choices.

GREEN SAUCE All incarnations of green sauce—Mexican, Italian, French, German—work well with fish.

MUSHROOMS Matsutake and button mushrooms are particularly good with fish. Salmon and matsutake, trout and morels, and freshwater bass with chanterelles are all classics.

OLIVES It seems odd, fat on fat, but olives work especially well with oily fish.

SAFFRON This spendy spice (the world's costliest by weight) lightens up most fish and seafood dishes, turning all to gold. Very few fish don't like it; sardines and mackerel are two of them. The best saffron is from India, Iran, and Spain. A very little goes a very long way.

TOMATOES Every fish, especially the dark oily ones like tuna, sardines, bluefish, and mackerel, plays well with tomatoes.

WASABI AND HORSERADISH Very few fish or seafoods *don't* work with these zippy condiments. I especially like them with lobster, as well as with heavy, oily fish like salmon, tuna, and mackerel.

WINE White wine with fish is typical, but I like using rosé a lot, too. White vermouth is always a winner, as is Japanese sake or a dry fino sherry. In some cases, a light red like a grenache or a pinot noir works well. This would also be a shorthand guide to what to drink with fish; in general, a wine that goes well in the pan will go well in your glass.

PAIRINGS BASED ON SPECIFIC FINFISH AND SHELLFISH

Below are the larger classes of fish and seafood and the pairings that are special to that group. You'll notice that most are saltwater species; virtually all freshwater species are white fish and would fall into the general ingredients- and accompaniments-pairing section above.

Clams

Clams really like being around strong flavors, much more so than, say, white fish.

ANCHOVIES Cured and mashed anchovies are especially good. Clams with anchovy butter is a classic.

CHINESE BLACK BEANS These are funky and often laced with chiles. Add them in a clam stir-fry.

CHORIZO Clams with either soft Mexican or hard Spanish chorizo is another classic. Really, any salted pork product will nuzzle up well with a clam. Talkin' to you, bacon.

ROMESCO SAUCE This garlicky Spanish sauce with sweet peppers is pretty much good on anything.

Crabs

ASPARAGUS Crabs with asparagus is another combination that just works. A shaved asparagus and crab salad is hard to beat.

AVOCADO I have to restrain myself from adding avocado to every crab dish I make.

CELERY It's a texture thing. Crunchy celery is a fantastic foil for soft, sweet crab.

MAYONNAISE I'm not normally a fan of mayo, but I like it with crab.

OLD BAY 'Nuff said.

PINEAPPLE Odd, but it works. Crab fried rice with pineapple chunks is amazing.

Lobster

ARTICHOKE HEARTS Don't worry about why. Lobster and artichokes is just a great combination. Butter and garlic round things out.

CHANTERELLE MUSHROOMS Chanterelles work really well with lobster, better than with crab. Look for them in the summer in most of the country and in winter in the Pacific Northwest.

COGNAC OR OTHER BRANDY The richness of lobster holds up to these alcohols.

OLIVE OIL There's no denying lobster's beautiful affair with butter, but olive oil—especially one of those pungent green olive oils you can get in the fancy oil section—is actually better. That hint of bitter and the green color work really well against the lobster.

Bluefish, Herring, Mackerel, Shad, and Other Oily Fish

OLIVES Going oil-with-oil works here, as there is a slight bitterness in olives that works against the strong fish to balance it.

CAPERS AND PICKLES The acidity and salt work to counterbalance the oiliness.

MUSTARD Again, something cutting and pungent to balance the oily fish.

SAKE Marinating these fish in this Japanese rice wine leaves them tighter and tasting cleaner.

VINEGAR Of all the fish and seafood, these species work best with vinegar. Their oiliness requires an acid more powerful than citrus.

ROSEMARY These are some of the few fish that work well with this resinous herb.

Salmon and Trout

BACON The strong flavor of bacon can overwhelm some fish. Not salmon.

CORN The sweet pop of good corn—primarily sweet corn—with the fatty salmon or trout is both colorful and balancing.

CUCUMBERS These are always welcome with white fish, but they work well with salmon and trout, too.

MISO This fermented soybean-based paste (sometimes made with barley or chickpeas) is powerfully flavored—too much for most fish. But salmon, black cod, and the bluefish clan like it quite a lot.

MOREL MUSHROOMS Combined with trout or the first salmon of spring, morels make a classic combination.

PINE AND SPRUCE Both are resiny and citrusy at the same time, and this works really well with fatty salmon and trout. Use the young growing tips of the branches.

Shrimp

Shrimp can handle quite a bit more than most seafood. There's not a lot that doesn't go well with it.

BACON Shrimp, too, likes bacon.

GARLIC Most fish and seafood like garlic, but shrimp loves it. Think shrimp scampi.

CHEESE Yes, cheese and seafood. Mexico has proven that shrimp (and clams) can play nicely with melty cheese.

Tuna

Tuna likes everything that the bluefish and mackerel clan likes, plus these:

AVOCADO Like avocado and crab, tuna and avocado just works.

Lots of fish do well with soy sauce, but tuna especially likes it.

WHITE BEANS Tuna—canned tuna in particular —paired with white beans is classic for a reason.

FREESTYLING

You're ready now to think about freestyling—making your own recipes using whatever's at hand or available in nearby stores. In essence, freestyling is a matter of hitting all the main flavor notes in a delicate balance—the essence of a successful dish. Easier said than done, right? Let me walk you through a classic to illustrate it—a simple fish sandwich.

First, you'll want a fillet of fish firm enough not to fall apart when put between two pieces of bread. Fortunately, pretty much any white fish will fit the bill, from panfish to walleyes and bass, to black seabass, Pacific rockfish, and snapper.

Most often, you will fry said fish. Why? Frying covers two bases: savory (the fish) and crunchy (the coating). The softshell crab BLT may be the gold-standard model; its perfect combo of fried, savory, and slightly crunchy crab makes it a strong contender as my deathbed meal. Grilling is a perfectly acceptable alternative to frying, but what you gain in Maillard reaction (browning/char) you lose in crunch.

On to the bread. It's your starch component, and while not 100 percent necessary for a meal, most of us want some form of starch to tide us over to the next meal. Besides, you need something vaguely bread-like for it to be a sandwich. If you've fried your fish, a classic hamburger bun will be perfect; its softness works well with crunchy fried fish. If you've grilled your fish, you'll want a good, hearty, crusty bread; the crust is your crunch. But remember, the act of biting down on a sandwich made from crusty bread will crush what's inside. A workaround is to scoop out a little of the bread inside the roll, creating little hollows. This prevents everything from escaping out the sides of the sandwich.

Now, what's in the sandwich besides fish and bread? A green thing, usually lettuce. This element is normally for color—we eat with our eyes—crispness, and moisture, and it contributes a welcome slightly bitter note. Believe it or not, most of us want a touch of bitter in a dish, even if it's as mild as parsley. But you can switch things up. Why not try French sorrel in place of lettuce and bring acidity and tartness to the party? Which brings us to the tomato slice. That tomato slice is there for more than its color. Its real job is to bring the acidity —which balances the fatty crust on the fried fish— and a bit of sweet. Yes, sweet is key, too. Not necessarily sugar sweet, although that can be great sometimes, but a hint of it.

Finally, you have the condiment on the sandwich. In this classic case, it's typically mayo or mustard. They do different things. Mustard hits the spicy note, awakening your taste buds. Mayo adds richness and is especially welcome when your fried fish is lean (properly fried fish is not terribly fatty).

See how much is actually going on with something so simple? That's what makes a classic a classic; all the culinary alchemy has been worked out for you. But it's not hard to do this on your own. You just have to remember to balance all the elements—savory, salty, sweet, sour, spicy, fatty. And no, you don't need all of them in one dish for it to work. But it sure helps.

To fully delve into this sort of freestyling would be a book unto itself, but you get the general idea. Before we move on, I do want to touch on another way to think about all this: through the lens of region and culture.

I once made a dish called Walleye Minot (the full recipe is on my website, Hunter Angler Gardener Cook) that celebrated a great fishing trip I had on Lake Sakakawea in North Dakota. I began working out the dish on the drive back to my hotel that night. My first thought was to make a fish risotto the way they do in Venice, but North Dakota is pretty much as far from Venice as you can get, both culturally and geographically. The solution, it turned out, was whizzing by the truck's windows:

thousands of acres of North Dakota barley. Barley, it so happens, makes an excellent risotto.

I decided I would make this dish as a hat tip to everyone in North Dakota who helped me so much; NoDak was definitely a highlight of my book tour that year. Sitting in the back of my truck was a bottle of buffaloberry syrup that had been given to me by my friend Beth Schatz-Kaylor of the blog *Rhubarb and Venison*. I decided to make a sweet-hot-sour gastrique with it to brighten everything up. By itself, the syrup tastes like the love child of cranberry and peach. To balance it, I added some malt vinegar, salt, and chile.

I filleted the walleye I'd caught, skinned the fillets, and portioned them out all pretty. I oiled the bones and heads with sunflower oil and salted them, then I roasted everything until it was well browned (see page 170 for the technique). This is what I would use to cook my barley risotto.

As for the fish, I salted the meat for an hour, then poached it very gently in butter. That left the skin, which, instead of tossing, I used to make walleye-skin chicharrones using the method on page 321.

The result: an incredibly flavorful barley risotto, topped with sweet butter-poached walleye, ringed with a little zippy buffaloberry sauce and topped with a light and crunchy fish-skin chicharron. No foams or molecular techniques were used to make this dish, but it certainly wasn't just a plate of fried walleye.

Here's how a simple concept—make a dish in which virtually every component is living in or around Lake Sakakawea on a particular day in October—came together. I was in North Dakota, a cold region where they grow barley and sunflowers and where most people are of German or Scandinavian descent. That set the tone. I chose butter as my fat because it made sense culturally, the way olive oil would with a Mediterranean dish. I wanted something like a risotto but used local barley instead. That hit the starch and fatty notes, the walleye the savory element, and the crispy skin the crunch. The final bright note was the gastrique,

▲ Walleye Minot.

which is basically a French sweet-and-sour sauce of vinegar—in this case, malt vinegar—and the local buffaloberry syrup. It all worked. As it turned out, it worked really well.

My point is that you might want to play with your fat, starch, sweet, sour, and spicy elements based on where you live. Are you in the Southwest? Tequila, lard, chiles, Sonoran flour, and mesquite or prickly pear syrup are all go-to ingredients for a great plate of fish or seafood. Now, I'm definitely not saying that if you're in North Dakota, you shouldn't cook tropical food. By all means, go for it. But you can create very satisfying—and, dare I say, unique—variations on classic dishes by paying attention to your local specialties. You can also riff on where the seafood came from, like a Caribbean stew made from fish you caught on a trip there, or a New England fish chowder with haddock. So long as you hit the savory, salty, sweet, sour, spicy, and fatty notes—which, by the way, you should become alert to when you eat someone else's food—you will go a long way toward never needing a set recipe again.

6

BROILING AND BAKING

BROILING

Broiling is considered an out-of-fashion method of cooking these days, and in some ways it is—unless you have one of those fancy salamanders, where you can precisely adjust the distance between the heat and the fish. That said, broiling has its place. Cooking something via fierce heat from above is especially good with long fillets of fish. Think anything too long for a frying pan or so thin you really don't want to move it.

My dad loves broiling. He has a dish that he makes all the time where he puts a haddock fillet in an individual broiling pan—those "sizzle plates" you used to see in restaurants, the kind that settle into a wooden charger—topped with butter, breadcrumbs, and maybe a hot pepper or some herbs. Simple, but he loves it. Once the dish is ready, he moves it to the wooden charger and eats. No need to ever move the fish.

Broiling is also an excellent way to achieve some sense of charring when you live in an apartment, or it's winter, or you're anywhere without access to a grill. Broiling can also give you a quick blast on the top of a dish to brown it quickly. For both of these applications, I put the rack as close as it can get to the flame or the electric heating element. You want to get browning as fast as possible without baking the fish.

Simple though it sounds, there's more to proper broiling than you might think. So many of us just pop a piece of fish or meat or some vegetables under the broiler and call it a day. Sometimes it comes out nice, sometimes it doesn't. It can seem like a mystery. But here are some tips and tricks to broiling fish, especially thin fish, that will serve you well.

First, your broiler is not a salamander. A salamander is what we use in the restaurant kitchen to brown the tops of things in a hurry. You place the food down and move the roaring hot gas flames as close as you need so the food is nicely browned in seconds. Nothing in the home can truly replicate this.

And let's face it, with broiled trout or any other fish you don't want that. What you want is perfectly cooked, moist fish that isn't blackened and blistered on top. Most fish tend to fare poorly when cooked hard, although a thick piece of swordfish, king salmon, or catfish can handle some blackening.

Trout, walleye, flounder, and small salmon are ideal candidates for broiling, for two reasons. First, you often catch them just a bit too large for a frying pan. Laying that fillet on a broiling pan is a perfect solution. Second, since the fillets are thin, you need not turn or otherwise disturb the fish while it cooks, so it stays nice when you serve. Any fillet that fits this description works, too. Small dorado and large Spanish mackerel fillets spring to mind.

So how to get there? First, salt your fish and set it out to come to room temperature. Salting the fish and letting it warm up a bit ensures that the fish will cook quickly all the way through. Of course, if you like your fish rare, move it right from the fridge to the broiling pan; you still need to salt it.

Get out a broiling pan, not a baking sheet. You can, of course, use a baking sheet if you must, but the extreme heat of your broiler, which averages 600°F for gas and about 550°F for electric, will often cause your baking sheet to warp with an alarming pop. I've seen this break fish fillets in two. Still edible, but no longer very nice to look at. (Incidentally, use the bottom piece of the broiling pan, the one under the wavy grill top with the holes in it. Line the pan with foil for easier cleanup.)

Next, pat your fish fillets dry and then coat them with oil or, better yet, melted butter. Why? Oil conducts heat better than water. So the roaring heat of a broiler when it hits an oiled surface will cook hotter than one that is wet. And butter browns better than most other oils, so it

◄ Pretty little kokanee salmon, from a mountain lake in California.

▲ Salmon tender waiting for gillnetters to bring in Copper River salmon, near Cordova, Alaska.

looks—and tastes—better when you're done. Oil the foil you're about to put the fish on, too. This makes it easier to move the fillet to a platter. If you want to serve just the meat by slipping it off the skin, then don't oil the skin. It'll stick to the foil.

Set your oven rack at the top. Normally, this is about four to six inches from the element. If it's less, move the rack down.

Preheat your broiler. I am amazed at how few people do this. You don't put things on a grill without preheating, do you? Let your broiler heat up for at least five minutes, and as many as fifteen.

How long does the fish take to cook? Well, that's a bit of voodoo. I generally like four minutes for a typical fillet about a half-inch thick. But that's my broiler. Broiling is not an exact science, and you need to watch it and, in many ovens, rotate the broiling pan midway through. Most broilers throw off heat unevenly, especially gas broilers.

Your fish is ready when it flakes all the way through. If you've basted it with butter, normally this is the point when the butter browns.

Now, how to get it off the broiling pan? Two large spatulas. I have a pair of long short-order-cook spatulas that I use, one in each hand, to carefully lift the fish from the broiling pan to a nearby platter. You don't have to do this, but it looks pretty, as you can see from the picture. And if you get a crack in the fillet? Cover it with whatever you're serving with the fish.

On to what you're serving with the fish. You'll see an array of mysterious and wonderful things with this broiled trout. In this case, it's lovage leaves, preserved mushrooms, preserved rowan berries, pickled mustard seeds, pickled angelica stalks, angelica oil, and black pepper. Esoteric, I know. But you should get an idea of what you're looking for: tart, bright, acidic flavors to balance the rich, fatty fish; something herby; and something else full of savory umami—in this case the preserved mushrooms, but it could be sautéed mushrooms, bits of bacon or ham, shellfish like clams, oysters, or mussels, or even some fresh or dried tomatoes.

There you go. You are now armed with the knowledge to whip up an amazing quick meal that will wow your family and friends. Play with it. Have fun. Enjoy!

BROILED TROUT

PREP TIME: 20 MINUTES | COOK TIME: 5 MINUTES | SERVES 4

1 or 2 large fillets of trout, char, or pink salmon, about 2 pounds
Salt
1 tablespoon vegetable oil
2 to 4 tablespoons unsalted butter
Black pepper

OPTIONAL GARNISHES
¼ cup lovage or parsley leaves
½ pound preserved or sautéed mushrooms (any kind)
1 tablespoon pickled mustard seeds
2 tablespoons berries either pickled or preserved in syrup (I used rowan berries)

Salt your fish well, and set out on the cutting board to warm up a bit. Preheat your broiler, and if it has a setting, set it to "high."

Pat the fish dry with paper towels, then oil it with the vegetable oil. Oil the broiler pan. Set the fillets skin-side down on the pan and dot the fish with bits of the butter.

Broil the fish for about 4 minutes, keeping an eye on it and rotating the fish if you see hotspots under your broiler. When the trout flakes, remove it from the oven. Using two spatulas, carefully lift the fish to a platter.

Grind some black pepper over the fish, and garnish with an herb of your choice, something pickled or otherwise tart—even lemon juice is fine—as well as something else savory, like sautéed or preserved mushrooms. Eat with crusty bread or with potatoes or rice.

NOTE Please don't get all hung up on the garnishes. They are my fancy, chefy touch. The point, again, is something herby, something tart, and something savory.

I normally don't like baked fish. With a few exceptions, which are below, it bores me to tears, it's an imprecise method, and it results in fish similar to, but inferior to, fish cooked in other ways. You will not see a simple baked fish recipe or a faux-fried fish in this book.

All this said, there are some good uses for your oven when cooking fish and seafood—first and foremost, to keep things warm while frying. Yes, that's a snide comment, but it's true. Another good use for baking is to cook through whole fish or very thick, meaty pieces of fish that you've seared on the stovetop first, a method called pan-roasting.

You can also bake hearty stews in a covered Dutch oven rather than cooking them on your stovetop. I generally do this at 325°F or so. That means that any of the stews you see in the soups and stews chapter (chapter 12) can be finished in the oven, after the initial searing and sautéing.

Finally, there are baked things that have fish or seafood in them that I really enjoy, like fish pie shepherd's pie style (English Fisherman's Pie, page 78), actual hand pies like pasties (Crawfish Pies, page 158), and mac and cheese. Mac and cheese with any crustacean is amazing (Shrimp Mac and Cheese, page 80). So there are some decent baking applications for fish, and I'll go over them here.

Pan-roasting is a technique for use with large or thick pieces of fish that you can't easily cook on the stovetop alone. Big slabs of king salmon spring to mind, as do thick blocks of halibut and the "meaty fish," such as tuna, swordfish, shark, marlin, or sturgeon. That said, if you wanted to pan-roast a thick hunk of flathead catfish or a big carp or buffalofish, that'd work, too. Another great use for this technique is to cook through a whole fish that you've grilled, fried, or seared on the outside. Plate-sized fish are best here. Basically, you sear the sides of the fish and then move it to the oven to finish.

With either fillets or whole fish, the easiest way to pan-roast is with an ovenproof pan. Just move the pan into a preheated 400°F oven until it's done,

which is about ten minutes per inch of thickness. Pro tip: *Don't forget that the handle is hot.* Ask me how I know.

The other option is to move the fish from the pan to some vessel in the oven: a roasting pan, baking sheet, another pan, or a rack. If I'm not just jamming my steel frying pan into the oven, I go for the rack option. I set one over a baking sheet to catch drippings. This is a good option because hot air can circulate all around the piece of fish, heating it quickly. I mostly do this with whole fish, however, because something like a salmon fillet will fall apart on a rack.

Note that unless you regularly cook giant blocks of fish, your fish will be in the oven for only about ten minutes. So it's important to have the oven preheated before you start searing.

As always, remember: you can always put something back in the oven to cook a bit longer if you need to. But you can't uncook it.

The final baking-related technique is baking in a shell. Shellfish, by definition, have a shell. And that shell can serve as a vessel. Not only does baking in a shell look cool, but it will add flavor and serve as good portion control—unless your guests won't think twice about eating forty-seven stuffed clams.

All baked-in-the shell dishes share similar traits. Usually the meat is ground, chopped, or shredded, mixed with some starchy thing—breadcrumbs being the most common—then highly seasoned. You can then either bake them or grill them. That said, I have found that heavily grilled crab and lobster shells turn bitter and can impart that bitterness to the food inside (see page 236 for my grilled clams recipe). Typically, these are appetizers for parties, but you can, of course, make a meal out of them. We do. And remember that clam shells can be reused. Scrub them clean after supper, and you'll have cool containers for a future round of baked clams already at hand. Crab and lobster shells are more fragile and don't keep well.

Keep in mind, too, that what's in the shell doesn't have to be the same animal that the shell came from. So if you want to stuff clam shells with fish or lobster or shrimp or oysters for the following recipe, go for it.

SERVING WHOLE FISH

There's an art to serving a whole fish. Many become flummoxed by the array of pointy bones in a fish's skeleton, and this, compounded with an unnatural fear of choking to death on a fish bone, scares many people away from eating whole fish. And then there's the whole staring eyeball thing.

Here's how to go about it. First thing to remember is to always remove meat in the direction of the tail. If you lift this way, you'll take meat and not bones; you're going with the grain of the flesh. When you're around the ribs, lift down and away—so, down toward the belly and back toward the tail. When you get the hang of it, you'll lift the meat right off the ribs.

Once you have half the fish done, pick up the tail and bring it up and toward the head. You'll lift off most of the skeleton this way. Discard it, or, in the case of smaller, oily fish like mackerel, sardines, or trout, save it for crispy fried skeletons (page 325). Now the second half of the fish's meat is easily removed.

That leaves the head. Unless you're dealing with a mega-head like that of a king salmon, amberjack, tuna, or a mighty codfish, most of the meat will be right behind the head at the top and in the two cheeks. Normally, only the worthy get the cheeks, as they are by far the best part. Choose wisely.

◀ A perfect kokanee salmon.

SNAPPER VERACRUZ

PREP TIME: 2 HOURS (MOSTLY MARINATING TIME) | **COOK TIME: 1 HOUR** | **SERVES 4 TO 6**

This is arguably the most famous Mexican fish dish, with the possible exception of fish tacos. Veracruz, on the Gulf of Mexico, is the state where the food is most like that of Spain: olives, capers, olive oil, paprika, roasted red sweet peppers, and parsley all play far more important roles in this part of Mexico than elsewhere in the country. The effect is very Spanish, and very good. Huachinango, or red snapper, is the common fish used, but any fish you can fit in a shallow pot will do; I use Pacific rockfish. Go for a bass-like fish first, so black seabass, snappers, perch, largemouth, spotted or smallmouth bass are all good options.

Serve your snapper (or whatever) with short- or medium-grain rice, ideally Spanish *bomba*. I like to serve this by lifting off portions of meat from the bones and setting it on the rice, spooning around some sauce.

2 whole bass-like fish, scaled and gutted, gills removed

2 limes

Salt

¼ cup olive oil

1 white onion, chopped

4 cloves garlic, minced

2 pounds tomatoes

¼ cup white wine

¾ cup fish, seafood, or chicken stock

12 to 15 green olives, sliced

¼ cup capers

2 bay leaves

2 teaspoons dried oregano, Mexican if possible

4 jalapeños, pickled or fresh, cut into strips

A pinch of cinnamon

2 tablespoons chopped parsley

Cut the limes in half and rub them all over the fish, squeezing out juice as you go. Salt the fish well inside and out and set them in the fridge for 2 hours.

Preheat the oven to 350°F. Heat the olive oil in a large pan and sauté the onion until soft. Stir in the garlic and cook for another minute. Turn the heat to low.

Purée the tomatoes with the wine and stock, then pour it into the pan with the onions and garlic. Turn the heat back to medium-high. The sauce will look strange at first, a sickly pink, but it will return to normal as it cooks. Add all the remaining ingredients except the fish and parsley, stir well, and simmer gently for 15 to 20 minutes.

In an ovenproof casserole, lay down some sauce. Set the fish on top, then cover with the remaining sauce. Set in the oven uncovered and bake for 40 minutes, or until the meat flakes easily away from the bones.

To serve, lift portions of the fish off the bones and serve over rice with the sauce. Garnish with parsley.

ENGLISH FISHERMAN'S PIE

PREP TIME: 20 MINUTES | **COOK TIME: 30 MINUTES** | **SERVES 6**

This is, more or less, a shepherd's pie with haddock or cod, and it will often have a mix of fish and seafood, most often fresh white fish, some smoked fish, and maybe lobster, crab, or shrimp. There's quite a bit of dairy in here, as well as cheddar cheese. It is one of the few fish dishes I like with cheese.

My advice is to either make the dish with leftover mashed potatoes or to make a batch of mashed potatoes especially for the pie. Once you have the potatoes, the dish comes together quickly.

POTATOES

2 pounds russet potatoes

Salt

¼ cup unsalted butter

Heavy cream or milk as needed
(about ¼ cup)

Make the potatoes first. Peel and cut them into chunks. Put them in a pot, cover with water by at least 1 inch, and toss in some salt. Bring to a boil and then drop the heat to a simmer. Cook until tender, then empty the pot into a strainer to catch the potatoes. Put the pot back on the burner and turn it to low.

Return the potatoes to the pot and let them steam off for a minute or two, shaking the pan as you go. This drives off more moisture to make for fluffier mashed potatoes. Add the butter and start mashing the potatoes with a potato masher. It will be a little dry, so add cream as needed to make smooth mashed potatoes, usually about ¼ cup. Turn off the heat and let the potatoes cool.

I will normally move the potatoes to a bowl and wipe out the pot for this next step, but you can use a clean pot, too. Pour in the cup of milk and cup of heavy cream and bring to the steaming point, about 160°F. Add the white fish and any uncooked shellfish you have, like shrimp. You don't need to do this for precooked crab or lobster or crayfish. Let the fish poach in the milk-cream mixture for 5 minutes, not letting the liquid simmer or boil. Turn off the heat and pour the liquid into a bowl, straining off the fish. Save both.

Now, if the pot you've been using is large enough to hold all the various fish, you can keep using it. If not, get a large sauté pan ready. Heat the butter in whatever vessel you're using over medium heat and, when it's hot, add the leeks, then a pinch of salt. Sauté the leeks in the butter until they're nice and soft, but not browned, about 6 to 8 minutes.

½ pound white fish (cod, bass, walleye, snapper, etc.), cut into chunks

½ pound smoked fish of any type, flaked

½ pound shrimp, crabmeat, crayfish tails, and the like, cut into bite-sized pieces

1 cup whole milk

1 cup heavy cream

4 tablespoons unsalted butter

2 leeks, split, cleaned, and cut into thin half-moons

Salt

¼ cup flour

½ cup lager beer or mild ale, at room temperature

2 teaspoons dry mustard

1 teaspoon prepared horseradish (optional)

¼ cup chopped parsley

3 tablespoons chopped chives

1 cup shredded cheddar cheese

Turn your oven to 350°F.

Add the flour to the pan and mix it in well. Cook this, stirring often, for 5 minutes. It will clump up, but that's OK. Slowly pour in the beer, stirring it in as you go, until it's incorporated. Do the same with the milk-cream mixture that you cooked the fish in. You want everything to be roughly the consistency of house paint, so you might not need all the milk and cream.

Stir in the mustard, horseradish, parsley, chives, and all the fish and seafood. Mix well and taste for salt, adding if needed. Turn off the heat.

Spoon this mixture into a casserole dish or some other shallow, ovenproof vessel. Spread the mashed potatoes over everything, then sprinkle the shredded cheddar on top. Bake for 20 to 30 minutes, or until you get some nice browning on the top.

Wait 10 minutes before serving, to let the pie set a bit.

"No good fish goes anywhere without a porpoise."

LEWIS CARROLL

SHRIMP MAC AND CHEESE

PREP TIME: 20 MINUTES | **COOK TIME: 30 MINUTES** | **SERVES 6**

Rare is the day that I mix cheese and seafood (English Fisherman's Pie, page 78), but crustaceans with mac and cheese is an exception. The taboo against mixing cheese and fish or seafood is largely an Italian one, and I absorbed it growing up in a heavily Italian American–influenced New Jersey. Few other cultures observe this prohibition, and Americans of all stripes love lobster mac.

Shrimp mac and cheese is more accessible, less expensive, and almost as good as the luxe original. I prefer spot prawns I catch while in Alaska, but really any shrimp will work, as will crawfish, crab, and yes, lobster. Shrimp mac is especially good with those little pink boreal shrimp from the northern oceans; those shrimp are also sustainably caught.

The key to any good mac and cheese is the cheese sauce. It's easy to make. You start with a flour-and-butter roux, cook it until it's a light beige, then mix in milk, half-and-half, or in this case, cream. Yes, cream is richer than milk, but with milk, you risk the sauce curdling if your pot is too hot. Cream is sturdier. If you do choose milk, it must be whole milk. As for cheese, I'm partial to a 50-50 mix of freshly grated cheddar and Gruyère, plus a little grated pecorino or Parmesan. Whatever you use, make it a mix of cheeses, which tastes better. Elbow pasta is traditional, but any short pasta is fine.

If you have leftovers, reheat them in a microwave or in a 350°F oven until warmed through. It does not freeze well.

5 tablespoons unsalted butter

1 large onion, chopped

2 cloves garlic, minced

1 small hot green chile (serrano), minced (optional)

5 tablespoons all-purpose flour

2 cups cream

2 cups shredded Gruyère cheese, loosely packed

1½ cups shredded cheddar, loosely packed

½ cup grated pecorino or Parmesan cheese

Salt and black pepper

1 pound elbows or other short pasta, cooked and drained

12 ounces shrimp, peeled

½ cup breadcrumbs

4 tablespoons fresh parsley, chopped

Cajun seasoning mix or Cavender's Greek seasoning (optional)

Heat the butter in a large pan over medium-high heat. When it's hot, add the onion and sauté, stirring often, until soft and translucent, about 4 minutes. Add the garlic and chile and sauté another minute. Preheat the oven to 350°F.

Add the flour to the pan and mix it in well. Cook this, stirring often, for 5 minutes, until it browns a bit. Pour in the cream about ½ cup at a time, mixing after each addition so that it's fully incorporated. Do the same with all the cheeses, adding about ½ cup at a time, and stirring it in before adding more. Add salt and black pepper to taste, then mix in the cooked pasta and shrimp.

Transfer all this to a casserole dish; I like to grease mine with butter, but this is not strictly necessary. Pat the mac and cheese into the casserole and sprinkle the breadcrumbs and parsley over it all. If you feel like adding some other seasonings, like Cajun or Cavender's, sprinkle maybe a teaspoon or two over everything now.

Bake uncovered for 15 to 20 minutes, until the top browns. Remove and let it sit 5 minutes before serving.

NOTE If you're using shrimp or lobster, cut them into small pieces.

STUFFED CLAMS

PREP TIME: 45 MINUTES | **COOK TIME: 25 MINUTES** | **SERVES 6**

Stuffed clams may be the official name of this recipe, but in our household, for a generation, they've been known as "clam things." My mom named them that, and she even had pretty green ceramic clamshell bowls strictly for the purpose.

I didn't know that she was making a variant of Rhode Island "stuffies" until I saw it on a menu in Rhode Island when I was a twentysomething. Stuffies are basically chopped clams, usually but not always quahogs (*Mercenaria mercenaria*), mixed with breadcrumbs or crushed crackers, with sautéed onion, celery, and green pepper, sometimes bits of bacon or linguica sausage, and often hot sauce and/or Worcestershire. You stuff the mixture into large, clean, clam shells, ramekins, or, if you happen to have the clamshell bowls, those would do nicely.

The main difference between stuffed clams and the better-known clams casino (also a Rhode Island invention) is that stuffed clams are generally made with larger clams that are ground or chopped. Clams casino is normally made with smaller, bite-sized clams like littlenecks.

Mom's recipe demands a particular ingredient I would never otherwise have in the house: Ritz crackers. Sure, you could use breadcrumbs, but it's just not the same. I buy the packages of Ritz that have several small sleeves of crackers, because, well, I never eat them as is, and I want them to be fresh for the next batch of stuffed clams.

Mom also uses butter, lots of it. But another perfectly good option is to fry some bacon, chop it up, add it to the mix, and use the bacon fat instead. I do deviate in one place from Mom's recipe: I roast my green peppers where she does not. I also prefer to roast Anaheim or poblanos instead of regular green peppers. You can do either.

Well, to be perfectly honest, I deviate from Mom's clam things in another way: I use the clams available to me, which are horseneck or butter clams, also called Washington clams. They are large, open-shelled clams of the Pacific Coast I dig every year. Any clam will work for stuffed clams, though. My preference would be ground sea clams, butter clams, horseneck clams, or a big chowder-sized quahog. Stuffed clams don't need pretty little topnecks or Manila clams.

And yes, you can make stuffed clams with canned clams, but I don't.

"A fishing rod is a stick with a hook at one end and a fool at the other."

SAMUEL JOHNSON

- 2 Anaheim, poblano, or green bell peppers, roasted, peeled, seeded, and chopped
- 3 cups chopped or ground clams, or 3 cans clams
- 5 tablespoons unsalted butter, divided (you'll need 3 tablespoons, melted)
- 1½ cups minced yellow or white onion
- 1½ cups minced celery
- Salt
- Tabasco or other hot sauce
- Worcestershire sauce
- 3 tablespoons grated Parmesan cheese
- 1 sleeve crushed Ritz crackers (or Saltines), or 2 cups breadcrumbs
- Black pepper
- Lemon wedges, for garnish

Once you have your green peppers ready and your clams ground or chopped, preheat your oven to 350°F. In a large frying pan, heat 2 tablespoons of the butter and sauté the onion and celery until softened and translucent, but not browned. Salt them as they cook.

Remove the vegetables to a bowl to cool. When they're cooled, mix well with the clams, the chopped green pepper, Tabasco, Worcestershire, cheese, and half the crushed Ritz crackers. Stir in enough of the clam juices to make a thick paste.

Stuff the mixture into clam shells, ramekins, or small ovenproof bowls. Top with the remaining crushed crackers and drizzle the remaining butter over them. Grind black pepper over them.

Bake uncovered for 20 to 25 minutes. I like to put the clam shells on a baking sheet so I can take them all out at once. Serve with lemon wedges.

DEVILED CRAB

PREP TIME: 30 MINUTES | **COOK TIME: 20 MINUTES** | **SERVES 4**

Along with the stuffed clams, I also grew up with the deviled crab, an old-school comfort food many of our moms made back in the day. Crabmeat, breadcrumbs or crushed crackers, onion and celery, seasonings, and a little butter. OK, maybe a lot of butter. The result is substantial, tangy, and herby, and yet the flavor of the crab still shines through. As with crab cakes, the best deviled crab is heavy on the crab and light on the devilling.

Deviled crabs are traditionally served in their own shells, but if you don't have the shells, use shallow ovenproof bowls or ramekins. I use our local Dungeness crab, but any crab will do. Blue crabs are the norm where they live, although I've even seen people make deviled crab with spider crabs, which is pretty trippy. In general, if you're using the shells, you want larger crabs—at least the size of a normal blue crab. That's not to say you couldn't use the shells of smaller crabs to make an appetizer, especially since deviled crab is a traditional starter for a larger seafood feast. The devil in the dish comes from the presence of cayenne or hot sauce. It's not actually spicy-hot, but there's just enough to keep things bright and interesting.

I am a big fan of using three specific, branded ingredients, which is a rarity for me. First, I prefer to use crushed Saltines for the breading instead of breadcrumbs; I like the variation in texture and the flavor. I also use Old Bay seasoning and a bit of Tabasco hot sauce. With these last two, I think the Old Bay is more critical, although I've made deviled crab with Cajun seasoning and it was almost as good.

Oh, about that butter. You need it. And lots of it. Sure you can use some sort of oil, but butter is important to my version of this dish. You need a full stick, too. You'll thank me later.

You can refrigerate the mixture for a few days beforehand, and you can freeze the stuffed crabs, well wrapped, for a few months.

1 cup minced onion or shallot

2 tablespoons olive oil

2 cloves garlic, minced

1 jalapeño or serrano chile, minced

1 pound crabmeat

1 tablespoon Worcestershire sauce

1 teaspoon Old Bay seasoning

½ teaspoon cayenne

3 green onions, chopped

3 tablespoons minced parsley

1 sleeve Saltine crackers, crushed (about 4 ounces)

Salt and black pepper

1 stick butter, melted (about ½ cup)

Lemons or limes, for serving

Cook the onions in the olive oil in a small pan over medium heat until they turn translucent, a few minutes. Add the garlic and minced chile and cook another minute or two. Turn off the heat and let this cool for 10 minutes or so.

Meanwhile, in a large bowl, add all the remaining ingredients except the melted butter and the citrus. Mix well. Preheat the oven to 400°F.

When the onion mixture has cooled, mix it into the crab mixture. Stuff the mixture into cleaned crab shells or whatever else makes you happy. Drizzle the melted butter over the stuffed shells evenly.

Bake for 20 minutes and serve with wedges of lemon or lime.

7
POACHING

YOU ALMOST NEVER actually boil fish. You can boil shellfish, but I generally prefer steaming, which is covered as a discrete method in chapter 10 (page 140). But you can poach it, either in a water-like liquid (use the sablefish recipe on page 88 as a model for your "water" poaching adventures) or in oil or fat (the butter-poached fish recipe on page 90 will turn your head). A general rule is that lean fish are better poached in oil, fatty fish in something like broth or sake or wine. This, as with everything in this book, is a guideline, not dogma. Butter-poached salmon is amazing—as is burbot poached in 7-Up, oddly enough.

In either case, you want your liquid to be below the simmer. That's typically around 160°F. Hot enough to kill germs and parasites, but not hot enough to wreak havoc with delicate fish flesh.

Poached fish and seafood are very delicate, and you need to move them from where they cook to where they will be served carefully. Using two spatulas helps a lot for larger pieces.

Butter-poached fish (or fish poached in olive oil or any good-tasting fat) is silky and luxurious, yet surprisingly light. It's ridiculously easy to pull off, and it works with anything from halibut to perch to salmon, lobster, shrimp, and snapper. So why isn't it done more commonly by more people? I'll tell you why. Every time a chef or cooking celebrity extols the idea of gently cooking fish in a flavorful fat or oil, you can almost hear the audience's concern: "What on earth am I going to do with all that excess butter?" It's a fair question, and it's why butter-poached fish is a lot less popular than fried fish—although, if you think about it, you're often using as much oil or butter in either case. The answer is the same as it is with fryer oil: save it and use it again. In both butter-poaching and frying, you simply run the melted butter or oil through a paper towel to strain out any bits and into a container. You can leave the oil on the counter, but you should keep the butter in the fridge. "But won't the reserved oil be fishy?" you ask. A little, but not unpleasantly so. It'll be fine with another fish or seafood dish, but you wouldn't want to put this butter on, say, chicken. For example, I poached a halibut in butter, and then used the butter again with some crab. "Then why not use salted butter?" Well, you could, but I find that in many cases, using salted butter results in very salty fish. Professionally, I never use salted butter, because I want to control the amount of salt. I recommend that you do, too. Feel better?

Let me tell you again why you really want to add butter-poaching to your cooking repertoire. It results in a wonderful, wonderful piece of fish. Now don't get me wrong, I love fried fish probably more than most people. But even I can get tired of it during fishing season, when I eat fish or seafood many times a week. When you poach in butter or olive oil or some other flavorful oil, you get just enough fat permeating the fish to make it silky. This is a huge deal with very lean white fish—particularly freshwater fish. Cook a piece of walleye or bass or bluegill this way and you'll be amazed. It can actually start to taste a little like lobster.

I normally just use butter, but you can flavor the butter with the herb or spice of your choice. Saffron or curry powder will turn the fish bright yellow, for example.

You cook the fish gently too, so it will not seize up like fish tossed into boiling water or fish that's over-fried. You get that pretty flake, and as the flakes begin to separate just a little, the butter seeps in. The texture is remarkable.

Finally, butter-poaching is ridiculously easy. Easier than frying, believe it or not. Salt fish, pat dry, melt butter, submerge fish in butter for ten minutes or so, remove, eat. Try it. You'll see.

◄ Black seabass and porgies caught near Montauk, Long Island.

SAKE-POACHED SABLEFISH

PREP TIME: 10 MINUTES | COOK TIME: 15 MINUTES | SERVES 4

Obviously, you don't have to use sablefish, but its high fat content really shines with this method. Salmon and any other fatty fish works very well here, and lean fish or shellfish are also good. In fact, the only things to avoid would be those that are not tender enough to be cooked so gently or so fast. Octopus and conch spring to mind. That said, if you had precooked and already tender mollusks on hand, by all means serve them with the Japanese seasonings in this recipe. And with fish, if you want to get cheffy, leave the skin on and use a culinary torch to sear it crispy.

1 pound sablefish, or other
   high-fat fish

2 cups sake

1 cup fish, shellfish, or
   chicken stock

3 bay leaves

Salt

Sesame oil

Soy sauce

Togarashi (Japanese spice mix)

Cut pieces of sablefish to serve. Leave the skin on.

Bring sake, stock, bay leaves, and pinch of salt to a boil.

Turn off heat. Set a saucer in the pot, then place the fish, skin-side up, on it, making sure the fish is submerged. Cover the pan and let sit about 6 to 10 minutes.

Very carefully remove the saucer, then carefully set the fish on a cutting board to rest for 3 or 4 minutes. Peel off the skin.

Serve the fish with greens of your choice (pickled mustard greens in my case), a little sesame oil, soy sauce, and togarashi, a Japanese spice mix that can often be found in the Asian aisle in many supermarkets. If you can't find togarashi, toasted sesame seeds are a nice touch.

VARIATIONS Clearly this recipe has a Japanese feel to it, but you can alter the poaching liquid and finishing ingredients for very different effects. A British take might be to poach in a light ale—something malty, not hoppy—then add a bit of melted butter, Worcestershire, and black pepper. A French rendition would be to poach in white or rosé wine, then hit it with butter or crème fraîche, then perhaps pepper or even quatre épices. I've seen fish poached in green tea, 7-Up, mushroom soaking water, Champagne, whey, you name it. And obviously, the classic is a light fish or shellfish stock, with a little wine added for acidity.

The point of the master recipe above is to show that a good poached fish will be:

▶ Cooked in something flavorful and aromatic

▶ Cooked very gently

▶ Finished with something rich—oil, fat, or dairy—something sour, something salty, and if you want, something a little spicy.

A plain slab of poached fish is drab. Don't be drab.

HOOK, LINE, AND SUPPER

BUTTER-POACHED FISH

PREP TIME: 20 MINUTES | **COOK TIME: 20 MINUTES** | **SERVES 4**

You can play with this recipe a lot by changing the fat—butter, olive oil, sesame oil, lard, duck fat—or the salad underneath the fish and, obviously, by altering the fish you use. I used California halibut because it is fantastic cooked this way, but almost any fish will work well here, especially freshwater fish. Oh, and yes, follow these instructions for lobster tails, too. The only sorts of fish I'd avoid butter-poaching would be dark, oily ones like mackerel, bluefish, herring, or shad. Other oily fish are nice this way, though, like tuna or salmon, sablefish (black cod), or yellowtail. See below and page 92 for some variations to play with.

1 to 2 pounds skinless boneless fish or shrimp

Salt

1 yellow squash

1 green squash, like a zucchini

1 large cucumber

3 to 6 radishes

¼ pound fresh green beans

¼ cup white wine or rice vinegar

1 pound unsalted butter

Olive oil (see below)

Black pepper

Salt the fish well and set aside. Slice the squash, cucumber, and radishes very thinly into rounds, ideally with a mandoline—although a knife is fine. Slice the green beans thinly on the diagonal. Toss all the vegetables with a little salt and vinegar and set aside.

Melt the butter in a pot large enough to hold at least 1 piece of fish—and ideally 2—at a time, but small enough so that the pieces of fish are submerged. You can use more butter if you want to, or you can top things off with olive oil. You want the butter to be between 150°F and 170°F. When the butter hits the right temperature, pat the pieces of fish dry with paper towels and submerge in the oil. If the fish sizzles at all, lower the heat. You want the fish to cook gently. Let the fish swim in the butter for roughly 10 minutes for every ½ inch of thickness. One way to do this is to put the submerged fish into a 325°F oven. If you're unsure, it's better to leave the fish in a little longer than you think. It'll be fine.

To finish the salad, add a little bit of the melted butter, or use olive oil, and toss well. Put some on everyone's plate. Gently lift out the pieces of fish and lay them on the salad. Grind lots of black pepper over everything. Serve with good crusty bread.

Ethiopian Spiced Butter

Poaching fish or seafood in this could change your life. Called niter kibbeh, you slow simmer 1 pound of butter with 2 minced shallots, 2 cloves minced garlic, 2 tablespoons minced fresh ginger, 12 crushed cardamom pods, 5 whole cloves, 1 inch of cinnamon, 1 tablespoon dried oregano, ½ teaspoon ground turmeric, and 1 teaspoon ground fenugreek.

Toast the cardamom, cloves, and cinnamon in a hot, dry pan until they are aromatic, about a minute. Cut the butter into cubes. Put everything into a pot and cook very gently for 30 to 45 minutes. Watch for browning, and when you see it, turn off the heat. Strain through cheesecloth and store in a clean glass jar. Niter kibbeh lasts for months in the fridge and forever in the freezer.

BUTTER-POACHED SEAFOOD

The timing on seafood other than lobster tails can be a little different than with fish. Shrimp, scallops, squid, small clams, oysters, and mussels will become tender in as little as five minutes; I do not recommend butter-poaching big clams. A few animals, while remarkable when butter-poached, can be tricky. Abalone, conch, and octopus are what I'm thinking about here. These can take a long time to become tender, sometimes more than an hour. You'll know they're ready when you can stick a needle or a thin knife point into the thickest part easily.

One useful tip: shell your lobsters or shrimp first, then smash them up with a hammer or a club of some sort. Melt the butter or heat whatever fat you plan to poach your seafood in and let it steep, not boil or even simmer, until the shells turn orange, about ten to twenty minutes. Strain the shells off the butter or fat and then use that to poach your now-shelled lobster or shrimp. This butter adds a lot of flavor to dishes like risotto or pasta.

VARIATIONS The fat or oil you use will make a big difference. Butter speaks of not only Western Europe, Canada, and the larger European tradition, but also India—particularly if you spice the butter. I can also tell you that lean fish poached in Ethiopian spiced butter, niter kibbeh, is out of this world (page 90). Olive oil is what you'd use if you wanted to go Mediterranean or Persian. Don't use expensive olive oil to poach in, but drizzle some of the good stuff on at the table. Most of the other really good fats are just too expensive to poach in; poaching in toasted sesame oil, unrefined canola oil, squash seed oil, and so on would break the bank. So here's what you do: poach in neutral oil, like refined canola, grapeseed, or rice bran oil, then, when you remove the fish, give it a good drizzle with the fancy, flavorful oil.

What about animal fats? Doable, but weird. I've poached fish and seafood in both duck fat and lard, and they're fine, but your brain goes a little crosswise when you eat it—silky porky walleye? Huh? The exception to this is schmaltz, rendered chicken fat. Lean white fish poached in schmaltz is scandalously good.

If you're playing with other cuisines, your side salad and your source of acidity will sometimes change, too. Asian ingredients with rice vinegar are a great option, but if you wanted to go Chinese in winter, you could go with roasted vegetables with Chinese black vinegar. English or Scandinavian? You might want to use malt vinegar. White wine vinegar in the Mediterranean, sour orange juice in the Caribbean, limes in most of Mexico and Central America, lemons in the Muslim world and India.

◄ An early encounter with a lobster, circa 1983.

▶ (next page) Spot prawns and Pacific pink shrimp, fresh out of the trap.

8
SEARING, SAUTÉING, AND STIR-FRYING

SEARING, SAUTÉING, and stir-frying are three cooking methods I use constantly for fish and seafood. I define searing as a method to give a piece of fish or a scallop a pretty, caramelized crust on one side while keeping the other side lightly cooked, so the overall item isn't hammered to death. Sautéing is where you use a smallish amount of oil in a pan, and the fish or seafood, coated with something or not, is moved around, more or less constantly. And it is this constant motion that defines stir-frying, which is just a modified sauté.

All three techniques use relatively small amounts of oil to cook things at high heat. The effect is to get some browning—that Maillard reaction we all know and love—without too much oil, all done fast enough so that you don't overcook the fish, and its accompanying vegetables are still bright and firm.

These methods work with most, but not all, types of fish and seafood. Notably, very delicate things like a sole or panfish fillet are terrible with these methods; they'll either break apart or are so thin that they'll overcook rapidly.

Searing is best with larger blocks of fish, thick fillets, or large scallops. I suppose you could sear a lobster tail, but it'd be very difficult to get that browning without destroying the meat. It's a fierce cooking process that caramelizes the side touching the hot pan, most definitely overcooking it, but for the purpose of rendering either the skin or the side of the meat you're searing ultra-crispy. It's a tradeoff most of us will happily make.

Sautéing the way I'm defining it is done primarily with shrimp, squid, crayfish tails, lobster tails, shucked clams, mussels and oysters, small scallops, and precooked crabmeat. Why no fish? Because the constant stirring and mixing of the ingredients will cause almost all fish to break apart. That said, there is a hybrid method that I'm calling "frying, then saucing," which I use often with fish. See details on that in chapter 9.

Stir-frying is more or less in the same boat as sautéing in terms of what things work well with this method, although the common Chinese step of coating and pre-frying before a stir-fry works very well with firm fish of all sorts.

Finally, there is a unique cooking method that began in the late 1970s called blackening, which involves ultra-high heat and lots of butter and spices and can damn well near destroy your frying pan. But it *can* be done safely at home with a variety of fish.

SEARING FISH (AND SCALLOPS)

If you've ever been to a nice restaurant and ordered fish, chances are you were served a piece of fish, either with the skin on or off, that was perfectly browned and seared on one side—and that side will be facing up—and then, when you dove into it, it was somehow not overcooked.

How do they do that? Short answer: they never flip the fish. Yep, this allows them (and us, because we do what the great ones do) to keep the fish on one side long enough to caramelize the proteins and sugars in the fish without cooking the thing to death. So how does the other side cook? You baste it with the hot oil or fat, effectively poaching it. There are some tips and tricks to do this right:

USE A SEASONED PAN

Ideally black steel or a stainless steel pan. That's what we used in restaurants. Cast iron does work but is very heavy, and non-stick pans hate the sort of heat you need to do this right.

GET YOUR PAN HOT

I mean *hot hot hot*. High heat for a minute or four. Then you add oil. You'll want your stove fan on high for this one.

USE OIL WITH A HIGH SMOKE POINT

This is not the place for delicate oils or fats, and certainly not whole butter. That can come later. Some good choices are refined safflower, canola, rice bran, or avocado oil. Refined peanut oil, the kind with no peanut aroma, works well, as will clarified butter (ghee), which happens to be my favorite.

Typically, this will be about 3 tablespoons. And, well, you need a spoon. A large soup spoon is a good choice.

Pat it dry with paper towels before you let it hit the pan. If it has skin, use a butter knife to scrape the skin before patting it dry; you'll be surprised how much ick comes off.

When it hits the oil, the fish will want to contract violently. Press the fish down for 30 seconds or so. (Yes, you really want a fish spatula if at all possible; this is where it shines above any other tool. See page 39.)

Tip the pan and spoon the hot oil over the fish until it turns opaque. With most fish, that's all you need to do. Just let the pan sizzle; it should sound like energetic bacon, so adjust the heat until you hear that noise. When you see brown edges on the side of the fish, shake the pan. If the fish moves, you're good to go. If they want to move but seem stuck a little, carefully try to slip the fish spatula under the fillet. If it comes up easily, you're good. If it's cemented to the pan, leave it be—*it will release*. This is why a fish spatula is so vital; it's very thin and flexible, and it has a sort of blade at the edge, which will scrape up any bits that are still attached when most of the rest of the fish has released.

If you have a thick fillet like king salmon, halibut, or a large striped bass, you'll need to keep spooning fat over the uncooked side for a minute or two, not necessarily all at once. Another option is to pop the whole pan into a 400°F oven for ten minutes. A really thick piece of fish can be seared on both sides. Put more of a sear on the side you plan to show the diner; sear the other side only as much as it takes to brown. It's a bit of an art, which is why the oven method is better for beginners.

Always serve seared-side up, and douse with a nice oil or whole butter right before you serve. I often do this in the pan at the last minute.

Some final tips: with thick fillets, it really helps to start with room-temperature fish. A good twenty-minute pre-salting helps all fish.

SAUTÉ

A proper sauté is a violent way to cook. High heat and constant motion are what's called for here, and this is anathema to most fish. They are simply too fragile to handle it. Seafood, on the other hand, really likes a good sauté—especially shrimp.

There are a few exceptions when it comes to fish. Hot-smoked fish, especially firm, lean fish like halibut, can handle the pan. And if you dust them in flour first, you can get away with sautéing very firm fish like sturgeon, halibut, swordfish, tuna, and maybe cobia or tautog. A few fish, like amberjack and yellowtail, are fatty enough that while they will stand up to a sauté, they aren't ideal flavor-wise. If you do this, make sure you use an oil with a very high smoke point (safflower or rice bran) and get that oil screaming hot before the fish hits the pan. The biggest mistake people make with any sauté is to not let their oil get hot enough. Your fish or seafood will stick to the pan if the oil isn't hot enough.

If you think about sautéing as Western stir-fry, you'll go a long way to understanding the method. Before you begin, everything needs to be ready; this is your mise en place, as it's known in the restaurant trade.

Most sautés are simple, with minimal ingredients. You want the fish or seafood to shine, with only one or two accompanying flavors.

I typically serve them with rice, polenta or grits, or bread, on tortillas, or with roasted potatoes. All of these should be ready before you start the sauté.

SIMPLE SAUTÉED SHRIMP

PREP TIME: 10 MINUTES | COOK TIME: 3 MINUTES | SERVES 4

Any shrimp will do here, but I love this with spot prawns. You want lots of garlic, a little chile, and enough lemon to balance the olive oil. This recipe is best done with shell-on shrimp that you peel at the table, but you can do it with peeled and deveined shrimp, too.

Other options are crawfish tails, big chunks of raw lobster, small shucked clams, squid, or bay scallops.

4 tablespoons extra-virgin olive oil

2 pounds large shrimp, squid rings, bay scallops, or shucked clams

4 to 6 cloves garlic, coarsely chopped or thinly sliced

1 or 2 small hot chiles, thinly sliced, or 2 dried hot chiles, crumbled

Salt

Juice of 1 lemon

1 or 2 tablespoons high quality olive oil

Heat 2 tablespoons of olive oil in a large sauté pan over high heat. When it just barely begins to smoke, add all the shrimp and toss to coat with the oil.

Add the garlic and chile and salt the pan well. Cook over high heat, tossing and/or stirring, until all the shrimp just barely turn pink, about 2 minutes, tops. Toss with the lemon juice and the remaining olive oil and serve at once.

NOTE These are also excellent served at room temperature or chilled as an appetizer.

HONEYED FISH WITH OUZO

PREP TIME: 15 MINUTES | COOK TIME: 10 MINUTES | SERVES 4

Greek fish with honey and ouzo is one of my all-time favorite fish recipes, and while I designed it for California white seabass, it is especially good with shrimp and the other seafoods mentioned in the recipe above. Use any firm fish you can cut into large chunks. This recipe has everything you could ask for: a crispy crust, tender fish, a hit of sweetness from the honey, and a blast of salty umami from the Worcestershire sauce.

I once made this recipe start-to-finish in a three-and-a-half-minute segment for a Tampa TV station back in 2011 while I was on my first book tour. That time, I made it with grouper. When I added the ouzo to the pan it flared up, of course—and in response, in what was one of my favorite moments of the entire book tour, I shouted, "*Opa!*" (this is a Greek dish, after all), and the TV host shouted, "Oompa Loompa!" I almost wet myself laughing.

This recipe comes together fast, so have everything ready before you begin. Try to get fresh oregano if you can find it, but good dried oregano will work, too. Serve this with rice pilaf, a green salad, and some crusty bread. As for a drink, choose a lager beer or a crisp white wine such as a Greek assyrtiko or an Italian pinot grigio.

1 to 2 pounds skinless sturgeon, swordfish, shark, or other firm fish

Salt

3 tablespoons olive oil

Flour for dusting

3 cloves garlic, minced

1 to 2 shots of ouzo or other anise-flavored liqueur

2 tablespoons Worcestershire sauce

2 tablespoons honey, ideally Greek thyme honey

2 tablespoons chopped fresh oregano, or 2 teaspoons dried

Lots of freshly ground black pepper

Cut the fish into chunks of between 1½ inches and 2 inches across. If you're using shrimp, peel and devein them. Salt the fish well and set aside while you chop the garlic and oregano.

Heat a large sauté pan over high heat for 1 minute. Add the olive oil. Dust the fish pieces in flour, shake off the excess, and lay down in the pan. Turn the heat down to medium-high and brown the fish. Add the garlic and cook for 30 seconds to a minute. Do not let it brown.

Take the pan off the heat and add the ouzo. It will flare up. Shout, "*Opa!*" Put the pan back on the heat, turn it to high, and scrape off any browned bits with a wooden spoon. Add the Worcestershire sauce, honey, and oregano and swirl to combine. Let this boil down until it's syrupy, tossing and swirling to coat the fish. Turn off the heat, grind fresh black pepper over everything, and serve at once.

OPTIONS If you use shrimp, squid, shucked clams, or scallops, don't flour them. If you use precooked crab, crayfish, or lobster, add them in with the ouzo.

SEARING, SAUTÉING, AND STIR-FRYING

97

HALIBUT PUTTANESCA

PREP TIME: 10 MINUTES | **COOK TIME: 20 MINUTES** | **SERVES 4**

Like the previous recipe, this dish comes together in a flash: chunks of firm white fish, floured and sautéed, then tossed with all the great flavors of a traditional Italian puttanesca sauce.

A what? Those who know Italian or even Spanish can guess at the origin of this sauce; its name, translated loosely, means "harlot-like." There are lots of legends about its name, but the one I like best is that the ladies of the evening, after a long night's work, could whip this up in the predawn hours—before any markets opened—eat a good meal, and finally catch some sleep.

And although I've never been a lady of the evening, my job as a line cook, and later as a late-night partier —that was me at those raves in the early 1990s—often had me wanting a decent meal at odd hours of the night. This sauce, usually with simple dried spaghetti but sometimes with other things, has been in my back pocket since college.

The key to a *puttana*'s puttanesca is that pretty much everything would either be in her pantry or growing on her windowsill. Fresh herbs, salted capers and anchovies, olives, an onion, maybe a clove of garlic or two. Some canned tomatoes, or fresh ones sitting on her kitchen counter. Maybe a hot chile or three. The result is powerful. Salty, herby, sour, and a little sweet (from the tomatoes). It's ideal for a big fish like tuna, swordfish, or sturgeon, but will work with shrimp or any very firm, white fish. I use halibut, mostly.

Normally, I'll dust the fish with regular flour, but there is an alternative that is both delicious and gluten free: chickpea flour. It will actually give you fish that is even more golden than with wheat flour, and it has a bit of a nutty flavor, too.

1½ pounds halibut or other firm fish, cut into chunks

Salt

2 cups regular or chickpea flour, for dusting

2 tablespoons safflower, rice bran, or other high smoke point oil

1 shallot or small onion, minced

2 cups diced tomatoes, fresh or canned

2 cloves garlic, thinly sliced

12 to 20 olives, sliced

2 tablespoons capers

½ teaspoon red pepper flakes

¼ cup chopped basil, parsley, or tarragon

2 tablespoons extra-virgin olive oil

Black pepper

Salt the fish well and dust with the flour.

Heat the safflower oil in a large frying pan over high heat. When it's hot, drop the heat to medium-high and brown the fish pieces in batches. Set the fish aside as it browns.

When all the fish is done, add the shallot and cook for 1 minute. Add the garlic and cook another 30 seconds.

Return the fish to the pan and add all the remaining ingredients. Toss to combine and cook for 1 to 2 more minutes. Serve with crusty bread, polenta, or rice.

VARIATIONS If you use squid or other shellfish, don't flour it and add it with the shallot. If you use precooked crab, crayfish, or lobster, add it with the garlic.

SALMON PICCATA

Piccata works for many things, not just the salmon in the picture. Piccata is an Italian sauce of butter, parsley, shallots, white wine, lemon, and capers that is especially good for pounded cutlets—historically, veal, but more commonly these days, chicken. Basically, it works with any light meat you can think of.

Piccata is a pan sauce, made after you've cooked the fish or seafood. You move the protein to a cutting board and make the sauce as it rests. Yep, it's that fast, so you need to have everything chopped beforehand.

First you add the butter and the shallots or onion and in some cases, garlic, although I don't put garlic in my piccata. That cooks quickly, and you splash in lemon juice or white wine or a combination—piccata has to have lemon juice in it—deglaze the pan, and then add a healthy spoonful or two of capers. I prefer the tiny nonpareil ones.

Now comes the only tricky part in making salmon piccata, or any other piccata, for that matter: mounting the butter. You do this by turning the heat to low and adding one tablespoon of butter at a time, swirling it around the pan until it incorporates into the sauce. Do not let this boil, or the sauce will break. Add the parsley and serve.

---

1 pound fish fillets

Salt

2 tablespoons olive oil

Black pepper

4 tablespoons unsalted butter, divided

1 shallot, minced, or
¼ cup minced onion

2 tablespoons capers

Juice and zest of 2 lemons

3 tablespoons white wine

3 tablespoons minced parsley

Salt the fish well and let it sit on the counter while you chop all the vegetables. Heat the olive oil in a sauté pan over medium-high heat. When the oil is hot, pat the salmon dry with a paper towel and set the portions, skin-side down, on the hot pan. As soon as they're all set down, jiggle the pan a bit to let them move. If they don't move, just leave them. Note: you want to put the fish skin-side down regardless of whether the skin is still there or not.

Let the fish sear. You want it to sound like bacon sizzling in the pan, maybe a little more energetic than that. Use a spoon to baste the top of the fish with the hot olive oil until the flesh turns opaque. After about 5 minutes, check to see if the fish is ready by jiggling the pan again. If the portions move, you're good to go. If not, carefully try to lift them with a spatula. If they're stuck to the pan, leave them. Continue cooking for a minute or two more, then try again. They will lift up easily when you have a perfect sear.

If you're using thick fish portions like the ones in the picture, you will want to flip your fish and cook it a few minutes on the other side. The way to do this is to flip one piece, jiggle the pan so that pieces slides around a little, then do the next piece. This way, they will release from the pan faster than the first side, and this prevents you from overcooking the fish. Only cook the fish for a minute or two on this second side. Note: This is not needed for thin portions.

When the fish is ready, move it, crispy-side up, to a cutting board and grind black pepper over it.

Add 1 tablespoon of butter to the pan, along with the shallots. Let this cook a minute, then add the capers and lemon zest. Mix well, let this cook about 30 seconds, then add the white wine. Use a wooden spoon to scrape up any browned bits from the pan. When this is done, add the lemon juice and the parsley. Turn the heat to low.

Now add 1 tablespoon of butter to the sauce and swirl the pan until it incorporates. Repeat this with the rest of the butter. You can, in fact, add up to a half stick of butter this way, and it's amazing, but very rich. Serve by putting a portion on each plate and pouring some sauce over each one.

NOTE If you're serving this with grits, polenta, or mashed potatoes, make them first and keep it warm while you make the fish.

NEW ORLEANS BBQ SHRIMP

PREP TIME: 30 MINUTES | **COOK TIME: 30 MINUTES** | **SERVES 4**

For those of you who are not familiar with New Orleans BBQ shrimp, this dish might seem confusing. After all, it's not, strictly speaking, barbecue. Legend has it that BBQ shrimp was invented in the 1950s at a NOLA restaurant, Pascal's Manale, when a guest who'd returned from a trip to Chicago described something like this to the chef at the time. The chef then created what was to become one of the iconic dishes of the city. It had little to do with whatever it was the guest had in Chicago, but it was—and is—amazing.

A couple of funny things about this recipe. Although its origins are in an Italian restaurant and it calls itself barbecue, it's really neither. New Orleans BBQ shrimp is deeply, intensely Creole-French. The only real connection with BBQ sauce is that this sauce hits the same notes: spicy (but not too much), sweet, salty, tart, rich. Just like a good barbecue sauce does. I've also heard tell that this sort of BBQ sauce as we know it now was not universally known until the 1970s, two decades after this sauce was invented.

There are no "weird" ingredients in this recipe, although I will warn you that you need a lot of Worcestershire sauce: a half cup, not just a few dashes. And trust me, the finished sauce really works.

You get that zing from the Worcestershire and Creole seasoning, some herbal notes, body from a full-on, French-style reduction, all rounded out with heavy cream and, well, a slightly obscene amount of butter. Don't skimp on the butter or cream in this recipe, or the sauce will be too sharp, almost unpleasant.

Once made, your BBQ shrimp can be reheated, but it won't be as good. Better to gorge yourself and regret it later. If you do somehow have leftovers, very gently reheat them and eat with bread.

Larger shrimp are preferable here, but any size will work. I prefer real Gulf shrimp, too. If you want to play with this recipe, try the sauce on lobster or any firm white fish.

1 to 2 pounds shrimp, with the shells (and heads if you can get them)

Salt

3 tablespoons bacon fat or olive oil

2 shallots, chopped

4 cloves garlic, chopped

1 teaspoon ground black pepper

1 lemon, sliced into rounds

½ cup Worcestershire sauce

1 tablespoon chopped fresh rosemary (optional)

1 teaspoon dried thyme

1 tablespoon Creole or Cajun seasoning

½ cup dry white wine

1 cup chicken or shrimp stock

3 tablespoons heavy cream

4 to 5 tablespoons chilled unsalted butter, cut into tablespoon-sized pieces

3 tablespoons minced fresh parsley

Peel the shrimp and remove the heads, if you have them, and set them aside. Devein the shrimp with a paring knife and salt the shrimp lightly. Set them aside.

In a sauté pan or sauce pot, heat the bacon fat over medium-high heat. When it's hot, add the shallots, garlic, and shrimp shells and heads. Sauté, stirring often, until the shrimp shells turn pink and the shallot is translucent.

Add the pepper, lemon, Worcestershire, rosemary, thyme, Creole seasoning, wine, and stock. Bring this to a boil, then drop the heat to a simmer and reduce the mixture for about 15 minutes. Strain it, moving the liquid to a wide sauté pan that will fit all the shrimp.

Bring the mixture to a boil and let it roll for 2 to 3 minutes. You ultimately want this to be a glaze, but you still need to cook the shrimp without overcooking them, so you'll need to use your judgment; the shrimp typically need about 3 to 5 minutes in the pan, maximum. So when the sauce just barely leaves a trail when you run a spatula through the middle of the pan, add all the shrimp and toss to combine.

Keep the shrimp moving in the sauce until it's syrupy, then turn the heat to its lowest setting. Stir in the heavy cream until it's well mixed. Now, one tablespoon at a time, swirl in the butter. Add the parsley, toss to combine one more time, and serve at once with rice, grits, or bread.

VIETNAMESE CRISPY FISH WITH CILANTRO

PREP TIME: 15 MINUTES | **COOK TIME: 15 MINUTES** | **SERVES 6**

This is a dish to make on a busy weeknight that comes together in about the same time it takes to make the steamed rice that goes along with it. It's Vietnamese comfort food: crispy pieces of fish bathed in a simple sauce, served with onions, chiles, and lots of the herb rau ram, or the more easily found cilantro. I discovered this recipe in my friend Andrea Nguyen's great book *Into the Vietnamese Kitchen: Treasured Foodways, Modern Flavors.* She uses catfish for her version, but I prefer a firmer fish such as lingcod. Really, any fish will work here.

The key to success with this dish is to not overcook the fish. The easiest way to achieve this is to get just one side of the fish crispy, letting the simmering sauce cook the rest of the fish gently. You can, of course, sear both sides if you want, but if you do, make sure you are really searing it quickly, over high heat.

2 pounds lean white fish, cut into 2-inch chunks

Salt

3 tablespoons peanut oil

1 large onion, about 3 cups, thinly sliced from root to stem

1 piece ginger about the size of your thumb, peeled and thinly sliced

1 tablespoon sugar

3 to 5 jalapeños or other hot chiles, seeded and thinly sliced

4 tablespoons fish sauce

4 tablespoons water

½ cup chopped rau ram or cilantro

Juice of 2 limes

Sprinkle salt over the fish. Heat the peanut oil in a large sauté pan or wok and add the fish. Sear the fish in the oil so one side gets a nice, golden-brown crust. Don't flip the fish; you'll finish cooking it later. Remove each piece of fish as it browns.

When all the fish is done, add the onions and ginger and a little more oil if needed. Stir-fry over very high heat until the edges of the onions begin to brown, about 3 minutes. Add the sugar, jalapeño chiles, fish sauce, and water and bring to a boil.

Add the fish and gently toss everything to combine. Cover the pan and simmer for 5 minutes. Gently mix in the rau ram and turn off the heat. Add the lime juice, and serve with steamed rice.

"Never leave fish to find fish."

UNKNOWN

WARM CRAB SALAD

PREP TIME: 20 MINUTES | **COOK TIME: 20 MINUTES** | **SERVES 4**

This is an example of a sauté where the fish or seafood is added at the last minute; everything *else* is sautéed, and since the crab is already cooked, it's just tossed in. I found a version of this recipe in Diane Kochilas's great cookbook *The Glorious Foods of Greece: Traditional Recipes from the Islands, Cities, and Villages.* It's from Roúmeli, Kochilas tells us, the region of central Greece encompassing Fokida, Boeotia, Evritania, Fthiotida, and the memorably spelled Aitoloakarnania.

According to Kochilas, this crab salad with peppers was originally made with freshwater crabs. I used Dungeness. Atlantic crabs work fine too, and this recipe would be every bit as good with precooked shrimp, crawfish tails, lobster tails, or small clams steamed open. Another great option is flaked smoked fish. If you go with uncooked fish or seafood, add the fish or seafood with the sliced peppers.

You might notice a lot of olive oil in this recipe. Yep, it's Greek food, folks. They use a lot. It's good for you, and it keeps your coat shiny. Use less if it makes you feel better. I don't. And while I call this a warm crab salad and that's how I like to eat it, it's very good at room temperature, too.

½ cup olive oil

1 large red onion, thinly sliced

4 to 6 bell peppers, of various colors, thinly sliced

2 to 4 hotter peppers, like poblanos, Anaheims, or jalapeños, thinly sliced

2 cloves garlic, thinly sliced

1 pound crabmeat

½ cup finely chopped dill

½ cup finely chopped parsley

½ cup finely chopped mint

Salt and pepper

Lemon juice

Heat the olive oil in a large pan over medium-high heat. Add the red onion and sauté, stirring often until wilted, about 10 minutes. Add all the sliced peppers, sweet and hot, and sauté another 5 minutes. Add the garlic and stir well.

Add the crabmeat and all the herbs, stir to combine, and add salt, pepper, and lemon juice to taste. Serve warm or at room temperature.

Like sautéing, stir-frying works best with seafood, not fish—unless you coat the fish first and then set that coating in hot oil. Technically, this is frying and then saucing, which I'm going to cover more in the frying section below, but since the final result is hot, fast, and quick, I'm including it here.

Most traditional stir-fries use shellfish like shrimp, squid, shucked clams, or scallops. But you will see coated fish quite often, too. I've included a couple of master recipes for stir-fries below, but it's important to remember to follow the lead of your neighborhood Chinese restaurant, where you'll see things like kung pao chicken *and* shrimp, sweet and sour pork *and* fish, and so forth—basically taking a master recipe and substituting chicken or pork or beef with shrimp or some other seafood.

If it's important to have everything ready for a sauté, it's even more important to have your ingredients set in a stir-fry, which in some cases can come together in three minutes.

An important word on stir-fries: if you're serving a crowd, double your mise en place, but don't cook it that way. You'll need to cook in batches, bringing each batch to the table as they're done. The reason is this: if you overload a wok, the wok will cool enough that your ingredients will stew and not fry.

And take another tip from Chinese restaurants: if you're stir-frying fish with a fried coating, you can do all the fish as much as an hour in advance, so it will be ready for that short blast at the end. Just leave the pieces of fish on a cooling rack set over a baking sheet.

CHINESE SWEET AND SOUR FISH

PREP TIME: 25 MINUTES | **COOK TIME: 10 MINUTES** | **SERVES 4**

This is arguably my favorite recipe in this book. Rather than being a strict interpretation of an existing Chinese recipe, it's a mashup of several recipes for Chinese sweet and sour fish, most of which use whole fish, and my recipe for General Tso's pheasant, which is in my book *Pheasant, Quail, Cottontail.*

It hinges on a Chinese technique called "velveting," a pre-frying trick that sets a thin batter onto meat, which keeps it tender; it's why the meat in a Chinese restaurant tastes different from when you do a stir-fry at home. Normally, velveting is a "cool" pre-fry at roughly 275°F. Here, we're actually frying at a full 350°F. The effect is more like the meat in orange chicken at Panda Express.

It's good. *Really good.* Shut-up-I'm-eating good. Make this recipe, I tell you. Make it tonight. Then go fishing and make it again.

I used Pacific rockfish, but you could use any relatively firm white fish. I'd suggest anything from walleye to striped bass to redfish to grouper, snapper, black seabass, catfish, smallmouth bass, halibut—even carp would be good with this if you chunk it and remove any bones.

It doesn't keep, so eat it when it's ready. Also, this is one of those few Chinese wok dishes that you can double.

»

MARINADE

4 tablespoons potato starch or cornstarch

2 or 3 egg yolks

1 tablespoon soy sauce

3 cups peanut or vegetable oil for frying

SAUCE

½ cup chicken or fish stock, or clam juice

1 tablespoon soy sauce

1 tablespoon sugar, more if you want it sweet

1 tablespoon Chinese black vinegar or malt vinegar

2 tablespoons tomato paste mixed with 2 tablespoons water

1 teaspoon potato starch or cornstarch

STIR-FRY

1½ pounds skinless fish, cut into bite-sized pieces

3 tablespoons peanut oil, lard, or vegetable oil

8 dried hot chiles, less if you don't want it spicy, broken in half and seeds shaken out

One 2-inch piece of ginger, peeled and minced

3 cloves garlic, thinly sliced

3 tablespoons chopped chives

2 teaspoons sesame oil

Mix together the ingredients for the marinade (except the oil), and then mix in the chunks of fish. Make sure the fish is well coated and set it aside while you chop everything else. Mix together all the ingredients for the sauce and set it aside.

Heat the 3 cups of oil in a wok or deep frying pan to about 350°F. If you don't have a thermometer, you'll know the oil is hot enough when a bit of flour flicked into it sizzles instantly. Line a baking sheet or tray with paper towels. Fry the fish in two or three batches, separating the pieces of fish the moment they hit the hot oil. Cook until they turn golden brown, about 3 minutes. Remove and let them drain on the paper towels.

When the fish is done, carefully pour off all but about 3 tablespoons of the oil. Add the chiles, ginger, and garlic and stir-fry over high heat for 30 seconds. Add the fish and stir-fry for a few seconds. Stir the sauce to bring the starch up from the bottom (where it will have settled), and pour over the fish. Let this boil furiously for 1 minute, then turn off the heat.

Stir in the chives and sesame oil and serve at once with steamed jasmine rice.

VARIATIONS This is pretty much a fish-only recipe, but you could sub in small peeled shrimp, bay scallops, or chunks of lobster. Or, if you wanted to make this with squid, you could substitute the egg yolks in the marinade for 3 tablespoons of sherry or Shaoxing wine, which will make a lighter batter more appropriate for squid.

KUNG PAO SHRIMP

PREP TIME: 25 MINUTES | COOK TIME: 10 MINUTES | SERVES 4

According to author Fuchsia Dunlop in her book *The Food of Sichuan*, kung pao shrimp is an American take on a traditional Sichuan dish—gong bao chicken—that is now popular back in Sichuan. My recipe is an amalgam of many I've read and eaten over the years. It's slightly modified from the kung pao pheasant in *Pheasant, Quail, Cottontail*.

SAUCE

2 teaspoons sugar

2 teaspoons soy sauce

1 tablespoon Chinese black
vinegar or rice vinegar

½ teaspoon potato starch or
cornstarch

1 teaspoon sesame oil

¼ cup chicken stock

MARINADE

1 tablespoon soy sauce

1 tablespoon Shaoxing wine or
dry sherry

1 tablespoon potato starch or
cornstarch

1 egg white

SHRIMP

1 pound peeled shrimp

10 dried hot chiles

4 cloves garlic

One 2-inch piece of ginger,
peeled and finely minced
(about 2 tablespoons)

5 green onions, cut into
½-inch pieces

2 cups peanut oil

1 teaspoon Sichuan peppercorns,
ground

¾ cup roasted peanuts

Whisk together all the ingredients for the sauce and set aside.

Whisk together all the ingredients for the marinade in a medium bowl.

If the shrimp are large, cut them into bite-sized pieces. I prefer to use small shrimp whole. Mix in with the marinade ingredients. Set aside for 20 to 30 minutes.

Meanwhile, break the dried chiles into pieces and shake out as many seeds as you can. This is also a good time to prepare the garlic, ginger, and green onions if you haven't already.

Set a wok over high heat and add the peanut oil. Heat this to 350°F. Fry the shrimp in batches, making sure they don't stick. I use a chopstick to keep them apart when they first go into the oil. You only want the coating to set, so fry them only about a minute or so. Move them to a tray lined with paper towels. Repeat with the rest of the shrimp.

Drain off all but about 3 tablespoons of the oil. You can reuse the excess oil several times; label it as "fish fry oil."

Heat the remaining oil in the wok over high heat. When you see a wisp of smoke, add the Sichuan peppercorns and the dried chiles and stir-fry a few seconds, until you can smell them. Add the garlic, ginger, and green onions and stir-fry another 30 seconds.

Add the shrimp, the sauce, and the peanuts and toss to combine. Bring to a rapid boil and stir-fry for 30 seconds.

Serve immediately over steamed jasmine rice.

BLACK BEAN LOBSTER STIR-FRY

PREP TIME: 15 MINUTES | COOK TIME: 20 MINUTES | SERVES 4

Unlike the recipe above, this dish, inspired by Cantonese food, which is what most American Chinese restaurants serve, is a bit more restrained. Another difference is that the coating on the lobster, or fish, or shrimp, or whatever, is not hard-fried; it is truly velveted, which is a bit more delicate.

In a perfect world, you would use Chinese fermented black soybeans (*douchi*) for this recipe, which can be found in Asian markets or online (they keep forever). Far easier to find, if less authentic—but perfectly fine—is the black bean garlic sauce you can find in the Asian aisle of your local supermarket. If this is what you use, only add two tablespoons, not three.

You have the same fish and seafood options you do with the sweet and sour fish recipe above, which is to say, pretty much anything goes.

Serve with steamed jasmine rice.

MARINADE

- 1 tablespoon potato starch or cornstarch
- 1 egg white
- 2 teaspoons Shaoxing wine or dry sherry
- ½ teaspoon salt
- ½ teaspoon white pepper

STIR-FRY

- 1 pound lobster meat, cut into bite-sized pieces
- 3 cups peanut or vegetable oil for frying
- 2 tablespoons minced fresh ginger
- 2 cloves garlic, minced
- 2 dried hot chiles, less if you don't want it spicy, broken in half and seeds shaken out
- 3 tablespoons fermented black beans
- ⅓ cup shellfish or chicken stock
- 2 tablespoons Shaoxing wine or dry sherry
- ½ teaspoon potato starch or cornstarch
- 3 chopped scallions
- 1 tablespoon sesame oil

Whisk the marinade ingredients together, then mix it into the chunks of lobster, making sure every piece is well coated.

Heat the oil in the wok on high heat until it hits 280°F. Pass the lobster through the hot oil in batches. I use chopsticks to place each piece in the oil so they don't all stick together. If you don't have chopsticks, use a butter knife to separate the pieces after lowering them in with a slotted spoon. Gently fry the lobster for about 1 minute to set the coating, then move it to a tray lined with paper towels.

When the lobster is done, pour off all but about 2 tablespoons of oil. You can reuse the rest of the oil several times; just mark it as "fish fry oil." Now's the time to mix the remaining starch with the stock.

Get the remaining oil in the wok hot and stir-fry the ginger, garlic, and chiles until they smell nice, about 30 to 60 seconds. Mix in the black beans, then return the lobster to the wok. Stir in the stock and the Shaoxing wine or sherry with the starch and boil it furiously until it all becomes a glossy sauce, about 2 minutes. Add the scallions, drizzle some sesame oil over everything, and serve.

9

THE ART OF FRYING FISH

LET'S FACE IT. If you were to walk up to a hundred random people on pretty much any street in America and ask them how they like their fish, the vast majority would say fried. I fall into that group, too.

What's so interesting about our hypothetical survey is that that single answer—fried fish—will conjure different things for different people. This chapter explores the global love of fried fish, from Japanese tempura to southern cornmeal, English beer batter to whole fish dusted in starch and fried in a wok. We'll walk through all sorts of ways to coat your fish or seafood before frying. Each creates a different result, and each is good in its own way.

Frying is also a first step in a whole range of dishes. I discussed several of them in the chapter on searing and sauté, notably the stir-fries, which often use frying as an initial step. In this chapter, I include cases where you fry then sauce a dish, like Louisiana courtbouillon and a Spanish dish with pine nuts and tomatoes.

As a general rule, you don't fry oily fish. I know, they love their fried mackerel in the Philippines, and I've seen salmon fish and chips. But I don't much like either. Here, we'll mostly be working with lean fish and seafood.

Nestled within these recipes you'll find some classic sauces that are useful for more than just fried fish. Tartar sauce, remoulade, and Thai dipping sauce, for example, are all good with both fried and grilled fish, and tartar sauce makes a nice base for a flaked fish salad, too.

Another thing you'll notice is that since this is frying, there is often a lot of oil involved. You can strain this oil after it cools and reuse it several times; I usually toss the oil after four fries. Be sure to mark it "fish fry oil" so you don't accidentally use it on chicken.

BEER-BATTERED FISH

PREP TIME: 20 MINUTES | COOK TIME: 40 MINUTES | SERVES 4

At some point, all of us have sat face-to-face with a pile of fish and chips. As this usually happens first when we're tiny tots, the experience can alter the course of our dietary existence. After that virginal fish fry, we emerge either as committed fish lovers or, like so many Americans, committed fish haters.

Only about half of Americans eat seafood more than once or twice a year, and I suspect that a big reason for such a gulf between fish eaters and fish haters is what was on that first plate of fried fish and chips. Try to think back to your childhood now. Did your mom cook her own fried fish, or did she open a box and shake out a few frozen fish sticks?

The key is batter. Batter—specifically beer batter—is why we love a good plate of fish and chips. "Golden brown" might be the two best words you can say in the kitchen (other than, perhaps, "More bacon?"), and the magic of a batter that is crispy yet light is a feat of culinary prestidigitation. While everyone has their own, beer batters are all basically the same: beer (what kind you use matters), flour, and a little salt.

So long as you watch temperature, you're fine. Sure, it can be sporty to have a half-gallon of 360°F oil roiling on your stovetop, but if you keep a sharp eye on that temperature, you're fine. Thermometers are a must. Soggy, greasy fish and chips happen because the oil was not hot enough. Oil that is too hot will burn the batter by the time the fish has been cooked. My sweet spot has always been about 360°F.

◀ Frying up a northern pike shore lunch in Manitoba, Canada.

»

Finally, what kind of fish to use for your fish and chips? I've eaten batter-fried fish six ways to Sunday, but all the best share a few characteristics: they're all firm, white, and lean. Cod, haddock, and pollock are classics in the East, as is halibut or lingcod in the West. In Wisconsin and Minnesota, walleye and yellow perch are king. In the South, it's all catfish until you get to the Gulf, where redfish take over. I've even used tilapia. But my absolute favorite? Shark. Dogfish and leopard shark are the perfect frying fish, and in fact are traditional in northern England fish and chips. The meat is white as snow, very lean, and firmer even than halibut.

Happily, none of these species is threatened, so you can eat them with a clean conscience. What's more, eaten cold the next day, fish and chips made with halibut or these little sharks tastes astonishingly like cold fried chicken. Go figure.

2 pounds skinless, boneless fish

Salt

½ cup self-rising flour

2 tablespoons vegetable oil

1 teaspoon salt

About ½ bottle beer

Oil for frying

Salt the fish and set it aside at room temperature. Mix together the flour, 2 tablespoons of vegetable oil, salt, and beer, stirring all the while. You want enough beer in the batter to give it the consistency of house paint or melted ice cream. Put into the fridge to rest for 20 minutes.

Now get your oil going. You want it to be 350°F to 360°F. Turn the oven to the "warm" setting and put a baking sheet inside. Place a wire rack on top of the baking sheet.

Take the batter out of the fridge. Dredge the fish in the batter and let the excess drip off for a second or two. Lay each piece gently into the hot oil. Do this by letting the bottom end of the piece of fish fry for a second or so in the oil before you let the whole piece get a bath. This helps prevent the fish from sticking to the bottom of the pot. Keep a chopstick or something similar around to dislodge any pieces that do get stuck.

Fry in batches until golden brown, about 5 to 8 minutes depending on how large the pieces are. Keep each batch in the warm oven while you finish the rest. Serve at once when you're done.

Serve with lemon, beer, and a sauce of your choice. Tartar sauce is a good idea, but remoulade is also good, as are aioli and the traditional malt vinegar and Tabasco.

VARIATIONS You can choose from a variety of beer styles, but I find that a simple lager or mild ale works best. Avoid hoppy beers; they'll be bitter. I rarely do seafood this way, but beer-battered shrimp or chunks of lobster tail are nice.

The two batters that follow are lighter and more delicate than beer batter and are slightly trickier to pull off, although neither is terribly demanding.

JAPANESE TEMPURA

PREP TIME: 25 MINUTES | **COOK TIME: 15 MINUTES** | **SERVES 4**

I first ate tempura in my twenties, as a young reporter with a girlfriend who loved sushi. At the time, I was running something like sixty miles a week and lifting weights, so eating enough sushi to fill me up would cost me half my paycheck. But tempura was on the menu, and that seemed more filling. But only a little. The batter was so light and airy, I found I could eat several orders of tempura shrimp. The tempura shrimp, meanwhile, ate my paycheck.

Tempura is a bit like beer batter but is lighter and, well, has no beer. Recipes for the batter range from flour and ice water to those that are more complex, which is where mine falls. The reason I do this is to make the batter pretty much foolproof. My batter is very light, and if your oil is hot enough, this tempura will be very crispy, too.

While it is always important with any fried food to move finished pieces to a rack set in a warm oven, it is vital with tempura, which can go soggy in a hurry.

Vegetable oil for cooking

1 pound peeled shrimp

Salt, for the shrimp

¾ cup rice flour or all-purpose flour

¼ cup corn, potato, or tapioca starch

¼ teaspoon baking soda

½ teaspoon salt

1 cup ice cold sparkling water

1 egg yolk

Heat your cooking oil to 360°F. While the oil is heating, salt the shrimp lightly. Mix all the dry ingredients for the tempura batter. Turn your oven to the "warm" setting, and place a baking sheet inside. Place a wire rack on top of the baking sheet.

When the oil is hot, mix the egg yolk and the sparkling water into the dry tempura batter ingredients and stir only until just combined; it's OK to have a few lumps. Dip a shrimp into the batter, then gently lower it into the hot oil. Repeat this with a few more shrimp, taking care not to crowd the pot. Fry the shrimp until golden brown, about 3 minutes. Make sure they do not stick to the bottom of the pot, and use a chopstick to dislodge any pieces that do stick.

When each batch is done, transfer it to the wire rack in the oven. When all the shrimp are done, serve at once with ponzu sauce (page 232), soy sauce, or any other dipping sauce.

VARIATIONS I've seen lots of things fried in tempura, and all are good. Shrimp is classic, but other options include oysters, small scallops, fish, pieces of lobster, snow or king crab leg pieces, and of course squid.

CHINESE SALT AND PEPPER FISH

PREP TIME: 15 MINUTES | COOK TIME: 20 MINUTES | SERVES 4

This is one of those classic dishes we Americans tend to give short shrift to, I suspect because there's no shiny sauce to go with it. It's something of a naked dish. You have nowhere to hide here, so if your batter is greasy, your black pepper stale, and your garlic burned, everyone will know it. That said, this is not a hard dish to master. It's of Cantonese origin, and my version is adapted from my friend Kian Lam Kho's fantastic book *Phoenix Claws and Jade Trees: Essential Techniques of Authentic Chinese Cooking.*

Key to this dish is very hot oil, as in 375°F, otherwise the fish will be greasy. You also want quality black pepper, the best you can find, because it's a major player in the flavor of this dish. At the very least, grind your own supermarket pepper as you serve. I would suggest a Tellicherry or Malabar black pepper. Finally, cake flour makes a difference in the batter. While not strictly needed, if you have cake flour, use it. The batter comes out lighter.

As to what fish to use, almost anything goes—pretty much any firm fish you'd want to fry, which is most of them. I'd avoid bluefish, salmon or trout, herring, or any other really oily fish. You'll mostly be using fillets of white fish, but this would be fantastic with whole fried smelt or shrimp, too.

Serve this with steamed rice—and chopsticks, which make it easier to pick up all the yummy bits that come along with the fish.

The quality of your ingredients matters here more than the specifics. If you don't like cilantro, use parsley, and any fresh hot chile will work—or leave it out. And use whatever nice fresh fish you can find.

»

Oil for frying (I use peanut oil)

2 tablespoons minced fresh ginger

2 tablespoons sliced fresh garlic

BATTER

½ cup flour, cake flour if you have it

½ cup cornstarch, potato starch,
   or tapioca

1 teaspoon baking soda

½ teaspoon salt

2 egg whites

½ cup ice-cold water or
   cold seltzer

FISH

1½ pounds fish, cut into chunks

1 heaping tablespoon coarse
   sea salt

1 tablespoon freshly ground
   black pepper

1 to 3 small hot chiles, like
   serranos, Thai, or cayenne,
   thinly sliced (optional)

Cilantro or parsley, for garnish

Heat enough oil to deep-fry the fish, about 3 to 4 cups, depending on what sort of pot or wok you use.

While the oil is heating, make the batter. Mix together the flour, starch, baking soda, and salt in a bowl. In another bowl, beat the egg whites into soft peaks. Add about ½ cup of ice-cold water (or cold seltzer) into the flour bowl, then fold in the egg whites.

Fry the ginger and garlic until the garlic just starts to brown, about 45 seconds. Use a skimmer or slotted spoon to remove it to a paper towel. Set it aside for now.

When the oil hits about 375°F, coat a few pieces of the fish in the batter and deep-fry them until golden brown, about 2 minutes. As they're frying, turn your oven to "warm" and set a cooling rack with a baking sheet underneath it for your fish. Move the finished fish to the rack and continue frying the rest.

When all the fish is ready, toss it with the salt and pepper, the reserved ginger and garlic, and the sliced chiles. Serve garnished with the cilantro.

"Govern a great nation as you would cook a fish.
Don't overdo it."

LAO TZU

I'm defining "breading" as coating fish or seafood with some combination of egg, flour, and breadcrumb-like thing. The traditional sequence is flour, then egg, then breadcrumbs. But as you'll see, there are lots of variations that result in very different effects.

FRIED FLOUNDER

PREP TIME: 20 MINUTES | **COOK TIME: 20 MINUTES** | **SERVES 4**

▲ Mom with an Atlantic fluke, circa 1980.

I have a history with fried flounder. A flounder, either a winter flounder or a fluke, was the first fish I ever caught. I can't remember the exact day, but I can tell you I was about four or five years old and it was aboard a party boat off the New Jersey shore. If I had to guess, it'd be the *Norma K II*. Mom loves flounder, and so did my stepdad, Frank. Mom taught me to keep the line under my finger while the bait was in the water, to better feel the delicate bite of the winter flounder, which are notoriously tricky to hook. We caught lots of them, as well as the larger fluke, which run once the weather warms.

Afterward, almost without variation, Mom would make fried flounder. Always dipped in flour, then egg, then breadcrumbs, always with "ta-ta" sauce, Yankee-mom New Englandese for tartar sauce.

These were the days of liberal limits, so the family could come home with coolers full of flounder. Mom always preferred to eat fish fresh, so we'd do a huge fish fry either that night or the night after. I have memories of her standing at the stove, frying fish after fish after fish. Each fried fillet would go on a paper towel to drain. Soon the stack would grow, sometimes a foot high.

I can hear you all thinking now just exactly what we all were thinking then: better get a jump on the fish fried last—only they would still be crispy. By the time we'd reached the fish fried first, they had become little more than a vehicle for ketchup—or ta-ta.

It never occurred to Mom, or to me until much later, that setting the finished fish on a cooling rack set over a baking sheet in a warm oven would solve that problem. I'm glad I know this now. Pretty sure I picked it up in college, when I fried a lot of fish in my dorm room at Stony Brook. Another tip I picked up later in life was to bread your fish early and set them in the fridge for a few hours. This helps the breading set up and stick to the fish—and yes, it really does make a difference.

Once made, if you have any leftovers, set them on a paper towel in a plastic container in the fridge. Then eat them cold with leftover tartar sauce the next day.

FRIED FLOUNDER, continued

TARTAR SAUCE

1 cup mayonnaise

2 teaspoons mustard, Dijon
   or brown

2 teaspoons lemon juice

A few drops Tabasco sauce

½ cup chopped pickles

1 teaspoon small capers

1 shallot, minced fine

1 tablespoon minced chives

Salt and black pepper

FISH

2 to 3 pounds skinless
   flounder fillets

Salt

1 cup flour

2 eggs

½ cup milk

1 tablespoon mustard

1 cup breadcrumbs

Oil for frying

For the tartar sauce, mix everything in a bowl and set it in the fridge. Salt the fish lightly on both sides and set aside.

Set up a breading station with three plates or shallow bowls. The first will have the flour; if you want more seasoning than I'm suggesting in this recipe, this is where you add it. The second will have the eggs, milk, and mustard all beaten together. The third will have the breadcrumbs.

Dredge the flounder in the flour first, pressing it into the fish and making sure you get the fish totally covered. Now sweep the fillet through the egg wash, again making sure you get it totally coated. Finally, set it in the breadcrumbs and press them in to make a good coating. Set each fillet on a plate or tray in the fridge and let it rest 1 hour, and up to all day.

When you're ready to fry, pour in enough oil to get to a depth of about 1 inch in a large frying pan. If you happen to be making the fries to go with this, make them first and hold them in the oven. Heat the oil over high heat. Set a rack over a baking sheet and put that into the oven. Set the oven to "warm."

When the oil hits 350°F, fry your fish, right from the fridge. This works because they are very thin, and you want a pretty, golden crust without overcooking the fish. Room temperature flounder fried this way will overcook. It takes about 3 to 5 minutes per side to get golden brown. Move each finished fillet to the rack in the oven. When they're all done, serve it up with the tartar sauce.

VARIATIONS This sort of breading is, to me, solely for lean white fish. I do not like it on salmon or other oily fish, and I don't much care for it on any seafood, either, although I've seen breaded shrimp. That said, any sort of "regular" fish will do.

THE ART OF FRYING FISH

SNAPPER BITES

PREP TIME: 20 MINUTES | COOK TIME: 15 MINUTES | SERVES 4

A snapper bite is basically fried snapper—or really, any firm white fish. The story of snapper bites is simple. My friend Joe Baya and I were visiting his dad, Emery, on Dauphin Island, south of Mobile, Alabama. We were there in time for opening day of snapper season, which is a big deal in the Gulf. Joe and Emery had a spot.

Red snapper like to live on structure—reefs, rockpiles, sunken boats, and such. And in Alabama, you can create your own mini-reef if you want to, so there are thousands of little bits of structure everywhere in state waters—the main reason that Alabama has so many red snapper, which can be hard to find in some Gulf states. Joe and Emery's spot was off where there were no other boats, a miracle on the opener. And Joe and I hadn't even finished tying new leaders when Emery's friend Joey had a huge snapper on the line. It turned out to be almost twenty pounds, a giant. As soon as we dropped a bait in the water, a snapper would hit it. It was ridiculous, amazing, unforgettable.

In minutes, all four of us had our two snapper apiece, none smaller than fifteen pounds. We couldn't have fished that reef more if we tried. Any grouper or other reef fish were safe from us because we simply could not get a bait past the snapper. So we left, happy and laden with red snapper.

Now, butchering giant red snapper is a bit unique. They're bass-like fish, sure, but they're a little tall in the saddle, like porgies, sheepshead, or a mega-bluegill, and when they're huge, you get different cuts off them. Off a giant side, you get a center-cut above the ribs, which is primo, then two tail-side fillets, one on either side of the centerline, which I cut out.

The primo "loins" we saved for another day. The tail-end fillets we ate immediately. They became snapper bites, the recipe for which I came up with on the spot. It's fried red snapper with a crust made from mashed up Saltine crackers, fried in peanut oil. The fish bits are soaked in a combination of beaten egg, ballpark mustard, Cajun seasoning, and a little heavy cream, then dredged in the Saltines.

We ate them without a sauce in Alabama, but when I made this again at home, I decided to serve them with a New Orleans-style remoulade. (Hat tip to my friend Chef John Currence for the inspiration for the remoulade, which appears in his awesome book *Pickles, Pigs & Whiskey: Recipes from My Three Favorite Food Groups and Then Some.*)

As I mentioned above, you don't need red snapper to make this recipe. Good alternatives would be black seabass, Pacific rockfish, lingcod, perch, walleye, chunks of big catfish, grouper, cobia, bass, halibut, or haddock.

"Only dead fish go with the flow."

UNKNOWN

NEW ORLEANS REMOULADE

½ cup Dijon or Creole mustard

⅓ cup mayonnaise

3 tablespoons chopped parsley

3 tablespoons minced shallot

3 tablespoons minced celery

¼ cup minced dill pickles

1 tablespoon minced garlic

1 tablespoon prepared horseradish

1 tablespoon cider vinegar

1 tablespoon olive oil

1 tablespoon lemon juice

1 teaspoon Creole or Cajun
    seasoning

1 teaspoon Worcestershire sauce

SNAPPER

2 pounds skinless snapper fillets

Salt

2 eggs, lightly beaten

¼ cup yellow mustard (or Dijon)

1 tablespoon Creole or Cajun
    seasoning

3 tablespoons heavy cream or
    half-and-half

Peanut oil for frying

1 sleeve Saltine crackers, smashed

Mix together all the ingredients for the remoulade and set aside. The remoulade can be made up to a week in advance, and making it the night before lets the flavors mellow.

Cut the fish into chunks of about two bites each. Salt lightly. In a bowl, mix together the eggs, mustard, Creole seasoning and heavy cream.

Pour enough peanut oil into a frying pan to come about a half-inch up the sides. Heat this to about 350°F.

While the oil is heating, dunk as many snapper bites in the egg wash as will fit. When the oil is hot, dredge the fish in the Saltines. You can do this in a bowl or in a plastic bag. Really press in the Saltines, and it's OK to have a few bits that aren't pulverized.

Fry the fish until golden brown on both sides, about 3 minutes per side. Drain on paper towels and serve with the remoulade and some lemon wedges if you have them.

MEXICAN FRIED FISH

PREP TIME: 10 MINUTES | COOK TIME: 10 MINUTES | SERVES 4

I've been obsessed with chicharrón de pescado ever since I first ate it at a little Mexican seafood place called Mariscos Lauro Villar in Brownsville, Texas. I was down there with my friends Jesse and Miguel chasing the wily chachalaca (a sort of grouse), and we saw a sign on the window that said "Chicharron de Catan." Huh? Fried gar? (*catan* being the local word for alligator gar; everywhere else in Mexico, the fish is called *pejelegarto*).

While I was intrigued, Jesse and Miguel were over the moon—they'd eaten gar before, and I had not. We walked into the unassuming restaurant—it's in a strip mall next to a liquor store that, by the way, has really good mezcal—and confirmed that the chicharron de pescado was indeed catan. "*Claro que si,*" the waitress said, "Yes, of course." We asked for two orders. It was amazing. What makes Mexican fried fish different from everyone else's fried fish is that they're going for a sort of cracklins thing with their fry—really kicking the spurs to it with the hot oil. So yeah, the fish is a bit overcooked, but it's super crispy.

Add gar to the equation and it's even better. Gar fish has a texture closer to chicken breast than to its fishy cousins: white as snow, meaty and firm. The dish was super simple. Fried gar on a plate with some shredded lettuce, a pickled jalapeño or two, limes, and our choice of hot sauces.

Flash forward to a recent teal hunting trip to the Galveston area of Texas, and, as it happened, a guy named Austin, who takes care of the ranch we were on, brought me a little gar to cook. This was a spotted gar, not a giant alligator gar, but it would do. The meat was just like the alligator gar in miniature, and Austin showed me the fine art of getting inside one of these prehistoric fish; the skin on an eighteen-inch fish was almost as thick as that of a six-foot alligator.

I seasoned the fish, coated it in egg and then flour, and then—and this is important—let it rest in the fridge for an hour. This helps the coating stick to the fish better. I fried it all in fresh lard, and *¡A huevo!* Was it good!

You don't need gar to make Mexican fried fish, but you do need a reasonably firm fish. We made it with largemouth bass as well as halibut, and both were good. Use what you have available.

2 pounds skinless fish,
    cut into chunks
Salt and black pepper
1 tablespoon garlic powder
2 eggs, lightly beaten
1 cup flour
Lard or oil for frying

Season the fish with salt, pepper, and garlic powder, then coat well with the beaten egg. Dust in the flour, pressing it in well. You want some eggy bits coated in flour to adhere to the fish; this give you a better texture. Put on a plate in one layer and set in the fridge for 1 hour.

Pour the oil into a large frying pan and get it very hot, about 350°F to 360°F. Fry your fish hard, about 3 to 4 minutes per side. You want them just past golden brown. If you can't fit all the fish in your pan, set up a rack on a baking sheet in your oven and set the oven to "warm."

Serve your fish with a selection of salsas or hot sauces and limes.

VARIATIONS This method does work well with seafood, but it seems a waste. Shrimp and other seafood will take this breading well and can handle the serious time in the fryer, but since they are expensive and more delicate than, say, gar, I'd use some of the less violent methods in this chapter.

CORNMEAL-CRUSTED SPECKLED TROUT

PREP TIME: 20 MINUTES | **COOK TIME: 20 MINUTES** | **SERVES 4**

Obviously, this recipe can be done with any white fish. Other good candidates would be catfish, bass, walleye, pike fillets, croaker, black seabass, haddock, Pacific rockfish, or freshwater sheepshead. You get the point. I wanted the salad to be very southern, thus the choice of black-eyed peas, turnip and mustard greens, and bacon. You can change it up as you like. Want a Nordic flair? Go with great northern beans, kale, and, well, bacon is universal.

FISH

4 to 6 skinless speckled
   trout fillets

1 cup milk

1 cup fine cornmeal, also known
   as "fish fry"

1 tablespoon Cajun seasoning

2 teaspoons ground black pepper

Peanut oil for frying

SALAD

2 cups chicken broth

2 cups water

1 cup black-eyed peas

¼ pound bacon

1 chopped onion

3 cloves garlic, chopped

3 cups chopped turnip or
   mustard greens

1 or 2 roasted red peppers, canned
   or freshly roasted, chopped

Salt and black pepper

Cider vinegar

Start by cooking the black-eyed peas. Bring the chicken broth and water to a boil and add the peas. Lower the heat to a very gentle simmer and cook until they're tender but not falling apart. While this is happening, cook the bacon in a large sauté pan. When the bacon is crispy, remove it and chop. Set the bacon aside for now. Keep the bacon fat in the pan.

Sauté the onion in the bacon fat over medium-high heat until the edges brown. Add the garlic and the greens and toss to coat in the bacon fat. Cook until the greens wilt. Turn off the heat, add back the bacon, then mix in the red peppers. Cover the pan and set aside for now.

Pour the milk into a shallow bowl. Mix all the breading ingredients. Pour enough peanut oil into a frying pan to come up about ¼ to ½ inch. Heat the oil to 325°F to 350°F. If you don't have a thermometer, the oil will be ready when a bit of the breading sizzles instantly when flicked into it. When the oil is hot, dredge the fish in the milk, then coat with the breading. Fry until golden brown, about 3 to 5 minutes per side. Drain on paper towels.

To finish, warm the black-eyed pea salad, add vinegar and black pepper to taste, and put some on everyone's plate. Top with the fried fish. Serve with beer or an uncomplicated white wine.

VARIATIONS This is a classic way to bread any sort of fish, oysters, shrimp, squid, and even clams, although a better clam breading follows this recipe.

FRIED CLAMS, NEW ENGLAND STYLE

PREP TIME: 10 MINUTES | COOK TIME: 20 MINUTES | SERVES 4

Face planting into a basket of fried clams is one of my earliest food memories. Crunchy batter, salty clams, that shellfishy meatiness that only a clam has—oysters and mussels are too dainty—and just a little whiff of an "ick" factor. After all, you eat the whole clam, foot, belly, and all. And who knows what clams eat, anyway?

I have this gauzy memory of being on the dock in Galilee, Rhode Island. It's somewhere around 1975, and I'm with my family. My sisters Laura and Liz are minding me. They'll correct me, but I think the ferry to Block Island was late that day, and we decided to eat something at one of the clam shacks that were right there. This was probably that tipping point moment into my addiction, because I ate a lot of clams that day. A lot. So many, I remember my sisters prodding my distended belly, half-joking that I might explode. Almost, but I didn't.

Once on the Block, I ate more clams, this time as Block Island clam cakes, another of my favorites (page 212). I gorged myself on clams at almost every meal that year and every vacation since then all through my childhood. Funny, we never ate clams when we were back home in New Jersey. Only when we were on vacation, or whenever we were in Massachusetts. The Bay State, I soon learned, is fried clam mecca. Mom's from Ipswich—and Ipswich is in Essex, Massachusetts, the home not only of Woodman's, but of several other legendary clam shacks (such as the Clam Box) that all vie for the title of Greatest Fried Clams on Earth. All have great clams.

Making fried clams is an art. The fat must be very hot, or the clams will overcook before the batter is golden and crispy. To my mind, you must have the whole clam in there too, belly and all. Yes, they serve them without the bellies, but that's for tourists or Howard Johnson's.

You want a little seasoning in the breading, but not much, or it will overwhelm the clams. Lemon wedges are a must, and many reach for either tartar sauce or ketchup. I like just lemon, then maybe a dash of hot sauce after I've eaten twenty or thirty.

The only part even remotely tricky about this recipe is finding the "corn flour," which is not the same thing as cornstarch. Corn flour is just finely ground cornmeal. The easiest way to find some is in the "ethnic" aisle, where you find Louisiana foods. It's called "fish fry," and if you look at the ingredients, you'll see that it's just superfine cornmeal. If you absolutely can't find any, just use more regular flour. It'll be fine.

1 pound shucked cherrystones, littlenecks, or western littlenecks or Manila clams

1 cup corn flour, as in "fish fry" mix

1 cup all-purpose flour

1 teaspoon salt

1 teaspoon freshly ground black pepper

½ teaspoon cayenne

1 cup buttermilk or evaporated milk

Oil for frying

Pick through the clams to make sure there are no bits of shell or obvious grit. Mix together all the dry ingredients in a bowl. Submerge the clams in buttermilk.

Preheat the oven to 200°F and put a rack set over a baking sheet inside the oven. Heat enough oil to float the clams, about a quart or so. What oil? Anything you feel like, but I prefer peanut oil or fresh lard. You want the oil hot, about 360°F.

When the oil is almost ready, coat a few clams in the breading. Don't do more than your fryer can handle in one batch, as you want the clams to go right from breading into the fryer. If you want super-extra-crispy clams, dip the breaded clams back in the buttermilk and again in the breading; I think this is too much, but some people like them that way.

Fry the clams until they're golden brown, about 90 seconds to 2 minutes. Move them to the rack in the oven and repeat with the remaining clams, making sure the oil gets back up to temperature between batches. Serve with homemade tartar sauce, malt vinegar, remoulade, ketchup, or hot sauce.

Fried clams almost have to be eaten with lemon wedges, potato salad, other fried things, maybe a lobster roll, and either beer or, if you feel all fancy, some white wine, maybe even Champagne.

VARIATIONS You will see both fish and seafood like shrimp and oysters fried in this style of breading. It's especially good with squid.

FRIED WHOLE FISH

Seen mostly in Asia, whole fish fried is made all over the world in one way or another. Fried trout is an American tradition, as is fried smelt. Whitebait—tiny fish, fried whole—is a thing in Britain. There are many, many more examples.

FRIED SMELT OR WHITEBAIT

PREP TIME: 10 MINUTES | **COOK TIME: 10 MINUTES** | **SERVES 4**

Smelt and whitebait are two small fish commonly eaten whole—heads, guts, and all—although the squeamish head and gut their smelt. Either way, these are unusual in that they are normally just dusted in flour and fried, then salted when they come out of the fryer. Whitebait is, essentially, "fries with eyes."

Oil for frying

12 ounces smelt, whitebait, or
    some similar fish

1 cup flour

Salt, finely ground if possible

Fill a pan of oil to about 1 inch deep, and heat to about 360°F to 375°F. While the oil is heating, dust the fish in the flour. Shake off the excess and drop about a quarter of them into the oil. Use a chopstick or something similar to separate them. Fry until nicely browned, about 2 minutes. Remove with a slotted spoon to a tray lined with paper towels. Salt them immediately, then do the next quarter, and so on.

Serve hot with aioli, mayo, remoulade, tartar sauce, or the like.

VARIATIONS You can play with the flour here. Chickpea flour is a great option, as is superfine cornmeal. I've used masa harina too, as well as nut flours. Generally speaking, these will be appetizers or snacks, rather than a full meal.

"Do not tell fish stories where the people know you; but particularly, don't tell them where they know the fish."

MARK TWAIN

PAN-FRIED TROUT WITH PEAS

PREP TIME: 15 MINUTES | COOK TIME: 10 MINUTES | SERVES 4

Pan-fried trout, dredged in flour and fried in butter with a little lemon. Few things are better. I start with a butterflied, deboned trout (page 53), fry it only on one side, and serve it with peas, parsley, and a lemon-butter sauce. If you don't have a butterflied trout handy, fillets or whole fish work fine. I just like the trout-as-schnitzel look of a flattened, boneless fish.

4 frying-pan-sized trout, butterflied, fillets or whole

Salt

About ¾ cup flour

¼ cup unsalted butter

1½ cups peas, fresh or thawed

1 cup chicken stock

Grated zest and juice of a lemon

3 tablespoons minced parsley

Black pepper

VARIATIONS Any fish you can butterfly will work here, as will shrimp, squid, scallops, chunks of lobster, clams, or even oysters.

Rinse the trout in cold water and pat it dry with paper towels. Salt it lightly on both sides, then dredge it in flour.

Heat the butter in a large frying pan over medium-high heat. If you think you can get all the trout into the pan at once, you're good to go. If not, get individual plates ready and set your oven to 200°F.

When the butter is hot, lay the trout skin-side down in the hot butter. Fry for 2 minutes, then use a large spoon to baste the meat side of the trout with butter. Keep basting with the spoon for a minute or two, depending on how thick the trout is. In the trout below, I only basted it for about 90 seconds. When the skin side of the trout is golden brown, use a spatula (or two) to gently remove the trout and flip it skin-side up onto a plate. If you need to fry more trout, put the plate in the oven.

When all the trout have been cooked, add the remaining ingredients to the pan and turn the heat to high. Boil furiously until the sauce reduces by half, then pour it over the trout. Serve at once with bread, rice, or potatoes.

HMONG CRISPY FISH

PREP TIME: 20 MINUTES | **COOK TIME: 20 MINUTES** | **SERVES 4**

It's a paradox that some of the easiest, most fun fish to catch are also among the hardest to cook well. Small bass-like fish—those with largish heads, prickly spines, and large rib cages—really need to be at least a good foot long to be worth filleting, and even that's a small fillet. What to do? The answer is to cook them whole. You get exponentially more meat off each fish, you waste less, and, well, it's just fun to tear into a whole fish at the table. There's something primal about it I really like.

Southeast Asia really does it well, where they are geniuses with fresh herbs, citrus, and chiles. This recipe is inspired by one I found in one of my favorite cookbooks, *Cooking from the Heart: The Hmong Kitchen in America*, by Sami Scripter and Sheng Yang. The Hmong are a group of Southeast Asians who fought with us against the communists in Vietnam, and after the war, thousands came here to live. There are large Hmong communities in Minnesota's Twin Cities, in San Jose, Fresno, and here in Sacramento.

The trick is to crispy fry plate-sized fish until the bones and spines soften, then tear into it. You end up eating about a third of the bones, which are reduced to crunchy, nutty tidbits. Crispy, meaty, crunchy, with the zing of citrus, the freshness of the herbs, and the occasional warm note from the fried garlic make this a near perfect plate of food.

This recipe works with any bass-like fish. I mostly use Pacific rockfish, but perch, large- or smallmouth bass, walleyes, black seabass, croakers, puppy drum, porgies, large crappies, and bluegills would all work. The ideal length for the fish is about the size of a big dinner plate.

FISH

2 to 4 plate-sized bass-like fish (see above), scaled and gutted

Salt

1 cup peanut or other vegetable oil

3 to 5 cloves garlic, smashed

Freshly ground black pepper

1 or 2 lemons, cut into wedges

4 green onions, sliced on the diagonal

Cilantro, torn into 1-inch pieces, for garnish

Take the fish out of the fridge and rinse under cold water, checking for any remaining scales. Remove the gills if they are still there. You can snip off the fins with kitchen shears if you want. Use a sharp kitchen knife to slash the sides of the fish perpendicular to the backbone. Make the slices at an angle. This opens up the fish to the hot oil and makes it cook faster. Salt the fish well and set aside.

Make the dipping sauce by combining all the ingredients in a bowl. Set aside.

A wok is the best thing to use for cooking these fish, unless you have a deep-fryer. I have both, and I still prefer the wok. A large frying pan will work, too. Heat the oil until it is between 330°F and 350°F. Fry the garlic until it is a lovely tan and remove.

Pat the fish dry with paper towels, then gently put one or two fish into the hot oil. It's OK if the tails and heads are not submerged. It will sizzle violently, so watch yourself. Use a large spoon to baste the fish with the hot oil as it cooks. Fry like this a solid 6 to 10 minutes, depending on how thick the fish is. You want it very crispy and golden brown. Carefully flip the fish—I use two spatulas to do this. Fry another 5 to 8 minutes. Repeat with any remaining fish. If you do have to do this in

DIPPING SAUCE

3 to 5 small hot chiles such as Thai, or 1 habanero, finely chopped

1 tablespoon minced lemongrass, white part only, finely chopped

3 tablespoons finely minced cilantro

3 tablespoons finely minced green onion or chives

Juice of a lemon

Zest of 1 lemon, grated

A pinch of salt

1 teaspoon sugar

2 tablespoons fish sauce

batches, let the cooked fish rest on a rack set over a baking sheet in a 200°F oven.

To serve, lay the fish on plates and grind a healthy portion of black pepper over them. Black pepper is a signature flavor in this dish, so be generous. Arrange the fried garlic and the remaining garnishes alongside. Serve with the dipping sauce and white rice.

Serve the fish with the garnishes around it and the dipping sauce in the middle of the table. Forks or chopsticks are a must, as is a big bowl of steamed white rice. A really good bite is some fish on top of a little rice, with a bit of the dipping sauce spooned over it.

THAI FRIED POMFRET

PREP TIME: 15 MINUTES | COOK TIME: 15 MINUTES | SERVES 4

I must admit that I had only a dim recollection of pomfret fish when I saw one in, of all places, Pelican, Alaska. I normally think of pomfret as something from India, so Alaska was an odd place to find this fish, which is most closely associated with the cuisines of South and Southeast Asia. A cousin of the more familiar pompano, pomfret shares the same body type as crappies, bluegills, spadefish, porgies, butterfish, and ocean perch—all of which can be substituted here.

Most recipes at least score the fish a few times, to open up the meat to the hot oil or grill. I prefer to cross-hatch the meat, which takes this one step further. It's also pretty. Simply slice down to the bones, but not through them.

I like to dust my pomfret in a 50-50 mix of cornstarch or potato starch and rice flour, then fry it hard in canola or some other high-smoke-point oil. All it needs then is a zippy dipping sauce. I went Thai and mixed lime juice, fish sauce, sambal oelek (any hot chile sauce will do), and minced garlic. Super easy and super tasty.

One added thing about cooking pomfret: the bones are soft enough to eat once fried crispy. I even like to deep-fry the backbone after we've eaten the whole fish; this softens the bones so you can eat them. They taste nutty and crunchy that way.

CHILE SAUCE

Juice of a lime

3 tablespoons sambal oelek, or
    other chile sauce

1 to 2 tablespoons fish sauce

1 to 2 tablespoons minced
    fresh garlic

FISH

1 or 2 whole pomfret, or enough
    crappies or bluegills to feed
    four people

Salt

½ cup cornstarch or potato starch

½ cup rice flour

Canola or vegetable oil for frying

Fresh cilantro or mint, for garnish

Make the chile sauce by mixing together all the ingredients. Set aside at room temperature. This sauce can be made up to a few days ahead of time.

Slice the fish in a cross-hatch pattern to expose the meat. Salt the fish well inside and out. Mix the starch and rice flour together then dust the fish with it, inside and out.

Heat about ½ inch of canola or vegetable oil in a very large pan. When the oil hits about 350°F, shake off any excess flour and fry the pomfret for about 5 minutes per side. One tip: if the tail overhangs the frying pan, break it off and fry it separately, then "reattach" it on the platter, covering the break point with sauce. No one will notice.

Place the fish on a platter and drizzle with the sauce. Fresh cilantro is a nice garnish, as is mint.

FRIED THEN SAUCED

This is a hard category in that it is very close to a sauté or a stir-fry. And it violates the Prime Directive of Frying: Thou Shalt Be Crispy. Yes, but. If the dish is served quickly after saucing, there is still some crispiness left, and the coating that is softening seems to add a layer of heft to the dish. It's hard to explain, but it works. This effect is common with Japanese ramen, which often has tempura in it, as well as with many other Asian dishes. I'll instead focus on two of my favorites: Louisiana courtbouillon and a Spanish dish with tomatoes and pine nuts that I can't bear to leave out of this book.

CATFISH COURTBOUILLON

PREP TIME: 25 MINUTES | **COOK TIME: 30 MINUTES** | **SERVES 4**

I've eaten catfish pretty much every way imaginable, but Louisiana Chef Don Link's catfish courtbouillon takes the prize, hands down. I had heard of catfish courtbouillon, pronounced something like "coo-be-YON," for years, but, well, I was kinda unimpressed. Then I sat at the bar at Cochon, in New Orleans. As I was working my way through the menu, I saw catfish courtboullion. If any place would make a good version of it, it would be Cochon. So I tried it. And was blown away.

Courtbouillon as I knew it was a sort of homey, one-pot gumbo-like thing, with chunks of catfish floating in a vaguely tomatoey stew. This was not that. Chef Link's version features a fillet of catfish, fried in cornmeal, sauced with everything in the traditional catfish courtbouillon—tomatoes, peppers, onions, celery, garlic, herbs—and served alongside simple steamed rice.

Somehow there was still a bit of crunch to the breading on the fish, and the sauce was light, bright, and just a shade zippy with cayenne and lemon. Of all the wonderful things I ate that night, this was the most memorable, because it shouldn't have been, but was.

Thankfully, Chef Link published his recipe in his excellent book *Down South: Bourbon, Pork, Gulf Shrimp & Second Helpings of Everything.* My version differs only slightly. I didn't want to mess with perfection.

Catfish is, of course, traditional, as is gaspergou (freshwater drum), but you can make courtbouillon with any fish you can get a skinless fillet from. Some good regional alternatives would be speckled trout, walleye, smallmouth bass, black seabass, Pacific rockfish, sand or Calico bass, snapper, or snook.

A word of warning. If you use commercial Cajun seasoning, don't add any salt to the dish until the end; chances are you won't need it, because those spice mixes are very salty to begin with.

»

SAUCE

2 tablespoons unsalted butter

1 small white or yellow onion, minced

2 stalks celery, minced

1 red bell pepper, minced

1 serrano or jalapeño pepper, minced

2 Roma or plum tomatoes, seeded and diced

4 cloves garlic, minced

1 teaspoon dried thyme

1 tablespoon Cajun or Creole seasoning

½ cup dry white wine

1½ cups chicken or seafood stock

FISH

5 tablespoons bacon fat or lard

½ cup flour

½ cup fine cornmeal, also known as "fish fry" (look for unseasoned Louisiana Fish Fry)

1 to 2 pounds skinless fish fillets

Salt

⅓ cup minced fresh parsley

¼ cup minced chives or scallions

5 to 10 basil leaves, torn up

Lemon juice

Make the sauce. Heat the butter in a large frying pan over medium-high heat and sauté the onion, celery, red pepper, and serrano until soft, about 5 minutes.

Add the tomato, garlic, thyme, and Cajun seasoning and let this cook another minute or two, then pour in the white wine and bring to a boil. Let this boil down by half, then add the stock and simmer this uncovered for 10 minutes. Turn off the heat, cover the pan, and set aside.

In another frying pan, heat the bacon fat. Mix the flour and cornmeal. Salt the catfish fillets, then dust them in the flour mixture. Fry the fish over medium-high heat until nicely browned, about 3 to 5 minutes per side.

Drain any extra fat, leaving only about a tablespoon. Add the sauce to the pan with the fish and add the herbs and lemon juice to taste. Swirl it all in the pan to mix. To serve, carefully lift a fish fillet with a long spatula, or two spatulas, and set on individual plates. Spoon some sauce over the fish, and serve with steamed rice.

"No human being, however great, or powerful, was ever so free as a fish."

JOHN RUSKIN

SHARK WITH PINE NUTS AND TOMATOES

PREP TIME: 15 MINUTES | COOK TIME: 15 MINUTES | SERVES 4

This is a knockout dish. I read about something called *tiburon con pasas y pinones* in Calvin Schwabe's classic book *Unmentionable Cuisine*. No real recipe, just ingredients. So I made it up from there. The dish Schwabe describes has both pine nuts and raisins in it. I don't much like raisins, so I left them out. You could put two tablespoons in if you'd like.

Shark is a firm white fish. I used leopard shark, which I caught in San Francisco Bay, but you could also use dogfish or any small shark that is not on any threatened list, which normally means you catch it yourself. If you're buying fish, use farm-raised sturgeon, tilefish, white seabass, tautog, halibut—really any very firm white fish you can cut into chunks.

Have everything ready before you start this dish, as it comes together fast. Serve with saffron rice, potatoes, or just crusty bread. White wine is a must with this, although an ice cold pilsner would be good, too.

1 pound skinless fillets of shark or other firm white fish

Salt

¼ cup pine nuts

3 tablespoons olive oil

Flour for dusting

2 to 3 cloves garlic, slivered

4 Roma or other paste tomatoes, seeded and diced

Black pepper

¼ cup white wine or water

2 teaspoons Spanish smoked paprika

¼ cup chopped parsley

Cut the fish into chunks about an inch across. Salt well and set aside.

Put a sauté pan over medium heat and add the pine nuts. Toast them well. Do not walk away at this point, because pine nuts can burn in a hurry. Toss the pan frequently to toast all sides of the nuts and to see if any are burning. Once you get a dark brown on even a few nuts, turn off the heat and pour the nuts into a bowl.

Wipe down the sauté pan with a paper towel and add the olive oil. Turn the heat to medium-high.

Dust the shark in the flour and sauté in the oil. I cook two of the four sides well, for 2 to 3 minutes per side, and then just "kiss" the other sides to lightly brown them. Set the cooked shark on a paper towel to drain.

Add the garlic and pine nuts to the pan and sauté. Add a little more olive oil if the fish soaked up too much. The second you see the garlic turn tan, add the chopped tomatoes and toss to combine. Grind some black pepper over everything.

Add the wine or water and scrape up any stuck-on bits from the bottom of the pan with a wooden spoon.

Sprinkle a little salt over the tomatoes, then add the fish back to the pan. Sprinkle with the smoked paprika and the parsley and toss to combine. Cook for only another minute or so, just to coat everything evenly. It is very important that you not cook the tomatoes so much they break down. Just a minute is all they need. Serve at once. I'd recommend a nice white wine, maybe a torrontés or an albariño.

STEAMED FISH SOUNDS to me like awful spa food. A dreadful, wan attempt to "eat healthy" resulting in desiccated, bland, unhappy fish, maybe with an overly hard floret of unsalted broccoli nearby. And indeed, many steamed fish recipes are exactly that. You will not find them here.

No, to me steaming is largely an initial step in further fish cookery—unless we're talking about shellfish, both mollusks and crustaceans. Steamed crabs, lobsters, and shrimp, not to mention mussels and clams, are wonderful. But even these don't rely solely on vaporized water to render them wondrous.

So why steam at all? In the case of shellfish, it is simply the easiest and, I would argue, one of the best methods to cook these creatures. You could argue that grilling over a wood fire is better, and you'd be right, but it's not easier. In the case of finfish, you get yourself an almost perfect blank canvas on which you can "paint" other flavors at will.

Thus my reference to steaming as a first step. Maybe the finest example of steamed fish in the world is the Chinese practice of steaming a whole fish, carefully moving it to a plate with lots of tasty accompaniments, then pouring a flavorful sauce or searing-hot chile oil all over it.

The other classic steamed fish recipe is the French *en papillote*, or, in English, fish in parchment. With this, you tuck a piece of fish set on top of vegetables and herbs, maybe a splash of wine, in an envelope made of parchment, then close it tight and bake it gently. Yes, you put the packets in the oven, but the method of cooking is steam within the parchment. It's nice, but I'll be honest: fish in parchment bores me to tears. But there is a Mexican variant to this I do like, and that is below.

What you'll find in this chapter are techniques for steaming fish and seafood well, and lots of options for when you do.

◀ Freshly steamed Dungeness crabs.

STEAMED SHELLFISH

Every crustacean known to humans, as well as all those tasty bivalves—clams, mussels, oysters, cockles, and so on—are excellent steamed. So are univalves, like limpets and other snails. One primary reason is because they all come with their own sauce. Shellfish, especially clams and mussels, hold a lot of moisture in their bodies. This is why steamed crabs and lobsters result in a superior texture to those that have been boiled.

Mollusks need to be steamed until they open, or in the cases of limpets or periwinkles, until the meat can be removed from the shell. Most recipes will ask you to do this in a large pan on the stovetop so you can arrange the clams or whatever in one layer. Here's a tip no one else seems to want to tell you: keep an eye on this process as the shellfish steams and remove each one as it opens. Bivalves will open at different rates, and if you wait for all of them to open, some will already be tough.

Also, everyone says to discard those that do not open. That is mostly true, but a little tap on the top shell of a recalcitrant mussel or clam while it's steaming can often pop it open. If it still doesn't open, it still might be good—*if* you did the tap test on them (page 22) all while they were still alive. *You judge a good clam or mussel when it's alive, not after you've steamed it.*

What you steam them in is up to you. Beer and wine are traditional, but cider (hard or soft), water, stock, tomato sauce, curry, and chile sauce all work. There's a reason why most recipes call for only one or two things, like, say, white wine and bay leaves: when they open, bivalves will expel grit along with their juice. By limiting what you steam open your shellfish with, you can then strain that liquid and add it to whatever final sauce you had in mind.

You can either serve steamed shellfish as is, or you can use the steaming process just to open them so you can then toss them into pasta or smoke them (see Smoked Oysters or Mussels on page 295). I've also steamed mussels open to get them out of the shell for fried mussels.

In general, steaming clams, mussels, and oysters takes no more than ten minutes, and the first ones will pop after only a couple of minutes.

A side note: in some cases, you'll find teeny little crabs in your broth. These were various species of pea crabs, and they lived their lives within the mollusks. They're not only edible, but also will add a little hit of crab to your mussel dish. Keep them as a sort of baby Jesus in the king cake kinda thing. Whoever gets the pea crab wins!

For crustaceans, steaming (or boiling) is a vital first step in the process.

All shellfish (mollusks, too) begin to rot very quickly once they die, often within hours or in some cases minutes. This is why you do your best to discard dead shellfish of all kinds even before you cook them. In rare cases, a dead one can taint the whole batch. Clams and most bivalves can be kept alive for days when treated properly, but this is more difficult with crustaceans.

You need to keep them alive in circulating water if that's what you want to do (see purging crawfish on page 26), or you can keep crabs and lobsters damp and cool *out* of the water. Never, ever submerge shellfish (except crawfish) in fresh water, as this will kill them. Far better to set your mess of crabs inside a cooler on top of a bag of ice, ideally with a wet towel or seaweed or burlap in between.

Yes, you can boil crustaceans, notably southern "boils," and if you really want a seasoning, like Old Bay or Zatarain's, to permeate the shellfish, boiling is a better cooking method. But in general, steaming is superior because you don't soak the meat in water. Boiled crustaceans can get waterlogged, and they are definitely messier to eat at the table.

If you have shelled shrimp, be very careful when steaming, as they can get hammered in a hurry. I've seen even large unpeeled shrimp cook through in three minutes when steamed in one layer.

You will also encounter precooked crustaceans, mostly Alaska and Dungeness crabs, but also crawfish tails and sometimes shrimp. These only need to be warmed, not cooked again.

STEAMED FISH

All fish can be steamed. Not all fish are wonderful this way. In general, thin skinless fillets are not steamed, because they fall apart very, very easily. Skin-on fillets can be steamed, because the skin holds the fish together, although it will still be eager to fall to pieces. Mostly we steam smallish whole fish, or sometimes steaks of very meaty fish like sturgeon, swordfish, or tuna, or a crosscut of a big catfish.

The same rules for grilling apply here. Make a few perpendicular slashes in the fish's side to help it cook more evenly. This will also open up the meat to allow more flavor to permeate it, both in the steaming process and afterward, when you pour over a sauce or hot oil or whatever.

How long to steam? Generally speaking, about eight minutes for every half-inch of thickness of the fish itself, up to ten minutes if the fish is on the bone. Another trick is to steam hard for six minutes per half-inch of the fish, then turn off the heat and let the fish finish cooking with carryover steam. This is a bit more gentle and results in a moister fish.

Any type of fish can be steamed, but in general, you see mostly steamed lean white fish (think walleye, bass, or snapper) or orange fish like salmon and trout. That said, I know people who love steamed bluefish and tuna. I do not.

THE SETUP

The process is simple. Get a big pot and set a vegetable steamer inside. This is that perforated, UFO-looking thing with legs that someone gave you for your wedding. In many models, you can remove the center post so a fish or various shellfish will fit better on it. These steamers are available in most supermarkets in their cookware sections, and online. Barring that, you can set a colander in the pot, or a round rack set on a bowl or mugs. Or you can buy a Chinese bamboo steamer, or really use anything perforated. You want steam to permeate the seafood.

Another fun trick is to make a nest of herbs and lemon slices and whatnot a few inches thick, add a little wine to moisten everything, and then set the fish or seafood on top of that.

Removing the steamed fish without massacring it can be tricky. This is why you need to have that in mind before you start steaming. Everything else in this chapter has a nice shell to hold it together. Fish, obviously, don't. Generally, you will need some way of removing the rack or steamer or whatever the fish is resting on from the pot. And then you need to move it to where it will be served, plate or platter. I just use tongs to grab the steamer itself, carefully lifting it out of the pot. I then slide long spatulas under the fish so I can move it to its final destination. If it breaks, not to worry. Reconstruct it and pour sauce over the break. No one will notice.

HOW TO STEAM FREESTYLE

Far be it from me to tell you that an austere slab of steamed skinless white fish is terrible, although it is. Still, if that's what you love, go for it. I, however, would want that fish dressed with something. What something? There are two schools of thought: the blank slate and the subtle plate.

Steaming is a wonderful way to cook fish and seafood because it allows whatever you're cooking to taste of itself. It's a clean, subtle way of cooking that, if you want, lets you really, really taste the inherent flavor of a fish, which in many cases is indeed nuanced and delicate. So you can choose to let your fish shine au naturel, with just salt and some complimentary flavors. There's a reason most steamed shellfish is eaten with drawn butter, and that's it.

A drizzle of a flavorful oil goes a long way, too. And it need not be olive oil, as much as I like olive oil. Butter is always welcome, but so is a roasted sesame oil, or pumpkinseed oil, or a good nut oil where you really get the aroma and flavor of the

▲ Steamed snow crab.

ingredient. Extra-virgin, unrefined canola oil is amazing. You get the idea. This addition of oil adds needed fat and a layer of flavor. And yes, flavored oils are great here, notably herb and chile oils.

You can also play with salt. Yes, you will have salted the fish prior to steaming it, but playing with fancy salts—and here I'm thinking of flaked salt like Maldon—make the salt a point of interest. Something crunchy-salty to contrast with the silky fish.

And not just salt itself, but salty things. Olives and capers are classic, as are brine-fermented pickled things. A piece of steamed fish on top of salty

STEAMING TIMES

These are general guidelines. You always want every crustacean to have turned red before you eat them. When in doubt, steam an extra minute or two.

▶ Live Crabs: 10 to 30 minutes, depending on size; the longer end of this scale is really for king crabs.

▶ Precooked crabs, as well as king and snow crabs: 5 to 10 minutes, just to reheat them.

▶ Shrimp: 3 to 10 minutes, depending on size.

▶ Crawfish: 10 minutes.

▶ Lobsters: 10 to 20 minutes, depending on size. Truly large lobsters, like 3-pounders, may need as much as 30 minutes.

▶ Clams, mussels, oysters, and limpets: 10 minutes.

pickled mustard greens is damn good. Anything lacto-fermented is a candidate here, but I've even seen Mexican chefs toss some fried chicharrón on top of steamed snapper for a porky-salty contrast. Play with it.

You may or may not want something tangy or acidic here. I usually do, but it's not 100 percent needed. Obviously, everyone here is thinking citrus, and you're not wrong. A squeeze of any sort of citrus really works well. Another great option is verjus, which is the juice of unripe grapes. It's a thing in France and Italy, and you can buy it in better supermarkets. Vinegar-pickled things fall into this category, as does, obviously, vinegar itself. This is where, like your fancy oils, you bust out the fancy vinegars. I'm not going to tell you that you can't use dark vinegars like balsamic, but I find them limited when it comes to fish—I will only use a dark, thick vinegar with dark, oily fish like bluefish, mackerel, some jacks, and the darker tunas.

Beyond that, you're thinking herbs, spices, alliums (onions and garlic), and chiles. Because you've gone subtle with the steamed fish, be judicious with these, as they all tend to be bold. If you want bold, read on.

Steamed vegetables are a good side here, as they will benefit from the same flavor enhancers you've added alongside the fish. The classic starch would be rice, but I prefer good, crusty bread, not sourdough in this case.

The second school of thought is to view the steamed seafood as a blank slate for bold flavors. Mayonnaise-like sauces are classic here, like hollandaise or aioli or something as simple as Sriracha mayo. Doing this adds fat and flavor in one fell swoop.

The Chinese practice of drizzling raging-hot chile oil falls into this, too. Not only are you adding fat and flavor here, but drizzling 350°F oil will crisp up steamed skin, adding another layer of flavor. And beyond that, they will add powerful aromatics like garlic and fresh ginger and scallions, each one bumping up the flavor quotient.

Steamed fish, flaked and then mixed with, say, a Mexican chile sauce and served on tacos, is wonderful. You can do the same thing with German mustard, Thai dipping sauce, or curry. Again, play with it.

CHINESE STEAMED FISH WITH CHILES

PREP TIME: 20 MINUTES | COOK TIME: 10 MINUTES | SERVES 2 TO 4

This is a bedrock method in China, as well as much of the rest of Asia. A fish, steamed until just cooked—which is when the meat pulls off the spine easily—tastes of itself. It is virtually the only way to taste the subtle differences between similar species. The best example of this where I live in Northern California is with Pacific rockfish—the gorgeous China cod, so named because the Asian American market will pay a premium for this fish, which is almost always cooked using the method below. If you do this, and if you steam any of the other myriad species of rockfish along with it, you'll detect that the China cod is sweeter, has a tighter flake, and has significantly more umami savoriness than the others.

You can create similar experiments with freshwater fish like smallmouth bass and walleye, or pike and perch. On the East Coast, black seabass is king for this method. In the Gulf, it's the smaller snappers, like mutton snapper.

Real purists, typically from Guangzhou, dress their steamed fish very simply, with slivered scallions, a little ginger and soy sauce, just to season the fish. This is what you want to do if you really want to taste differences in similar fish. But I prefer bigger flavors, so I look to Sichuan. As you can see, these fish are dressed with lots of fiery chiles, as well as with Sichuan peppercorns in addition to ginger, scallions, and garlic.

My version of this dish (see the front cover of this book for a photograph) is an amalgam of those I've eaten in Sichuan restaurants and from the great Chinese cookbooks *The Food of Sichuan*, by Fuchsia Dunlop, and *Phoenix Claws and Jade Trees*, by Kian Lam Kho.

2 whole fish, about 1 pound each, scaled, gutted, and gilled

Salt

One 1-inch piece of ginger, sliced then smashed with the side of a knife

5 scallions, chopped, green and white parts separated

¼ cup Shaoxing wine or dry sherry

3 tablespoons peanut oil

2 tablespoons minced ginger

6 cloves garlic, minced

As many red chiles as you can stand, chopped

2 tablespoons soy sauce

¼ cup fish or chicken stock

1 tablespoon ground Sichuan peppercorns, green if possible. You can buy green Sichuan peppercorns online. Get some. They're worth it—intensely citrusy and altogether wonderful.

Slash the fish several times perpendicular to the backbone. Salt them well.

Put the ginger and the white parts of the scallions, along with 2 tablespoons of the Shaoxing wine, in the bottom of your steamer. Add water until it almost comes up to the level of the steamer. Set the fish in your steamer and place it in the pot. Turn the heat to high and cover the pot. Steam, covered, for 10 minutes. Lift the lid and carefully test to see if the meat will lift off the spine at the thickest part. If it does, turn off the heat. Recover the pot and make the sauce.

In a wok, heat the peanut oil over high heat on your hottest burner. When it's hot—you'll see a wisp of smoke rising—add the ginger, garlic and chiles all at once. You might need to step back, as that many chiles rises a steam that's basically mace.

Stir-fry this for 1 minute, then add the remaining Shaoxing wine, soy sauce, stock, the green parts of the scallions, and the ground Sichuan peppercorns. Bring this to a raging boil and then turn off the heat.

Carefully move the fish to a platter and pour the sauce over them. Serve with steamed rice.

MEXTLAPIQUES, OR "FISH TAMALES"

PREP TIME: 45 MINUTES | COOK TIME: 20 MINUTES | SERVES 6

Leave it to Mexico to get me to love a variation of steamed fish in parchment. Of course, their version uses corn husks instead of parchment and the little packets are either cooked on a comal or a grill. So it's a sort of hybrid steaming and charring. No wonder I like it.

The origins of this method of cooking appear to be Aztec; they're definitely pre-Columbian. It's a nifty setup: either small whole fish or chunks of larger fish, along with vegetables, mushrooms—almost anything, really—tied up in corn husks and seared on a hot iron flat-top or over a grill. You will see these most often in the State of Mexico, which surrounds Mexico City on three sides.

There's no set recipe here. Anything goes. That said, you'll make better mextlapiques (pronounced mex-tlah-PEE-kays) by using the principles I've been talking about this whole book: salty, spicy, sour, sweet. A simple, classic example here would be a pico de gallo surrounding the fish—diced white onion soaked in lime juice, cilantro, tomatoes, chiles, and maybe a little garlic. To this I add chopped up escabeche—the pickled jalapeños, onions, carrots, and garlic you see as an accompaniment to tacos everywhere. This adds heat and acidity. A drizzle of your favorite hot sauce is another good option. So would slices of tomato, zucchini, or onion. You could line the corn husks with hoja santa leaves if you happen to have them; they add an anise-y, root beer-ish flavor that works very well with fish. Or you could precook some vegetables and add them to the packets. Sautéed mushrooms or caramelized onions would be especially good.

Sealing your mextlapiques takes a little practice. Here's how I do it. I first soak my corn husks for several hours to get them pliable. I then pick through them and find odd ones that I will use to make the strings. You'll need to pull strips off these and then tie two together; it's a rare husk that's tall enough to make a string long enough to tie around a mextlapique. You need two strings per packet.

You then want to lay two husks down, overlapping by about an inch or so, fat end to fat end. Place a rectangle of fish in the center. Salt it. If you want, this is when you spoon on a little hot sauce. Arrange the vegetables over and around the fish. Usually about two tablespoons is enough. Fold the husks over on the left side, then the right, to close the packets. Now fold over the end closest to you. Tie this off with a string. Double knot it. Now fold over the other end. Tie that one off, too. You're good to go. The packets can be made and kept refrigerated for up to a day, although it is better to cook them when you are done making them.

Either grill the mextlapiques or sear them over a comal or cast iron pan set over medium heat. You want significant blackening on the corn husk. It generally takes ten to twenty minutes to cook each one, so you'll want to use a grill for big groups. A comal is fine for just a few people. You can eat your mextlapiques solo or with rice or corn tortillas.

What follows is a simple version, to give you an idea of proportions.

2 pounds fish fillets, or something
similar (see below for options)

Salt

1 white onion, minced

Zest and juice of 3 limes

Fresh or pickled jalapeños,
chopped

3 Roma tomatoes, diced

¼ cup chopped cilantro

2 teaspoons dried Mexican
oregano, crushed

Olive oil, for drizzling

About 20 corn husks

Salt the fish and set it aside. Don't cut it yet.

Make the modified pico de gallo. Mix the lime zest and juice with
the onion first and set them in a bowl, then chop all the other
vegetables, adding them to the bowl as you finish. Add the oregano
and salt to taste.

Make your packets as I outline above and cut the fish to fit them. You
want to be easily able to wrap the fish, so leave room on all sides.
Generally, this means a block of fish about 2 to 3 inches wide by about
4 to 5 inches long. Spoon a couple of tablespoons of the salsa over
them, and drizzle with oil. Seal the packet and repeat with the rest.

You will likely have one mextlapique with the trim. It's fine, as you end
up eating this with a fork anyway.

VARIATIONS Any seafood will work here, too. Just make sure they
don't have shells! In the case of octopus, you will need to precook it
until it's mostly tender. And in the case of crab, it'll be cooked already,
so this would go better with larger slices of vegetables. Literally any
fish works here, and if you want to get funky, there is a version of
mextlapiques that mixes charales, which are, more or less, smelt, with
beaten eggs and they are then, somehow, tucked into the packets and
grilled. The egg binds it all together.

STEAMING

SPANISH CLAMS AND CHORIZO

PREP TIME: 20 MINUTES | **COOK TIME: 20 MINUTES** | **SERVES 4**

There is nothing more Iberian—meaning Spanish, Basque, or Portuguese—than the combination of shellfish and pork. It's a magical pairing, unless you're Kosher, in which case it's a double whammy of "nope, can't eat that." Indeed, some food historians think this combination originated with the Spanish Inquisition as a way of testing Jews who had supposedly converted to Catholicism. Yikes.

Anyway, it's a damn good plate of food, and it's fun to eat. The triple play of savory umami from the chorizo and clams, tartness from lemon juice, and saltiness from both the broth and the sausage makes this dish a classic for a reason. You want Spanish chorizo, not Mexican; Spanish chorizo is a hard, dry-cured sausage, while Mexican is soft and fresh. Also try to get real Spanish pimenton, smoked paprika, and get the best loaf of bread you can find. And please don't slice your bread all dainty-like. Tear it into pieces as you eat, using it to coax yummy things onto your fork and to soak up the fantastic broth. Eating a bowl of clams should be primal, and the torn bread just seems more natural.

I use western littleneck clams for this recipe because that's what I can gather here in Northern California. You could use any small hardshell clam, and Manila or eastern littlenecks are just as good or even better than the western clams I use.

Serve with a dry rosé or a light red, like a Spanish garnacha, California gamay, or French Beaujolais. Hard cider is another good choice here, as would a full-flavored white wine like a Spanish verdelho.

25 to 50 small hardshell clams

1½ cups white wine

¼ cup olive oil

1 large onion, thinly sliced

4 cloves garlic, thinly sliced

1 to 3 dried hot chiles, broken up

½ pound dry Spanish chorizo or other hard salami, sliced

A pinch of saffron (optional)

2 teaspoons Spanish smoked paprika

Juice of a lemon

2 tablespoons chopped cilantro or parsley

Black pepper

Lay the clams in a wide pan, like a big frying pan, in one layer; you may need to do this batches. Pour 1 cup of white wine in the pan and turn the heat to high. Cover the pan and steam the clams open. Keep an eye on the pan and check every minute or two and remove each clam as soon as it pops open. Move the opened clams to a bowl. Keep doing this, adding and removing clams, until they're all opened. Tap on the shells of those clams that don't seem to want to open, and sometimes they'll pop. If they stay resolutely closed, toss them.

When I make this dish, I remove all but a few of the clams from their shells because it's easier to eat this way; I leave a few clams in the shells for garnish. Some people just like to pick through the whole shebang, and if you're one of those, go for it.

OPTIONAL Strain the clam juice through a paper towel to remove grit. You can use this for the finished dish.

Wipe out the pan you cooked the clams in and heat the olive oil over medium-high heat. When it's hot, sauté the onions until they're soft and the edges have browned a bit. Add the garlic, chiles, and chorizo and cook for another minute or two.

Crumble the saffron over the pan and sprinkle the paprika over everything. Add the remaining white wine, the clams, and enough of the strained clam juice (or water) to halfway cover everything. Boil this furiously for about 90 seconds. Turn off the heat, add the lemon juice, herbs, and black pepper. Serve at once with a big loaf of crusty bread.

VARIATIONS This recipe would work well with precooked octopus, or you could sub in squid or shrimp and follow the recipe as is; it will likely take about 5 to 10 minutes for everything to steam properly. Chunks of firm fish would also work, but you'll want something that won't fall apart.

SEAFOOD TAMALES

PREP TIME: 90 MINUTES | **COOK TIME: 1 HOUR** | **SERVES 12**

There is an entire genre of seafood tamales in Mexico and Central America, mostly involving shrimp. They range from delicate little bites to the basically impossible to eat tamales barbones of Sinaloa, which consist of an entire shrimp, shell, head, everything, encased in steamed masa dough.

What follows is a recipe for seafood tamales from Nayarit. It's an amalgam of several recipes I have encountered, but I'm most indebted to Alondra Maldonado Rodriguera's shrimp tamales recipe in her fantastic book, *Sabores de Nayarit: Icónico*.

After you've steamed these, if you have leftovers, pop them into the freezer; they freeze well. My advice on reheating them is to set the tamales directly on the comal or heavy pan, in the husks and with no oil. Let them char slowly over medium heat until the husk is pretty burned and the masa has reheated. This is a far superior way to enjoy these tamales, so much so I prefer it to the initial steaming. And yes, you can do this with tamales fresh out of the steamer, just increase the heat to high to get the char without overcooking the tamales.

Note: Definitely try to get fresh *masa para tamales* from your local Mexican market, as this will be superior to making your own dough from masa flour. I'll give you measurements for both.

Also, you will note that this only makes twelve tamales or so. Obviously, this is not many by Mexican standards, and you can certainly double, triple, or otherwise scale up this recipe.

MASA

2 or 3 guajillo or California or
   New Mexico dried chiles

4 dried arbol or other small hot
   chiles

1 tablespoon dried Mexican
   oregano, crushed into a powder

2 cloves garlic

½ cup small, dried shrimp, crushed
   into a powder (optional)

2 pounds fresh masa for tamales
   (it will have lard already in it)

or

3 cups masa harina plus 2 cups
   hot water and ½ cup lard or
   shortening

1 tablespoon salt

You will need dried corn husks, too. Generally about 20 or so, because even though you're only making a dozen tamales, some of the husks won't be good, and you also want to line your steamer with them. Start by dunking a bunch of husks in boiling water. Turn off the heat, weigh them down, and let them soak at least 1 hour, or up to 8 hours. Also remember you can dry out those you end up not using and use them again down the road.

Start by making the masa. Pour boiling water over the guajillo and arbol chiles and let them soften about 20 minutes. Remove the stem and seeds and put them in a blender with the oregano, garlic, and dried shrimp, if using. Blend smooth, adding a little of the chile soaking water if you need to get it all to blend properly. Set this aside.

If you have masa for tamales from a market, it will already have lard and likely salt in it, so you can go from there. If not, put the masa harina in a large bowl with the salt and mix well. You want it to be like a wet pasta dough—not a batter, not something you can knead easily. In between.

If you have a stand mixer, add the lard to it and whip it well on high speed until it's fluffy, then add the masa to it bit by bit, making sure it has been incorporated before adding more. If you are using premade masa for tamales, you'll want to put it into a stand mixer, too.

3 tablespoons corn or peanut oil

1 medium white onion, chopped

Salt

1 poblano or 2 Anaheim chiles,
    seeded and chopped

1 to 4 serrano chiles, minced

3 cloves garlic, minced

1 pound small to medium shrimp,
    peeled, deveined, and chopped

2 tablespoons small, dried shrimp,
    crushed into a powder (optional)

Once you have your basic masa dough in the stand mixer, let it run on low speed and add the contents of the blender. Once this is totally incorporated, you are ready to rock. The overall consistency should be spreadable, but not pourable (too wet), and not like pasta dough (too dry).

To make the filling, heat the oil in a pan over medium-high heat and sauté the onion until translucent, about 4 to 6 minutes. Add salt while you are cooking the onions. Now add the remaining ingredients and cook until the shrimp are nicely done, about 3 to 5 minutes. Turn off the heat, mix well, and taste it. You can add a little lime juice if you want, or some more salt. If you're using the dried shrimp, which are usually salty, you probably won't need to add more salt.

Now you make your tamales. Put a corn husk in front of you, inside up and wide side farthest from you. You'll know the inside because the husk will want to curl upward. Smear some masa into the center of the husk, leaving about 1 inch from the top and several inches on the bottom; you'll be folding the husk in half in a moment.

Place a heaping tablespoon or so of the filling in the center of the masa and, using the husk, fold the masa over it. You might need to close the top of the tamal by hand. Fold the sides of the husk over, then fold the bottom up to close the tamal. Some people will simply place the folded tamal in the steamer as they go, letting each one keep the others sealed, but I tear off strips of husk to make string, which I use to tie them securely. Make sure the open ends of the tamales faces up.

Keep doing this until you run out of filling or masa—my measurements will get you close, but husks come in different sizes—and then steam them for 1 hour. Let them sit a few minutes off the heat but in the steamer before serving.

I like these with a salsa verde, but any salsa that makes you happy will work.

11

SANDWICHES AND OTHER HANDHELD THINGS

FISH AND SEAFOOD in a handheld portion is a thing all over the world. A whole book could be written just about this. From a New Orleans po'boy to Indian samosas, fish tacos, Vietnamese banh mi, New England lobster rolls, to a good ole' fried fish sandwich, we humans like to eat our fish on the go. Perhaps the quintessential fish sandwich, at least here in the United States, is the venerable "tuna-fish" sandwich, about which I write in chapter 16 (the recipe is on page 257).

As you think about the recipes that follow, think about the elements that make up a good handheld meal. Whether it's a sandwich, a taco, a seafood roll, or a pie, there are, of course, two: the hand holder (the wrap) and the filling. I'll cover these in each of the four recipes that follow. Tacos rate a subcategory of their own, and the general principles described in the taco intro can be applied to either of the two taco master recipes, Lobster Tacos (page 161) and Tacos Gobernador (page 164).

A SIMPLE FISH SANDWICH

PREP TIME: 20 MINUTES | **COOK TIME: 20 MINUTES** | **SERVES 6**

What makes a good fish sandwich? It starts with the fish, which for me needs to be firm, white, and lean. I'm not a fan of sandwiches made with fillets of salmon or mackerel or the like; too soft and too fatty. Cod, haddock, bass, walleye, or rockfish are ideal. And it's gotta be either grilled or fried. Breaded, as in this case, is easier, although a good beer-battered deep-fried fish is damn tasty, too.

Bread choice is key—really good, crusty bread can be so sturdy that biting into a sandwich made with it can mash everything inside, except for equally sturdy ingredients, such as shrimp or lobster. So in most cases, with fish and seafood, softer bread is better. Buns? Anything from good rye bread to hamburger buns to hoagie rolls will do, but I am partial to poppyseed kaiser rolls. It's a New Jersey thing, I think.

And you want to include something either spicy or tart. A green thing is always nice, usually lettuce, or my favorite, sorrel leaves. Bacon likes seafood, so it's usually welcome here, too. Mix and match until you have some favorites, and then you can freestyle at will.

That leaves the sauce. I've had fish sandwiches with everything from ketchup to mustard to horseradish, remoulade, Asian dipping sauces, you name it. But the Big Daddy of sauces for a fish sandwich is tartar sauce. But I hate store-bought tartar sauces, so I make my own. Too hard? Not so. A tartar sauce is basically mayo with a little mustard and some chopped pickles, plus a random onion product, hot sauce, and salt. Easy-peasy. That recipe accompanies the fried flounder recipe on page 121. Incidentally, that fried flounder makes a fantastic base for a fish sandwich.

If you want to get beyond fish for this sandwich, crawfish tails, shrimp, clams, oysters, or mussels, breaded and fried, are awesome, and they essentially turn this sandwich into a New Orleans po'boy. Dust the shellfish in cornmeal and fry, and serve with the remoulade on page 123. Even better? Dust a soft-shelled crab in flour, fry crispy, and use in place of fish in this recipe. You'll thank me later.

»

◄ A mess of speckled sea trout caught near Matagorda Bay, Texas.

FISH

4 to 6 strips of bacon

4 skinless fillets of rock cod or
    other bass, seabass, walleye,
    or the like

Salt

Oil for frying (I prefer peanut oil)

1 cup flour

2 eggs, lightly beaten

1 cup breadcrumbs

FIXINGS

4 large lettuce leaves

4 to 8 slices tomato

Buns for the sandwiches
    (I prefer kaiser rolls)

If you're making homemade tartar sauce (page 121), do this first by mixing everything in a bowl. Cover the bowl with plastic wrap and set in the fridge.

Fry the bacon slowly in a pan until almost crispy; you want a little bend in your bacon for a sandwich. Set the bacon aside and discard the fat in the pan, or reserve it for another recipe.

Get all your fixins' ready for the sandwiches, and get three shallow containers for the dredging station: one for the flour, one for the beaten eggs, and one for the breadcrumbs.

Take the fish out of the fridge and salt them. Pour the oil in the pan in which you fried the bacon and heat it over medium-high heat until it's about 350°F; if you don't have a thermometer, flick a little flour into the oil. When it sizzles immediately, you're ready. Turn the heat down to medium for a moment.

Dredge the fish fillets in flour, then dip in the egg, then in the breadcrumbs. If you want a really thick and crispy crust, dip the fillets in egg and breadcrumbs a second time. Turn the heat on the oil to high (adding the fish will drop the heat of the oil, which is why you want to kick the heat up for a minute or two here to compensate). Gently lay the fillets into the pan, making sure the fillets aren't touching each other. Let them fry for a minute or so, then lower the heat. If you can't get all the fish into the pan at once, fry in batches.

Fry the fish until they're golden brown, about 2 to 5 minutes per side; use the longer range if your fish fillets are thicker than an inch. Set on paper towels to drain.

Spread the tartar sauce on both sides of the buns, then add the lettuce, fish fillets, tomato, and bacon. Open a beer and enjoy!

CRAB ROLLS

PREP TIME: 20 MINUTES | **SERVES 4**

I grew up with lobster rolls. After all, my mom is from Massachusetts, the capital of Lobster Roll Nation. I'd never heard of crab rolls. Then, one day, I wandered into Obrycki's in search of food during a layover in Baltimore/Washington International Airport. Crab rolls were on the menu. OK, I'll bite, I thought. So I ordered them.

"Good call," the bartender said. "They're my favorite." Sure they are. Everything's your favorite when you're the bartender. I expected a glob of mayo-based crab salad in a tired hot dog bun.

An Obrycki's crab roll is not that. Yes, there's mayonnaise, and yes there's a bit of celery and the obligatory Old Bay seasoning—I think it's the law to include it with any crab dish within 150 miles of the Chesapeake Bay—but this sandwich (can you call something on a hot dog bun a sandwich?) was all about the crab. While not as minimalist as a New England lobster roll, which can be nothing more than buttered lobster in a split-top roll, this crab roll is full of crab with only the Old Bay-lemon-mayo to tie it all together. Celery is a minor player, added entirely for texture, not as a filler. I wrote notes about this amazing lunch on a napkin, determined to reverse engineer it at home.

This is what I came up with. While probably not the exact Obrycki's crab roll, it's close, and it's really good. I used Dungeness crab because that's what I had, but any crab will do. Obviously, they use blue crab in the Chesapeake. Oh, and good luck finding split-top rolls outside of New England; that's one thing I won't buy online. Just use a good quality hot dog bun or something similar. I won't come to your house to beat you up if you used, say, a kaiser roll or even a tortilla.

Try to get good quality crab. It matters. Tinned crab isn't very good here. Once made, the salad will keep a couple of days in the fridge.

1 pound lump crabmeat

¼ cup unsalted butter, melted

2 tablespoons lemon juice

¼ cup mayonnaise

2 tablespoons minced chives

1 stalk celery, minced

½ teaspoon Old Bay seasoning

½ teaspoon black pepper

4 hot dog buns

Toss the crabmeat in the melted butter. Mix all the remaining ingredients except for the buns in a large bowl. Fold the crabmeat into this.

Grill or toast the buns; you can spread some butter on the buns first if you'd like. Fill with the crab mixture. Serve with pickles and potato chips.

NOTE You can substitute precooked flaked fish, crawfish tails, shrimp, or lobster for the crab.

CRAWFISH PIES

PREP TIME: 2 HOURS, MOSTLY CHILL TIME FOR THE DOUGH | COOK TIME: 20 MINUTES | SERVES 8

"Jambalaya and a crawfish pie and filé gumbo." Hank Williams's legendary song says it all. Now, you can absolutely make this filling and use it for the English Fisherman's Pie recipe on page 78. This is a commonly seen form of this amazing savory pie. But that's not how I like my crawfish pies. Yes, pies, as in more than one. My idea of a great crawfish pie is what I would pick up at gas stations and random Cajun butcher shops from Vinton to Metarie. Hand pies. Pies you can eat while zipping down I-10, keeping a sharp eye out for the sneaky state cops hiding in wait for you.

These are, more or less, empanadas. A flour-based dough filled with crawfish tails and other good things, fried in peanut oil, or, if you're feeling extravagant, lard. Think of the dough as a master recipe for any sort of filling you fancy. This is a fantastic empanada dough, one you'll want to memorize for non-seafood fillings, too. One hack I use that works very well is a tortilla press lined with plastic, which flattens the dough into perfect circles very well. You can, of course, roll them out with a rolling pin, too.

This recipe can be doubled if you're making a big batch of pies. Once made, they can be frozen after they're fried. To reheat, stick in the oven to fry them again briefly.

DOUGH

2¼ cups all-purpose flour

½ teaspoon baking powder

½ teaspoon salt

½ cup unsalted butter or lard

1 egg

⅓ cup ice water

2 teaspoons white vinegar

Make the dough first. Mix the flour, baking powder, and salt in a bowl. Add the butter or lard, and, with your fingers, incorporate the fat into the flour until it all looks like cornmeal. Mix in the egg, ice water, and vinegar, then knead the mixture well for a few minutes. Separate it into eight balls, put into a plastic bag, and set in the fridge for at least an hour, 2 hours is better, and up to a day.

To make the filling, heat the butter in a pan over medium-high heat and sauté the onion, celery, and jalapeños until soft, then add the garlic clove and cook another minute. Add the crawfish meat, some black pepper, and Cajun seasoning, then sprinkle the flour over everything. Mix well, and then add the broth. Cook this, stirring often, until most of the liquid has been absorbed. Turn off the heat.

When the mixture is cool, stir in the parsley, green onions, Worcestershire, Tabasco, and the beaten egg.

Once the dough has chilled, start the process. Set a cooling rack over a baking sheet in the oven and set the oven to "warm." Pour about an inch of oil in a large, heavy pan—you want the pies to be mostly, if not completely, submerged in oil. Set the oil over medium heat as you make the pies.

FILLING

2 tablespoons butter or peanut oil

1 small onion, minced

1 celery stalk, minced

1 to 2 jalapeños, seeded
   and minced

1 clove garlic, minced

8 to 12 ounces crawfish meat

Black pepper

1 tablespoon Cajun seasoning

1 tablespoon flour

½ cup chicken or seafood broth

2 tablespoon chopped parsley

3 green onions, minced

Worcestershire sauce

Tabasco sauce

1 egg, lightly beaten

Oil for frying

Keep all the dough balls in the fridge as you work. Take one out and flatten it into a disk—a tortilla, if you will. Put a tablespoon or two of the filling into the center, then use the plastic that is lining the tortilla press to fold this over into a half-circle. Seal the pie with your fingers, then move it to a clean cutting board. Crimp the edges with the tines of a fork.

Repeat this process until you have enough pies to fill your frying pan. Increase the heat to 325°F and slide the pies in. Fry them until golden, about 4 or 6 minutes, flipping them as needed.

As they're frying, build more until you have another frying-pan's worth. Repeat the process.

As the pies finish, set them on the rack in the oven to stay warm.

"Fish in another man's pond and you will catch crabs."

HABEEB AKANDE

SAMOSAS

PREP TIME: 2 HOURS, MOSTLY CHILL TIME FOR THE DOUGH | COOK TIME: 20 MINUTES | SERVES 8

These are more or less the same as crawfish pies, but the filling is different. If you can find them, add a teaspoon of ajwain seeds to the dough. These are available online or in Indian markets. You can skip them. Most Indians will use ghee (clarified butter) for the fat, but butter will do if you can't find ghee.

2 tablespoons ghee or peanut oil

1 small onion, minced

2 jalapeño peppers, seeded
   and minced

2 cloves garlic, minced

1 tablespoon ginger, minced

½ teaspoon turmeric

1 teaspoon garam masala

8 to 12 ounces chopped shrimp,
   crab, or crawfish meat

2 tablespoons chopped cilantro

3 green onions, minced

Sauté the onion, jalapeños, garlic, and ginger in the ghee until soft, then add then add the spices and shrimp. Mix well. Allow this to cool, and add the herbs. If you think this might be too loose a mixture, you can add ½ cup of mashed potatoes to bind it up.

Folding samosas is a little different from folding the crawfish pies. You will want to separate the dough into twelve pieces, not eight, since they're smaller. Flatten into a tortilla, then put the filling in the center. Fold into a triangle by using the plastic to fold each side over the other to seal. Fry the same way as the crawfish pies.

"Don't bargain for fish which are still in the water."

INDIAN PROVERB

Fish and seafood tacos are common all over Mexico, but especially on the coasts, as you might expect. They vary in as many ways as there are *taqueros,* but with a few exceptions, they have a similar structure. The fish or seafood is typically cooked simply, grilled or fried. Use the Beer-Battered Fish recipe on page 113 for any fried-fish taco. For a grilled-fish taco, simply grill fish steaks, hefty fillets, or whole fish, flake them, and put on a tortilla.

To get a taste of real Mexican fish tacos, you'll want corn tortillas, although there are a few fish tacos commonly served on flour tortillas in Baja and the Sonoran coast. Both are, in the end, fine; use what makes you happy.

Fish and seafood tacos are also, mainly, light. Tacos gobernador, as you will see in the next recipe (page 164), is a bit heavier, but even that isn't a gut bomb. Most variations on fish or seafood tacos are simply the fish in question, a light salsa like pico de gallo, perhaps some finely shredded cabbage, and, often, a flavored cream sauce. This is almost always Mexican crema, which is a thin version of sour cream, mixed with puréed avocado, or chipotles in adobo, or some other exciting flavor element. Mexican crema is easy to find in any Latin market and in any larger supermarket if you happen to live where there's a Latino community nearby. If you can't find Mexican crema, use regular sour cream thinned with a bit of heavy cream until it flows like barbecue sauce.

Are there any fish or seafood species that aren't good on a tortilla? It's hard to think of any. Shellfish? Done as ceviche or fried, they're all good. Oily fish? Best grilled, but otherwise great. Crustaceans? Ideal. Dense, meaty fish? Awesome grilled or diced small—and then sautéed, another cooking option for a fish taco; it works because dense fish like sturgeon, shark, swordfish, or marlin won't fall apart. Smoked fish? Awesome. Raw fish? Probably not as such, but ceviche is great on a tortilla. Let your mind flow, and play with it.

LOBSTER TACOS

PREP TIME: 30 MINUTES | COOK TIME: 20 MINUTES | SERVES 4

Lobster tacos might sound extravagant, but they're a thing on both the Pacific Coast of Mexico and the Yucatan Peninsula. I've seen them fried and grilled, and that's nice, but I still prefer my lobster steamed and then bathed in butter, or straight up butter-poached, for that matter. I simply put a few tails on a steamer tray in a pot with a little water in it, steam for about ten minutes, remove them from their shells, and dunk them in melted butter. After you eat a piece—'cause you have to, you know?—cut them into bite-sized pieces and toss them with a variant on the standard pico de gallo we all know and love. That variant is called salpicon, which at its core is a pico de gallo with shredded cabbage and often chopped radishes added to it. You see seafood mixed with this a lot all over Mexico, sometimes stuffed into a roasted poblano, which is kinda awesome.

That's really all these tacos are. Simple, buttery lobster tossed with good things that add crunch, spice, tartness, a little sweetness, and that herbal touch you get from cilantro.

>>

If you wanted to add to this, a good option would be to whip together Mexican crema with your favorite Mexican hot sauce—Huichol, Culichi, or Cholula would be my recommendations—and drizzle that on top. Want a bit more heft? Smear some refried beans on the tortilla before you top with the lobster and salpicon. Could you add cheese? I suppose, but I wouldn't. Not here.

No lobster handy? Peeled shrimp would be an almost perfect substitute, and crawfish, crabmeat, squid, or octopus would really shine here, too. Little steamed clams would be nice, and sure, you can use chunks of fish. If you go the fish route, you want dense, meaty fish like tautog, shark, swordfish, sturgeon, cobia, grouper, amberjack or yellowtail, pike, or flathead catfish.

1 white onion, diced

½ cup lime juice

Salt

1 teaspoon dried Mexican oregano (optional)

1 cup finely shredded cabbage

6 small radishes, chopped

1 to 3 habaneros, minced (see recipe note)

3 Roma tomatoes, diced

½ cup chopped cilantro

12 corn tortillas

1½ pounds lobster tails

⅓ cup melted butter

Start by soaking the onion in the lime juice. Sprinkle salt over it and mix well. Now cut all your other vegetables. Doing it this way will take the sting out of the onions.

Chop all your other vegetables and add them to the bowl with the lime juice and onions. Mix well and add the oregano and salt to taste. Have this ready for the lobster.

Heat your tortillas now. If you're making your own, make them after the salpicon but before you steam the lobster.

Set a steamer tray in a pot and pour enough water to come up to just below the level of the tray. Cover the pot and bring this to a boil. Lift the lid, set the lobster tails on the tray, cover the pot, and steam for about 10 to 15 minutes. Big Maine lobster tails can take 15 minutes, but little Caribbean or Pacific lobster tails will only take about 10 minutes.

Meanwhile, melt the butter in a little pot. When the lobster is ready, remove it from the shells and cut into bite-sized pieces. Put the lobster in a bowl and toss with the melted butter.

Mix the lobster with the salpicon, add it to tortillas, and have at it!

NOTE This makes a spicy taco. If you want things less picante, tone down the peppers. Maybe go with one habanero, or downgrade to serranos. If you're really not into heat, use supermarket jalapeños, which are typically not very hot.

TACOS GOBERNADOR

PREP TIME: 45 MINUTES | **COOK TIME: 20 MINUTES** | **SERVES 4**

Tacos Gobernador, "governor's tacos," is one of those modern classics of Mexican cuisine. Interestingly, it's the second such seafood classic from Sinaloa, a state known for good seafood; the other is Aguachile, a modern take on ceviche (page 284). Tacos gobernador is also one of the many Mexican dishes that combines shrimp and cheese, a combination I have learned to love over the years—breaking from the "no cheese and seafood" rules I grew up with.

You can make these tacos on a griddle or a grill, and there are variations to tacos gobernador all over the Pacific coast of Mexico. The original is from Sinaloa, and legend has it that in 1987, the chefs at Los Arcos in Mazatlan invented these tacos to impress the governor of Sinaloa, who was visiting them. But even searching for the original recipe from Los Arcos turns up variation. Some versions claiming to be the original include celery and, oddly, machaca, which is finely shredded dried beef. Most do not, however, and I suspect this could be a mix-up in conversations between cooks; *machaca de camaron* is a term in Pacific Mexico for chopped shrimp. I've seen cooks from other parts of Mexico miss this and add the dried beef.

All variations of tacos gobernador that I've seen and eaten—and there are a lot of them—include the following:

▷ Shrimp. Usually medium or large shrimp, cut into pieces.

▷ Cheese. Always melty cheese, usually queso Chihuahua or asadero or Oaxaca. Most are easily available in Latin markets, but mozzarella is a very good substitute.

▷ Always onions, usually white, sliced or chopped.

▷ A bit of chopped garlic.

▷ Chiles of some sort. I've seen chipotles in adobo, but mostly I see roasted, skinned, and seeded poblanos, cut into rajas, strips. Anaheims or green bell pepper is a decent substitute.

▷ Often, dried Mexican oregano and/or fresh chopped cilantro.

▷ Sometimes tomato, sometimes not. Apparently not at Los Arcos.

▷ Butter is the fat, although I actually prefer lard, and I've seen olive oil.

▷ Corn tortillas are traditional, but I've seen tacos gobernador served on flour tortillas in Baja.

The exact combination is up to you. The cheese adds heft to the taco, and the little edges that brown or even burn are one of the highlights. Even with all that, tacos gobernador are still light enough that a half dozen will quickly disappear.

Making these is a bit more like making a quesadilla than a traditional taco. You warm the tortillas, then add some cheese, and, once the cheese starts melting, add the remaining filling and fold the taco over to get it to stick. You're shooting for an open quesadilla, as you can see in the picture.

Be warned: tacos gobernador are as messy as they are delicious. Eat with plenty of beer and some hot sauce.

2 large poblano peppers, skinned, seeded, and cut into strips

2 tablespoons butter, lard, or olive oil

1 white onion, thinly sliced

2 cloves garlic, minced

4 small, hot chiles, chopped (optional)

2 Roma tomatoes, seeded, and diced

1 pound peeled shrimp, cut into bite-sized pieces

Salt

½ teaspoon Mexican oregano (optional)

2 tablespoons chopped cilantro

½ pound shredded melty cheese (see notes above for options)

Corn tortillas

Roast the poblanos and set them in a plastic bag to steam the skins off. Skin, then remove the tops and all the seeds. Slice them into strips crosswise. You can dice them if you prefer.

Heat the butter in a large pan over medium-high heat. Add the onion and sauté until wilted, about 3 to 5 minutes. Add the garlic, the small, hot chiles if using, tomatoes, shrimp, salt, and oregano if using, and toss to combine. Sauté until the shrimp turns pink, about 3 to 4 minutes. Mix in the cilantro and turn off the heat.

Heat tortillas on a comal, griddle, large frying pan, or grill. Set the tortilla down, then add a generous portion of shredded cheese on it. As soon as the cheese starts to melt, spoon some filling into the center and fold the taco over. Press down with a spatula to set the taco, let it char just a bit on that first side, then flip to brown the other side. Serve at once.

SANDWICHES AND OTHER HANDHELD THINGS

12
SOUPS, STEWS, STOCKS, AND BROTHS

THIS IS A BIG chapter, but it could have been so much bigger. Fish and seafood shine in soups and stews all over the world—everything from minimalist clear dashi with perhaps one perfect clam at the bottom, to gumbos and fish stews with practically the entire fish counter in them. I've shied away from several international classics, notably bouillabaisse, cioppino, zuppa di pesce, and the like. Not so much because I don't like them, but because there are so many wonderful recipes for these dishes out there already. And there's a more practical reason: many of those stews require so many different kinds of seafood that they become very expensive to put together.

So for the most part, these recipes are either for one fish, or a fish and a seafood. There's no reason not to use more species if you happen to have them lying around, but I wanted to make things a little easier, especially for everyone in the center of the country. While you'll be able to catch the fish no problem—crappie, bass, and walleye, for example, are all good in soups—you'll still need to run to the market for clams or shrimp or crab or whatever. No need to make things baroque.

A few general tips. Most of the recipes in this chapter can be made ahead and reheated, but unlike bird or mammal-based soups, they are *not* better the day after. Fish and seafood is always best that first day. When you reheat them, do so slowly with the lid on the pot; all you want is to bring them back to temperature, not to boil them. And for God's sake, don't microwave fish!

Virtually every fish or seafood you'll encounter won't need more than ten minutes in the pot, so add them late in the game. The only foods in this book that can withstand long cooking are squid, abalone, and octopus; they can all benefit from several hours in the pot.

◀ Simmering skeletons of rockfish aboard the *F/V Heather Anne* for fish soup.

BROTH JAZZ

You will find set recipes for various fish and seafood stocks and broths in this chapter, but to be very honest, I rarely follow them to the letter. Don't get me wrong, they're all tested and good recipes, and you should follow them to the letter if you're unfamiliar with making fish or crab or shrimp stock. But once you're familiar with them, you can freestyle quite easily.

At their core, these stocks are an exercise in getting the most out of the fish and seafood you bring home, while at the same time mitigating any fishiness or weird smells. You have lots of choices before you start. Cook the fish or seafood first or not? Clear stock or milky? Tomato or no tomato? Are you looking for flavors evoking a certain cuisine, or do you want a neutral stock? All have places in the kitchen. For the record, milky or cloudy stocks are common in dishes like ramen, or where you will add ingredients later that will turn the broth opaque anyway, like tomato or coconut milk. And they're quicker to make.

The number one rule for all fish and seafood stocks is to not boil them. A bare simmer is all you need or want. Boiling makes for fishy, cloudy, chalky stock. The second iron-clad rule is that fish and seafood stocks are not cooked very long. Never more than ninety minutes, and I prefer closer to forty minutes or even less in some cases. And because of this, you'll want to add only as much water as will come up maybe one inch above the level of the fish skeletons or crab shells. Because these stocks don't simmer for hours, they don't reduce much, and so you don't need an enormous amount of water at the get-go.

After that, it's jazz.

Sometimes I start with slightly charred and grilled fish heads and skeletons. Sometimes I use the leftovers from whole smoked fish. A very good, if labor-intensive, method is to pat dry your skeletons and heads and sear them hard in a little oil; this makes a pretty brown stock. In winter, I might coat the bones and heads with some oil and brown them in a 400°F oven. Or do none of that at all. Note that grilled and charred crab and lobster shells can get bitter, so avoid this.

Adding tomato paste or any other tomato product will give you a lovely rich color and add savoriness to the broth, but it's not always wanted. I do tend to add tomato to crab and lobster broth.

I rarely add alcohol to basic stocks or broths, but people do, both for the flavor and, in the case of wine, acidity. Some add a splash of vinegar for the same reason.

If I have them handy, I'll add a handful of dried mushrooms, usually porcini, to the broth for umami. Shiitake stems are another great option here. And best of all are matsutakes, but they can be hard to find.

And while every European stock starts with a mirepoix of carrots, onion, and celery, I don't always do that. Chinese stocks might only use smashed fresh ginger, some chopped scallions, and maybe a star anise or three. Bay leaves are a must in a European stock, as is parsley, but they will not taste right if you're shooting for Asian flavors.

Most of these additions are to offset fishy smells. General fish handling tips will minimize this, too. Rinse your fish in salty water to remove slime, which is a main cause of stinky broth. Grilling, searing, or roasting heads and bones helps a lot, too. Another thing you can do is pull a trick from Asia, where they will bring the fish or seafood bits to a boil, then toss that first water out. This will make a cleaner, clearer broth.

One more key to minimizing fishiness is to keep the cooking temperature low and the cooking time short. A lovely fish broth can turn into a smelly mess by boiling it for an hour. Remember: gently simmer for less than one hour for best results. And if you have ingredients that normally take more than one hour to give up their goodness—like mushrooms, for example—start them first and add the fish or seafood bits later.

STORING STOCK

I'm a terrible snob when it comes to storing fish or seafood stock. I just won't do it. I use it within a week in the fridge, then I toss anything I don't use. Wasteful? Maybe, but I fish a lot, so there will always be another carcass in the kitchen soon. I do this because stored fish and seafood stock gets fishy in a hurry. Pressure-canning it is the worst, as the high heat involved really amps the stink. It's obviously safe to eat when properly pressure-canned, but I can't stand the stuff. Frozen fish and seafood stock is OK. I've done that, and it's fine, but not nearly as good as fresh. I will freeze some seafood stocks, like those made from lobster or shrimp shells. But even that's a rarity for me. Instead, I'll freeze the raw materials. I often have bags of shrimp shells in the freezer, and I'll store crab and lobster shells, too, because I get them so rarely compared to fish carcasses, which I can get whenever I want. There's no reason not to freeze fish carcasses, except that they're bulky.

Now, there is a nifty side effect of freezing fish stock, and this works only with fish, not seafood: when it thaws, all the particulates and impurities adhere to the gelatin in the stock, leaving a crystal clear broth underneath. This is excellent for fancy fish soups, where clear broth is vital. Is it as good as a classic French consommé? Nope, because classic consommé still has the gelatin in it, which adds body. But the freeze-then-thaw trick is a helluva lot easier.

If you do this, thaw the stock in the fridge slowly. I tend to freeze broth in quart Mason jars, so what I do is let the broth thaw enough so that I can hack it to bits with a butter knife to get it out of the jar, then put the whole shebang in a paper-towel-lined strainer set over a bowl—in the fridge. As the broth slowly thaws, what drips through is crystal clear. It can take a couple of days, though, so be forewarned. And you can't speed it up.

FISH STOCK

PREP TIME: 15 MINUTES | COOK TIME: 1 HOUR, 45 MINUTES | MAKES 1 GALLON

Fish stock isn't like normal stock. It's a fairly quick affair. My venison stock takes all day, or even overnight. My fish stock asks only fifty minutes or so of your time. Strain and enjoy. A long-simmered fish stock gets cloudy and bitter and fishy. I don't recommend it.

What fish? Really almost anything. I've made fish stock with bass, walleye, perch, black seabass, white seabass, lingcod, Pacific rockfish, stripers, tilefish, porgies, redfish, sea trout, spotted bass, bluegills . . . you get the point. Do not use oily fish if you intend on using the stock for anything other than a soup with the meat of the same fish, like the Salmon Head Soup on page 200. Stock made from oily fish is pretty much good only the day you made it, and maybe the next day. Maybe.

Be sure to rinse the heads and bones well to remove slime, and be absolutely certain to snip out the gills. Gills in your stock will ruin it, as the blood in them will cloud your stock and give it an "off" flavor very quickly.

»

2 to 5 pounds fish bones
  and heads

3 tablespoons olive oil, divided

Salt

1 large onion, chopped

1 large carrot, chopped

1 fennel bulb, chopped (optional)

3 stalks celery, chopped

1 cup white wine or vermouth

A handful of dried mushrooms
  (optional)

2 to 4 bay leaves

1 star anise pod (optional)

1 to 2 teaspoons dried or
  fresh thyme

3 or 4 pieces dried kombu kelp
  (optional)

Chopped fronds from the
  fennel bulb

Preheat your oven to 400°F. Rinse the fish heads and bones and pat dry with paper towels. Coat them with a thin layer of oil and salt them well. Arrange on baking sheets in one layer and roast in the oven until lightly browned, up to 1 hour.

When that time is nearing its end, heat the remaining olive oil in a large stockpot over medium-high heat. When the oil is hot, add the chopped vegetables and cook, stirring often, until they are all soft, but not browned. This should take about 10 minutes or so.

Add the fish bits, then the white wine, and then all the remaining ingredients, plus enough water to cover everything by about an inch or two. Bring to a simmer, then drop the heat to a bare shimmy, about 175°F if you want to be precise. It should not boil under any circumstances, and keep an eye on things to ensure that it doesn't. Simmer like this for 30 to 45 minutes, definitely no more than 1 hour.

Turn off the heat. Set a fine mesh strainer over a big bowl, then put a piece of paper towel or cheesecloth in the strainer. Ladle the stock through this setup into the bowl. When you get to the bottom, skip the dregs down there, as they will be filled with sediment. The stock will never be as good as it is right now, but it can be refrigerated for up to a week and frozen for up to 6 months.

NOTE You'll notice that my stock differs from others in that I use mushrooms and dried kombu kelp, which is a sort of seaweed. Dried mushrooms are easily available in most supermarkets, but you'll need to go to an Asian market for the kelp. You can skip it if you want.

ALTERNATE METHOD Heat a large frying pan and add a tablespoon of neutral oil. When the oil is hot, sear your skeletons and/or heads until they're well browned, adding them to the stockpot when they're ready. Scrape the pan as you go and add the browned bits to the pot. You'll need to keep adding a little oil between batches. This will take 30 minutes or so for a normal round of fish stock, but it makes a lovely broth. When the last round of skeletons is done, use the white wine or vermouth to deglaze the pan, using a wooden spoon to scrape up the browned bits; this goes into the pot, too.

SEAFOOD STOCK

PREP TIME: 15 MINUTES | COOK TIME: 1 HOUR | MAKES 5 QUARTS

Seafood stock, usually crab stock for me, is a mainstay in my kitchen during Dungeness crab season, which in California runs from November through June. But you can legally catch red and rock crabs all year long, and they make a fine stock, too. I've used pretty much every species of crab in North America for this recipe —even spider crabs. After picking the meat out, I use the leftover shells to make this rich broth.

You can use lobster or crayfish shells for this recipe, and it will be very similar. If you use this recipe for shrimp or fish, it'll be fine, too, just a change of pace from the previous fish stock recipe. I find that the best bits for a good seafood stock are the shells from the legs, as well as the top shell. If you use the inner shell bits from the body, be aware that there's a lot of fat in there that can cloud the stock. If you aren't worried about that, go right ahead.

Use this stock in seafood soups and stews, as a base for the Crawfish Bisque on page 184, or in the Crab Curry on page 196.

As I mentioned in the chapter opening, the vegetables in here are open to substitution; the only ones you really need are the onions (or leeks) and celery. I also think fennel adds a lot here. If you can't find it, add fennel seeds, or even a shot of ouzo or other anise-flavored liqueur.

4 tablespoons olive oil

1 large onion, chopped

4 cloves garlic, chopped

3 stalks celery, chopped

2 carrots, chopped

Tops from 1 fennel bulb chopped

½ pound fresh mushrooms, or a handful of dried, chopped

3 tablespoons tomato paste

1 to 2 pounds crab, lobster, or crawfish shells

1 cup white wine

3 bay leaves

2 tablespoons black peppercorns

½ cup chopped parsley

Salt

Heat the olive oil in a large stockpot and sauté the vegetables over high heat for 5 minutes, stirring often, until the onions are translucent. Add the tomato paste, stir well, and cook over medium heat for another 2 or 3 minutes, until it darkens.

Add the shells and bodies and smash them all with a potato masher. Mix well to coat with the tomato paste and to disperse the veggies. Cook for another 5 minutes, stirring a couple of times.

Add the white wine, bay leaves, peppercorns, and parsley and bring to a boil. Let this cook for a minute, then pour in enough cold water to cover everything by about an inch; normally this is about 10 cups. Let this simmer very gently for between 45 minutes and 1 hour. Add salt to taste.

Turn off the heat. Set up another large pot or bowl and put a fine-meshed strainer over it. Line the strainer with a plain paper towel or a piece of cheesecloth and ladle the stock through this setup into the large pot or bowls. Don't try to get the last dregs of stock, as this will be full of debris. Discard the shells and the other solids.

Let the stock cool for 15 to 30 minutes, then use or pour into quart jars. The stock will keep for a week in the fridge. It will freeze well for 2 months, but after that, it deteriorates rapidly.

JAPANESE DASHI

PREP TIME: 5 MINUTES | COOK TIME: 20 MINUTES | MAKES 1 QUART, AND CAN BE SCALED UP

Dashi underpins much of Japanese cuisine, and you can't really make a Japanese soup without it. At its core, dashi is a broth made from kombu, a dried kelp, and shaved dried, fermented bonito, called *katsuobushi* in Japanese. I mean, yeah, sure you can get an instant mix, and if you make a lot of Japanese food, it's fine for a worknight. But making dashi from scratch will let you in on why this is a cornerstone of one of the great cuisines of the world.

Now, if you can get your hands on an actual block of katsuobushi, awesome. You will shave off flakes as you need them for the dashi, and it'll be fantastic. More common will be bags of shavings, called *hanakatsuo*, which is what I use.

If fish stock is an ephemeral thing, dashi is even more so. You don't make batches to store; you make it as needed. Dashi is light and aromatic and should be made and used. Storing it is unnecessary; after all, the main ingredients are dried and shelf stable.

I am indebted to Shizuo Tsuji's classic book *Japanese Cooking: A Simple Art* for this recipe. I've tried others, but this is simple and wonderful.

---

1 quart cold water

1 ounce kombu

1 ounce bonito flakes

Pour the cold water into a pot and add the kombu. Turn the heat to medium, or even medium-low. You are gradually infusing the seaweed into the water. As soon as you see the water begin to simmer, remove the kombu. You can actually reuse it, as I'll explain below. Boiled kombu gets smelly.

Now bring the stock to a simmer and add the bonito flakes. Bring the stock to a full boil, then turn off the heat and move the pot off the burner. Cover the pot and let it sit for a minute or two.

Strain it through the standard paper towel set in a strainer over a bowl. This is your dashi, and it should be used that evening. Don't make it more than an hour or so in advance, and don't let it boil again.

Tsuji notes that you can reuse both the kombu and the bonito flakes to make a secondary dashi that works well as a base for noodle soups and such. For this, you put the once-used bonito and kombu in a pot and cover it with 1½ quarts of cold water. Bring this to a boil, then immediately drop the heat to a bare shimmy, not even a simmer. Let this cook, uncovered, for 20 minutes. You'll make a better secondary dashi if you toss in another half-ounce of fresh bonito flakes at this point, turning off the heat and removing the pot from the burner. Strain this stock, and you're good to go. Now you discard the used kombu and bonito flakes.

SOUPS

Debris Soup, a Model for All Fish Soups

Fillets do not make the best fish soup. There, I said it. What does? *Every other part of the fish.* The reasons are two: fat and collagen. Fillets are almost entirely lean muscle, even on fatty fish like salmon and mackerel. All the best parts lie elsewhere: the bellies, collars, the fins, the head. There is one reason so many cultures have fish-head soups. A fish head, especially a big one that happens to have the collar still attached, may be ugly to look at, but it's a glory to eat. Let me walk you through it.

Most of you reading this know about fish cheeks, the muscles fish use to close their jaws. Predatory fish tend to have the biggest cheeks, although pound for pound, those of the coral-eating parrotfish are pretty impressive. Cheeks are twin gold coins to be fought over. Then there are the lumps of meat directly behind the head; they're nice, but, seeing as they are extensions of the fillet, they happen to be lean and firm. The throats of fish, not to be confused with the collars, are under the bottom jaws and consist of two morsels of silky meat bonded to some seriously gelatinous frames.

Working backward, you get to the collars, which, on a decent-sized fish, have the good stuff. Like the meat at the back of the head, the top of the collar is regular fillet meat. Nice, but nothing to write home about. The treasures lie in pockets behind the pectoral and pelvic fins. On either side and behind these fins are lens-shaped muscles that are by far the best part of the fish—fatty, silky, yet firm, they taste meatier than anything else in the fish world. And they are jewels when found floating in the soup.

What's more, fish heads and fins are loaded with collagen, which makes a superior broth. I once made a fish broth out of skinless fillets, just to see what might happen. It was terrible. Boring and thin. At the very least, you need the racks—the skeletons—but a broth made solely from heads will be better still.

▲ A lingcod cheek. Cheeks are fantastic in soups.

Put all this together and you have the makings of a sublime soup. Soup, remember, differs from stew in that the broth is the star; in a stew, what's floating in the broth is the star. You could make a smooth, puréed soup like a bisque with the meat and broth from fish debris, but better still would be a simpler soup featuring the meat, the broth, and a few other ingredients to play harmony.

In general, you'll want something green, whether it be leafy greens or herbs. You might want to add something for heft, like potatoes or other root vegetables, or perhaps pasta, barley, beans, or rice. If you choose to do so and if you care about a pretty broth, cook them separately and then add them later; cooking the grains in the final broth muddies it. I tend to split the difference by making quite a lot of broth, cooking the grains or beans in some and leaving the rest for the finished soup. I like some acidity to perk things up, so a few peeled tomatoes, crushed by hand, or some citrus or vinegar are always nice. But, at least in this case, keep things simple, and savor that silky fin meat and cheeks, and slurp that amazing broth.

SIMPLE SPANISH FISH SOUP

PREP TIME: 90 MINUTES, MOSTLY TO COOK THE BEANS | **COOK TIME: 20 MINUTES** | **SERVES 4 TO 6**

Use this recipe as a master, subbing in similar ingredients as you have them on hand. See the variations below.

1 cup dried beans (cranberry or white beans)

2 quarts fish stock, divided

Salt

2 to 4 slices bacon

1 yellow onion, chopped

1 clove garlic, minced

1 pound freshly peeled, or canned plum tomatoes, crushed by hand

A pinch of saffron

1 cup dry sherry, vermouth, or white wine

1 pound cooked, flaked fish, preferably from the collars and head (see above)

¼ cup minced Italian parsley

Black pepper

Cook the beans in 1 pint of the fish stock plus another pint of water. Simmer gently until tender, add some salt, and set aside in their cooking liquid.

In a soup pot, fry the bacon slowly until crispy, then remove it and chop. Set it aside, too. Eat a piece if you want.

Sauté the onion in the bacon fat over medium heat until soft but not browned, about 6 to 8 minutes. Add the garlic and cook another minute.

Crush the tomatoes into the pot. You want them in rough, irregular shapes, which is why you want to start with whole tomatoes, not pre-crushed ones, which are too smooth for this soup. Add the saffron.

Mix it all well, then pour in the wine and bring it to a boil. Pour in the rest of the fish stock. Bring this to a simmer and let everything cook gently for 10 minutes. Add the fish and stir to combine. Rinse the cooked beans under cold water and then add them to the pot. Let all this cook for 5 minutes, then add the parsley, chopped bacon, and black pepper to taste.

Serve at once with a glass of white wine.

VARIATIONS Looking at what purpose the ingredients serve in this recipe gives you an idea of how to change it to suit various cuisines. The heft, which comes from the beans here, can also come from rice, pasta, or barley, for example, cooked separately in some broth (as we did here with the beans).

The bacon adds a bit of fat and smoky flavor. Adding a bit of anything smoked will get you there, even if it's not fatty. Chipotles and olive oil will give you the same effect, more or less, as would a bit of smoked fish and butter. Onions and garlic are a given, but you could vary what form they take. Leeks, shallots, garlic scapes, you name it.

Tomatoes are used all over the world, but if you want to skip them, add citrus juice for a bright note or malt vinegar if you want to take this Scandinavian. The saffron is an emblematic spice of Spain; for something Caribbean, try allspice; for Chinese, use Sichuan peppercorns. Try curry powder or lovage—the list is a long one. All are strong flavors that evoke a place.

The alcohol is also very Spanish, but you could switch to lager for a German touch, ale for British, sake for Japan, or just skip it altogether. And whatever soft aromatic green herb makes you happy can work in place of the parsley.

CHOWDERS

For the purposes of this book, the difference between a chowder and a soup is the presence of dairy. I am staking out a position here, because there is a tomato-based thing called Manhattan clam chowder and a Rhode Island clear clam chowder, neither of which have dairy. Both are great, but neither are chowders the way most Americans think of them.

Clams—the stars of our first chowder—are in my family's DNA. My mom, after all, is a native of Ipswich, Massachusetts. And if there is a place more clam-centric than Ipswich, I can't think of it; there's even a clam nicknamed the "Ipswich clam." The rest of America knows it as the steamer. To me, clams mean vacation. Summertime. Happiness. I've written about my fond memories of digging hardshell clams on Block Island in my first book, *Hunt, Gather, Cook*, and even today, living three thousand miles from New England, clamming in the mudflats of California brings joy to my heart the way nothing else really does.

I owe all of this to my mom. It was she who taught me how to dig and eat clams. So imagine my surprise when it finally dawned on me, sometime in my teenage years, that Mom really didn't care all that much for clams. Don't get me wrong; she led our clamming expeditions on Block Island, her version of Stuffed Clams (page 82) is one of my favorites, and no one else's New England clam chowder can ever compare to hers. But for Mom, clams and clamming bring back bittersweet memories of her own childhood on coastal New England. It was just after World War II, and while times weren't as hard as during the Depression, the beauty of the shoreline was mixed with some hard, smelly work. Every Friday during those summers, it was up to Mom and Uncle David to gather steamer clams for dinner and quahogs for chowder. I asked her to tell me about it a few years ago. This is her story:

> The steamer or "piss clams" were dug at low tide, and we walked to the flat from our cottage in Ipswich carrying our large clam bucket, a pitchfork, and a small tin can for the sea worms [which Mom sold as bait].
>
> The steamers were plentiful then, and the water wasn't polluted, so it was safe to eat the clams that we dug. The clams were easy to find, as when the tide goes out, the clams bury themselves deep into the mud and leave a small round air hole, which is a dead giveaway that the clam is there. For some reason, the clams like to all live together in the same area, so once we started to dig, we found plenty of them.
>
> We tried hard not to pierce their soft shells with the pitchfork and mostly were successful. We did this by not digging quite as deep as where the clams lay and then used our hands to finish the job. As we dug away the mud, we sometimes got cuts on our hands from the sharp empty clamshells that were sticking up at odd angles. No manicure in those days!
>
> But what a delight it was to reach into the mud and come up with a juicy, spitting (they spit out a long stream of salt water when picked up to try to frighten you away), healthy steamer clam to plunk into the bucket!
>
> After we had a bucket full of steamer clams, we got our rowboat and went to the enormous sand bar off the south end of Plum Island, which juts out into Ipswich Bay. We would pull our boat up onto the bar and drop the anchor. If the tide turned and started coming in, we would keep careful watch and keep moving the boat higher up onto the bar.
>
> The process to find the giant sea clams (what we locally called quahogs) is to wade waist deep in the water out onto the bar and start to wiggle your toes in the lovely sandy bottom. When your heel, foot, or toe hit something very hard you knew you had found your first quahog! Then you had to dive down under the

water and using two hands dislodge the sea clam from its hold on the sand. This is easier said than done. The quahog has an enormous "foot" which it proceeds to stick out into the sand to help anchor it in place. So it is a tug-of-war to get the thing up and out of the sand.

Because we were waist deep in water, we had to be upended very much like you see the ducks and swans do when they are looking for food. Fortunately, it only takes two or three of these large clams to make a very tasty chowder.

Sounds pretty fun to me. But when she described what she had to endure when she returned home, I got a sense of why Mom isn't all that keen on clams to this day. Clams, as you know if you've ever cleaned one, are pretty gnarly. And remember, she was ten or eleven years old at the time:

My job was to make the chowder. This meant I had to clean those enormous, nasty quahogs. To this day, I really don't enjoy eating clams of any kind. The quahogs had huge, nasty bellies which I had to separate and throw away, and they had a five- to six-inch-long translucent round tube in them that was slippery and hard. I don't know how the clam used it but it was yucky! That too had to be removed and thrown out [the tube is called the crystalline style; it's part of the clam's digestive system].

That left the luscious, pink-colored, firm, meaty foot (the part that the quahog used to try to anchor itself in the sand so I couldn't pull it up) and two large, round, white muscle hinges. These I was happy to grind up for the chowder.

I'm pretty durable, but even I get skeeved out a bit by that freaky translucent tube; when you clean a clam, it seems to be alive—almost rocketing out of the clam belly when you cut it open. And, as they say, it was a brave person who first ate a clam. While not quite so mucus-like as a raw oyster, a raw clam doesn't scream out, "Yummy!" Even though it is.

Nonetheless, I grew up eating clams. Which means Mom made them. And all her clam recipes are fantastic, especially her New England clam chowder. For the first thirty-odd years of my life, I just thought Mom's chowder was unique to our family. It is a white chowder like most New England versions, but unlike the chowders in much of Massachusetts, Mom's is soupy and brothy, not thick and creamy. It was only when I delved more seriously into food that I realized that this was a recognized variety of chowder; it is Maine style. I asked Mom about this, and she reminded me that her mother grew up in Wiscasset, Maine. Mystery solved.

Looking back on all this, I'm struck by how important it must have been for Mom to raise us all as bona fide clam lovers, even though it was not something she herself still liked to eat. It was both an act of regional pride (Yankees eat clams. Period.) and, more importantly, an act of love. I am thankful for that, and for all the other acts of love Mom has shown me over the years, both large and small. Every time I eat this particular New England clam chowder, I think of her. I love you, Mom. I hope I did your chowder proud.

MAINE CLAM CHOWDER

PREP TIME: 15 MINUTES | **COOK TIME: 1 HOUR** | **SERVES 8**

This is a recipe that goes back in my family probably a century or more. It's easy to make, with one exception, and it is an important one: you cannot allow this to boil, or even simmer, once the milk has been added. It will curdle. There are two ways to help stop this from happening. First, you can heat the milk and evaporated milk to steaming before adding it to the chowder pot. Or you can do what Mom often does, which is to let the chowder base cool to room temperature before adding the milk and then reheating it; this process is called *ripening*.

Finally—and this is a hack I've developed—you can skip the milk and evaporated milk altogether and use heavy cream, which will not curdle. If you do this, add a half pint.

2 tablespoons butter

¼ pound salt pork or bacon, minced

1 large onion, about 1½ to 2 cups, chopped

2 pounds potatoes, about 3 to 4 cups, peeled and diced

1 quart clam juice

1 pound chopped clams, about 1 pint

One 12-ounce can evaporated milk (do not use lowfat milk)

3 cups whole milk

Black pepper

In a large soup pot, heat the butter over medium heat and add the diced salt pork and onions. Fry this slowly until the onions are soft and translucent. Do not brown the onions.

Mix in the potatoes and the clam juice and add enough water to just barely cover the potatoes. Bring this to a simmer and cook until the potatoes are tender, about 15 minutes.

When the potatoes are just about tender—not completely cooked—add the chopped clams and turn off the heat. Let this cool for at least 30 minutes. You can make this chowder base up to a day ahead if you'd like.

Once the chowder base is pretty cool (below 100°F), add the evaporated milk and whole milk and turn the heat on low. Gently bring the chowder up to eating temperature, and be very careful not to let it simmer. Add some freshly ground black pepper to taste and serve hot.

NOTE Resist the urge to add any herbs or spices other than black pepper to this chowder. New Englanders in general, and Mainers specifically, are as spare in their words as they are in their cooking. A word on the clams. I'm using gaper (horseneck) clams from California because that's what I have. A real Maine chowder uses sea clams or quahogs, which are the dominant clams in markets on the East Coast. Canned clams are OK too, although not as good. Eat this chowder with Yankee cornbread—Mom calls it johnnycake—and a salad.

VARIATIONS Any firm white fish can sub in for the clams, and little boreal shrimp are a nice change of pace here, too. Chunks of lobster will work, as will oysters. If you want to make this more like a traditional southern oyster stew, sub in oysters and their liquor, omit the salt pork and potatoes, and use heavy cream instead of milk. Unlike Maine clam chowder, oyster stew is often garnished with parsley.

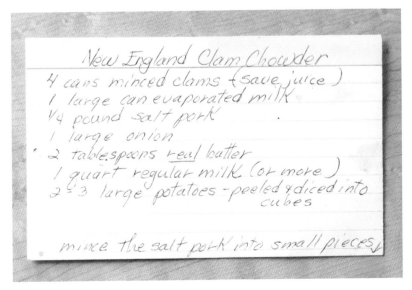

New England Clam Chowder
4 cans minced clams (save juice)
1 large can evaporated milk
1/4 pound salt pork
1 large onion
2 tablespoons real butter
1 quart regular milk (or more)
2-3 large potatoes - peeled & diced into cubes

mince the salt pork into small pieces

▲ Mom's original recipe card.

LAKE ERIE PERCH CHOWDER

PREP TIME: 20 MINUTES | COOK TIME: 40 MINUTES | SERVES 8

I don't get to fish for perch very often, since they're not native to the West. But whenever I visit my friends Joe and Dorrie, who live near Cleveland, I try to get out and catch some yellow perch in Lake Erie. Why Lake Erie? More than 85 percent of the continent's commercial catch of yellow perch comes from there, and I'd heard stories of recreational anglers having hundred-fish days and of perch topping two pounds—a monster for a fish that averages about five ounces. I had to get me some of that. Yeah, I hear you. Isn't Lake Erie horrifically polluted? Isn't it near the Cuyahoga River, which famously caught fire in 1969? That was a *long* time ago. The lake has cleared up dramatically since the 1990s, thanks to serious anti-pollution laws, and, oddly, the invasive zebra mussel, which filtered out even more pollution from the lake. This helped the mayfly larvae, which the perch love to eat, return in force. Another invasive species, the round goby (a little fish), also arrived in recent years and has quickly become another favorite food of the yellow perch. As a result, perch numbers have increased almost every year since their crash in 1994.

It's a ton of fun to fish urban waters. There's something about fishing while watching other people work that is perversely satisfying. It's even more fun to know that it's safe to eat the fish there. We've come a long way from the 1970s.

Cleveland has one of the most vibrant Polish communities in America. And perch makes a phenomenal chowder. And Cleveland-style Polish perch chowder was born. So a perch chowder with butter, potatoes, onions, and fish stock was where I started. And the Polish? Easy. I decided to toss in a link of Polish kielbasa, a pinch of marjoram and dill, and for the dairy, I skipped the regular cream and went with sour cream. How was it? Lemme tell ya. If the Browns ate this, they might win the Super Bowl.

3 tablespoons unsalted butter

1 large yellow or white onion, about 2 cups, chopped

1½ pounds Yukon Gold or other waxy potatoes, peeled and diced

1 quart fish or clam stock

2 cups water

½ teaspoon marjoram

Salt and black pepper

1½ pounds skinless yellow perch fillets, cut into chunks

6 to 8 ounces Polish kielbasa, sliced

¼ cup chopped fresh dill or parsley

1 cup sour cream, served tableside

Melt the butter in a Dutch oven or other heavy pot over medium heat. When it stops frothing, add the chopped onion and cook gently until soft and translucent. Do not let it brown.

Add the potatoes and coat with the butter. Cook for 1 to 2 minutes to let the butter absorb a bit. Sprinkle everything with salt. Pour in the fish stock, water, and marjoram, and add salt and pepper to taste. Simmer gently for about 20 minutes, or until the potatoes are tender.

Once the potatoes are tender, add the perch and the kielbasa and simmer another 10 minutes. Turn off the heat and add the dill.

Ladle into bowls, and let everyone add sour cream at the table. Serve with lots of beer and some crusty bread.

SALMON CHOWDER

PREP TIME: 20 MINUTES | COOK TIME: 90 MINUTES | SERVES 8

Ritual and tradition are powerful forces, both for good and for ill. Such it is with me and chowder. I grew up eating chowder, all sorts of chowder, really, but my mom's is the best. My first tentative steps to break with Mom's chowder dogma came with the perch chowder above. This was the next step.

I live in northern California, where the chinook salmon is, well, king. This is the very southern end of its range, and what, ecologically speaking, could be called the Pacific Northwest—and it is the Pacific Northwest, with its vast salmon runs, trout in the mountains, steelhead in the rivers, and char in the snowy north—is where I drew my inspiration here. This chowder has bacon, corn, lots of herbs, and a homemade stock. None of this would fly in Mom's clam chowder. But here's the thing. People move west to escape tradition, to be free to be whomever they wish to be. Why can't their chowder follow suit?

You can use any salmonid fish for this recipe. Actually, you can use any fish—except something like sardines, mackerel, or bluefish. What makes this chowder great is the broth you make from the heads and bones, and while you're perfectly OK making this with store-bought stock, it won't be as good. Serve with crusty sourdough bread and a hoppy West Coast IPA or crisp white wine. Oh, and this chowder is actually better the next day; just heat it up very slowly on the stovetop. Don't let it boil.

SALMON BROTH

Salt

3 to 4 pounds salmon heads, fins, and bones, gills removed

Salt

2 tablespoons safflower, grapeseed, or canola oil

1 onion, chopped

2 carrots, chopped

2 stalks celery, chopped

1 cup white wine

1 handful of dried mushrooms, preferably matsutake

2 bay leaves

To make the broth, bring a large pot of water to a boil and salt it well. Add the salmon bones, heads, and fins. When the water returns to a boil, let this cook 1 minute. Remove the salmon bits (save them!) and discard the water. Blanching this way removes the scum from the stock and will give you a cleaner-tasting broth when you're done.

Wipe out the pot, add the oil, and turn the heat to medium-high. When the oil is hot, sauté the onion, carrot, and celery, stirring often, until the onion is soft, about 4 to 5 minutes. Add the wine, the dried mushrooms, bay leaves, and use a wooden spoon to scrape up any browned bits from the bottom of the pot. Let the wine boil for a minute or two, then add the blanched salmon bones and enough cool water to cover everything by about ½ inch. Bring to a very gentle simmer (barely bubbling) and cook like this for 45 minutes.

Get a large bowl for the broth and set a strainer over it. Line the strainer with a plain paper towel or cheesecloth. Turn off the heat on the broth and ladle it through the strainer and into the bowl. Don't bother trying to get the last little bit of broth out of the pot, as it will be full of debris. Discard the contents of the pot and reserve the broth.

CHOWDER

1 tablespoon unsalted butter

¼ pound thick bacon, cut into batons

1 cup chopped yellow or white onion

2 stalks celery, chopped

1½ pounds potatoes, peeled and diced

5 to 6 cups salmon broth, or 4 cups chicken broth plus 1 to 2 cups water

Salt

1 to 2 pounds skinless, boneless salmon meat, cut into chunks

1 cup corn, fresh or thawed

⅔ cup heavy cream

Black pepper

2 tablespoons chopped fresh dill or chives, for garnish

To make the chowder, melt the butter in a Dutch over or other soup pot set over medium heat. Add the bacon and fry, stirring and turning often, until crispy, about 6 to 8 minutes. Add the onion and celery and sauté until soft, about another 4 to 5 minutes. Add the potatoes and the salmon broth and bring to a simmer. Add salt to taste. Cook until the potatoes are tender, about 15 to 20 minutes.

When the potatoes are tender, add the chunks of salmon and the corn. Cook gently until the salmon is just cooked through, about 5 minutes. Turn off the heat and stir in the heavy cream, black pepper, and dill.

"It has always been my private conviction that any man who puts his intelligence up against a fish and loses had it coming."

JOHN STEINBECK

CRAWFISH BISQUE

PREP TIME: 35 MINUTES | **COOK TIME: 3 HOURS** | **SERVES 8**

Few recipes concentrate the flavors of the main ingredient better than a French bisque. This is no mere soup or stew. It's a full-on barrage of flavor that makes everyone stop talking at the table. You just want to savor this soup in silence. Such an experience has its price, however. This is not an easy recipe, nor is it quick. Save this one for weekends, holidays, or date night, as it takes most of the day to make. But it is more than worth the effort to transform the humble crawfish into one of the highlights of French haute cuisine.

To get the full effect here, you need to make your own broth and butter from the shells of the crawfish. The butter, especially, is a little persnickety, but it adds so much flavor to the soup that you'll be sad if you don't make it. The reason crawfish butter is so good is that a great deal of the flavor in lobsters, crabs, shrimps, and crawfish is fat soluble, not water soluble. So what you can't extract by making broth, you get by making the butter. Ah, those crafty French.

Why crawfish? Well, I live three thousand miles from New England, where the best lobsters live. And yes, I know I could use California spiny lobsters, but they're not as good here. I could, of course, use Dungeness crab, any other crab, or shrimp, too.

The broth and butter can be made well ahead, and frozen for months before you make the soup. Once you have them in hand, the bisque comes together in less than 30 minutes.

The end result is pure luxury. You sit there looking at a soup so rich with crawfish, crabs, or lobsters that the whole thing is a warming, welcoming orange. The texture of the bisque is velvet, and you taste the seemingly impossible combination of silky cream, buttery crawfish, and tangy hot sauce. Yes, hot sauce. A few splashes is all you need to add a touch of acid and heat to the bisque.

The key for me, however, is the crawfish meat in the bisque itself, which gives you something to aim for when you're eating this with a spoon. Not every bisque includes this, but I think it really needs it, especially if you're serving this as a main course.

CRAWFISH BUTTER

¼ pound cooked crawfish heads and shells from the tails

½ pound unsalted butter

TO MAKE THE CRAWFISH BUTTER Smash the shells to a pulp. This can be done in a mortar and pestle or in a strong blender or food processor—or with a mallet in a bowl. You really want to mash everything well so you get more flavor from the shells.

Melt the butter in a small saucepan and add the shells to it. Cover and put into a 170°F oven and let this cook for 90 minutes, stirring now and again. Strain the butter through a fine-meshed sieve that has a paper towel set inside it; this filters out all the debris.

Pour into a container and let it cool. Tip: for long storage, let the butter solidify and pop it out of the container, leaving behind the gellified liquid at the bottom of the container. Leaving this in contact with the butter over time can make it go rancid.

CRAWFISH BROTH

¼ cup safflower, grapeseed, or other neutral oil

3 to 4 pounds crawfish heads and shells from tails

1 fennel bulb, chopped with fronds

2 large carrots, chopped

2 cups chopped onion

4 cloves garlic, chopped

1 ounce dried mushrooms (optional)

One 6-ounce can tomato paste

1 cup dry vermouth

5 bay leaves

BISQUE

6 tablespoons crawfish butter, divided (see above)

⅓ cup chopped onion

2 tablespoons vermouth or brandy

5 cups crawfish broth (see above)

⅓ cup rice

Salt

1 pound crawfish meat

2 tablespoons heavy cream

Chopped dill, parsley, or chives, for garnish

TO MAKE THE BROTH Heat the oil in a large stockpot over medium heat. Add the crawfish shells and smash them to bits with a potato masher. Crush and stir them as they cook until they're all in pieces. Let this cook for a few minutes, then mix in the fennel, carrot, and onion. Cook for 5 minutes, stirring often. Mix in the garlic, dried mushrooms, and tomato paste. Turn the heat as high as it will go and stir-fry this for 2 minutes.

Add the vermouth and stir well. Let this boil for 1 minute, then add enough cool water to cover the shells by 1 inch. Add the bay leaves and let this simmer gently for 90 minutes to 2 hours. Do not let it boil.

Strain the broth by pouring it through a fine-meshed sieve with a paper towel set inside. Set aside or chill quickly and store.

TO MAKE THE BISQUE Heat 2 tablespoons crawfish butter in a large soup pot over medium-high heat. Sauté the onion until soft and translucent. Do not let it brown. Pour in the vermouth or brandy and let this boil for a minute.

Add the crawfish broth and rice and bring it to a gentle simmer. Simmer until the rice is soft, about 25 minutes. Add salt to taste.

Pour the soup into a blender along with ¼ pound of crawfish meat. Purée, in batches if you need to.

Wipe out the soup pot and return the puréed soup to it. Heat the bisque over medium-low heat just to the steaming point. Add the rest of the crawfish meat and heat for 2–3 minutes. Mix in the heavy cream, then stir in the remaining crawfish butter 1 tablespoon at a time. Serve at once, garnished with the herbs.

Serve this with crusty bread and a green salad as a main course, or as part of a larger meal. Cajuns make a slightly different version of this bisque and serve it with a spoonful of rice in the center of the bowl, which is another serving option.

VARIATION You can turn this into a very good rendition of southern she-crab soup by cutting the tomato paste in the broth by half and by puréeing in the roe from several crabs into the bisque. Drizzle a little sherry into the bisque at service.

GULF FISH STEW

PREP TIME: 15 MINUTES | **COOK TIME: 45 MINUTES** | **SERVES 8**

The best stews combine ingredients that really make their origin shine. After a fishing trip to Mobile Bay with my friend Joe Baya where we targeted sheepshead, I came home with lots of fish. Sheepshead is a cousin of the porgy or scup and looks a little like a gigantic panfish or surf perch—if it was in jail. I used to catch them as a kid in New Jersey, where we'd call them "convict fish," for their black-and-white stripes. They're immensely fun to catch, and their diet is high in crustaceans and mollusks, so their meat is almost crab-like—white, firm, flaky.

Sheepshead make a great stew fish, but many other fish would work here, too. Bass fillets, snapper, grouper, black seabass, Pacific rockfish, perch, lingcod, chunks of pike, and, above them all, tautog, which is the finest stew fish in North America.

The inspiration is a dish known as Alabama camp stew, which is normally made with a selection of canned ingredients so you can make it in deer camp. Canned tomatoes, corn, and beans, and, well, canned pork, which I'm not a fan of. While this stew does use canned tomatoes, I made my own hominy from heirloom Tennessee corn, and I used dried black-eyed peas. You can use canned hominy (or some other corn), and canned beans, too.

I also used dried okra I had in the pantry. I happen to like reconstituted okra a lot, better than frozen, but any sort of okra would be good. Another thing I like in this stew is the use of chicken (or in my case, pheasant) broth instead of a fish broth. You can use either, but the chicken broth tames the fish-ness of the stew. The fish then becomes a welcome guest in the stew, not a main player.

This stew uses a special seasoning blend common in the South called Cavender's seasoning. I've seen it in supermarkets here in Northern California, but if you can't find it, skip it or add some garlic and thyme. A final piece to this stew is very, very southern: Conecuh sausage. Those of you who know, know. For those of you who don't, Conecuh is to Alabama as Taylor ham is to New Jersey: a breakfast meat with a cult following. It's a proprietary recipe, and there's nothing exactly like it. That said, any smoked sausage you like will do.

The result is a rich stew that gives you different flavor combinations at every bite. The fish is present, as I mentioned, but not overwhelming. If you want a more seafoody stew, I suggest adding things that sheepshead eat: shrimp and crab. Both would be great additions.

»

3 tablespoons bacon fat or
vegetable oil

1 large yellow or white onion,
chopped

½ pound fresh okra, sliced
(or 1 cup dried)

2 teaspoons Cavender's
seasoning (optional)

1 quart chicken or seafood stock

1 quart water

1 cup crushed tomatoes

Salt

2 cups cooked hominy or other
corn (canned or frozen is fine)

2 cups cooked black-eyed peas
or butter beans (canned or
frozen is fine)

1 pound Conecuh or other smoked
sausage, sliced

2 pounds sheepshead or other
fish, cut into 1-inch chunks

¼ cup chopped chives or parsley

Saltine crackers (optional)

In a large soup pot, heat the bacon fat over medium-high heat and sauté the onion, stirring often, until it just begins to color around the edges, about 5 to 8 minutes.

Add the okra and Cavender's seasoning and stir well. Sauté this for 3 minutes or so if you have fresh or frozen okra. If you're using dried, just mix it around a bit.

Pour in the stock, water, and crushed tomatoes. Bring to a simmer and add salt to taste. Add the hominy, beans, and sausage. Simmer, don't boil, for 15 minutes.

Add the fish and simmer another 10 minutes. Stir in the chopped chives and serve. If you want to bulk this up a bit, crush Saltines into the soup while eating.

"Fish, to taste right, must swim three times—
in water, in butter, and in wine."

PROVERB

SEAFOOD GUMBO

PREP TIME: 30 MINUTES | COOK TIME: 2 HOURS | SERVES 8

I've had lots of seafood gumbo in my day, and I've made more than a few. But nothing has blown me away like the version I ate at Peche, a New Orleans seafood restaurant run by Chef Don Link. Where most seafood gumbos revolve around a peanut-butter-colored roux, include tomatoes, are lighter, and feature okra, Link's gumbo had its shrimp and crabs swimming in a classic "dark chocolate" Cajun roux, no tomato at all, and was thickened with filé powder.

The effect is heartier, darker, like a squall roaring over Lake Pontchartrain, but everything in the bowl points to the seafood. It was less like eating a soup than it was like eating seafood with a gumbo sauce. It was a revelation. It was so much better than any others I'd ever had. I couldn't stop thinking about it. I needed the recipe. Fortunately, I found it in Link's excellent book, *Real Cajun*.

As I suspected, his seafood gumbo hinges on great broth and a serious roux—and of course, great seafood. Chef Link uses crab, shrimp, and oysters. I'd just returned from down South, laden with Gulf shrimp and fish. I'd smoked some tripletail throats (belly and collar), which, when flaked out, tasted almost exactly like crabmeat. They'd go into the gumbo in place of the crab. I'd also just come home from a San Francisco Bay fishing trip, so I had some fresh halibut, too. All three would go into this gumbo. You can use any combination of fish and seafood, but you really need at least shrimp in there to go along with whatever fish you choose. And please get Gulf shrimp, or at least American shrimp. It makes a difference.

Now comes the only hard part of this recipe, the roux.

There are lots of ways to make a roux, but I prefer the traditional method of mixing flour and oil or fat in a pot and stirring over medium heat until it's ready. How long? As Chef Emeril Lagasse likes to joke, "three beers." He's right. To get a roux dark enough for this seafood gumbo, you need almost an hour of almost constant stirring. It's the price you pay for magic.

The only other special thing you need to make this recipe is filé (fee-lay) powder, the dried leaves of the sassafras tree. You can find it in some supermarkets, and you can buy it online. Or if you live in the East, where sassafras lives, dry some leaves and grind them to a powder.

You'll likely have leftovers. It reheats beautifully for a few days afterward (store the leftovers in the fridge, of course). And it freezes well, too.

»

3 quarts seafood stock (page 171)

1 cup peanut oil

½ cup bacon fat

2 cups flour

1 large onion, chopped

1 green bell pepper, chopped

2 stalks celery, chopped

1 to 5 jalapeño peppers, chopped
(optional)

1 tablespoon garlic powder

2 teaspoons paprika

2 teaspoons chile powder

1 teaspoon black pepper

2 teaspoons dried oregano

1 teaspoon cayenne

½ teaspoon celery seed

Salt

2 pounds shrimp or crawfish

2 pounds firm white fish, cut
into chunks

1 pound crabmeat (optional)

1 pint shucked oysters (optional)

1 tablespoon filé gumbo powder

Hot sauce

½ cup chopped green onions

Heat the seafood stock in a pot. You want it steaming, not simmering. In another large soup pot, heat the oil and bacon fat over medium-high heat. Stir in the flour and make sure there are no lumps. Cook this roux until it's the color of dark chocolate, which will take anywhere from 40 minutes to an hour. You will want to use a wooden spatula or spoon to stir. You will also want to lower the heat as the roux browns, until it's at low heat when the roux is ready. Drink beer and listen to Cajun music while doing this. It helps.

When the roux is ready, add the chopped onion, bell pepper, celery, and jalapeño peppers to the pot and mix well. Cook this, stirring often, for about 5 minutes.

Stir in the garlic powder, paprika, chile powder, black pepper, oregano, cayenne, and celery seed. Ladle in some seafood stock and mix well. Turn up the heat to medium-high and keep stirring in the seafood stock until the gumbo thins out. Typically, you will need anywhere from 6 to 9 cups.

Add salt to taste and simmer gently for 30 minutes to an hour, stirring from time to time. The roux should not break, but if oil starts pooling on the surface of the gumbo, skim it off.

Add all the seafood and the filé powder. Simmer this gently for 15 minutes. Add salt and hot sauce to taste and serve, garnished with the green onions, along with some rice or potato salad.

NOTE If you don't have bacon fat lying around, just use 1½ cups of peanut oil.

EAST AFRICAN FISH STEW

PREP TIME: 1 HOUR | **COOK TIME: 40 MINUTES** | **SERVES 6**

There's something about tropical food that's just exciting—vivid colors, summertime ingredients, exotic flavors, and a constant balance of sweet-salty-sour-spicy that makes you want to eat more then you really ought to. But when you try to cook it yourself, too often you get hung up on hard-to-find ingredients. And while I use a couple here, there are easy substitutions available in any supermarket that make this stew accessible anywhere.

What is an "African" fish stew anyway? After all, Africa is a big place, far larger than the United States—larger even than North America—and made up of myriad cultures. Well, this dish takes its inspiration from the Swahili Coast in East Africa, where it's hot, there are lots of fish, and there's a significant Indian influence on the cuisine. You could easily find something like this stew anywhere from Mozambique to Kenya, a 2,500-mile stretch that covers most of Africa's east coast. The recipe relies on vegetables, fish, shrimp or crab, coconut milk, and a bit of curry powder.

You can buy curry powder in pretty much any supermarket in America, and canned coconut milk isn't much harder to find. What's more, coconut water—the water inside a coconut you see people drinking on desert islands—has become some sort of fitness fad, and cartons of it are popping up all over in markets. If you can find coconut water, you can use it in this stew in place of regular water to add one more layer of flavor.

Other than that, this stew is super easy to make: onions, sweet peppers, potatoes, some tomato, a few chiles, any fish you want, some shrimp or crab, and cilantro for garnish. Easy-peasy.

I serve this fish stew alongside coconut rice: medium- or long-grain rice cooked in coconut water and a little coconut milk (half a cup per cup of uncooked rice). But regular rice, or even just bread, would be fine.

2 to 4 pounds fish heads and
    bones, gills and guts removed

2 quarts coconut water or just
    plain water

1 cup chopped onion

2 stalks celery, chopped

2 carrots, chopped

3 bay leaves

A 1-inch piece of ginger, chopped

STEW

2 tablespoons red palm oil,
    peanut oil, or vegetable oil

2 cups chopped onion

One 8-ounce can tomato sauce

1 to 2 tablespoons curry powder

1 large potato, peeled and cut into
    1-inch chunks

2 sweet bell peppers, diced

2 plum tomatoes, diced

1 to 2 habanero chiles, minced
    (optional)

1 cup coconut milk

1 pound fish, skinless and
    boneless, cut into 1-inch chunks

½ to 1 pound peeled shrimp or
    crabmeat

¼ cup chopped cilantro

Add the fish heads and bones to a large soup pot and cover with water. Bring to a rolling boil, then immediately pour the contents of the pot into a colander, saving the heads and bones, but tossing the water. This step makes a cleaner broth. Wipe out the pot.

Now, return the heads and bones to the pot, along with all the other broth ingredients. Bring to a bare simmer and let this just shimmy a bit for 45 minutes to 1 hour, no more. Strain and use for the stew.

In a large, heavy pot like a Dutch oven, heat the oil over medium-high heat and sauté the onion until soft, but not browned.

Add the tomato sauce, curry powder, and potatoes and stir well. Pour in about 6 cups of the broth you just made, or chicken stock. Bring to a simmer and taste for salt. Simmer gently until the potatoes are almost tender, about 20 minutes.

Add the sweet peppers, the diced tomatoes, the chiles, and the coconut milk. Stir well and simmer gently for 10 minutes.

Add the fish and shrimp and simmer until the shrimp are nice and pink, about 5 to 10 minutes. Add the cilantro, cook another minute, then serve.

"Love is the net where hearts
are caught like fish."

MUHAMMAD ALI

SOUPS, STEWS, STOCKS, AND BROTHS

VIETNAMESE CLAYPOT CATFISH

PREP TIME: 30 MINUTES | **COOK TIME: 30 MINUTES** | **SERVES 4**

Other than southerners in the US, no culture loves catfish more than the Vietnamese. There are scores of Vietnamese catfish recipes, but this one, claypot catfish, may be the most famous. And while it's called claypot catfish, I confess I cooked it in a regular pot. The original dish calls for Asian caramel sauce, but it's hard to find and a pain to make. So I used molasses instead, and it was really, really good.

What sort of catfish to use? Well, catfish *can* be muddy tasting, especially bullheads, which can live in stagnant water. Channel catfish, which is the variety you can buy as farmed catfish, tends to be cleaner. Blue and white catfish are also of higher quality, as are saltwater gafftopsail cats. You can also use any other fish you'd like in this recipe.

This recipe is for small cats, less than eighteen inches long. You steak the cats without skinning them, which saves a lot of work, because while there's more than one way to skin a cat, all are a pain. You do have to flake the meat off the bones as you're eating it, but it comes right off. The skin helps thicken the sauce. If this freaks you out, remove the skin. I won't hate you for it.

The flavor? Meaty, sweet, salty, a little spicy, with a sauce that begs to be spread over steamed rice.

You'll need Asian fish sauce for this recipe (page 307), but it's readily available in large supermarkets, and, obviously, in Asian markets. In a pinch, you can substitute Worcestershire, but it's really not the same. I also call for lard, which really makes a difference in flavor, but you can use oil if you must. Serve this with plain white rice and a beer.

---

2 teaspoons brown sugar

1 teaspoon black pepper

2 tablespoons molasses

2 tablespoons fish sauce

2 pounds catfish steaks

2 tablespoons lard

3 cloves garlic, slivered

3 scallions, cut into 1 inch lengths

1 or 2 hot chiles, such as Thai or
    serrano

Mix the brown sugar, black pepper, molasses, and fish sauce and coat the fish in it. Let this stand for 15 to 30 minutes.

In a pot just large enough to contain the fish, heat the lard over high heat and sauté the garlic, scallions, and chile for 2 minutes. Do not let them brown.

Add the catfish and all the marinade. Mix well, turn the heat down to medium-low, cover, and simmer for 10 minutes.

Pour in enough water to almost cover the catfish, then turn the heat to medium-high. Cook this uncovered until the sauce reduces by half, about 10 to 15 minutes. Be sure to turn the fish over a couple times so both sides get coated by the sauce.

Turn out the fish into a bowl, and serve with white rice. Have a bowl on the table for everyone's fish bones.

CRAB CURRY

PREP TIME: 15 MINUTES | **COOK TIME: 20 MINUTES** | **SERVES 4**

When life gives you crabs, sometimes you need to do something other than make crab cakes or just eat the meat with a little drawn butter, right? How about crab curry? This version is from Goa, in western India. Goan food is a combination of Indian and Portuguese, and culinarily speaking, it's one of the more exciting places to go.

This is a from-scratch curry—no premade curry powders—and while it looks complicated, it's not. Just have everything laid out before you start, and you can have this curry done in less than forty-five minutes.

You do need the tamarind in the recipe, however, as it is a defining feature of Goan curries; you can buy tamarind paste in Asian and Latin markets and online.

How spicy is this? Pretty spicy, although the chile heat can be adjusted depending on how many you put in the curry. I like it hot, so I put in four to five serranos, but you may want to use less.

Finally, if you don't have lots of crab around, there's no reason on earth not to do this curry with shrimp, lobster, or even a firm fish.

1 tablespoon coriander seeds

1 tablespoon black peppercorns

6 cloves

8 cardamom pods, or
   1 teaspoon ground

1 tablespoon turmeric

1 teaspoon ground cumin

2 teaspoons fenugreek (optional)

2 medium onions, 1 chopped fine
   and 1 sliced

2 tablespoons fresh ginger,
   minced

2 or 3 small fresh chiles, such as
   serrano or Thai, chopped

1 tablespoon vegetable oil or
   clarified butter

2 cloves garlic, minced

One 14-ounce can coconut milk

¼ cup grated coconut, fresh, if
   possible

1 heaping tablespoon
   tamarind paste

Salt

1 pound crabmeat

⅓ cup chopped cilantro

Make the curry mix by toasting the coriander, peppercorns, cloves, and cardamom pods in a dry skillet until they're fragrant and the coriander just starts popping. Take off the heat and let cool a minute or two and then grind fine in a mortar or spice grinder. Mix well with the turmeric, cumin, and fenugreek.

Sauté the chopped onion, the ginger, and the chiles in the same pan with the oil or butter until soft. Do not brown. Add the garlic and cook for another 2 minutes, stirring occasionally.

Take the onion mixture off the heat and put it into a blender. Add the curry spice mix to it, then about ¼ cup of water. Blend into a purée.

Pour the coconut milk into a pot and heat it over medium-high heat until it simmers. Add the sliced onion and grated coconut and let this cook for 3 to 4 minutes at an active simmer.

Add the curry from the blender and mix well, then add the tamarind paste and mix again. Taste for salt and add some if needed.

Mix in the crab and cook until just heated, maybe 2 to 3 minutes. Stir in the cilantro and serve over rice.

NOTE If you use ground versions of the spices, don't toast them.

THAI FISH CURRY

PREP TIME: 30 MINUTES | **COOK TIME: 30 MINUTES** | **SERVES 4**

There are lots of Thai curries of various colors, but I prefer to go green with fish and seafood. Pretty much anything goes with this curry in terms of protein, and I'm hard-pressed to think of a creature that won't taste good swimming in this sauce. I typically use California halibut, rockfish, lingcod, or leopard shark, all white-meat fish local to me. But I've made it with oily fish and salmon, too. And shrimp, crab, and lobster are classic. So have fun with it.

I'm giving you a recipe for homemade curry paste because I prefer it that way. I have Asian markets near my house, but many supermarkets sell Thai green curry paste in little jars, and the Mae Ploy brand is especially good. You can buy that in Asian markets or online.

This recipe makes more curry paste than you need, but it keeps in the fridge for several months.

CURRY PASTE

1 teaspoon ground cumin

1 teaspoon ground coriander

1 teaspoon black pepper

1 teaspoon white pepper

4 whole cloves, or ¼ teaspoon
    ground cloves

1 teaspoon salt

5 cloves garlic, coarsely chopped

½ cup minced shallot

1 bunch of rau ram or cilantro,
    about 1 cup chopped

Juice and zest of 2 limes

2 medium dried shrimp, or
    1 tablespoon shrimp paste
    (optional)

3 tablespoons minced galangal
    or ginger

1 stalk lemongrass, white and light
    green parts, minced

1 tablespoon fish sauce

Lots of green chiles (see method)

CURRY

2 tablespoons peanut
    or coconut oil

1 white onion, thinly sliced

6 ounces snow or sugar snap peas

4 tablespoons green curry paste

1 cup coconut milk

2 tablespoons sugar

3 tablespoons fish sauce

1½ pounds skinless, boneless fish,
    cut in chunks

Some chopped red chiles for color

½ cup Thai basil leaves

To make the curry paste, put everything in a food processor and buzz to combine. A word on the chiles, however. They give you a lot of the color in the paste, so you'll want a fair number. I've made this with about ½ cup of coarsely chopped green Thai chiles and it's fantastic, but very hot. If your heat tolerance isn't quite there yet, use a similar amount of serranos or jalapeños. Typically, you'll need to add around ¼ cup of water for the paste to come together fully. As I mention in the headnotes, this can be made well in advance.

To make the curry, heat the peanut or coconut oil in a pan over medium-high heat and sauté the onion until slightly browned on the edges, about 6 to 8 minutes. Add the snow peas, curry paste, coconut milk, sugar, and fish sauce and mix well. Simmer this gently for 5 minutes. Add the fish and red chiles into the pan and simmer another 5 minutes. Turn off the heat, mix in the Thai basil, and serve over jasmine rice.

"At high tide the fish eat ants;
at low tide the ants eat fish."

THAI PROVERB

SALMON HEAD SOUP

PREP TIME: 15 MINUTES | COOK TIME: 40 MINUTES | SERVES 6

Despite its gruesome sounding name, salmon head soup is actually a refined, Japanese-style miso soup with noodles. It doesn't even take very long to make, and this soup is so, so satisfying. You'll never toss those fish heads again. And while I prefer to use large salmon heads here, you can use this recipe to make a generic fish head soup by switching up the species. Cod and striped bass heads are common in the Northeast, grouper and snapper in the Gulf, lingcod and halibut in the Pacific. Inland, I'd use big pike or lake trout. All these are lean fish, however. Salmon heads make this a luxurious broth—it's the fat—so if you want to substitute other species that will give you a similar effect, try lake trout, large char or other trout, catfish, cobia, sturgeon, amberjack, or tuna.

Two important things to remember when you use salmon or other fatty fish: never let this broth boil, or it will get overly fishy and cloudy (think making a tea rather than boiling a soup); and it doesn't keep well. Eat your fish head soup that evening or the day after. Beyond that, things can get stinky.

You'll need some Japanese ingredients to make this dish, but they're not terribly hard to find—easy, actually, if you have an Asian community near you.

2 to 4 large salmon heads, gills
   removed

1 small onion chopped, about 1 cup

One 2-inch piece of dried kombu
   seaweed (optional)

One 3-inch piece of slivered ginger

Salt

¼ cup mirin (sweet rice
   cooking wine)

1 tablespoon soy sauce

Asian noodles (ramen, udon,
   or rice noodles)

3 tablespoons white miso paste

Chives and sliced chiles,
   for garnish

Wash the salmon heads well to remove any blood or gills. Gills will ruin the broth by making it bitter and cloudy. Cover the heads with water in a large pot or Dutch oven. Add the onion, kombu, and ginger and bring to a bare simmer. Do not let this boil. Simmer gently for 20 to 30 minutes.

Strain the broth and save the heads. Pick out all the meat from the heads, especially the cheek meat. Reserve in a bowl.

Return the broth to a clean pot and add the mirin. Heat but do not let boil. Add the soy sauce. If the broth still needs salt, add salt—not more soy sauce, as that will make the broth too dark.

Bring another pot of salted water to a boil. This is for the noodles. Cook the noodles according to the directions on the package.

Ladle out some broth into soup bowls. Add a heaping teaspoon of miso (or more) to each bowl and stir to combine. Portion out the noodles to each bowl. Add the salmon meat on top of the noodles. Each person should get at least one cheek. Cover with more broth, garnish with chives and sliced chiles, and serve at once.

◄ Roly-poly fish heads.

13
FRITTERS, CAKES, AND BALLS

I COULD HAVE included the dishes here with the leftover-fish recipes in chapter 16, since in many cases, you're using leftover, or at least previously flaked, fish or seafood. But there are enough examples of this sort of snack that don't rely on precooked fish that this deserves its own chapter.

Typically fried, these discs and globes of goodness can sometimes reach iconic heights—think Chesapeake crab cakes or conch fritters. But in most cases, they are simply a fantastic, accessible way to serve fish or seafood to the skeptical, or to start a larger seafood feast.

CRAB CAKES

PREP TIME: 30 MINUTES | **COOK TIME: 20 MINUTES** | **SERVES 6**

I'm pretty sure I'd be arrested if I did not include a crab cake recipe in a fish and seafood cookbook. Of the myriad versions of this icon of the mid-Atlantic states, I'm leaning heavily on one by my friend Bryan Voltaggio, of *Top Chef* fame, who happens to be a hunter and an angler from Maryland. My recipe differs slightly from his, but his was my inspiration.

1 pound crabmeat

1 sleeve Saltine crackers, pounded into meal

2 green onions, minced

¼ cup mayonnaise

1 egg

½ teaspoon salt

½ teaspoon hot sauce

2 teaspoons Old Bay seasoning

1 teaspoon Worcestershire sauce

1 teaspoon dry mustard

Grated zest and juice of a lemon

1 clove garlic, minced

½ cup Wondra flour

Oil for frying

HORSERADISH CREAM

½ cup sour cream

1 tablespoon prepared horseradish

2 tablespoons whole milk

Salt and black pepper

◄ Blue crabs ready for cracking, part of a Louisiana crab boil.

Mix everything together in a bowl except the crushed Saltines, Wondra flour, and oil.

To make the horseradish cream, mix everything together well. You can tinker with the ingredients as needed. Remember, you want to be able to drizzle this on, so it shouldn't be too thick.

Heat enough oil to come up about 1 inch up the sides of a heavy pan; I use cast iron. Heat it to between 325°F and 350°F.

While the oil is heating, add enough of the crushed Saltines so that the cakes will come together. Start with ¼ cup. You might need more, but you won't need less. Form the cakes with your clean hands—wetting them every so often helps a lot—and set them aside. Mix the remaining crushed Saltines with the Wondra flour.

When the oil hits temperature, coat the cakes in the flour-Saltines mix and fry until golden brown on both sides, about 3 to 4 minutes per side. Serve with a salad and some horseradish cream.

VARIATIONS These cakes can be made with pretty much anything. I do this with raw salmon "spoon meat," the meat scraped off the carcass, more than I do it with crab. Any fish will work here, so long as you chop or flake it. You can use precooked fish too, but I prefer using raw because the result comes out better. Chopped shrimp, lobster, or crayfish tails work, and while you could use clams, mussels, or oysters, I prefer the clam cake recipe on page 212.

SALMON PATTIES

PREP TIME: 25 MINUTES | **COOK TIME: 10 MINUTES** | **SERVES 4**

What's the difference between these salmon patties and a fish cake? To me, it's mostly a matter of the binder. Fish cakes to my mind have mashed potato or lots of bread or breadcrumbs in them, whereas patties are more meat-centric. Possibly it is a distinction without a difference. Who knows.

It's tricky to make a salmon patty that holds together without some sort of binder, however, so I do use a little bit of torn-up bread and one egg white—just enough to keep the patties moist and together. These still have a good feel to them, though.

This recipe has a Scandinavian feel to it, with a bit of sour cream and dill. Salmon + sour cream + dill = a perfect combination, to my mind. The little bit of sour cream in the patty helps keep it moister; dried out salmon patties are a sad thing, but all too common. I also go bunless, serving the patties with a zippy summer salad and topping everything with a little homemade salmon caviar. It's as close to spa food as I get—light, relatively low in fat, clean.

SALMON PATTIES

1½ pounds raw salmon meat

2 slices bread, crust removed and torn to bits

2 tablespoons minced onion

1 egg white

1 teaspoon white pepper

1 teaspoon salt

2 tablespoons sour cream

Zest of 2 lemons, grated

2 tablespoons dill, chopped

Salmon caviar (optional)

FENNEL-WATERCRESS SALAD

1 fennel bulb, thinly sliced

½ red onion, thinly sliced

Juice of 2 lemons

Salt and black pepper

1 cucumber, peeled if the skin is bitter

1 tablespoon pickled mustard seeds (optional)

2 teaspoons sugar

3 tablespoons sunflower, walnut, or squash seed oil

2 cups watercress

Either grind your salmon, the bread, and the onion through the fine die of the grinder (this is how I do it) or pulse it a few times in a food processor. Put the mixture in a bowl and mix in the egg white, white pepper, salt, sour cream, lemon zest, and dill. Form into patties. Put the patties in the fridge while you make the salad.

Toss the sliced fennel and red onion with a little salt and the lemon juice and let it marinate for 20 minutes. Cut the cucumber lengthwise and remove the seeds with a spoon. Slice it thinly and add it to the bowl with the fennel and onion. Stir in the pickled mustard seeds, black pepper, sugar, and sunflower oil and set aside.

I like to grill my salmon patties. Get your grill very hot and scrape down the grates with a wire brush. Dip a paper towel into some vegetable oil and use tongs to wipe down the grill grates. Set the salmon patties on the grill and cook with the grill cover up for about 3 minutes. Flip and grill for another 3 minutes or so.

When you're ready to serve, toss the watercress in with the rest of the salad and serve with the salmon patties. Top the patties with the salmon caviar if you have it.

FISH CAKES WITH WILD RICE

PREP TIME: 20 MINUTES | **COOK TIME: 15 MINUTES** | **SERVES 4**

Americans tend to reject fish with more bones than they think are appropriate. This is a shame, because many of these fish are fantastic to eat, once you deal with the bones. And making fish cakes is a prime way to do that. Pike, especially, is a wonderful fish. Very firm, very white, as mild to eat as it's fun to catch.

Whereas the crab cakes are mid-Atlantic and the salmon patties are Scandinavian, these fish cakes are firmly, solidly in the upper Midwest, or Manitoba if you're Canadian. The wild rice in the cakes is both native to the region and adds a bit of color and texture to the fish cakes. Just make sure you cook the wild rice completely before adding to the fish cakes, because the cakes cook up quickly.

Pike cakes are a natural because of the fish's many bones. True, it's not that hard to fillet a pike, and I have detailed instructions on page 45, but it's easier to fillet as normal, gently poach the fish, and flake the meat. You only need a half-pound for this recipe, so vacuum-seal any extra and freeze for later. You'll want to make these fish cakes again.

How do they taste? Just really good. There's no single overwhelming flavor, although you do pick up the mustard and the chives in every bite. The fish is mild, the mayo keeps everything moist, and the Worcestershire and lemon brighten things. This is good midwestern food without the blandness that mars that region's culinary reputation. And they're easy to make and can be done start to finish in thirty minutes, if you've precooked the wild rice. I often cook a batch then freeze it for when I need it. Do this, and you have a light, easy, thirty-minute meal.

Needless to say this recipe can be done with any white fish. Trout would also work well, here, especially Great Lakes lake trout or steelhead.

½ **pound cooked, flaked pike or other white fish**

1 **egg**

1 **cup breadcrumbs**

½ **cup cooked wild rice**

¼ **cup minced onion, red if you have one**

2 **tablespoons mayonnaise**

1 **tablespoon mustard, Dijon if you have it**

1 **tablespoon Worcestershire sauce**

1 **teaspoon lemon juice**

½ **teaspoon salt**

½ **teaspoon black pepper**

2 **tablespoons fresh chopped parsley**

1 **tablespoon fresh chopped chives**

¼ **cup butter, lard, or vegetable oil for cooking**

Greens for a salad

Make sure any little bones are out of the fish. Mix everything (except the butter and salad greens) together in a large bowl. Divide the mix into 8 roughly equal parts and form into patties. If you have time, set the patties on a cookie sheet in the fridge for 30 minutes to firm up. You can skip this step if you're rushed.

Fry the patties in the butter until golden brown, about 3 to 5 minutes per side. Serve with a green salad with a nice vinaigrette, or try my saffron aioli below.

SALT COD FRITTERS

PREP TIME: 1 HOUR | **COOK TIME: 30 MINUTES** | **SERVES 8**

Salt cod, bacalao, baccala, or bacalhau, it's all the same: codfish, salted down and air-dried to make it invulnerable to decay. Salt cod and its cousin stockfish (cod dried without salt) have been so important to world history there's even been a book written about it (Mark Kurlansky's *Cod: A Biography of the Fish that Changed the World*, a James Beard Award winner). You can buy salt cod in many supermarkets, especially around Christmas, or you can make your own with the instructions on page 305.

To eat salt cod, you must rehydrate it in many changes of water, which can take two days in the fridge. It will never fully rehydrate, but that texture change is what makes bacalao so special; rehydrated salt cod has much more of a meat-like texture than fresh codfish.

My all-time favorite way to eat bacalao is as these *buñuelos*, or fritters.

I have a history with salt cod fritters. Back in 2004, when I moved to NorCal, I was the capitol bureau chef of the *Stockton Record*. As such, I hung around the political bars. A lot. My favorite haunt was a place in Sacramento called Spataro's, after the chef, Kurt Spataro.

Much to my amazement, I saw on the menu a little appetizer of salt cod fritters, for just $3, no less! At the time, this was exotic in Sacramento, but I'd eaten them before in New England and elsewhere. Salty, crunchy on the outside, pillowy inside, almost always served with some sort of aioli or mayo. I don't know how many hundreds of salt cod fritters I ate while covering the political scene, but it was a lot.

My salt cod fritters are potato-based, and are more herby than most. I like that hit of fresh herbs. I serve them with a saffron aioli, but really any sauce that makes you happy would work.

One key to cooking your fritters is to have a cooling rack set on a baking sheet in the oven; set the oven to 225°F. Because the starches in potatoes brown quickly, you don't want to fully fry your fritters or they'll be unappetizingly dark. Better to fry until golden brown, set them on the rack in the oven to fully cook through.

They are crunchy on the outside, soft in the center, herby and meaty, and only vaguely fishy. Not bad for a slab of fish that sat uncovered in a fridge for almost a year, eh?

In theory, you can make these fritters from any cooked, flaked fish, but they are best with shredded, rehydrated bacalao. Once fried, these are great the next day, either fried again to reheat, or in a 350°F toaster oven for about 20 minutes.

»

> "He who wants to catch fish
> must not mind getting wet."
>
> SPANISH PROVERB

½ pound flaked, reconstituted salt cod

1 russet potato, peeled and cut into 1-inch chunks

4 cloves garlic, minced

1 tablespoon lard or butter

¼ cup minced fresh herbs (parsley, chives, basil)

⅓ cup flour

1 egg, lightly beaten

¼ teaspoon baking powder

Salt and black pepper

Oil for frying

SAFFRON AIOLI

Large pinch of saffron threads

2 tablespoons hot water

2 cloves garlic, minced

2 teaspoons lemon juice or white wine vinegar

1 teaspoon salt

1 or 2 egg yolks

¾ cup olive oil

To make the aioli, which can be done a few days in advance, crumble the saffron threads into the hot water in a small bowl. Let them steep 10 minutes.

In the bowl of a blender, briefly buzz the garlic, lemon juice, salt, and egg yolks to combine. Add the saffron and the water and buzz until smooth. With the motor running, drizzle in the olive oil until the whole thing emulsifies into a mayonnaise-like consistency. Taste for salt and acid, adding a little lemon juice and salt if needed.

To make the fritters, pulse the salt cod in a food processor until it's finely shredded. Boil the potato in salty water until it's tender, about 15 minutes. Drain and set the pot back on the stovetop over low heat. Return the drained potatoes to the pot and let them steam for a minute or so; this prevents the mashed potatoes from being soggy. Mash them very well. Alternatively, run the cooked potatoes through a ricer or a food mill.

Sauté the garlic in the lard or butter until it just barely begins to color, about 2 minutes. Let this cool a bit and add it to a large bowl with the salt cod and mashed potatoes. Add in the herbs and flour and mix well.

Once the mixture is cool, mix in the egg and baking powder, and add salt and black pepper to taste. If you're averse to tasting a mixture with raw egg, taste before you add it. Let this mixture chill in the refrigerator for at least 30 minutes and up to overnight.

Get at least 2 inches of oil hot in a heavy pot, or use a deep-fryer. You want the oil about 350°F. As the oil is heating, scoop out a tablespoon of the salt cod mixture and roll it into a ball. Line up these balls on a cutting board so you have them ready to go. Set a cooling rack on a baking sheet and set that in the oven. Set the oven to 225°F.

Fry the fritters for about 3 minutes each, or until they are golden brown. Move them to the rack in the oven to keep cooking a bit. Once your last fritters are in the oven, wait 5 minutes before serving.

CONCH FRITTERS

PREP TIME: 30 MINUTES | **COOK TIME: 20 MINUTES** | **SERVES 8**

Conch fritters are to the Florida Keys what crab cakes are to the Chesapeake: iconic, ubiquitous, with as many variations as there are cooks. Conch is a giant snail that lives in the Caribbean, similar to northern whelks, which can be substituted. There is a distinct Caribbean flair to these, and they are often served with Calypso sauce, which is, more or less, a standard habanero hot sauce of puréed chiles, onion, garlic, lime, dry mustard, vinegar, and maybe a little rum.

I love these fritters spicy. Unlike everything else in this chapter, these are supposed to have a kick to them, with no need for sauce. Of course, you can reduce the chiles if you need to. But it needs to have something, even if jalapeños scare you.

One vital aspect of a conch fritter is that the conch needs to be ground. Chopping isn't enough, because the meat is so tough. If you don't have a grinder, pound the conch very thin, to the point where it's ripping in places, and then mince it as fine as you can.

Any shellfish will work here, and I imagine you could use finfish too, though I've not tried it myself.

1½ cups conch meat, ground fine

1 cup flour

2 teaspoons baking powder

1 egg, lightly beaten

½ cup milk

A pinch of dried thyme

Salt and pepper

1 cup minced white or
   yellow onion

1 cup minced green pepper,
   Anaheim, or poblano

1 to 3 Scotch bonnet or
   habanero chiles, minced

2 cloves garlic, minced

1 tablespoon ketchup or
   tomato paste

3 tablespoons chopped cilantro
   or parsley

Oil for frying

Mix everything but the fryer oil in a large bowl. It's a wet batter, so you'll need either wet hands to roll them into a ball or a spoon to dole out batter by the tablespoon or so.

Heat your oil in a deep-fryer or large, heavy pot to 325°F. You want the oil deep enough to submerge the fritters. Set a cooling rack over a baking sheet in the oven, and turn the oven to "warm."

Gently drop your fritters into the hot oil, a few at a time. After a second or three, use a chopstick or butter knife to dislodge any that have stuck to the bottom of the pot. Fry until golden, about 3 minutes, then move to the oven while you make more.

Serve hot. If you have any leftovers, they can be refried a little to reheat, or they can be heated in a toaster oven at 350°F for 15 minutes.

CLAM CAKES

PREP TIME: 15 MINUTES | COOK TIME: 15 MINUTES | SERVES 8

This is the New England version of those conch fritters above. And if you think they're just like crab cakes or fish cakes, only with clams, you would be terribly, tragically wrong. Because as much as I like crab cakes, a true Rhode Island–style clam cake is so, so much more.

Think clam beignet, or donut hole. Only savory. Crispy, golden brown on the outside, pillowy and light on the inside. Steam rises from the first bite. The slightest aroma of brine surrounds you. Tiny chunks of clam nestle themselves in the folds of the pillow, offering surprising bites of chewy meatiness as you down one of these little glories after another. And another.

With the possible exception of the Pacific Northwest, no region can boast mastery of the humble clam like New England. And within New England, it is Rhode Island that does it best. I have never seen these clam cakes any other place. They are a masterpiece of street food. To me, they are why you arrive early at the port of Galilee to await the Block Island ferry.

When I was a boy, I was partial to gigantic plates of fried clams (page 128). When I grew a little older, I discovered these clam cakes. They are to me the gateway food of Block Island, which is the place I learned to forage and the place whose natural beauty I still hold closest to my heart.

Normally, Rhode Island clam cakes are served with Tabasco and tartar sauce. But I could not keep thinking about how much these were like New Orleans beignets. So I decided to break from Rhode Island tradition and add a little bit of the Big Easy to this recipe: remoulade.

This recipe is best made with freshly ground clams, although it would still be good with finely chopped clams. Canned would be OK, and better to make it with canned than not at all, but please, please, please make this at least once with fresh clams. You will not be sorry.

Use cake flour if you can get it; it will make a lighter, fluffier cake. All-purpose is fine if you can't find cake flour. Use a "regular" beer, not a fancy one. Think Budweiser. Be sure to keep your oil as close to 350°F as you can. The cakes will come out greasy if your oil gets too cool. Fry in batches to prevent this.

Remoulade (page 123)

Canola or other vegetable oil
    for frying

3 beaten eggs

½ cup buttermilk

½ cup clam broth

½ cup cold beer

2 teaspoons maple syrup

1½ cups chopped or ground clams

1 teaspoon salt

2½ teaspoons baking powder

3½ cups cake flour, or
    all-purpose flour

Make the remoulade first and set aside. Heat the oil to 350°F.

Mix all the liquid ingredients together except the beer. Mix all the dry ingredients together. When your oil is hot, add the beer to the liquid ingredients and mix gently. Stir in the dry ingredients just until combined.

Drop a tablespoon of batter into the hot oil at a time. Do not crowd the pot. Let them sizzle for 30 seconds or so, then dislodge any that are stuck to the bottom with a chopstick or wooden skewer. Fry until golden brown on both sides, about 5 minutes.

Drain on paper towels and serve while hot with the remoulade, Tabasco or tartar sauce. And beer. Lots of beer.

VARIATIONS Obviously you can use oysters too, but finely ground or chopped whelk, conch, squid, octopus, cuttlefish, or shrimp would all be excellent alternatives. Can you use fish? Of course, but it would be different.

SICILIAN TUNA MEATBALLS

PREP TIME: 30 MINUTES | **COOK TIME: 30 MINUTES** | **SERVES 6**

Tuna is a staple in the Mediterranean diet, and just as with other meats, little is wasted. Meatballs made from scraps of tuna appear in several cultures, but the Sicilians seem to eat them the most. This recipe is an amalgam of about a dozen I've read, and it works well either as a stand-alone dish or, American-style, served with tomato sauce and spaghetti. If you don't tell anyone, many of your guests will think they're made from beef or pork.

If you can't get fresh tuna (you cannot use canned tuna here), use salmon, trout, amberjack, yellowtail, mackerel, bluefish, king mackerel, wahoo, or any dark, fatty fish.

½ cup chopped fresh mint

⅓ cup shelled pistachios
    or pine nuts, chopped

1 cup minced onion

⅔ cup breadcrumbs

1½ pounds tuna

Zest of 1 lemon

1 tablespoon salt

1 egg

Flour for dusting

Olive oil for frying

FENNEL-TOMATO SAUCE

4 tablespoons olive oil

1 cup fennel, finely chopped

½ onion, finely chopped

Salt

1 clove garlic, chopped

¼ cup ouzo, or other
    anise-flavored liqueur

1 quart tomato sauce, crushed
    tomatoes, or chopped fresh
    tomatoes

1 tablespoon honey

1 tablespoon mint or lemon
    verbena, chopped

To make the sauce, heat the olive oil over medium-high heat in a wide, deep pan or a large pot. When the oil is hot, add the fennel and onion and sauté for 4 to 5 minutes, until translucent. Sprinkle salt over everything. Don't let the vegetables brown—turn down the heat if you need to. Add the garlic and sauté for another minute or two.

Pour in the ouzo and let this boil until it is reduced by half. Add the tomatoes, honey, and mint and mix well. Taste for salt and add some if needed. Let this simmer gently for 30 minutes.

Puréeing the sauce in a blender makes a better sauce for long pasta like spaghetti, but if you're going to serve this sauce with short pasta, like penne or bowties, you can skip this step.

To make the meatballs, chop the tuna into ½-inch pieces. Put the tuna, mint, pistachios, and the onion in a food processor and pulse to combine. You want a rough mixture, not a smooth paste. Put the tuna mixture into a large bowl with the breadcrumbs, lemon zest, salt, and egg and mix well with your clean hands for a minute or so. You want everything combined well and you want the proteins in the egg and tuna to bind the mixture.

Using an ice cream scoop or large spoon to scoop out the meat, roll into meatballs. You should be able to make about 20 golf ball–sized meatballs. Roll each meatball in flour and fry in enough olive oil to come halfway up the sides of a large frying pan. You will probably need about 1 cup. Fry gently until browned over medium heat, about 15 minutes, and set each finished meatball on paper towels to drain.

To finish, stew the meatballs in the tomato sauce until heated through, about 5 to 10 minutes, and serve alone or with pasta.

The meatballs can be made a day ahead; once cooked, they'll store in the fridge for a couple days or in the freezer for a couple months.

GERMAN FISH MEATBALLS

PREP TIME: 30 MINUTES | COOK TIME: 15 MINUTES | SERVES 4

I got the inspiration for this recipe from the always inspirational Mimi Sheraton, whose book *The German Cookbook: A Complete Guide to Mastering Authentic German Cooking* is a masterpiece. The fish meatballs could not be simpler: ground fish (of any type), mixed with egg, breadcrumbs, and herbs. Poached very gently in salty water, they come out light and fluffy. The green sauce adds several layers of flavor to round things out.

You should know that this is not a traditional Hessian green sauce, which has crushed up hard-boiled eggs in it or sometimes mayonnaise. My version is lighter, and it's much better for the kind of hot days we get here in Sacramento. But I really like the German tradition of using lots of different herbs to make the sauce, so I kept that in my rendition.

It is a lovely, light supper. The fish is moist and almost bouncy, the sauce an equal combination of buttery goodness, tangy creaminess from the sour cream, and a rat-a-tat jolt of the various bitter-sweet-aromatic herbs as you taste each one. As a main course, I'd serve this with new potatoes or bread. But it would be fantastic alone as a summertime appetizer.

Keep in mind that pretty much any fish will work, but the Germans do this a lot with freshwater fish like pike, perch, and the like. Similarly, feel free to mix and match herbs to your liking. Other good candidates for the sauce would be tarragon, thyme, radish or turnip greens, watercress, basil, borage, lovage . . . you get the point.

»

FISH BALLS

1 pound ground fish

2 eggs, lightly beaten

2 teaspoons salt

6 tablespoons plain breadcrumbs

2 teaspoons minced fresh dill

2 teaspoons minced fresh parsley

GREEN SAUCE

¼ cup unsalted butter

1 large shallot, about ⅓ cup, minced

1 cup fish stock or chicken stock

2 tablespoons minced spinach, amaranth, or lamb's-quarters

¼ cup chopped sorrel (optional)

¼ cup minced parsley

2 tablespoons chopped dill

2 tablespoons minced garlic chives or regular chives

1 sage leaf, minced

Salt and black pepper

½ cup sour cream, at room temperature

To make the meatballs, simply mix all the ingredients in a bowl and form into small meatballs, about the size of a walnut. To cook, bring a large pot of salty water to a boil and gently lower the fish balls one at a time into the water. They will sink. Turn the heat down to a bare simmer—if you let it boil again, it can destroy your fish balls. Simmer gently until the meatballs float. Look for a total cooking time of about 10 minutes or so.

Remove the fish balls from the hot water and set aside.

While you're heating the poaching water, make the green sauce. Heat the butter in a large sauté pan over medium-high heat. When it's hot, add the shallot and sauté until it's translucent and soft, about 3 minutes or so. Don't let them brown. Add the stock and bring to a boil. Boil hard for a few minutes until the sauce reduces by about one-third.

Turn the heat as low as it will go and stir in all the herbs. Let them all wilt. Add salt and black pepper to taste and turn the heat off.

When all the fish balls are ready, turn the heat back on under the sauce to warm it, and coat the fish balls with the sauce. When the sauce boils again, turn off the heat, let the bubbling subside, and add the sour cream, stirring constantly. Adjust for salt and black pepper once more and serve at once.

"Fish without wine is like egg without salt."

AUGUSTE ESCOFFIER

PIKE QUENELLES

PREP TIME: 30 MINUTES | **COOK TIME: 20 MINUTES** | **SERVES 6**

Pike quenelles or dumplings are an ancient preparation in Europe, dating back at least to the Renaissance. It makes perfect sense if you've ever worked with pike. They're a bony fish, and they require some special handling. This recipe modernizes the venerable quenelle and serves it in an unexpected-but-rockin' broth. A quenelle (keh-NELL) is just a dumpling made with two spoons. You can, of course, just make little balls out of the mashed pike, but these look more refined and are not hard to make.

Most recipes for fish quenelles would have you serve them in über-rich sauces that involve cream or cheese or both and are just impossibly heavy, at least to me. That said, the Germans do another thing with their myriad dumplings: they serve them in clear broths. The obvious choice would be a fish broth, but I developed this mushroom broth, and it's a winner. This is a dark, rich umami bomb. You'd think it would overpower the light fish, but they balance. The quenelles tame the broth a bit, and the broth boosts the dumplings, which are subtle.

You'd get a whole different experience if you changed the broth, which I encourage you to do if you make this recipe several times. The dumplings become the canvas to paint on. Served with, say, a fish fumet or a carrot consommé, it'd be a very light soup course. This mushroom broth makes it a main course.

The bottom line is that this dumpling recipe can be your go-to not only with pike, but with any bony fish, or really with any fish where you can't get a nice clean fillet—perch, panfish, small catfish, carp, you name it. And orange dumplings made with salmon are cool.

You can play with the seasonings, too. Add some minced fresh herbs. Skip the nutmeg and white pepper and go with something exciting—maybe mustard or freshly grated horseradish? Or even zippier: cayenne or chipotle powder and cilantro. Have fun. Play.

»

DUMPLINGS

2 slices white bread, crusts
removed

1 cup whole milk

1 pound pike meat, or any fish

1 egg white

About 1½ teaspoons salt

½ teaspoon white pepper
(optional)

A few gratings of nutmeg,
about ¼ teaspoon

BROTH

1 carrot, peeled and chopped

2 stalks celery, chopped

1 small onion, chopped,
about 1 cup

1 tablespoon olive oil

3 cloves garlic, black or roasted

½ to 1 ounce dried morel
mushrooms

½ to 1 ounce dried porcini
mushrooms

¼ to ½ ounce black trumpet
mushrooms (optional)

1 quart broth (chicken, duck,
vegetable)

3 cups water

Soy sauce

Start with the broth. Sauté the carrot, celery, and onion in the olive oil until they're soft and the onion is translucent, about 5 to 7 minutes. Add the garlic cloves and mash them into the vegetables.

Add the mushrooms and pour over the broth and the water. Bring to a simmer, cover the pot, and simmer gently for at least 90 minutes; 2 hours is better. Strain the broth through a paper towel set in a fine-meshed strainer into a bowl. Season it with the soy sauce. Pour into a clean pot and keep warm.

To make the dumplings, soak the crustless bread in the milk for a bit, and then mash it into a paste with a fork. Run the fish through the fine die of a meat grinder, or chop it coarsely and buzz it into bits with a food processor; don't let it become a paste, though.

Mix the fish into the bread paste with the remaining dumpling ingredients. Bring a large pot of salted water to a boil. Form quenelles or little balls of the pike mixture—use teaspoons for soups like this, tablespoons for serving by themselves—and drop them into the boiling water. When the dumplings float, cook them for a minute more and then put them in the bottom of soup bowls.

When all the dumplings are made and in the bowls, bring the broth to a bare simmer and pour over the dumplings in the bowls. Garnish with something green, like parsley, chervil, chives, or lovage.

▶ A basket of beeliners, off the coast of Mississippi in the Gulf of Mexico.

14

GRILLIN' AND CHILLIN'

THIS CHAPTER DEALS with all aspects of outdoor cooking except slow smoking, which is in its own chapter (chapter 18, page 288). Let me start by noting that grilling is not barbecue. Grilling is hot direct heat, and barbecue is low indirect heat. Both work for fish and seafood. But if I had to pick just one, it would be grilling. Because fish and seafood are so delicate, relative to meat from mammals or birds, a shorter time on the fire is better, with a few exceptions. Direct grilling also creates the crispy char that we all love, which adds a significant layer of flavor on often mild meats. Most fish and seafood can be grilled or barbecued, even small, delicate fish like sardines, which are, arguably, best eaten after being grilled over a hot, smoky fire. But as a general rule, the more delicate the fish, the more it needs to be intact to grill. It's nearly impossible to grill, say, a flounder fillet without it breaking or drying it out hopelessly. But you can grill a whole flounder, even a small one like a sand dab.

You might think that shellfish aren't good on a grill, and you'd be correct if you were talking about shucked shellfish. But slapping a dozen oysters on the grill until they open up, then giving them a minute or three with some thick, aromatic smoke, is a wonderful way to serve them. Clams, too.

You do need to watch out when grilling crabs, lobsters, and crayfish. All can be grilled with good success, but if you let them go too far and the shells blacken, it can impart a bitter flavor to the meat inside. So keep an eye on it.

Another general tip when grilling whole fish is to cook them a little longer than you think you need to. This is because you want the flesh to easily come off the bones, and the sacrifice you make in perfectly cooked meat is offset by skin that is even more smoky-crispy-crunchy than it would have been otherwise.

TIPS TO KEEP FISH FROM STICKING

The smaller the fish, the hotter the grill. Sardines need fiendishly hot grills, big bass less so. The idea is to cook the fish through and crisp the skin at roughly the same time. Smaller fish cook faster, and so they need higher heat to achieve this.

▶ Always have clean grill grates. This is the number one issue with fish sticking. Clean your grates, people!

▶ Wait for the grates to be hot before putting fish on. This is key when grilling, not as important with slow barbecue.

▶ Slick the grates and the fish with oil right before putting them on.

▶ Don't mess with the fish. Flip only once. It will release eventually, and you can test it with a fish spatula or some other thin metal spatula, but you want the fish to be almost completely released before flipping. Patience!

"I'm going to gut you like a fish."

MIKE TYSON

BRINING YOUR FISH BEFORE GRILLING

Although I don't often brine grilled whole fish, I do brine-grilled Fish on the Half Shell (page 230) and Barbecued Fish (page 228). Brining fish that are about to hit a hot grill does help the flesh retain moisture, but it can limit your ability to achieve that perfect crispy skin, which is why I typically avoid it for the whole grilled fish; the skin is a big part of the feast. You have to decide what's more important to you. You don't need to brine very long or use a strong brine. My go-to is two tablespoons of Diamond Crystal kosher salt to one quart of water, for about four hours. Any longer and you run the risk of the fish getting too salty. When you're done, rinse, pat dry, and slick it up with oil.

Grill baskets are useful, but not necessary. They're very nice for open fire cooking, but not needed on a proper grill. Grill baskets are also persnickety to clean. I'd only suggest them if you do a lot of open fire cooking.

Most people skewer a fish through the mouth, running it under the backbone in the cavity, then through the meat below the backbone and out the tail. This is a pretty good setup, but it's not as good as a Japanese method that uses three bamboo skewers. In this configuration, you angle the three skewers perpendicular to the fish so that they come together on one side, usually the belly. What this does is prevent the fish (or squid or octopus) from spinning on the skewer, and by angling them together you have a handle to flip the fish easily.

Even better is when you butterfly a fish (page 53), so you can then skewer it using the Japanese method, going in and out of the fish's flesh, keeping it flat. This is my preferred method for skewering small fish. And butterflying is very much like spatchcocking a chicken.

GRILLED WHOLE FISH

PREP TIME: 20 MINUTES | **COOK TIME: 15 MINUTES** | **SERVES 4**

Why grill whole fish? Several reasons. First, they look fantastic. Second, cooked properly, a grilled whole fish will stay together better than a grilled piece of fish. Third, you get crispy charred bits, which we all know and love. Finally, and probably most importantly, you get to eat more of the fish by wasting less. You get the collar, the cheeks, and those amazingly nutty tail fins (I'm serious. Try a crispy tail fin and tell me I'm crazy. I dare you).

You can grill almost any whole fish, but in general, the best fish to grill whole are bass-like fish that have substantial skeletons and relatively thick skins: porgies and sheepshead, Pacific rockfish, black seabass, walleyes, snapper, croakers, sea trout, smallmouth bass, and the like.

Here are some tips:

▸ Size. You will have to flip the fish on the grill, so I generally won't grill a whole fish larger than about twenty inches.

▸ They need to be scaled, gutted, and gilled. Gills impart an off taste to the fish and must be removed. Crispy fish skin is amazing, so you want to be able to eat it.

▸ Slice the fish several times perpendicular to the backbone—this opens the fish to heat better, so it cooks evenly. Three to five slashes are good.

▸ Coat them in oil and only salt . . . for now.

▸ Flipping a whole grilled fish is an art, but not a hard one to master. If your fish is well oiled, your grates are clean, and you happen to have one of those long flat spatulas that short-order cooks use to flip pancakes and eggs and burgers and such, you're in business. Two regular spatulas work, too.

After the fish are grilled, you can add more flavors if you like. A salsa or vinaigrette is fun, as is barbecue sauce. But for me, it's mostly just a hit of lemon and black pepper.

A tip: Peel the skin off the top side of the fish, set it aside, and place the fish so the now-skinless side faces down on the platter. This way you have saved more crispy skin for people to eat. If you don't do this, the skin facing down will get soggy and sad.

»

1 or 2 whole fish, scaled, gutted,
    and with gills removed

Olive oil

Salt

Lemon

Freshly ground black pepper

Wash the fish well and make 3 to 5 slashes in the meat perpendicular to the backbone on each side of the fish. You are doing this to open the interior of the fish to the heat, so it will cook more evenly. Make more slashes closer to the head, where the fish is thicker, than toward the tail, which cooks first. Snip off any sharp fins with kitchen shears or scissors if you want. Leave the tail, as it will crisp up and taste wonderfully nutty. Seriously. Try it.

Coat the fish with olive oil and salt it a little more than you think you ought to; salty fish tastes good! Let the fish sit at room temperature for 20 minutes to an hour.

Get your grill crazy hot, at least 500°F, and scrape the grill grates well to clean them. When you're ready to lay the fish down, dip a paper towel in some oil and grab it with tongs. Wipe down the grill with the oily towel and then immediately lay the fish down on the grill grates. Let them sizzle nicely for a minute or so.

Turn the heat down to medium and cover the grill if you have a gas grill, or just leave the fish on the open grill if you're using wood or charcoal and the grill is very hot. Let the fish cook for a total of 5 to 10 minutes on this side, depending on how thick it is. As a general rule, fish will need 10 minutes per inch of thickness. Estimate this thickness measuring to the fish's spine; remember, you're flipping the fish.

To turn the fish, have your tongs in your off hand and a big spatula in your dominant hand. Gently turn the fish over. It should come off the grates cleanly. If not, *don't force it*. Let the fish back down and wait another minute or two. Now come back at it with the spatula, using pressure to pry it off the grates. You don't want to pull the fish away from the grates and have half the skin and meat stick to the grill. Once the fish is flipped, let it cook for another 5 to 10 minutes.

Once the fish is ready—check by making sure the meat is fully cooked at the spot closest to the bone in the slash that is closest to the head of the fish—put it on a platter and serve, with a sauce or without.

GRILLED FISH STEAKS

PREP TIME: 15 MINUTES | **COOK TIME: 20 MINUTES** | **SERVES 4**

In general, you grill fish steaks the same way you grill beef steaks, which is to say hot and fast, possibly rare at the center, flipping only once. Most of us are looking for pretty grill marks, and if you want them, let your fish sit on the grill for a minute or two longer than you think it should. How long? Depends on how hot your grill is, but about ten minutes per inch of thickness, and if it's me, every fish steak is at least an inch thick. If you suspect that you left the fish on a bit too long to get the grill marks and you're worried about overcooking, paint the top with a bit more oil, and when you flip it, place it on a clean spot on the grill—and cook it only half as long.

This is a simple recipe from Sicily for a nicely grilled tuna steak with an easy-to-make summertime salad. Tuna is a major part of Mediterranean cuisine, although Mediterranean fishing has hit resident tuna populations hard. Fortunately, yellowfin, blackfin, albacore, and skipjack are all good choices here in North America—even bonito would work. But whatever species of tuna you choose, slice out the very dark centerline of meat; it's perfectly edible, but it has a strong, fishy flavor most people don't like. Cats, though, won't say no.

Doneness is a personal choice. I love the "black and blue" technique with tuna, where the outside is nicely cooked but the center is still raw, even cool. Many Europeans hate this, however, and if you do, too, go ahead and cook the tuna longer over lower heat.

A grill is important here, but you could sear the tuna in a pan if you had to. I just like the flavor that charcoal or wood brings to the dish. It turns humdrum tuna into something special, and the smoky flavor really completes a dish that has it all. This salad is spectacular, folks. Salty, sweet, tart, herby, savory.

Any sort of fish you can steak will work here; I used yellowfin I caught off San Diego. If you don't have access to good fresh tuna, salmon steaks, sturgeon, shark, swordfish, marlin, and monkfish all work here.

You definitely want good bread to serve with this, but grilled potatoes would be another option, as would steamed rice. To drink, a big white wine like a chardonnay would be good, as would the hot-weather whites from the Rhone, like viognier. Obviously, Sicilian whites are a great choice if you can get them. A dry rosé is another great choice. As for beer, this is lager or pilsner food, but a lighter-bodied pale ale would be another good choice.

»

"If the fish had not opened its mouth,
it would not have been caught."

PROVERB

FISH

1 to 2 pounds tuna steaks

Salt

Olive oil to coat fish

SICILIAN SALAD

1 small onion, thinly sliced
   from root to tip

¼ cup extra virgin olive oil

1 clove garlic, minced

2 Roma or plum tomatoes, diced

15 to 20 black olives, pitted
   and halved

15 to 20 green olives, pitted
   and halved

2 or 3 roasted red peppers, diced

1 tablespoon capers

Salt and black pepper

1 teaspoon dried chopped
   oregano, or 2 teaspoons fresh

2 tablespoons chopped fresh basil

2 tablespoons chopped fresh mint
   (optional)

Salt the tuna steaks and set aside while you chop the vegetables for the salad.

To make the salad, sauté the sliced onion in 2 tablespoons of olive oil over high heat until they brown a bit on the edges, about 4 minutes or so. Add the garlic, cook another 30 seconds or so, then turn off the heat. Add the tomatoes, olives, roasted red peppers, and capers to the pan and toss to combine. Add the remaining olive oil and salt and black pepper to taste; you might not need more salt, as the olives and capers are salty. When the salad has cooled a bit, toss in the oregano, basil, and mint.

When you're ready to cook the fish, get your grill nice and hot and clean the grates well. Pat the tuna dry and coat with oil. Using tongs, grab a crumpled piece of paper towel you've dipped in some vegetable oil and wipe down the grill grates.

Grill the tuna for at least 2 minutes per side, depending on how thick the pieces are and how well-done you like your tuna. Grind some black pepper over the fish. Slice it crosswise and serve atop the salad with some crusty bread and a good white or rosé wine.

CUTTING FISH STEAKS

I don't know why fish steaks aren't more popular. They were, back in the 1980s, but for some reason, the gods of taste turned from them. A fish steak can be something special; it holds together well since it will have the skin on it, the meat will be more tender than a fillet because of the bone, and you get a taste of everything the fish has to offer—belly meat, prime fillet, and those little pockets of fat near the dorsal fin.

Any large fish can be made into steaks. We mostly see salmon, swordfish, tuna, and shark steaks, but I've made them with catfish, big red drum, cobia, striped bass, lingcod, and halibut.

If you ask for them, or cut them yourself, please, for the love of all that's holy, cut them no thinner than an inch thick. This is America, and we deserve big, thick, juicy steaks—no matter what animal they came from.

BARBECUED FISH

PREP TIME: 30 MINUTES | **COOK TIME: 45 MINUTES** | **SERVES 4**

Barbecued fish. Two words you don't hear together a lot. That's a shame, because fish cooked slow and low over smoky heat is an unquestionably great way to eat them. The technique is simple. Brine fish for four hours up to overnight in a solution of two tablespoons kosher salt to one quart of water; freshwater fish should get three tablespoons of salt. If you're barbecuing fillets, salt them and put them into the fridge for thirty minutes before cooking.

Keep the skin and scales on the fillet, like you're doing redfish on the half shell (page 230), and for the same reason: the skin and especially the scales will protect the fish from the heat and allow you to really go slow and low. If you have whole fish or a pre-scaled fillet, you will still be fine, just be sure to thoroughly oil the skin and the grill grates.

At their purest form, you will taste fish, and smoke, and a little salt; this is how I cook whole fish. I will then either flake off the meat and use it in something else, like a taco or a salad like the Vietnamese Smoked Fish Salad on page 260 or present it on a platter for people to pick off. It's a dramatic presentation.

And this method, to my mind, is how you "smoke" lean fish like walleyes, bass, snapper, Pacific rockfish, or seabass. Because they lack fat, none are great smoked in the traditional way. But if your aim is simply to cook them to regular doneness in a slow, smoky fire, they can shine.

With fillets, you can barbecue them in a more traditional way, that is, with a sauce or rub. A really robust sauce like a Kansas City–style BBQ sauce might be too much for most fish but just right for, say, a strongly flavored fish like bluefish, king mackerel, amberjack, or tuna. More often, I'll use a mustard-based South Carolina BBQ sauce, which works really well with fish. Only apply your sauce once. Too much sauce overpowers the fish.

Wood choice is up to you. Fish is not barbecued for hours and hours, so the smoke flavor is mild.

---

2 whole fish, scaled and gutted, or 4 fish fillets, skin and scales left on

Salt

Vegetable oil for greasing the skin of the fish

½ cup BBQ sauce of your choice (optional)

Follow the salting procedure I mention in the headnote. Clean your grill grates well. Preheat the grill to anywhere from 200°F to 225°F.

When you're ready to barbecue, slick the skin of the fish with some vegetable oil. Do this from the head end of the fillet toward the tail, so you're going with the grain of the scales if they're still there.

Paint the flesh side of the fillets with the BBQ sauce of your choice (if you're using it), or give it a nice dusting of a barbecue rub you like. If you want to stay simple, grind some black pepper on it.

Set the fillets skin-side down in the grill, cover the grill, and cook as slowly as you can stand. A thin, ½-inch fillet, barbecued at 200°F, will be perfect in 45 minutes. A whole fish can take up to three hours at very low temperatures. Remember: slower is better, so you get more smoky flavor. It's ready when the meat flakes easily.

Serve your fish on the skin—you eat it by picking the meat off the skin with a fork—with some lemon or lime wedges, a nice vegetable, and either rice or potato salad.

FISH ON THE HALF SHELL

PREP TIME: 90 MINUTES | **COOK TIME: 20 MINUTES** | **SERVES 4**

Redfish on the half shell is a classic Gulf Coast dish, and it is easily translatable to many other kinds of fish. As bass-like fish tend to grow large, their meat gets coarse, and their scales get big. Just like a bull redfish. This can make them challenging to cook, but the Gulf anglers' technique of redfish on the half shell is the answer. You fillet the fish, but *leave the skin and scales on.* You do this with redfish because the scales on a drum of any color, red or black, are big and tough.

Why leave the scales on? Because that armor shields the meat, allowing you to set the fish, ideally coated in Cajun seasoning, on a smoky grill and allow it to cook to perfection without destroying it. When it's ready, you slide a spatula under the meat but above the skin, and the meat will slip off, leaving the charred skin and scales. And since the scales are basically made of the same stuff as your fingernails, they won't stick to your grill too badly, so you can take the whole thing off if you want. It's a genius preparation for big fillets. Try it with any large bass, snapper, tripletail, grouper, big black seabass, or sheepshead, and of course black and red drum.

I brine the fish in this case, because it helps it retain more moisture as it cooks. You don't have to, but it's a nice insurance policy against drying out the fish.

FISH

2 tablespoons kosher salt

1 quart water

2 to 3 pounds large fish fillets, with the skin and scales still on

3 tablespoons vegetable oil

2 to 3 tablespoons Cajun seasoning

3 tablespoons unsalted butter

CAJUN SEASONING

1 teaspoon black pepper

½ to 1 teaspoon cayenne pepper

1 teaspoon celery seed

2 tablespoons sweet paprika

1 tablespoon garlic powder

1 tablespoon dried thyme

1 tablespoon dried oregano

Mix the salt and water until the salt dissolves. Brine the fish in the fridge for 1 hour. Remove, pat dry with paper towels, and put on a rack in a cool, breezy place for 30 minutes. While you're doing this, get your grill nice and hot.

When your grill is ready, coat the fish with the vegetable oil, then sprinkle the meat side of the fish with the Cajun seasoning. Lay the fish on the grill with the fat side of the fillet over the hottest part of the fire and the tail sections out toward the edge where the fire is a bit cooler. Let the fish grill undisturbed until the meat is fully cooked; it will just begin to flake when that happens. This can be done in an uncovered grill if it's not too windy and if the fillet is less than 2 inches thick. If you're worried, cover the grill or tent the fish with some heavy-duty foil.

When the fish is done, gently remove it with a large spatula or two spatulas if you need to. Move it to a platter and dot the top of it with the butter. Serve when the butter melts alongside the starch of your choice—rice, potato salad, or maque choux are great choices.

GRILLED OCTOPUS

PREP TIME: 10 MINUTES | **COOK TIME: 2 HOURS** | **SERVES 4**

I wish I could tell you that I first ate grilled octopus while sitting at a seaside bistro in Argos, staring out at a Peloponnesian sunset and knocking back tumblers of ouzo, made milky with ice. But I can't. Sadly, I've never been to Greece. The Fates seem always to prevent me. I can, however, tell you that this Greek-inspired recipe is so wonderful that I'd happily feed it to Aphrodite, or some mortal facsimile thereof, like Holly, who just so happens to be part Greek. Holly loves grilled octopus, and so do I.

There are any number of methods to tenderize octopus, but over the years, I've found the best way is to slowly braise them in their own juices over a bed of mixed herbs; I learned this technique from the great food scientist Harold McGee. After the octos are tender, the grilling part adds some char and scorch. Serve your grilled octopus simply, with lemon, a drizzle of fine olive oil, and a grind of fresh black pepper.

Bread is a must, as are olives. I like feta cheese with my octos, too. And you need either an austere white wine—I recommend a Greek assyrtiko or a French Sancerre—or lots and lots of ouzo or raki or tsipouro.

I used small octopus for this recipe, but it works just as well with larger ones, too. If you use a big octo, you'll need to braise it longer, and you'll want to cut it into chunks when you're ready to grill. Octopus is readily available at both Asian and Latin markets. There is no good substitute for octopus.

3 pounds octopus

3 to 4 bunches of herbs, such as parsley, oregano, fennel fronds, and green onions

4 to 6 bay leaves

¼ cup olive oil

Juice of a lemon

2 tablespoons chopped fresh oregano

1 chopped fresh hot chile, or ½ teaspoon chile flakes

Fine olive oil

Freshly ground black pepper

Lemon wedges

Bring a large pot of salted water to a boil and blanch the octopus for 90 seconds. Remove the octopus and let it drain on a colander.

Meanwhile, preheat the oven to 300°F. Line the bottom of a brazier, a Dutch oven, or other large, ovenproof pot with the herbs and bay leaves. Lay the octopus on the nest of herbs, cover the pot, and cook in the oven until tender, which will be somewhere between 90 minutes for a small octopus to 4 hours for a really gigantic one. Two hours is about normal.

When the octopus is tender, cut it into chunks that won't fall through your grill grates. Leave small octopi whole. Mix the olive oil, lemon juice, oregano, and chile and marinate the octopus in this for at least 1 hour, and as much as a day or two.

To finish, get your grill blazing hot. Make sure the grill grates are clean. Grill the octopus over high heat until you get a little bit of charring here and there; they're already cooked, so you're just adding flavor. Drizzle your grilled octopus with really good olive oil, grind some black pepper over them, and serve with a wedge of lemon—and a shot of ouzo.

NOTE You can marinate your octopus for as long as a day or two beforehand and they will still taste fine. You can also braise on one day and grill on another. Once they've been braised, the octopi will keep a few days in the fridge. You can serve this hot or at room temperature, so it really is a perfect make-ahead appetizer.

GRILLED FISH COLLARS

PREP TIME: 10 MINUTES | COOK TIME: 20 MINUTES | SERVES 4

I remember the first time I had hamachi kama. Obviously, it was at a sushi restaurant, really the only place you can find grilled yellowtail collar. It was a little sushi place in Sayville, Long Island, and I had no certain idea what I was ordering. At the time, I thought it was tuna—there are no yellowtail in the North Atlantic, but there certainly are yellowfin tuna. And I knew what a fish collar was, having eaten them off the striped bass I'd been catching.

I wasn't prepared for the experience. Striped bass collars are nice, but nothing like the fatty, meaty, charred goodness of hamachi kama. Not until I moved out West and started grilling salmon collars was I able to approximate that meal. I still order hamachi kama at restaurants, but since yellowtail is a Southern California fish, by and large, making it at home was out of the question. Until finally, after several attempts, I caught a nice yellowtail off San Clemente Island.

Now, keep in mind that the hamachi kama you order in a restaurant won't ever be as glorious as the one you see in the picture, largely because they never serve the collars off such large yellowtail. Or at least I've never seen one this big.

Do you need to have yellowtail to make hamachi kama? Kinda, yeah. That's what a *hamachi* is. That said, really good substitutes would be the collars off salmon, really big trout like lakers, almaco jacks or amberjacks, very large bluefish, and small tuna like blackfin or skipjack, as well as wahoo, cobia, or king mackerel. You want a fish with some fat.

Do you have to grill your collars? I'd say yes, but if you can't, you can broil them. Just keep an eye on the collars so they only burn a little.

You will want to start making hamachi kama a day in advance, so you can have the collars well marinated. I generally use a simple ponzu sauce marinade, which is basically a soy sauce-citrus mixture.

Grill your collars over high heat, painting them with sesame oil, until they're cooked through and a little charred. Generally, this is pick-it-up-and-eat-it food, but you can pick at hamachi kama with chopsticks or a fork.

Serve with a salad, steamed rice, and plenty of beer.

PONZU SAUCE MARINADE

¼ cup lemon juice

¼ cup lime juice

¼ cup orange juice

1 cup soy sauce

¼ cup mirin or other rice wine

FISH

4 yellowtail collars
   (or substitute, see above)

Sesame oil

Mix the marinade ingredients together and put them, along with the yellowtail collars, into a heavy plastic bag or lidded container. Marinate overnight or up to 1 day. If the collars are not submerged, turn them periodically so they are in good contact with the marinade.

The next day, pour the marinade into a small pot and bring it to a boil. Reduce it by half, and set it aside.

Pat the collars dry with paper towels and coat with a film of sesame oil. Get your grill nice and hot, and clean the grates.

Grill your collars over high heat, basting with the reduced marinade, for about 10 to 20 minutes, depending on how large your collars are and how hot your fire is. You want them fully cooked and a little charred. Serve with steamed rice and a salad.

GRILLED LOBSTER TAILS

Grilling lobster tails is a thing in Florida and Southern California, where the spiny lobster lives, and it is indeed a fun way to cook them in hot weather. It's a bit alien to me, given that I grew up on Maine lobsters eaten, more or less, in only one way: steamed or boiled, with melted butter. But the grill adds that element of smoke, and you can baste the lobster with that melted butter if you want. Or you can go with any number of other flavors, like olive oil, or sesame oil, or salsa, or ponzu sauce (page 232), or chimichurri or . . . you get the point.

This is more of a method than a recipe. There are a lot of ways to prep a lobster tail for grilling, but the easiest way I've found is to use shears to cut the shell on the top of the tail back to the fins. By doing this, you will likely cut the tail meat too, and that's OK, because you're going to open the tail like a book to grill it. You want the bottom of the shell intact; doing this, as opposed to cutting the tails in half completely, allows the shell to protect the meat somewhat. I will also use my fingers to work the raw meat away from the shell a little, which will make it easier to remove later.

Get your grill hot. This is a hot and fast cook, not slow and low. Clean the grates.

Paint the lobster meat with oil or melted butter and set the tail, meat-side down, on the grates. Press the tail down with your tongs or a spatula for about 30 seconds. Grill the meat side for about 4 or 5 minutes, then turn. Paint the meat with more melted butter or oil.

Grill the shell side for another 5 or 6 minutes, then remove. Add more seasonings of your choice; I go with an herb butter, but a single chipotle from a can of chipotles in adobo, puréed with melted butter or olive oil, is another great option.

"The best way to observe a fish is to become a fish. "

JACQUES YVES COUSTEAU

BAJA GRILLED CLAMS

PREP TIME: 20 MINUTES | COOK TIME: 15 MINUTES | SERVES 6 AS AN APPETIZER

This is a Baja California interpretation of the "clam things" of New England (Stuffed Clams, page 82). In all likelihood, this is an example of convergent evolution, culinarily speaking—clams, cooked in their shells, with good things added. You need reasonably large clams here, at least cherrystone size if you're using quahogs. They use "chocolate" clams in Baja, which are so called because of their pretty, milk-chocolate-colored shells. I used Washington clams I dug off the Marin coast here in California.

Loreto is the spiritual home of almejas rellenas, which means stuffed clams in Spanish. They will cook them in foil, which to me kinda defeats the purpose of grilling them; you want that smoke, no? But I get it. Most Baja recipes put everything in there raw, and unless you create an oven effect on the grill, it won't work. I sidestep this by precooking most of the ingredients, leaving only the clams and the cheese to cook on the grill.

Cheese? *Sí, amigo, queso.* Unlike Italian cuisine, Mexican cuisine has no taboo against cheese and seafood. It took some doing to break it out of my mind, but I can assure you this is really good.

1 poblano or 2 Anaheim or
    Hatch chiles, roasted, peeled,
    and seeded
1 to 4 small hot chiles like arbol
    or Thai, chopped
6 big clams about 4 inches across,
    or the equivalent in slightly
    smaller clams
¼ pound bacon
1 small red onion, minced
2 cloves garlic, minced
¼ cup cilantro
½ pound shredded melty cheese,
    like Oaxaca, Chihuahua, or
    mozzarella

If you haven't roasted the peppers yet, do that first. Blacken their skins on a gas burner or under a broiler or on the grill. Put the peppers in a paper or plastic bag to steam for 30 minutes, then use a butter knife to scrape off the skins. Remove the stem and seeds and chop roughly.

Shuck the clams, saving the shells and the liquor. Chop them if they're not too big—Pismo or chocolate or large cherrystones fit this description—or grind them if they're huge, like big surf clams, quahogs, horseneck clams, or Washington clams. You can chop the big guys too, but they can be very tough.

Strain the liquor free of debris. You'll need some, but not all; the remainder will freeze well and is great in fish soups and stews.

Fry the bacon in a pan until crispy. Remove and chop. Add the onion and sauté for about 3 minutes, just to get it soft. Add the garlic and both the hot and green chiles and sauté another minute, then turn off the heat. Add the bacon back and mix well. When this mixture cools, stir in the clams and cilantro and a tablespoon or three of the clam liquor. This can be done ahead of time, although the bacon will lose its crispiness.

When you're ready, break the clam shells into their two halves and stuff with the clam mixture. Top with a healthy bit of melty cheese and set onto a hot grill. Once the cheese melts, you're ready to go.

15
PASTA, RISOTTO, AND OTHER STARCHES

THIS IS AN area where freestyling shines. Once you know how to make a decent plate of pasta, fried rice, risotto, or grits, you can whip up any of those dishes with any number of fishes. Arguably, this is also a haven for leftover fish and seafood, since in most cases it is tossed in at the end. What follows are a few master recipes for starchy dishes where fish and seafood play an important but supporting role, and a couple where fish are integral to the dish itself.

A few initial notes:

RICE MATTERS.

Long-grain rice does not cook like short-grain rice, and you cannot make risotto with long-grain rice. Similarly, perloo is nasty and sticky when made with short-grain rice. Most supermarkets sell a variety of rice, so getting the right kind has become a lot easier.

FRESH OR DRIED PASTA IS EQUALLY GOOD, JUST DIFFERENT.

In the recipes below where the fish or seafood is just tossed in at the end, like the smoked salmon pasta, freshly made pasta works well. But I really prefer the Spaghetti With Crab Sauce on page 241 with dried spaghetti.

GRITS MATTER, TOO.

Buy the best you can find, the kind that come in cloth bags, if at all possible. And for the love of all that's holy, don't use quick grits. Make something else instead. Polenta can sub in for grits, however, although it is a slightly different product.

▲ Shrimp risotto with saffron and peas, see recipe variations on page 251.

◄ Western Littleneck clams.

CLASSIC LINGUINE AND WHITE CLAM SAUCE

PREP TIME: 45 MINUTES | COOK TIME: 10 MINUTES | SERVES 6

This is arguably the most popular clam dish in the New York/New Jersey area I grew up in, challenged only by linguine in red clam sauce. I've adapted my rendition of white clam sauce from Marcella Hazan's recipe in her classic book *Essentials of Classic Italian Cooking*, which is to Italian food what Julia Child's *Mastering the Art of French Cooking* is to French food. As a New Jersey native, I was surprised to see tomato in Marcella's white clam sauce, but it's only one large plum tomato, seeded and diced, more an accent than the base of a sauce.

This recipe is traditionally made with linguini, and you can, by all means, use it. I prefer the lighter touch of angel hair or capellini pasta, but honestly, any pasta will do. There are lots of versions of pasta with white clam sauce, many involving obscene amounts of olive oil and garlic.

At old-time "red sauce" places, I've had plates of clam linguini literally swimming in garlic and olive oil. Blech. I use western littleneck clams for this dish because that's what I have around me. I've also used Manila clams and eastern littlenecks. Any small hard-shelled clam works here. Mussels or oysters work well here too, as would crab or lobster or small squid.

20 to 30 small hardshell clams

1¼ cup white wine, divided

5 tablespoons olive oil, divided

2 cloves garlic, thinly sliced

½ teaspoon red pepper flakes

1 pound linguine, angel hair, or other pasta

1 large fresh plum tomato, seeded and diced

3 tablespoons fresh basil, torn into pieces

Black pepper

Make sure the clams are clean; scrub them with a stiff brush under cold water if you need to. Lay them in a large, wide pot no more than 2 clams deep. Pour over ¾ cup of the white wine. Cover the pot and bring to a boil. Turn the heat down to a simmer and steam open the clams. Pay attention and pluck out each clam as it opens—this prevents them from being overcooked. Remove the clams from their shells and cut into bite-sized pieces, unless they're already bite-sized. Put them in a bowl with a tablespoon of the olive oil and toss to coat. Set aside for now.

Discard the shells. Strain the liquid in the pan by pouring over a fine-meshed strainer with a paper towel set inside it that has been set over a bowl. Reserve the strained liquid.

Wipe out the pan and add the remaining olive oil. Turn the heat to medium-high and sauté the garlic for about 1 minute; don't let it brown. Add the red pepper flakes and the remaining white wine. Boil this for 1 minute, then add the reserved clam juice. Turn off the heat.

Boil the pasta in a large pot of salty water. When it's almost done—very al dente, as in just barely crunchy in the center—move the pasta to the pan and turn the heat to high. When it begins to boil, toss the pasta with the sauce constantly so the pasta is evenly coated. Add the reserved clams and the tomato while you're doing this. The pasta should be fully cooked in 30 seconds to 1 minute. When it's perfect, turn off the heat, add pepper and mix in the basil. Serve at once.

SPAGHETTI WITH CRAB SAUCE

PREP TIME: 15 MINUTES | COOK TIME: 2 HOURS | SERVES 6

Crab and tomato go together like cats and random things tossed onto the floor. That is to say that crab and any form of tomato play well together, from a simple salad with freshly chopped tomatoes to this spaghetti with crab sauce. I first had a version of this dish many years ago; my brother-in-law Mark made it with lobster while I was visiting in Massachusetts.

It is a sauce of two parents: Italian and thrifty Yankee. Mark being both, he made the sauce using just the legs and bodies of the lobsters, parts many people throw away. But Mark knows that plenty of meat lurks within lobster bodies, and he'd patiently pick it out before making this sauce. As he did so, it occurred to me that there would be no reason why it would not work with crabs, too. Or crayfish.

I've tinkered with the original recipe to streamline it. In the old version, I had trouble getting all the shell out of the sauce. I've fixed that here.

This sauce is insanely good. Good in the way only years of tinkering can get to. Sharp, sweet, garlicky, just a little spicy, with a strong hit of anise flavor from fennel and ouzo. It may look like just a regular tomato sauce with bits of crab in it, but it's not. I assure you.

This recipe is a two-step process: making the sauce base and then the sauce itself. You can make the base a day ahead if you like. Any crab will do here, but I use a combination of red crabs, rock crabs, and Dungeness crabs. The only tricky ingredient here is ouzo, the Greek anise-flavored liqueur. Most liquor stores have it, but you can sub in sambuca, raki, pastis, Pernod, or any other anise-flavored liqueur. Still can't find it? Go with brandy; that's what my brother-in-law does.

SAUCE BASE

3 tablespoons olive oil

1 cup chopped onion

Shells from 3 Dungeness crabs
    or 4 large rock crabs,
    or 10 blue crabs

2 cloves garlic, crushed

Tops from 1 fennel bulb, chopped

3 or 4 bay leaves

½ cup ouzo

Salt

To make the sauce base, put the olive oil and onion in a stockpot and cook, stirring occasionally, over medium heat until the onions is soft and translucent, about 6 to 8 minutes. Add the crab shells and the garlic and stir to combine. Use a potato masher to smash the crab shells into small pieces. Cook, stirring often, for 5 minutes.

Add the tops from the fennel bulb, the bay leaves, ouzo and a healthy pinch of salt. Add enough water to cover everything by 1 inch. Bring to a simmer and cook for 1 hour. Turn off the heat and strain the liquid through a paper towel set in a colander. Reserve.

To finish the sauce, heat the olive oil in a Dutch oven or other large, wide pot over medium-high heat. Sauté the onion and chopped fennel until they are soft and translucent, about 6 to 8 minutes. Add the garlic and cook another minute.

Mix in the tomato paste and cook for 3 to 4 minutes, stirring often, until it darkens and turns the color of brick. Add the ouzo, the tomatoes, and 2 cups of the crab sauce base. Stir well and bring to a simmer. Taste for salt and add the Tabasco to taste. Simmer uncovered for 30 minutes, stirring from time to time.

FINISHED SAUCE

2 tablespoons olive oil

½ cup chopped onion

½ cup chopped fennel bulb

3 cloves garlic, minced

1 heaping tablespoon
   tomato paste

¼ cup ouzo

One 28-ounce can crushed
   tomatoes

2 cups of the crab sauce base

Tabasco or other hot sauce

1 to 2 pounds dried spaghetti

1 cup cooked crabmeat

Chives, green onions, or parsley
   to garnish

Boil your pasta. Once the pasta is ready, add the crabmeat to the sauce and stir gently. Mix the pasta with a little of the sauce, then portion it out. Top with more sauce, and garnish with chives.

Once you make this sauce, it will last up to 3 days in the fridge before it starts to get funky.

"Give a man a fish and you feed him for a day; teach a man to fish and you feed him for a lifetime."

MAIMONIDES

SMOKED SALMON PASTA

PREP TIME: 10 MINUTES | **COOK TIME: 20 MINUTES** | **SERVES 4**

I love the flavors in this recipe. Homemade whole wheat pasta, smoked salmon, tarragon, parsley, and lots of sweet butter. This is a pasta for the Pacific Northwest, for Salmon Nation. Big flavors, hearty, unpretentious. No tweezers, fancy plating, or hard-to-find ingredients here.

I make my own smoked salmon and my own whole wheat pasta. Note that I use hot-smoked salmon, which will flake, not cold-smoked, which will not. I chose whole wheat pasta— actually bigoli—which I made with an old-school Italian torchio, because it has heft and the homemade spaghetti is rougher in texture than machine made; this roughness allows each strand of pasta to hold onto more sauce. I urge you to use whole wheat, spelt, or some other heartier, darker pasta here. It matters.

As for the salmon, in this case, I used a chum salmon I smoked over alder and glazed with birch syrup. Chum (also known as keta or dog salmon) are excellent candidates for smoking, but any species will do. As would any kind of trout; smoked lake trout would be ideal. New Englanders should use smoked mackerel or bluefish, southerners smoked king mackerel, mullet, or wahoo.

The rest is pretty simple, and this recipe comes together in less than 30 minutes if you have everything ready.

1 pound whole wheat pasta

¼ cup unsalted butter

1 large shallot, minced

½ pound smoked salmon, flaked

¼ cup white wine or vermouth

2 tablespoons chopped tarragon

2 tablespoons chopped parsley

Black pepper

Bring a large pot of water to a boil. Add enough salt to make the water taste quite salty, like seawater. Add the pasta.

In a large sauté or frying pan, heat the butter over medium heat and add the shallot. Sauté the shallot, stirring often. You want it soft but not browned. Add the flaked salmon and spread it in one layer in the pan. Let this cook to sear a bit. Don't move the fish for at least a minute, maybe two.

Pour in the wine and use a metal spatula to scrape everything off the bottom of the pan. When most of the wine has boiled away, mix in the herbs and add a fair bit of black pepper, maybe a couple teaspoons' worth; you want to taste black pepper in this dish. Turn the heat to low.

To finish, move the pasta from the boiling water to the pan, and toss. I like to add maybe ¼ cup of pasta cooking water to the mix to emulsify everything. Toss and serve at once.

VARIATIONS The structure in this dish: a distinctive fat, a strong-flavored smoked fish, a light acidic liquid, and fresh herbs. You could make this super German by using squash seed oil, lager beer, and lovage instead of the butter, vermouth, and tarragon. Or you could go Asian and use sesame oil, sake or Shaoxing wine, and cilantro, and use soy sauce instead of salt.

CRAB FRIED RICE WITH PINEAPPLE

PREP TIME: 20 MINUTES | **COOK TIME: 10 MINUTES** | **SERVES 4**

I love fried rice in general, and crab fried rice in particular. The flakes of crab work really well in fried rice, better than most other meats. True fried rice is essentially a "garbage plate" dish made with whatever is lying around. Toss it all together with an egg, last night's rice, and bam, there's dinner.

I got the idea for my crab fried rice from an excellent primer on preparing Asian food called *Steamy Kitchen's Healthy Asian Favorites*, written by my friend Jaden Hair. Lots of Asian countries make fried rice, and looking at her recipe it's clear that this is at its core a Thai or Vietnamese fried rice; the fish sauce is a dead giveaway. If you want to get sporty and make your own fish sauce, the technique is on page 307.

This can be made with any sort of crab. You can get those refrigerated jars of pasteurized crabmeat that are good. I used fresh pineapple, but you don't need a whole pineapple for the recipe. So canned will work if you don't feel like eating the rest for a snack. If you're a novice to fried rice, you need to remember one vital thing: *start with cool cooked rice*. I usually use day-old rice or at least rice I've made in the morning. Once made, this is best eaten immediately, although I've reheated it for lunches later, and it was perfectly fine.

To view this as a master recipe, know that you can substitute the crab for literally any cooked fish or seafood. A few, like flaked sardines, might be weird, but for the most part, any flaked fish, crayfish, lobster, clams, oysters, squid, or cooked octopus would be nice here.

To make it more Chinese and less Southeast Asian, skip the lemongrass and pineapple and fish sauce and sub in diced carrots, peas, and soy sauce.

---

3 tablespoons peanut oil, lard, or
  other vegetable oil, divided

2 to 3 eggs, lightly beaten

3 to 4 green onions, chopped

1 tablespoon minced fresh ginger

1 clove garlic, minced

1 tablespoon minced lemongrass
  (optional)

3 to 5 dried hot chiles, broken up
  and partially seeded

½ pound pineapple, cut into
  chunks

3 cups cooked, cooled rice

¼ cup roasted cashews (optional)

2 to 3 tablespoons fish sauce
  (or soy sauce)

½ pound crabmeat

⅓ cup chopped cilantro

Heat 1 tablespoon of the peanut oil in a wok or large non-stick sauté pan over high heat. Use your hottest burner, too. The second the oil begins to smoke, pour in the beaten eggs and swirl them around in the pan to coat it in a thin layer. Let this cook for a couple of seconds, then use a spatula or wooden spoon to break it up into pieces. Tip it out of the pan and into a bowl. Set aside.

Wipe the inside of the wok with a paper towel and add the remaining peanut oil. Let this heat up for a minute or so, and the moment it smokes, add the chopped green onions, ginger, garlic, lemongrass, and chiles and stir-fry for 30 seconds to 1 minute over high heat.

Add the pineapple, rice, cooked eggs, fish sauce, and cashews and stir-fry for 2 minutes. Now let the mixture cook undisturbed for 1 minute; this gives it a little color. Add the crabmeat and toss well and repeat the process for 1 more minute. Turn off the heat and mix in the cilantro.

LOWCOUNTRY PERLOO

PREP TIME: 30 MINUTES | COOK TIME: 30 MINUTES | SERVES 6

In Charleston, South Carolina, rice was once king. And this Lowcountry perloo was once one of that region's crowning dishes. Perloo. Such a strange name, and spelling. It gets even stranger when you see it spelled purloo or perlo. But if you say it, and you've been exposed to the cooking of certain parts of the Middle East, India, or East Africa, you'll recognize that this is a version of pilau. And if you eat it, you will taste echoes of its more famous cousin, Louisiana jambalaya.

Perloo's origins lie in Africa. West Africa, to be exact. The concept of a one-pot, rice-and-whatever dish exists wherever rice is grown, and in Senegal, there's a dish known as jollof rice, with its own variations throughout that part of Africa. Two centuries ago, Charleston was the entry point for roughly 40 percent of all African slaves to this country, and the city's cuisine reflects those African roots.

Even the rice is African, *Oryza glaberrima*, which is a different species than the Asian rice we all buy today. And while African rice hasn't been grown commercially in the Lowcountry since the 1920s, it's recently been revived as Carolina Gold rice, which is a hybrid of the old African rice and Asian varieties (you can buy Carolina Gold rice online).

Many varieties of perloo exist. I've seen them loaded with pig parts, with chicken, rabbit, or game. But perloo is mostly about seafood, and that seafood means shrimp, crab, and oysters. What shrimp? Well, American shrimp, of course. I strongly urge you to seek out real American, usually Gulf, shrimp. Our shrimp industry is as sustainable as any in the world, it doesn't destroy the environment the way Southeast Asian shrimp farming does, and, importantly, it supports American jobs. Any size shrimp will do.

Some sort of smoked pork is vital to a good perloo. Bacon is what I use, but salty country ham or salt pork will also work. Jowl bacon is ideal. And yes, I've seen sausage in perloo too, but to me, that tips it a bit too close to jambalaya.

This makes enough for a crowd. So if you're not a crowd, reheat your perloo in a microwave for thirty seconds or so, or do what I do and reheat it on the stovetop in a covered non-stick pan over very low heat for about twenty minutes.

2 pounds shrimp, with shells (and heads if possible)

2 bay leaves

1 onion, chopped

1 large carrot, chopped

2 stalks celery, chopped

¼ pound thick-cut bacon

2 cups chopped white or yellow onion

2 cups chopped celery stalks

1 yellow bell pepper, diced

2 large cloves garlic, minced

2½ cups rice

½ cup white wine

One 14.5-ounce can fire-roasted tomatoes

1 datil, fish, or habanero chile, minced (optional)

½ pound crabmeat (optional)

½ pound shucked oysters (optional)

⅓ cup chopped parsley

Black pepper

Peel all the shrimp and put the shells, and heads if you have them, into a pot with the bay leaves, onion, carrot, and celery. Cover with 7 cups of water and bring to a simmer. If you're using oysters, add the oyster liquor, too. Simmer gently for 30 minutes while you chop everything else for the perloo.

As the stock is simmering, slowly fry the bacon in a large, heavy pot. When crispy, remove the bacon, eat a slice, and chop roughly. Set the bacon aside.

Sauté the 2 cups chopped onion, 2 cups chopped celery, and the diced yellow bell pepper in the bacon fat until soft but not browned. Add the garlic and rice and cook, stirring often, for 3 minutes, until the rice turns translucent.

Add the white wine, tomatoes, and chile pepper to the pot and stir well.

Set up a fine-meshed strainer with a paper towel in it. Ladle two or three ladles of the shrimp stock through this strainer into the rice pot. Stir well. Cook, stirring often, until the liquid is absorbed. Repeat this process until the rice is tender.

Add one more ladle of shrimp stock to the pot, along with the shrimp, crabmeat, oysters, and parsley. Mix to combine, cover the pot, and turn the heat to its lowest setting. Cover for 5 minutes to let the shrimp cook, then mix in the bacon and black pepper and serve.

FISH RISOTTO

PREP TIME: 1 HOUR | **COOK TIME: 45 MINUTES** | **SERVES 6**

If there's one episode of Anthony Bourdain's old show *No Reservations* that sticks with me, it's his trip to Venice. In that episode, Bourdain has risotto di go, an ethereal dish that hinges on a magical fish broth made from gobies. Called *go* in Venetian dialect, a goby is a tiny fish that's no good for anything but making broth. Any true, authentic risotto di go must have the goby from the Venetian lagoons. Alas, this is impossible outside Venice. But the technique of making this risotto is repeatable—and unforgettable.

No matter what fish you make it with, a Venetian fish risotto is always a little soupy, always hinges on a rich, pampered broth, and is almost always as white as innocence itself. It is one of the most beautiful things you can create from such humble beginnings. Done perfectly, a bowl of this risotto will restore your faith in humankind and make you misty with thoughts of a simpler age, a quieter time.

It all begins with the broth. You cannot make a great fish risotto with anything other than fish broth made immediately prior to making the risotto. Yes, you can make passable ones with broth from a few days ago, thawed broth, or even a little clam juice. But it will not be the same. Not by a long shot.

Clean, golden fish broth is why risotto di go, or any other good fish risotto, is such a beloved dish. Heads, backbones, fins all go into the pot; only the guts and gills, which are bitter, are tossed to the seagulls.

This is not a difficult recipe to make. And you can make it no matter where you live, as most any lean white fish will work. What's more, the fish broth you need for it comes together in less than an hour. It's the method for making the risotto that takes time to perfect. But this is one of a very few fish cooking techniques that everyone should master. After all, who wouldn't want to make magic from little more than rice and a bucket of bones?

I used striped bass for the broth in this recipe, but you can use any lean white fish. I've done this with yellow perch from Lake Erie, and it was sublime, and codfish, walleye, smallmouth bass, black seabass, Pacific rock cod, and ling all work fine. The fennel is important, so if you can't find a fennel bulb, add a tablespoon of fennel seeds to the broth. It's also vital that you use short-grained rice, preferably proper risotto rice—long-grained rice lacks the particular starch needed to make a risotto.

BROTH

- 2 to 3 pounds of fish heads, bones and fins, gills removed
- 3 tablespoons olive oil
- 2 stalks celery, chopped
- 1 large onion, chopped
- 1 bulb fennel, including fronds, chopped
- 4 cloves garlic, minced
- 2 tablespoons green peppercorns
- 3 bay leaves
- ½ cup chopped parsley
- Salt

Bring a pot of water to a boil and drop in all the fish heads and bones. Let this return to a simmer and cook for 5 minutes. Turn off the heat and discard the water. Pick off about 1 cup of fish from the carcasses and heads and set aside in the fridge.

Clean the pot or use another, and heat the olive oil over medium-high heat. Sauté the celery, onion, and fennel for 3 to 5 minutes, stirring often. Do not let it brown. Add the garlic and cook another minute.

Add the blanched fish carcasses, green peppercorns, bay leaves, and parsley and cover with enough water to submerge everything by 1 inch. Bring to a bare simmer, then drop the heat a little until the broth is just steaming, about 160°F. Add salt to taste. Let this cook gently like this for 45 minutes.

FISH RISOTTO, continued

RISOTTO

2 tablespoons olive oil

1 large shallot, minced

2 cloves garlic, minced

1½ cups risotto rice

1 cup white wine

Salt

About 1 cup flaked fish meat

2 tablespoons unsalted butter

1 tablespoon lemon juice

2 tablespoons minced parsley

Once the broth has been cooking for 30 minutes, start the risotto. Heat the olive oil in a medium pot over medium-high heat. Sauté the shallots for about 90 seconds, until they turn translucent. Add the garlic and cook another minute. Add the risotto rice and stir to combine. Cook, stirring often, for 3 to 4 minutes.

While the rice is cooking, get a fine-meshed sieve and a ladle ready. Add the white wine to the risotto and stir to combine. The rice will almost immediately absorb it. When the pot is nearly dry, add two ladles of the fish broth—poured through the strainer to make sure all that's in the risotto is broth, not debris.

Stir the risotto almost constantly until the rice absorbs the broth. Taste for salt and add a little if needed. Repeat this process of adding a ladle or two of strained broth and stirring until it has absorbed until the rice is fully cooked, but still al dente. You want it just past the point where there is a little chalkiness at the center of each grain of rice. This normally takes 35 minutes or so.

When the rice is ready, stir in the remaining ingredients. The risotto will tighten up, so add a final ladle of fish broth right before you serve. This risotto needs to be a little soupy; the Italian term is *all'onda*, or "under the waves."

VARIATIONS Any fish or seafood works here. I love seafood risottos especially, and there are a few combinations that are classic: shrimp with saffron and peas (photo on page 239), crab with tomato and chile, squid and its ink. You can make the broth from the same animal that's in the rice, or start with the same fish broth in the recipe above, but add the other seafood at the end. In the case of those combinations, the saffron and tomato paste (a big pinch and about a tablespoon) go in with the white wine, and the squid ink, which you can buy online or in specialty stores, goes in right at the end.

FISH AND GRITS

PREP TIME: 20 MINUTES | **COOK TIME: 30 MINUTES** | **SERVES 4**

Several years ago, I saw a painting on the wall of the hunting lodge my friend Larry Robinson owns in Texas. The painting showed a gray fish leaping out of the water near a buoy. It looked like the prehistoric ancestor of a bluegill, only larger. I asked Larry what it was. "That's a tripletail," he said. "Best eating fish out there."

I've caught and eaten most of the fish that swim in North America's lakes, streams, and oceans. But somehow this tripletail fish had eluded not only my hook, but even my notice. How on earth was it possible that there was a fish with this reputation as table fare that I didn't even know about? It's probably because when I fish the waters of the Deep South, it's normally either inshore for redfish and speckled trout, or over wrecks for snapper.

Tripletail. *Lobotes surinamensis.* I had to catch one.

Tripletail like to live inshore, but it's pelagic, meaning it hangs out in the middle or top of the water column. And, just like in Larry's painting, it loves structure, like buoys or pylons. Sometimes they float around on their sides, looking like debris; small fish congregate underneath them to get some shade, and whump! Dinner.

Years passed before I would finally get my chance to fish for them. In 2017, my friend Joe Baya offered to take me out to experience what the Alabama coast had to offer. He added, somewhat offhandedly, that he and his dad were good at catching tripletail. I think there was some other talk about shrimp and tuna, but at the time, all I could hear was the word "tripletail." Yes, I'm in. Name the time. I'll be there.

Fishing for tripletail is a lot like bluegill fishing, oddly enough. You use a bobber and bait, only much bigger. We used live shrimp for bait. You cast toward some sort of structure, let the current take the bait past the object, and watch the bobber. Tripletail don't always strike hard.

I cast out to a buoy and immediately got wrapped around the chain. Damn. "I think that's a fish," Joe said. No way, it's just the chain. I reeled in gently, trying not to snag the hook. The chain pumped its head twice. Hard. *Holy crap!* Now I felt the fish, and it was a good one. I finessed it in closer to the boat, a gray hubcap. Huh. Not much of a fighter. Then it saw the boat, tore off about fifty yards of line and changed my mind about the fighting abilities of *Lobotes surinamensis.* Now all I felt was nervousness. This might be the only chance I got. Don't. Screw. It. Up. Fortunately, I didn't, and Joe netted the fish with the skill earned by netting scores of these things. And all of a sudden, I had my first tripletail, a spectacular fifteen pounder! To say I was excited is an understatement. To not only catch a tripletail, but to get a really good one, was awesome. It still gets my blood up writing this.

Fish and grits was the first way I prepared it. This is a riff on Lowcountry shrimp and grits—bacon, fresh tomatoes, some mushrooms, green onions, and lots of lemon. The tripletail itself is seared simply in bacon fat.

The tripletail lived up to its reputation. Firm, clean tasting, with a meaty texture very close to grouper, and reminiscent of striped bass. Tripletail has thick, wide flakes, and the meat is pearly white. It was worth the wait.

You can use any firm white fish here. Grouper or striped bass are ideal substitutes, but snapper, catfish, walleye, redfish, seabass, or Pacific rockfish or lingcod are great, too. Get the best grits you can afford.

3 cups water

2 cups fish or chicken stock

salt

2 cups grits

1½ pounds tripletail fillets, or
    similar fish

¼ pound bacon

Black pepper

1 pound fresh mushrooms,
    chopped

4 tablespoons butter

¼ cup cream

¼ cup shredded cheese
    (I use white cheddar)

5 or 6 plum tomatoes, diced

3 or 4 green onions, chopped

Zest and juice of 2 lemons

Worcestershire sauce

Boil the water and stock and add salt to taste. Start stirring it and pour the grits in slowly; this prevents lumps. Drop the heat to a simmer and cook, stirring frequently, for about 20 to 30 minutes.

Meanwhile, salt the fish fillets and set aside on the counter. Fry the bacon in a large pan to render the fat. Remove the bacon, chop, and set aside.

Pat the fish dry with paper towels and place in the hot bacon fat, the flattest side down. Keep the heat at medium-high. Use a spoon to ladle bacon fat over the top of the fillets until they turn opaque. Keep doing this for about 1 minute. Do not flip your fish unless the pieces are more than 1 inch thick. When you have a nice sear, remove the fish from the pan and set, seared side up, on a cutting board. Grind black pepper over it.

If you have less than about 2 tablespoons of bacon fat in the pan, add some more. Add the mushrooms and sear them well. They'll sear, then give up their water. Let this happen without moving the mushrooms. This should all take about 3 minutes or so.

Right before serving, stir the butter, cream, and cheese into the grits until the butter and cheese melts in.

When the mushroom water subsides, add the remaining ingredients and stir-fry them about 90 seconds. To serve, give everyone some grits, then some fish, then pour the mushroom-tomato mixture over.

"Fishing is not an escape from life, but often
a deeper immersion into it . . ."

HARRY MIDDLETON

CLAM DUMPLINGS

PREP TIME: 1 HOUR | COOK TIME: 10 MINUTES | SERVES 6

These dumplings are inspired by a Sichuan recipe for pork dumplings in Fuchsia Dunlop's amazing book *The Food of Sichuan*, plus some conversations with my friend Kian Lam Kho, author of *Phoenix Claws and Jade Trees*. Clam dumplings do appear here and there in China, although shrimp are more common.

I really like the combination of smoky pork and clams, although you need to be sparing with it. A batch I made with ultra-smoky Benton's bacon overpowered the clam; the dumplings were great, but the clams disappeared. I find the best combination is to mix a bit of bacon in with the ground pork. I grind the pork, bacon, and clams all at once, but you can finely chop the bacon and clams by hand.

See how pretty those dumplings are? Part of it is the wrappers, which are store bought. Yeah, I took that shortcut. It was originally just to test the filling, but I really like the look of them, the way they dimple up; my handmade ones don't do that. So there you go. This recipe got easier.

If you have leftovers, freeze them on a plate until solid, then put them in a freezer bag. They will get brittle quickly, but will still be good for a few months.

Feel free to substitute really anything for the clams. I'm hard-pressed to think of a fish or seafood that won't be tasty ground with pork and put in a dumpling.

DUMPLINGS

1 slice bacon, chopped

¼ pound lean pork, cut in chunks

¾ pound clam meat

2 tablespoons finely grated ginger

3 tablespoons finely minced green
    onions or chives

1 small hot chile, such as a Thai
    chile, minced

¼ teaspoon white pepper

1 tablespoon soy sauce

1 tablespoon Shaoxing wine or
    dry sherry

1 tablespoon sesame oil

1 egg, lightly beaten

Round dumpling wrappers

SAUCE

⅓ cup soy sauce

3 tablespoons Chianking black
    vinegar or malt vinegar

3 tablespoons chile oil

1 clove garlic, minced

A pinch of sugar

To make the sauce, mix everything together and let it sit at room temperature.

Mix together the bacon, pork, and clams, then grind through a fine die on your grinder. I use a 4.5 mm die. If you don't have a meat grinder, use a food processor to pulse the mixture into a paste. Put the mixture into a bowl and add the grated ginger, green onions, chile, and white pepper.

In another bowl, mix together the soy sauce, wine, and sesame oil.

Mixing the meat in one direction with a clean hand, drizzle in about a third of the liquid in the other bowl. Keep stirring with your fingers until that liquid has been incorporated. Repeat with the next third of the liquid, then again once that has been incorporated. Now mix in the egg. You should have a loose but cohesive filling.

Get yourself a little bowl of water. Set out a baking sheet that has been dusted with semolina or cornmeal or lined with parchment paper.

Set a wrapper in front of you, and spoon about a tablespoon of filling into the center. Dip your finger into the little bowl of water and outline the wrapper to moisten it. Fold it over and seal carefully, then set it on the baking sheet. Repeat until you're out of filling or wrappers.

Boil the dumplings for about 3 to 4 minutes total, then move to a shallow bowl and top with some sauce.

16
SALADS, COLD DISHES, AND LEFTOVERS

THIS IS SOMETHING of a grab bag of recipes. But they all have something in common: they are bits of things in other things. No great big slabs of fish or whole lobsters here. Rather, they're made with fish or seafood you made previously, in some cases quite a while ago if you're using your own home-canned tuna. Some are hot, some not. Some are fancy, some are simple, and one, the iconic tunafish sandwich, is a cultural touchstone.

MY TUNAFISH SANDWICH

PREP TIME: 15 MINUTES OR LESS | SERVES 4

It is perhaps the most recognizable and loved fish dish in America. Pretty much every man, woman, and child has, at one point, eaten one. I used to eat them for lunch in junior high school. I still eat them. At its core, an American tuna sandwich—why we added "fish" to the end of the word I am not entirely certain—consists of presliced bread, maybe some lettuce or tomato, and flaked, canned tuna mixed with mayonnaise, celery and/or onion, and some other flavoring elements.

Below you'll see how I like my tunafish sandwiches (a term I've christened here to mean any fish or seafood sandwich made like the tuna sandwiches we all know and love), but first, I want to give you some ideas on how to make this classic your own.

Let's start with the tuna. It need not be canned tuna, or even tuna at all. I've made fish salads of this sort with more or less everything that swims or walks on the bottom. Caught walleyes or crappies? Use them. Leftover shrimp? Chop them small and go for it. Lobster salad, especially in a lobster roll, is one of the stations of the cross in any New England culinary pilgrimage.

I've also used home-canned sturgeon and salmon, as well as pretty much every sort of canned tuna there is. Even there, are you using oil-packed or water-packed fish? Your choice. I prefer oil-packed, but in this one case, water-packed is better because of the mayo you're about to add.

My secret? I really like to mix simply flaked fish, canned or not, with flaked, smoked fish. You could also use 100 percent smoked fish, too.

Firm fish, soft fish, lean fish, fatty fish, seafood—all will work. That is one of the beauties of a tunafish sandwich.

I don't need to tell you that anything goes as an accompaniment. Traditional is lettuce and tomato, but I also like a slice of bacon or three (thin cut), shaved fennel, pickled greens, and roasted green chiles. I personally don't like melted cheese—the venerable tuna melt—but many people do.

What about the sandwich part? Clearly you can stand over the bowl and eat your fish salad over the sink if you want. But any sort of bread is fine, including wraps and tortillas. I once roasted some chiles, seeded and peeled them, then stuffed them with a Mexican-inspired salmon salad. Toasted bread or untoasted? I like both. You could even get super fancy and stuff some of your salad into a ramekin and serve it on a charcuterie board. After all, tuna salad, cut very small, is basically a rillette.

◄ Rods at the ready aboard a San Diego tuna boat.

Finally, there is the salad itself. Flaked fish is the only absolute, although mayonnaise really needs to be in there for it to be a recognizable tunafish salad. Fish salads without mayo are amazing, but not what we're talking about here. That said, you can sub in other mayonnaise-like things, like remoulade, (page 123) or even Miracle Whip if that floats your boat.

You also need something crunchy to offset the soft texture of the fish. Most people use some sort of onion (I like shallots), as well as minced celery. Minced fennel bulb is pretty awesome, too. Anything fun to eat raw, cut small and crunchy, will work.

The salad requires zing, too. Depending on my mood, I do this with either horseradish or Dijon mustard, but you could add any other mustard, or hot sauce, if that's what you like.

I will often hit two points at once by mincing pickles into the mix, especially spicy pickles.

Finally—and this isn't entirely needed—you'll want something to offset the whiteness of the salad. I typically use the leaves from the celery I'm cutting, as well as a bunch of minced flat-leaved parsley. But this herbal component can be any soft herb you like to eat: cilantro, thyme, chervil, lovage, sage, cilantro—hell, even epazote.

How do you get there? Little by little. The beauty of a tunafish salad is that everything is cooked, so you can add, mix, taste, add, mix, taste until your salad is where you want it.

Here's what you need.

---

12 ounces flaked fish,
  smoked or not
4 tablespoons mayonnaise
1 tablespoon Dijon mustard
⅓ cup minced shallot
1 stalk celery, minced
2 tablespoons minced parsley
1 tablespoon minced leaves from
  the celery (optional)
1 tablespoon capers
2 tablespoons minced pickles
Salt and black pepper

Mix everything in a bowl to combine, and serve as you'd like.

"A countryman between two lawyers
is like a fish between two cats."

BENJAMIN FRANKLIN

VIETNAMESE SMOKED FISH SALAD

PREP TIME: 20 MINUTES | **SERVES 4**

This smoked fish salad is a hat tip to all the Southeast Asians fishing for shad on the American and Sacramento rivers near my home. Other than a few transplanted easterners and an even fewer number of local non-Asians, few people eat shad here in the West. I happen to think that shad is best smoked, and I've been making my own smoked shad for many years. But any smoked fish will work for this light, bright salad. Smoked bonito or smoked lake trout are good choices, as would be smoked salmon.

And honestly, really any fish cooked any way you want, so long as it can be flaked, will work. So don't get all hung up on shad or smoked fish, although I happen to like both in this dish. Smoked foods add a mellow, savory base to all the other flavors in this salad, which are crunchy, tart, and spicy. The key here is the mix of fresh vegetables, some roasted peanuts, fish or seafood, and a zippy dressing that brings it all together.

I serve this all by itself on hot days, but smoked fish salad is nice over rice, or, if you chop everything a bit smaller, as a sandwich filling.

This dish doesn't exist in Vietnam, so far as I can tell, but it definitely has the flavors we all look for in that fantastic cuisine. Sweet, sour, salty, meaty, and spicy—and to this I add smoky. Any sort of flaked fish, smoked or not, will work here.

DRESSING

2 tablespoons fish sauce

2 tablespoons lime juice

1 tablespoon water

1 tablespoon sugar

1 clove garlic, minced and mashed

1 tablespoon sambal chile sauce,
   or 1 to 2 small hot chiles,
   minced

¼ cup sesame oil

SALAD

1 pound flaked fish (ideally
   smoked)

1 large carrot, peeled and
   shredded on a grater

¼ cup chopped cilantro

⅓ cup roasted peanuts

3 to 6 green onions, thinly sliced

20 cherry tomatoes, sliced in half

1 to 3 serrano or jalapeño chiles,
   thinly sliced

1 tablespoon minced ginger

Make the dressing by mixing all the dressing ingredients together in a small bowl. If you'd like, you can purée it all in a blender. The dressing will keep for a week or so in the fridge.

Mix the salad ingredients in a large bowl and add dressing to taste. Serve slightly chilled.

CALIFORNIA CHRISTMAS CRAB SALAD

PREP TIME: 20 MINUTES | **SERVES 4**

Let me start by saying, "Sorry, rest of the country," as this is a decidedly California crab salad. While most of the rest of the nation is dealing with snow and ice, here in California, our winter bounty is bursting: Dungeness crab, persimmons, pomegranates, avocados, citrus. This recipe has it all.

For most of you, crab is a summer thing. It was for me too, until I moved here in 2004. I soon learned that crab in California is a fall and winter thing, and what's more, it's traditional—even required in some families—for Dungeness crab to be eaten at Thanksgiving and Christmas, normally Christmas Eve. I grew up in New Jersey, where the Feast of the Seven Fishes is a thing, so this sat well with me.

I happen to love crab salad, but I normally do a sort of Mexican route—essentially adding crabmeat to pico de gallo. This is different. Avocado and crab is a classic. Pomegranate and persimmon is a classic. Turns out they all play well together, sauces with lots of fresh citrus juice and California olive oil.

This is a holiday salad, as everything in it is in season in California between Thanksgiving and New Year's. Obviously, everything will be better if it is all freshly picked, crab included, but you can get away with pre-picked crab.

3 or 4 lemons

1 shallot, peeled and sliced very thin

Salt and freshly ground black pepper

1 firm fuyu persimmon, peeled and diced

2 avocados, skinned and diced

½ cup pomegranate arils, about ¼ of a pomegranate

¾ pound crabmeat

2 tablespoons minced parsley

3 to 4 tablespoons olive oil (use the good stuff)

Zest one or two of the lemons with a fine grater; I use a microplane. Put the zest into a large bowl. Juice all the citrus into the bowl and add the sliced shallot. Let this marinate while you cut everything else.

Add the remaining ingredients to the bowl and gently mix to combine. Serve as is, or in hot corn tortillas, or on crackers or tortilla chips.

VARIATIONS While this recipe may look specialized, filled with ingredients hard to get in most of the country—and it is—it is really a model for all fish or seafood salads that are oil and acid based. As I've mentioned, simply adding cooked fish or seafood to an everyday pico de gallo is wonderful. Ditto for the classic Greek salad of cucumbers, tomatoes, red onion, and feta; try this with shrimp, which like feta cheese. Pretty much any of the salads in this book—and there are a lot of them—can be turned into a main course by simply flaking fish or adding cooked seafood into it. I am especially fond of doing this with the black-eyed pea salad that goes with the Cornmeal-Crusted Speckled Trout on page 126.

Your bottom line is to add a flavorful oil, citrus or vinegar, herbs, and something crunchy to the seafood. Follow that and you can't go wrong.

PULPO A LA GALLEGA
(SPANISH OCTOPUS WITH PAPRIKA)

PREP TIME: 20 MINUTES | **COOK TIME: 90 MINUTES** | **SERVES 6**

Man, is this good! I can't tell you when I first ate this Spanish classic, but it was probably sometime in my late teens, and probably at a Spanish restaurant on New Jersey's Route 22 whose name escapes me now. But I remember it being real-deal Spanish—or at least what I imagined it might be, considering I've never been there.

Pulpo a la gallega is basically an octopus salad. According to the late, great cookbook author Penelope Casas in her *The Foods and Wines of Spain*, *a la gallega* is anything cooked with paprika and olive oil. Everything is good with paprika and olive oil, as far as I'm concerned, but octopus is especially good. And while most octo salads are summertime fare, pulpo a la gallega works in any weather. I think it's the paprika and garlic that gives you a warming feeling when you eat it.

Since this recipe is good either warm or at room temperature and because it keeps for several days, it is a perfect make-ahead recipe for parties and big dinners with guests. I like dipping into it while watching TV; it's perfect to munch on with good, crusty bread.

You'll note that my method of cooking octopus does take a while, but it's the best way I know to concentrate the flavor of octopus while at the same time tenderizing it.

2 to 3 pounds octopus

1 bunch parsley

Tops from a fennel bulb

1 sprig oregano

2 to 3 green onions, coarsely
   chopped

2 bay leaves

½ cup extra-virgin olive oil

4 cloves garlic, crushed and
   minced

1 tablespoon paprika

1 teaspoon smoked paprika
   (optional)

¼ teaspoon cayenne

Salt and black pepper

Lemon wedges to serve

First you'll need to tenderize the octopus. Boil a large pot of salty water. Cook the octopus for 2 minutes, then remove to a cutting board. While the octos are cooling, turn the oven to 225°F.

Line a heavy lidded pot with the parsley, fennel fronds, oregano, green onions, and bay leaves. Trim fatty bits from the octopus and clean out the heads (normally this last step has been done for you, but not always). Cut the octopi into large pieces and nestle into the pot of greens. Cover the pot and cook for 90 minutes to 4 hours, depending on how large and tough the octopi are. I typically shoot for 2 hours. Don't worry about the lack of liquid in the pot; the octos will release enough to make a flavorful broth.

When the octopus is tender, remove from the pot, coat with some of the olive oil, and either grill or broil until you get some char marks, about 8 to 10 minutes.

Toss the octopus with the rest of the olive oil, garlic, the paprika, smoked paprika and cayenne. Add salt and black pepper to taste and serve with lemon wedges, at room temperature or slightly warm. Serve with bread.

PAN DE CAZON

PREP TIME: 1 HOUR | **SERVES 6**

This is a specialty of the Yucatan Peninsula that is normally made with precooked shark. It's a stacked enchilada—its name literally means "shark bread." Any precooked flaked fish works fine here, as does lobster and crabmeat. I suppose other seafoods would work, too.

Admittedly, this is an involved recipe for leftover fish, but it's worth it. The result is a show stopper. You make a zippy tomato-chile sauce, some thin refried black beans, add some fish and corn tortillas, and you're good to go. All of the elements can be made ahead and heated up when you want to eat.

One tip: Char-grill the fish beforehand, so you have a bit of blackened goodness here and there in the fish. You'll notice it in the finished dish.

Everything should be reasonably hot as you put the enchiladas together, as they will cool to nicely warm as you eat them. Remember, these are normally served in tropical Yucatan, so they don't have to be blazing hot.

TOMATO SAUCE

1 to 3 habanero chiles

6 Roma tomatoes, sliced in half lengthwise

1 small onion, cut in half

2 tablespoons fresh epazote, chopped

Salt

3 tablespoons lard or oil

BEANS

3 tablespoons lard or oil

1 small white onion, chopped

1 habanero, chopped

2 cloves garlic, chopped

1 sprig epazote, chopped

½ pound cooked black beans

A can of beer (Mexican lager or any macro-brew)

If you're doing this all in one shot, start by soaking the red onions in the sour orange or lime juice to make a quick pickle; this is your garnish.

Make the tomato sauce. If you have a comal, set it over a strong burner and get it hot, like 500°F. If you don't have a comal, use a flat-top or cast iron pan. Lacking both of these, you could use a grill on high or a broiler. Once your cooking surface is hot, set the habaneros, tomatoes (cut-side down), and onion on the comal. You want them to blacken pretty well. You'll need to move the habaneros around so they get charred in multiple places.

When everything is nicely charred, put the tomatoes and habaneros in a blender along with the epazote. Roughly chop the onion and add about ½ cup to the blender. Save the rest for another recipe. Purée, then add salt to taste.

Heat the lard in a small pan, and when it's hot, pour in the sauce. It'll spatter, but stir it well and everything will incorporate. You want the sauce to be the consistency of house paint, which is to say thinner than you might otherwise want a tomato sauce to be because you'll soon be coating tortillas with it. Thin with some of the beer you have ready for the beans.

Now, for the beans, heat the lard in a small pan and sauté the onions and habanero a few minutes, then add the garlic, epazote, and beans. Stir well and cook for a few minutes, then add salt to taste. Purée. Similarly, you want these to be fairly thin refried beans, so add beer until they are the consistency of pancake batter. You want them easily spreadable.

»

TO FINISH

1 small red onion, sliced

¼ cup sour orange juice or lime juice

1½ pounds flaked shark or other fish

18 small corn tortillas

Avocados, for garnish

Keep both the sauce and the beans warm.

Put the shark in a bowl, then ladle out some tomato sauce and coat the fish with it.

Get all your tortillas hot.

You build your enchiladas by dipping a tortilla in the tomato sauce, shaking off the excess, then setting it down on a plate. Spread some beans on it, then some shark. Repeat. For the final tortilla, spread some beans on it then set it, bean side down, onto the shark. Pour a little more tomato sauce on top, spread it so it covers the top tortilla, then garnish with the pickled red onions and some avocado. Serve at once.

SALMON RILLETTES

PREP TIME: 15 MINUTES | **COOK TIME: 15 MINUTES** | **SERVES 8**

Rillettes, pronounced "ree-YETS," are one of my favorite appetizers. A rillette is basically a really rough pâté that's just barely spreadable. And salmon rillettes are every bit as good as the customary pork or duck. Far easier to make than a proper pâté and equally less fussy, rillettes are to pâté as Armagnac is to a fine Cognac: just as good, but a little rougher around the edges.

Another way to look at a rillette is that it's a lot like a salmon salad (or egg salad), except it's been beaten to a pulp. You eat it on crackers or toasted bread, so it needs to be spreadable enough to stay where you put it. Best part is you don't want the prime cuts to make your salmon rillettes; anglers, this is a great use for the meat you scrape off the carcass with a spoon and for that last six to eight inches of fillet on the tail end.

If you're buying your salmon, don't make rillettes from top-of-the-line Pacific salmon loin cuts. Make it with cheaper pieces, or with lesser salmon, such as pinks or chum salmon. Any trout or char will work, too.

You'll also want some smoked salmon, too. The flavor will be different depending on whether you use hot-smoked or cold-smoked fish, however. I use cold-smoked fish here, which is more delicate. A rillette with a piece of hot-smoked salmon will be pretty assertive, but still very good. Only thing you want to watch for is hot-smoked salmon that's been really heavily smoked; it's too firm and will not properly incorporate into the rest of the spread.

Rillettes are perfect outdoor food, too. You pack it into little jars—a half-pint Mason jar is ideal—melt some butter on top, let it solidify in the fridge, cover the jar and you're good to go. Bring along some crackers or bread, and you have a helluva meal at a picnic, on the boat, streamside, or wherever you find yourself.

Serve the rillettes on toast or crackers as an appetizer or a snack. It's really good onboard while you're fishing for more salmon and trout.

½ pound fresh salmon or trout, skin and bones removed

½ pound smoked salmon or trout, skin and bones removed

¼ cup sour cream or crème fraîche

3 to 5 tablespoons unsalted butter, at room temperature

2 tablespoons lemon juice

Zest of 1 lemon, finely grated

3 to 5 tablespoons minced chives or parsley

Salt and black pepper

About 1 tablespoon prepared horseradish

Pickled mustard seeds or trout caviar (optional)

Bring about a quart of water to a boil. Salt it well. You can add some flavorings if you want, such as bay leaves, herbs, or onions, but I rarely do. Slip the fresh salmon into the water and turn off the heat. Cover the pot and let this sit for 15 minutes or so. Remove the salmon, and when it is cool enough to handle, flake it into a large bowl.

Break up the smoked salmon and add that to the bowl, along with the sour cream, 3 tablespoons of butter, lemon juice, lemon zest, and chives. Use a heavy fork to mash everything together. You want a rough spread, not a smooth pâté. Add the remaining 2 tablespoons of butter if the rillettes look dry.

Add salt, pepper, and horseradish to taste. Cover the rillettes with plastic wrap and set in the fridge for an hour or so before serving. Spoon over some pickled mustard seeds or caviar when you serve.

Once made, pack the rillettes tightly into jars; try to remove all air pockets. Once packed, melt some butter over the top of the rillettes, cover, and store in the fridge. It will keep for at least a week this way, and up to 2 weeks if you keep resealing the butter cap between each use. You can also freeze the finished rillettes for several months.

SMOKED BLUEFISH PÂTÉ

PREP TIME: 20 MINUTES | **SERVES 10**

Bluefish is just about as polarizing a food as there is. You either love it or hate it. *Pomatomus saltatrix* is a pelagic fish that normally travels in big schools, eternally in search of food. They're a lot like a pack of wolves, or oceanic piranha. All that traveling means bluefish have lots of red slow-twitch muscle, which in fish is very, very strong and unpleasant to eat.

What's more, the "white" meat, really bluish gray in a bluefish, is pretty soft. Oh yeah, and uncooked it doesn't freeze worth a damn. So what's to love? Well, cooked fresh, bluefish is fantastic—if you cook it right. I prefer mine grilled, slow barbecued, or better yet, smoked.

Smoked bluefish pâté may well be the best thing you can do with blues, especially big blues larger than ten pounds (they can grow to twenty-five pounds). Basically it's fish, cream cheese, capers, lemon, onion, and dill. Super simple, so good on crackers for a summertime lunch or appetizer.

I'd been wanting to make it for a while, and I got my chance when I returned to Long Island—my old stomping grounds—to do some fishing with my friend, Chef Anita Lo. We fished out of Montauk, ostensibly for black seabass and gigantic porgies, which we laid into something fierce. All the while, though, I was hoping to get into some bluefish. Why? I can catch fish that taste like seabass and porgies here in California, but we have nothing like bluefish in the North Pacific.

About halfway through the trip, Anita hooked a big fish on a porgy rig. It wasn't coming up, either, and lest you think it's because Anita is just a fancy-pants big-city chef, I can assure you that she's a real-deal angler; we've fished together in Alaska, and she proved herself then. About five minutes into the fight, we all reeled up to watch the show. Tuna? Tilefish? World-record seabass? Shark? Shark. Had to be a shark. Finally, about fifteen minutes in, we saw the fish. It was a bluefish. A big one. And it was hooked in the gill plate, so it could swim freely. No wonder Anita was having a tough time. Nearly twenty minutes in, we gaffed the fish and brought it aboard. Easily fifteen pounds, maybe more than that.

It was the only bluefish we caught that day, but it was enough. Anita can catch blues whenever she wants, so she was nice enough to give me the fish, which we filleted and I brought home on the airplane. I smoked it the next day, and it was awesome. Tasted like the old days.

If you want to smoke your own bluefish, here's how I did it. I had about 3½ pounds of skin-on fillets. I mixed half a pound of kosher salt with half a pound of brown sugar and packed the fish with it. I put that in the fridge for four hours, then I rinsed off the cure and patted the bluefish dry. I let the fish dry uncovered in the refrigerator overnight. The next day, I smoked it over alder for four hours, never letting the temperature top 200°F.

This recipe assumes you have cooked bluefish, preferably smoked bluefish. You can find smoked bluefish in most markets in the Northeast. Or you can make your own. Or you can just cook up some bluefish—on the grill is best—and then use the cooked flaked meat.

No bluefish near you? Try these fish as substitutes: mackerel (of any kind), shad, herring, sardines, freshwater sheepshead (drum), whitefish, cisco, wahoo, dorado, or any jack. You want an oily fish that isn't salmon.

½ pound cooked (smoked)
  bluefish (for alternatives, see
  above)

¼ pound cream cheese, softened

½ cup minced red onion

1 tablespoon chopped dill

1 tablespoon small capers

Zest and juice of 1 lemon

A few splashes of Tabasco or
  Worcestershire sauce

2 tablespoons brandy or bourbon
  (optional)

Salt and pepper

Remove all the red meat from the bluefish and either discard or give it to your pet. It's very fishy, and most people (including me) don't like it. Toss all the ingredients in a large bowl and mash them together into a rough pâté. If you want a smooth pâté, double the cream cheese and mash everything up even more. Serve with crackers or flatbread.

Once made, this pâté will keep in the fridge for a week to 10 days. It doesn't freeze well, so my advice if you smoke your own bluefish is to seal it into ½ pound portions so you can make this whenever.

FISH OR SEAFOOD ESCABECHE

PREP TIME: 20 MINUTES | **COOK TIME: 25 MINUTES** | **SERVES 6**

It's likely that the Arabs invented this method of cooking fish or seafood then sousing in a vinegary sauce sometime in the Middle Ages. It spread to Spain during the Moors' conquest of the peninsula, and there are versions of it all over the Mediterranean and the Latin world. This is a version from Tabasco, a state in southern Mexico.

I make this with oysters, which are simply poached open before making the recipe; their liquor is used as the broth. You can do the exact same thing with little clams or mussels. But escabeche is every bit as good with fish. In that case, you flour and fry the fish before poaching in the vinegary broth. Normally, you would use fresh sardines, but small mackerel are good, as are jacksmelt, really large anchovies, and herring. Barring that, a great freshwater option is small trout—the little mountain trout are perfect here. No small trout? You could try this with bluegills, little bass, or perch.

6 to 8 whole cloves

6 to 8 allspice berries

1 teaspoon black peppercorns

½ teaspoon cumin seeds

1 cup white wine, sherry, or
   cider vinegar

3 bay leaves

Zest and juice of 2 lemons or limes

3 tablespoons olive oil

1 small white onion, sliced root
   to tip

1 large carrot, peeled and diced

6 cloves garlic, chopped

2 hot chiles, such as serrano or
   arbol, seeded and chopped

2 dozen oysters in the shell, or
   1 pint shucked oysters with
   their liquor

½ cup white wine or water

Start by toasting all the whole spices—the cloves, allspice, peppercorns, and cumin—in a dry pan until they smell nice, maybe a minute or two. In a mortar, crack them all, but do not grind to a powder.

Add this to the white wine, along with the bay leaves, and bring to a simmer. Turn off the heat, add the lemon or lime juice and zest, and cover the pot. Let this cool, and then strain out the solids.

In another pan, sauté the onion, carrot, garlic, and chiles in the olive oil until the onion is soft and translucent, about 6 to 8 minutes. Turn off the heat. Add the contents of the sauté pan, along with any oil in it, to the strained vinegar mixture. Wipe out the sauté pan.

If you have pre-shucked oysters, just add them to the pan, bring the liquor up to a simmer until the oysters all cook—just a minute or two—and then add the oysters, plus maybe 2 tablespoons of the liquor, to the vinegar mixture. You're done.

If you have oysters in the shell, add them, plus the additional ½ cup of white wine to the pan, cover it, and turn the heat to high. Keep an eye on the oysters, and as soon as one opens, pluck it out and shuck it into the vinegar mixture. Doing this will keep you from overcooking some oysters while waiting for them all to open.

When all the oysters have opened, strain the liquid from the pan to remove debris, and add 2 tablespoons of it to the oyster-vinegar-vegetable mixture.

Serve warm or chilled, on its own as an appetizer, or on top of tostadas, or with crusty bread.

For small fish, follow these instructions:

First, make the spiced vinegar from step one above.

Ideally you would butterfly your fish; instructions for that are on page 53. Anything larger than a sardine, you can fillet. Lay the fish on a small tray or baking sheet in which lemon juice, salt, and water cover the whole bottom of the sheet. You want the fish to be laying in a shallow pool of lemon juice-salt-water. Leave them there for 30 minutes, turning once.

Meanwhile, sauté the onions, carrots, garlic, and chiles in 3 tablespoons of olive oil until they are just starting to color around the edges. Add the spiced vinegar from above and simmer 10 minutes. Turn off the heat and set aside. Stir in the zest.

Pat the sardines dry and dust with flour. Any sort of flour will do, but chickpea flour is a fun option; it is often used in southern Italy and adds a nutty flavor.

Fry the sardines in some more olive oil until golden brown and set aside to drain on a rack or in one layer on paper towels.

Pour some of the vinegar mixture into a plate with a well or a shallow bowl. Add the sardines, then cover with the remaining sauce.

NOTE Either version of this dish is just as good covered in the sauce and left to marinate for up to three days in the fridge. If you use pre-shucked oysters, replace the ½ cup white wine with their oyster liquor.

SALADS, COLD DISHES, AND LEFTOVERS

17
I LIKE IT RAW

RAW FISH IS a pleasure that, for many Americans, is relatively new. There are no traditional American raw fish dishes, with the exception of clams and oysters on the half shell. Other cultures, however, celebrate the freshest fish by eating it raw, or slightly "cooked" or "cured" with something acidic or salty. Even with sashimi or sushi, arguably the purest form of raw fish, the rice underneath the sashimi or in the sushi is laced with vinegar. Done right, raw fish and seafood feels clean, pure, fresh. There is very little like it in the world of gastronomy. There is a reason sushi, ceviche, and poke are so popular.

You see raw fish and seafood paired with ingredients known to be antimicrobial or that help preserve the fish, thus the vinegar or citrus and the presence of salt. You will also see mustard, chiles, and horseradish where those ingredients are common (as wasabi is in Japan). All not only add zing to the mild fish flesh, but can also help stave off the wee beasties—not that a dip in soy sauce or a bite of fish with a habanero will save you from parasites. See the section on food safety for details on how to eat raw fish safely.

A general rule when you want to freestyle raw fish and seafood is to follow the safety instructions on page 32, which normally means blast-freezing the fish for a couple days in a box freezer or a week or more in a regular freezer; many normal freezers are not cold enough to entirely eliminate any parasite risks, but if you set it at -4°F, normally as low as it will go, the fish will be safe after about a week in the freezer.

Beyond the issue of parasites, raw fish should be the finest and freshest you can provide. This means taking care of the fish or seafood from the moment it comes over the rail. See the section "Catching Your Own: Fish Care from Water to Freezer" on page 23 for details.

Good raw fish ranges from caught that moment—I know tuna anglers who keep everything for ceviche except the tuna in Tupperware

▲ Me shucking clams on Block Island, circa 1976.

in a cooler, waiting for that tuna to come over the rail—to several days old.

It's a myth that fish doesn't age like meat. It does, only on an accelerated timeframe. Tuna, salmon, skates, and even white fish like sturgeon or grouper are all better a day or three after being caught. That's not usually a problem if you're buying it, but it's a good thing to keep in mind if you're catching your own fish. The exceptions are shellfish and crustaceans. First off, raw crustaceans are a dicey proposition. There are lots of parasites that cause you havoc if you eat raw crabs or shrimp. I do not recommend eating raw crustaceans at all, unless they've been properly frozen beforehand.

Raw shellfish, oysters, and clams, are indeed best the moment they're opened. But of course, they can be kept alive for days in the right conditions, and in many cases need to be purged of sand and grit first (page 29).

◀ A pristine Olympia oyster, ready for slurping.

SUSHI AND SASHIMI

I love both, having first encountered them relatively late in life. I'll never forget it. It was an early lunch date with my girlfriend. I was about twenty-five years old. She wanted to go, and I, of course, said yes. I remember it being expensive, and, well, as a distance runner training for a marathon at the time, not very filling. After we parted, heading back to our respective jobs, I swung by the Italian deli to pick up a bag of arancini, rice balls stuffed with cheese and then fried crispy.

To this day, sushi is a treat, something someone else makes for me. It's still expensive, especially if you want to fill up on it. I've never learned the craft of it, so I can't help you here. There are books on home sushi making, but my recommendation is to enjoy it out, made by a professional, on date nights.

You always want to serve raw fish and seafood cold; it's supposed to be refreshing and clean. There's something deeply unsettling about biting into a warm piece of raw fish.

Another general tip, besides serving it cold along with something exciting, is to mix your raw whatever with something crunchy. The classic mignonette on raw oysters is a perfect example of this: minced shallot in a vinaigrette hits two points at once; it's a texture thing. Raw fish and seafood, with a few exceptions, are soft, almost silky. You want to contrast that.

Following are some basic raw fish and seafood preparations from all over the world. Let's start with one from my childhood—cocktail sauce.

COCKTAIL SAUCE

Yep, the basic cocktail sauce you see with shrimp cocktail, which is pretty close to a raw preparation. We used to eat it with clams on the half shell back on Block Island in the 1970s. At its most basic, it's just ketchup mixed with prepared horseradish. The ratio is up to you. Me? I like my nose to get blasted.

Here's a slightly fancier version.

½ cup ketchup
2 to 3 tablespoons prepared horseradish
A few dashes of Worcestershire sauce
A few dashes of hot sauce

Mix well and serve cold, either with lemon wedges alongside, or you can squeeze the juice of a lemon into the sauce. Once made, this keeps well, tightly covered, for a week or so.

MIGNONETTE

A bit classier than cocktail sauce, mignonette serves the same purpose: to fancy up shellfish on the half shell. I first encountered this one in restaurants when I was a kid. My ten-year-old self, taking a dignified stab at the French, felt ritzy asking for "mig-non-et" instead of the cocktail sauce I was used to.

Ideally, you'd use a quality white wine or champagne vinegar, but I've used rice vinegar, pineapple vinegar, sherry vinegar, and homemade fruit vinegars, too. Just don't use distilled white vinegar, for God's sake.

2 shallots, minced fine
½ cup really good vinegar
Freshly cracked black pepper

Mix everything and keep it cold for at least 1 hour before serving, which tames the shallots. Keeps a couple days in the fridge.

My friend Nate Grace digging steamer clams near Gloucester, Massachusetts.

CEVICHE

Ceviche is raw or cooked fish or seafood marinated in citrus, almost always accompanied by onion, chiles, and some sort of herb, typically cilantro. It is of Latin American origin, and many countries claim it, notably Peru and Ecuador.

Normally, ceviche is cubed raw fish or shellfish, or precooked crab, lobster, or shrimp. Lime is the most common citrus, but many variations exist. I prefer a mix of lime, grapefruit, and lemon juice. Sour orange juice is great, too. Minced or thinly sliced onions are a must, as is some sort of hot chile.

Traditionally, the fish in ceviche is fully "cooked" by the citrus, whose acidity denatures the proteins of the fish, making it appear cooked. This takes a few hours. But many chefs are tossing together their ceviches at service, giving the fish only a short time with the citrus. This is fine if your fish is pristine.

In Mexico, most ceviche is basically your standard pico de gallo salsa—tomatoes, onions, chile, and cilantro—with chunks of seafood tossed in. Avocado is common, too. This is what we in America are most used to. Peruvian ceviche is often served with a slice of cooked sweet potato and the huge-kernelled corn they are known for, and Ecuadorean ceviche tends to be tomato-heavy.

I find that lean white fish work best for ceviche, although I do like it with salmon, too. Any sort of snapper, grouper, black seabass, porgy, sea trout, white seabass, or yellowtail will work, as will prefrozen freshwater fish like walleye or perch.

---

1 pound prefrozen lingcod,
   rockfish, or other lean,
   white fish

2 Roma or other paste tomatoes,
   seeded

4 limes

1 lemon

1 grapefruit

1 habanero or rocoto chile pepper,
   or more

Salt and black pepper

½ small red onion, thinly sliced
   from root to tip

1 ear of corn, kernels sliced off

3 tablespoons chopped cilantro

Slice the fish into bite-sized pieces. Cut the tomatoes into pieces the same size as the fish and set them aside for later. Grate the zest of 1 lime, the lemon, and the grapefruit; I use a microplane grater to do this. Finely mince the habanero. Juice all the citrus. Add all the ingredients except the tomatoes and the cilantro to a bowl or plastic container with a lid and refrigerate for 30 minutes to 3 hours.

Add the tomatoes and cilantro, mix well, and serve cold with chips or on tostadas.

NOTE Marinating times make a difference when you're making ceviche. Depending on the size of the fish pieces, you will need at least thirty minutes and normally an hour for the citrus to "cook" the fish. Up to about three hours is fine, but beyond that, the ceviche, while still good, becomes more of a pickled fish thing. It's a subtle difference, but you can taste it. Citrus matters, too. You always want the dominant citrus in the marinade to be either limes or lemons, which are far more acidic than oranges, grapefruits, or tangerines. Add these fruits as an accent to the ceviche; I'm especially fond of a little grapefruit in the mix.

POKE

This is a Hawaiian dish that has grown very popular on the US mainland. Meaning "to cut crosswise" in Hawaiian, poke is cubed raw fish with soy sauce or sea salt, seaweed, and candlenuts. Nowadays, you will almost always see green onions, sweet Maui onions, sesame oil, and macadamia nuts instead of the hard-to-find candlenuts. I've seen pretty much anything you can imagine in a poke bowl, however. Other good additions would be avocado, wasabi, or lime juice right at the end—you don't want your fish to turn color—and hot chiles. The Japanese rice seasonings called togarashi or furikake are also good additions.

Tuna and its cousins or cooked octopus are the norms here, but salmon is common in the United States. Any fish safe to eat raw will work, as will cooked shrimp or chunks of cooked lobster. Use this recipe as a guide, not as gospel. One of the best things about poke is your ability to have fun with it. Any high-quality tuna or other fish, as mentioned above, will work here. Precooked shellfish and crustaceans are good, too.

1 small sweet onion, like a Maui or
   Vidalia, thinly sliced

3 tablespoons lime juice

1 to 2 pounds high-quality tuna,
   cut into dice

3 to 5 thin green onions, or chives,
   thinly sliced

½ cup macadamia nuts, coarsely
   chopped

1 avocado (slightly underripe),
   cut into chunks

¼ cup soy sauce

2 tablespoons sesame oil

1 tablespoon togarashi or furikake
   seasoning, or sesame seeds

Slice the onion thinly and soak in the lime juice while you chop and cut everything else. Mix everything together gently in a large bowl, then serve in individual bowls.

CRUDO AND AQUACHILE

Similar to Japanese sashimi, only with less ceremony, these—and their relatives, tiradito and carpaccio—are a class of simple raw fish dishes that are almost always an appetizer or starter. Crudo and carpaccio are Italian, the difference being that carpaccio is pounded flat, while crudo is thinly sliced, like the rest of these dishes.

Crudo is influenced by Japanese sashimi, although some Italians would deny this. Peruvian tiradito is actively a Latin-Asian fusion, thanks to the influx of Japanese immigrants to that country in the 1800s. Aguachile is similar. It's a Mexican dish, most often done with shrimp.

Tiradito and aguachile are basically instant ceviches, in that they always have a spicy, acidic element, but that element is added right when you serve, so the fish is still raw, not "cooked" by the acid. Italian carpaccio and crudo are not normally marinated with anything acidic, but lemon is a traditional accompaniment; you add it as you eat. You see capers a lot here too, as a textural and salty note. Always get the smallest nonpareil capers, if you can find them.

The point of these dishes is to enjoy super-fresh chilled seafood with punchy accompaniments. They are openers to a larger meal.

CRUDO

PREP TIME: 20 MINUTES | **SERVES 8**

You'll need a dense fish you can slice very thin. Tuna is traditional, but many other fish will work. I've seen it done with scallops, slices of lobster tail, and even large shrimp sliced lengthwise. Yellowtail and amberjack are also great.

Crudo requires good olive oil if you want it to be Italian. If you are taking it in another direction, you will need some sort of really special oil. If you wanted to make it very Canadian, for example, use extra-virgin canola oil, which is amazing. Raw sunflower or roasted pumpkinseed oils are good too, for northern European crudo. Hard to beat sesame oil for an Asian twist.

Italian crudo also features excellent salt and fresh pepper. This is where you break out the fancy flaked salt and the pepper grinder with the spendy Malabar or Tellicherry peppercorns. Since there is so little to this dish, every ingredient needs to shine.

Finally, you'll see capers and herbs in many renditions of crudo, normally basil. It should always be a soft herb, like basil, parsley or cilantro, not tougher ones like sage or rosemary.

1 pound boneless, skinless fish

High-quality extra-virgin olive oil, for drizzling on the dish

2 to 3 tablespoons small capers

Grated zest and juice of 2 lemons

1 small bunch of basil, thinly sliced or torn

Flaked salt, such as Maldon

Freshly ground black pepper

Using a very sharp knife, slice the fish into thin slices, and arrange them on a serving plate.

When you're ready to serve, drizzle each plate with the olive oil, scatter some capers, grated lemon zest, and basil over each plate, then some flaked salt and black pepper. Right as you serve, drizzle the lemon juice over it all, or give everyone a lemon wedge.

AGUACHILE

PREP TIME: 20 MINUTES | **SERVES 4**

Aguachile, meaning "chile water," is Mexico's take on sashimi. Commonly done with shrimp, aguachile is a cousin of ceviche. What makes aguachile different from ceviche? Unlike ceviche, aguachile is only doused with the zippy marinade a few minutes before serving, so it's quite raw.

Most often, you'll see it with raw shrimp, but I prefer it with the sorts of fish you see at a sushi bar, ideally tuna or yellowtail, which is what you see in the picture.

Aguachile as we know it is not an old dish, and most sources think it only took its current form in Sinaloa during the late 1970s. Most people north of the border know only that Sinaloa is home to the infamous drug lord El Chapo, but it's a beautiful state in northwest Mexico—one with a lot of shoreline. West Coasters may know of the Sinaloan city of Mazatlan, which has been a prime destination for spring break for decades. It's likely that the current incarnation of aguachile came about there. Before that, aguachile had no fish or seafood. It was a humble dish of wild chiltepin chiles, raw onions, and fresh cheese.

My aguachile recipe is close to what you would see in Sinaloa, although again, most cocineros there use shrimp. Mine has hot green chiles, cilantro stems, and cucumber buzzed with lime juice, very thinly sliced red onions or red shallots, fresh cilantro, avocado, and most importantly, crushed wild chiltepin chiles. You will also often see cucumbers as a garnish.

What fish to use? Well, my advice is to buy anything sold for sushi or sashimi, including shrimp. You should know that eating raw, never-frozen shrimp is risky. Any number of studies have shown that a significant percentage of raw shrimp have harmful bacterial or parasites that are invisible to the naked eye (page 17). Prefrozen shrimp are OK.

SAUCE

1 stalk celery, coarsely chopped

½ cucumber, seeded but not peeled

2 serrano or jalapeño chiles, sliced

½ cup cilantro (stems are fine)

½ cup lime juice

¼ cup water

AGUACHILE

2 large shallots or 1 small red onion, thinly sliced

1 pound skinless yellowtail fillet, or other piece of fish you can thinly slice

1 avocado, thinly sliced

Chopped cilantro, for garnish

Crushed, dried chiltepin chiles, for garnish

Put the sauce ingredients in a blender and purée. Set a fine strainer over a bowl and pour the contents of the blender into it. Let this drain 20 minutes. Do not push anything through, as you want this liquid to be clear. Salt it to taste.

Once you've sliced the shallots or red onion, douse it with some lime juice to take away its raw sharpness.

Slice your yellowtail or other fish into pieces about ¼- to ⅛-inch thick. Not super thin, but fairly thin.

Pour some marinade on a plate or shallow bowl and arrange the fish on top and garnish with the sliced avocado, cilantro, shallot, and chiles.

NOTE If you can't find dried chiltepin chiles, use any hot dried chile you can crumble up. Or skip it.

TARTARE

Think of tartare as micro poke: small bits of raw fish served with good things around it. Unlike poke (page 280), which is designed to be a meal in itself, tartare is almost always a starter and almost always meant to be served on or with something, like a cracker. And whereas poke is Hawaiian, tartare is of Eurasian origin, so what's normally served with the fish will typically be European ingredients. That's not to say you couldn't take the poke recipe and cut everything smaller.

When you break down tartare, you usually see a set of accompanying ingredients that meet the same requirements we see with all raw fish dishes:

▶ Something salty
▶ Something crunchy
▶ An oil
▶ Something tart, like vinegar or citrus
▶ Often an herb or other aromatic thing

Follow these rules—as always, tasting as you go—and you'll be in good shape.

You mostly see tuna and salmon tartare, but once you properly freeze and thaw your fish, the sky's the limit. There's a reason for the prevalence of salmon and tuna, however: fat. Fatty fish make better raw fish in most cases, and tartare is no exception. Denser fish are also better, because you need to cut your tartare small. With softer fish, it helps to mince the fish when it's partially frozen. And mince you must; ground fish tartare is, at least to me, nasty. Tartare is entirely judged by the skill of your knife work, so you want well-defined dice small enough to fit a portion on a cracker; this is called a *brunoise* in French cooking.

Make sure you cut your fish with a sharp knife, as a dull knife will smear any fish fat and damage the way the tartare feels in your mouth when you eat it. I can't stress enough that you want little dice, not a mush.

Now, as for the cracker, you can go as low-brow as Saltines or as high-brow as the salmon-skin crackers I do in the recipe below. A good middle ground is a table water cracker, which is vaguely classy without requiring too much extra work on your part.

▼ Salmon tartare

SALMON TARTARE

PREP TIME: 20 MINUTES | SERVES 6

This tartare is inspired by one my friend Dan Klein made while we were in Cordova, Alaska, fishing for Copper River salmon some years ago. We'd gathered salmonberries that day, and he chopped them into his tartare, topped with fresh salmon caviar, and served it on a salmon skin cracker. The result was brilliant.

I wanted my tartare to go north, in honor of Alaska. So I went Scandinavian. I added a little horseradish, dill, and toasted pumpkinseed oil. Pumpkinseed oil is not actually a Scandinavian thing, it's an Austrian thing, but it's amazing. The oil is dark and viscous, and it looks a little like motor oil. But it has an intense roasted-nutty flavor that I can't get enough of—it's every bit as wonderful as the finest olive oil. Added to this tartare, it immediately hits you with a sense of cool Northern Europe.

This is a party appetizer, something to impress your guests or special someone. It requires a little effort to make the salmon-skin chips, but if you forgo them and use table water crackers (my second choice), this comes together in a snap. Just be sure to make more than you think you need. They will get eaten fast.

You will need high-quality salmon (preferably wild salmon) and a nice oil, and I urge you to at least look for salmon roe caviar; it's available in little jars at most good supermarkets in the canned fish section.

Sub in any good quality fish here, and keeping in mind the rules of a good tartare, feel free to play around with this. Remember, the shallot is the crunchy thing, there's the oil, lemon zest, and juice, herby dill, zippy horseradish, and the salty pop of the caviar.

1 pound salmon fillet, with skin if possible

1 shallot, minced, about ¼ cup

1 to 2 tablespoons pumpkinseed oil or some other nice oil

Zest of 1 lemon

1 tablespoon fresh chopped dill

1 teaspoon prepared horseradish

Salt and black pepper

1 tablespoon lemon juice

2 ounces salmon caviar (optional)

OPTIONAL SALMON-SKIN CHIPS Slice the skin off the salmon with a fillet knife and gently scrape off any meat sticking to it. Pat the salmon skin dry with paper towels and lay flat, cut-side down, on a non-stick skillet. Turn the heat to medium and place another flat, heavy surface on top of the skin. I use another pot. Let this cook for 5 to 8 minutes. Listen for it sizzling under the weight, and do not check the skin for at least 3 minutes—this prevents it from curling up. Once the cut side looks crispy, turn the salmon skin, salt the side you just cooked, and repeat the process with the other side of the skin.

When the salmon skin is crispy, take it out of the pan and let it cool for a minute or two. Use a sharp chef's knife to cut it into cracker pieces. Let it cool completely.

TARTAR Meanwhile, make the tartare by finely chopping the salmon into small dice. Do not put it into a food processor and do not chop it into mush. Put the chopped salmon into a bowl and mix in the shallot, pumpkinseed oil, lemon zest, dill, and horseradish. Salt and pepper it to taste and set it in the fridge to chill for up to a few hours.

When you're ready to serve, mix the lemon juice into the tartare and scoop little piles of it on each salmon skin cracker. Top with a dollop of salmon caviar and serve. Have some table water crackers around to serve after the salmon-skin crackers are devoured.

THIS IS ONE of my favorite chapters in this book. Not only do I love the processes of salting, smoking, and pickling, but they are all methods that work very well with fish and seafood, having been perfected over millennia.

Evidence for salted fish exists before the written word, and various forms of dried and salted fish and seafood exist in most cultures. Little dried shrimp are a fixture in Mexican cuisine, dried fish and squid are all over Asian cuisines, ranging from India to Korea, dried fish are common in West African cooking, and salt cod and its wind-dried cousin stockfish—both normally cod—are a bedrock ingredient in both Caribbean and European cultures. Rakfisk—salted fermented trout and char—is a thing in Norway, and heavily salted, dried bottarga—fish roe from mullet and tuna—are common in the Mediterranean. Salted herring—rehydrated, fried, and served with cornmeal pancakes and Karo syrup—is a very old-school breakfast where I used to live in Fredericksburg, Virginia.

Less dramatically dried products abound as well. Caviar—salted fish roe—springs to mind, and gently salt-cured fish shows up all over the world. This more gentle salt-curing is the first step in cold-smoking, and you should really think of cold-smoked fish as salt cured and then smoked rather than wholly smoked. Cold-smoking after that salt cure does preserve fish for quite some time, while hot smoking, which is far more common in North America, does not. I'll cover both styles in this chapter.

Finally there is pickling, which can extend the life of fish and seafood for a few weeks to months—depending on your tolerance for fishy smells.

I generally like pickled fish and seafood as an appetizer, and I do not like it long pickled. I know some people who will keep a jar of, say, pickled pike, in their fridge for months. So far as I can tell, it's safe to eat, but it will take on a very strong smell and be very acidic. That's why you will not see canned pickled recipes in this book, and it's why my pickling recipes are small. Make some, eat, then make some more. It will be a lot better.

SMOKING

Let's start with hot smoking, which is what most people do here in North America. It's a process more or less like barbecue, rather than cold-smoking, in that you normally smoke at temperatures above 150°F and, in the case of fish and seafood, below 225°F. It will preserve the product a bit longer than if the product had been cooked regularly, but not dramatically so. A piece of smoked salmon left in the fridge for two weeks will get a bit slimy and unappetizing.

There are two main ways to brine your fish before you smoke: brining or dry-salting. Note that there is no such thing as a "dry brine," since brines, by definition, have water in them. It's dry-salting. Brining is better when you're smoking a load of fish or seafood, since you can dunk lots of fish in a brine inexpensively. I prefer dry-salting though, because it's a bit more precise and you're done faster.

Why the salt? You need to in order to remove excess water from the fish, firm it up, season it, and to preserve it somewhat. If you don't salt or brine fish or seafood first and you then cook it slowly over a smoky fire, you are barbecuing. It's awesome, but it's a different thing for a different chapter (chapter 14, page 219).

My general rule for salting a fish for smoking is to thickly coat it in salt for one hour per pound. More specifically speaking, that is one hour per pound of each piece. So if I have a half-pound piece of fish I want to smoke, I will coat it thickly in salt—you can even bury it in salt if you want—for thirty minutes. See what I mean about fast? You can have twenty pounds of salmon, or bluefish, or whatever ready to dry in less than an hour if they're all in smallish pieces. But that would require a lot of salt. The Smoked Sablefish recipe on page 297 is your master recipe for dry-salting.

WHICH FISH TO SMOKE?

This is a surprisingly controversial topic. People, mostly male anglers, want to smoke everything. And while that's everyone's God-given right, not every fish takes the smoke well— particularly any lean fish. Yes, I hear all the time that this person makes great smoked flounder or bass or walleye, but I've eaten them all, for decades, and no, they're not great. They're OK, perfectly edible, but all are lacking in something. And that something is fat.

All the best smoked fish in the world are fatty. Period. Look at any culture on any continent, and their most prized smoked fish or seafood is fatty. Why? Smoke adheres better to fat than it does to lean meat.

What fish are we talking about? All of the orange fish, the salmonids (salmon, trout, char, grayling), which includes the whitefish family, like ciscoes, Great Lakes whitefish, chubs, and sheefish; all the mackerels, which includes their friends the jacks and the wahoo, as well as all the tuna; all the marine "little fish," including anchovies, sardines, herring, mullet, smelt, and hooligans, which are so oily they can be lit on fire once dried; swordfish, marlin, and other billfish; freshwater drum and some catfish; oysters and mussels; eels, meaning American eels, not moray or conger eels; and sablefish, arguably the finest white-fleshed fish to smoke.

Beyond that, your results will be, well, OK. I'm not saying don't ever smoke, say, cod or haddock. It's just that smoking is not the best treatment for them. If you want to cook a lean fish over a smoky fire, that can be amazing, but use my barbecue recipe on page 228.

As for a brine, I go with one-third cup Diamond Crystal kosher salt to one quart of water. I mention the brand because salts are cut differently. By weight, that's two ounces, or about fifty-seven grams, per quart or liter—yes, I know that quarts and liters are slightly different, but this brine doesn't have to be *that* precise. So if you use a different brand, go by weight.

What about sugar? Sugar works too, as it will also pull moisture from fish and seafood. I generally use it in a secondary role, so I don't measure it as precisely as the salt. It will help remove moisture and firm up fish, but it won't penetrate to the center of the fish.

Nor will any other herb or spice. This is a myth perpetuated by the fact that some swear by baroque brines with twenty-three ingredients, saying they can taste it. The soup you just made will stick to the surface of the fish, but it won't seep into the middle of it. No need for complicated brines. If you want added flavors, add them in a mop or baste as you are smoking or a spice mix you add after the brine but before the pellicle.

The pellicle. This is that shiny, tacky sheen you get on a salted or brined fish after you've let it dry for a while. You need it. Sopping wet meat doesn't take smoke well, but neither does bone-dry anything. You need some moisture to allow the smoke to stick.

What smoke? Alder. I use alder if at all possible. It's a light smoke that allows the fish to taste of itself. Fruit woods are fine, as is maple, but hickory, pecan, and mesquite are, to my mind, too heavy for fish and seafood. The lone exception to this is if you're making smoked marlin Mexican style, in which case you do need mesquite.

The smoked salmon recipe on page 292 is your master recipe for all smoked fish fillets; smoked whole fish (page 298) are a slightly different deal from smoked fillets or big blocks from larger fish. But regardless of the fish, there are several things you'll want to get you started:

A smoker

I've used a Traeger and a Bradley, an open fire and various offset smokers. All are good in their own way. No matter what smoker you use, you'll need two things: to be able to know your smoking chamber's temperature, and to control the heat, at least in a rough sense.

Wood

The only downside to a Traeger smoker is that you need to use their wood pellets. As a guy who used a Brinkmann wood-fired BBQ for years, fueling it with scraps of almond and other fruitwoods, buying wood can be annoying, but you get better precision with this method.

Salt

Buy a box of kosher salt from the supermarket. Do not use regular table salt, as it contains iodide and anti-caking agents that will give your fish an "off" flavor. I use Diamond Crystal.

▼ Smoking a pair of **Pacific rockfish.**

Something sweet

Salmon in particular loves sweet. I prefer to sweeten my smoked salmon with birch syrup; it's just like maple syrup, only tapped from birch trees instead. But maple syrup is just as good. Just use *real* maple syrup, OK? Honey works, too. Molasses is too strong.

A large plastic container

Buy the big, flat ones from the supermarket. They stack easily in a normal fridge, so you can have two different brines going. And they clean easily and are pretty cheap.

A wire rack

You need to rest your brined fish on a rack with plenty of air circulation to form the all-important pellicle, and you will use it to rest the smoked fish before storing it.

A basting brush

You probably already have this in your kitchen, but if not, pick one up. Get the flat kind, like you use to paint detail on window trim.

SMOKED SALMON

PREP TIME: 15 MINUTES | COOK TIME: 4 HOURS | MAKES 5 POUNDS

I smoke a lot of salmon, and I'm proud of this recipe, although it would be the height of arrogance to say that what I do is the be all, end all of salmon smoking recipes. Lots of people smoke their salmon in lots of ways, and many of them are good. But I've been smoking fish for many years, and I've developed a system that works well.

How do you eat it? Well, you can just eat it plain, or you can flake it and make it into a smoked salmon salad, you can pound it with butter and make salmon rillettes, serve it in deviled eggs, tossed with pasta—anything you'd like.

When you're ready to start, you'll need smallish pieces of salmon about ¼ to ½ pound each. Any salmonid fish will work with this recipe. I've done it with king salmon, sockeye, coho, chum, and pink salmon, dolly varden, plus kokanee, steelhead, and all sorts of trout.

I prefer to smoke salmon with its skin on, but I've done it with skinless pieces and it works fine.

FISH

5 pounds salmon, trout, or char

Birch or maple syrup for basting

BRINE

1 quart cool water

⅓ cup Diamond Crystal kosher salt, about 2 ounces of any kosher salt

1 cup brown sugar

Mix together the brine ingredients until they dissolve and place your fish in a non-reactive container (plastic or glass), cover, and put into the refrigerator. This curing process eliminates some of the moisture from the inside of the fish while at the same time infusing it with salt, which will help preserve the salmon.

You will need to cure your salmon at least 4 hours, even for thin fillets from trout or pink salmon. In my experience, large trout or char, as well as pink, sockeye, and silver salmon need 8 hours. A really thick piece of king salmon might need as much as 24 hours in the brine. Never go more than 36 hours, however, or your fish will be too salty. Double the brine if it's not enough to cover the fish.

Take your fish out of the brine and pat it dry. Set the fillets on your cooling rack, skin-side down. Ideally, you'd do this right under a ceiling fan set on high or outside in a cool, breezy place. By "cool" I mean 60°F or cooler. Let the fish dry for 2 to 4 hours (or up to overnight in the fridge). You want the surface of the fish to develop a shiny, tacky, lacquer-like skin called a pellicle.

This is one step many beginning smokers fail to do, but drying your cured brined fish in a cool, breezy place is vital to properly smoking it. The pellicle seals it and offers a sticky surface for the smoke to adhere to. Don't worry, the salt in the brine will protect your fish from spoilage. Once you have your pellicle, you can refrigerate your fish for a few hours and smoke it later if you'd like.

»

Start by slicking the skin of your fish with some oil, so it won't stick to the smoker rack. Know that even though this is hot smoking, you still don't want high temperatures. Start with a small fire and work your way up as you go. It's important to bring the temperature up gradually or you will get that white albumin "bleed" on the meat (albumin, a protein, is that white, creamy substance that can form on the surface). I can control my heat with my smoker, so I start the process between 140°F and 150°F for up to an hour, then finish at 175°F for a final hour or two.

NOTE A smoker's temperature setting doesn't necessarily correspond precisely to the actual temperature inside the smoker. Smoking is an art, not a science. To keep temperatures mild, always put water in your drip pan to keep the temperature down. If your smoker is very hot, like a Traeger can get, put ice in the tray.

After an hour in the smoker, baste the fish with birch or maple syrup, or honey; do this every hour. This is a good way to brush away any albumin that might form. In most cases, you will get a little. You just don't want a ton of it. Even if you can't control your temperature this precisely, you get the general idea. Your goal should be an internal temperature of about 130°F to 140°F. (Incidentally, yes, I keep the smoke on the whole time. I don't find this to be too much smoke, but if you want a lighter smoke, finish the salmon without smoke or in a 200°F oven.)

You must be careful about your heat. Other than failing to dry your salmon long enough, the single biggest problem in smoking salmon is too high heat. If you see lots of white albumin "bleed," your heat is too high; a little albumin formation is normal. Here's what happens: if you cook a piece of salmon at too high a heat, the muscle fibers in the meat contract so violently that they extrude albumin, which immediately congeals on the surface of the fish. It's ugly, and it also means your salmon will be drier than it could have been. You prevent this with a solidly formed pellicle, and by keeping your heat gentle.

If you let your heat get away from you and you do get a white mess on your salmon, all is not lost. Just flake it out and make salmon salad with it: The mayonnaise in the salad will mask any dryness.

Once your fish is smoked, let it rest on the cooling rack for an hour before you put it in the fridge. Once refrigerated and wrapped in plastic, smoked fish will keep for 10 days. If you vacuum-seal it, the fish will keep for up to 3 weeks. Or freeze your fish for up to a year.

One last piece of advice. Try to fill your smoker with fish. The whole smoking process takes a while, and your smoker doesn't care if its full or half empty, so you might as well make a big batch.

SMOKED OYSTERS OR MUSSELS

PREP TIME: 30 MINUTES | COOK TIME: 90 MINUTES | SERVES 8 AS AN APPETIZER

I'm generally not a fan of canned meats and fish. Very few of them are as good as fresh (olive oil–packed albacore being a notable exception), and many go from wonderful to foul when punished by the rigors of the pressure-canning process. None, in my experience, suffers more than smoked oysters or mussels.

Mussels are delicate little creatures. Oddly shaped, they seem to be conjured from some as-yet-undiscovered Georgia O'Keefe painting. Eaten as soon as they pop their shells, they are wonderful bar food. Messy, briny, usually studded with bits of garlic and greenery, accompanied by lots of beer or wine, a crust of bread to soak up the broth—eating mussels is only slightly less primal than sitting around cracking crabs or peeling crawdads.

Mussel season in California is open from November to April, and I try to make it early in the season, when the mussels are fat. Both California mussels, *Mytilus californianus*, and the non-native blue mussel, *Mytilus edulis*, are all over the coast, waiting to be picked if you have a fishing license. But don't ask me for my spot; I'm not telling. And as a side note, if you live in California, you must call 800-553-4133 before you pick; this hotline lets you know if there are any quarantines. Eating quarantined mussels can kill you, so don't forget that phone call.

You will need to clean your mussels first (page 29). If you're smoking oysters, chances are you bought them, so they will be clean already.

Once your oysters or mussels are ready to rock, steam them open in small batches, removing each one just as it pops open. When they are open, strain the liquid in the pot through a paper towel or cheesecloth and reserve.

Use a small, sharp knife to remove all the meats—with mussels, I try to get the little "scallop" muscle that keeps it in its shell, too—and drop them into the strained broth.

Now you smoke the mussels for a couple hours, then toss them in some really good oil. Voila! A masterpiece. You can just sit there and eat them, or you can make a seafood salad with them, add the smoked mussels to pasta or rice, or set them out as a party appetizer. If you make too many, please don't pressure-can them. I vacuum-seal my extras and freeze them. Thawed, they are almost as good as fresh.

I prefer fruitwoods for this one, but alder or maple are fine, too.

---

4 pounds mussels or oysters

1 cup dry vermouth or white wine

1 cup water

¼ cup high quality olive oil, or other oil such as walnut or hazelnut

Make sure all the mussels or oysters are clean. You can debeard them now or do as I do and cut the beard off after the mussels are steamed. Bring the vermouth and water to a boil and add some shellfish in a single layer. Cover and steam until they're open, which should take between 1 and 3 minutes. Move opened oysters or mussels to a bowl or baking sheet and add more fresh ones until you've steamed open all the mussels.

Strain the cooking liquid through a paper towel or cheesecloth (to remove all the debris) into a bowl. Set aside.

»

Use a small, sharp knife to remove the oysters or mussels from the shells, trying your best to get the little "scallop" muscle that holds the mussel in its shell—it's tasty! Use the knife to cut off the beard if you have not done so already. When it's done, drop each mussel into the strained broth. Make sure all the mussels soak for at least 20 minutes and up to 1 hour in the fridge.

Fire up the smoker. I use apple or cherry wood, and I like the temperature to be around 145°F, or whatever you can manage below 200°F. Keep in mind that mussels are small, so you'll need a pretty fine grate to prevent them from falling through. I use dehydrator grates. Smoke the oysters or mussels for 1 to 2 hours—you don't need a whole lot of time here, just enough to get a smoky flavor without overcooking the mussels. Don't let the smoker get too hot!

When they're done, toss the meats in the oil and eat, or store in a glass jar in the fridge for up to a week. Freeze what you don't eat.

SMOKED SABLEFISH

PREP TIME: 15 MINUTES | COOK TIME: 3 HOURS | MAKES 3 POUNDS

This is your master recipe for smoked fish that uses dry salting. Smoked sablefish, a stalwart of the smoked fish case in Jewish delis all over New York City, is a classic example of this.

Sablefish is incredibly rich. It's as fatty as good salmon but with a more neutral flavor. It has a very fine flake, edible skin, and pin bones that are brutal to remove when the fish is uncooked. Smoked sablefish is like eating silk. It makes you feel wealthy, like you're eating something only royalty has the right to consume. Fortunately, it's not that spendy.

This is as close as I've come to classic Jewish deli-style smoked sable. Basically, it's a dry cure and a light smoke, with the addition of some honey for sweetness and then that paprika that's so distinctive. Fresh or frozen sablefish (black cod) fillets are becoming more and more available. My local Whole Foods carries them frozen, and I've even seen whole black cod sold fresh.

If you can't get sablefish, other fish you might try this recipe on would be bluefish and mackerel, especially Spanish mackerel. The meat will be different, but this method responds well to all oily fish.

1 cup kosher salt

¼ cup sugar

2 tablespoons garlic powder

2 to 3 pounds sablefish fillets, skin on

Honey, for glazing the fish

Sweet paprika, for dusting the fish afterward

Mix the salt, sugar, and garlic powder in a bowl. Pour a layer of the mix into a lidded tub that will hold the fish. I cut the fillets into pieces I imagine I will want to serve, so about two to three per side of a large fish, probably just two pieces per side with a typical fish. Set the fish skin-side down on the salt. Use the remaining salt mix to massage into the meat of the fish. You want it covered with as much salt as the fish can hold. Cover the container and set in the fridge for one hour per pound of fish.

Remove the fish and rinse it briefly under cool water. Pat it dry. Set it back in the fridge, this time uncovered, overnight.

The next day, get your smoker ready. I prefer alder wood for fish, but any mild wood will do. Maple is nice, as is beech or a fruitwood. Smoke the fish at about 165°F for 2 to 3 hours. You want the fish cooked through, but just barely. After the first hour of smoking, paint the fish with honey. Repeat every hour.

When the fish is ready, move it to a cooling rack and paint it with the honey one last time. Let it cool at room temperature for about an hour. When it has cooled, use tweezers to pull out all the pin bones running down the center of the fish. They should slide out easily. Now dust the top of the fish with the paprika. Let this set for about 30 minutes, then put the fish in the fridge. You can serve it now or when chilled. If you want to package it up to store it long-term, wait a day before vacuum-sealing it—this will let the paprika adhere to the fish.

Once made, your smoked fish will keep a week or so in the fridge, and up to six months vacuum-sealed in the freezer.

SMOKED WHOLE FISH

PREP TIME: 20 MINUTES | COOK TIME: 2 HOURS | MAKES 4 FISH

I grew up with whole smoked whitefish—chubs—in Jewish delis. Golden-lustery wrinkled fishes that smelled like a campfire and were amazing eaten straight off the butcher paper they came in, maybe with a little mustard.

But for most of the country, a whole smoked fish usually means a trout, a mackerel, or a mullet. Really any fatty fish generally smaller than eighteen inches works with this recipe. If I had to choose my all-time favorite small fish to smoke, it would be a kokanee, which is a small landlocked sockeye salmon.

To salt or to brine? That's a decision largely based on how many fish you're smoking and what sort of containers you have. If I'm smoking only a few fish, I'll dry-salt them. If I have a mess o'trout, I'll make a salt-sugar brine and soak the fish in that.

How long? For dry-salting, generally about one to two hours. Brine? You can go a lot longer, and it will create a more cured, salty, and firm product the longer you leave it. I like a day-long brine; that is, brine in the morning and remove around dinnertime.

You then need to dry the fish in a cool place. I set them in the fridge in a rack overnight. You need this step to create a tacky, sticky pellicle on the outside of the fish. This helps the smoke adhere to the trout. Skip this step and it won't be as nice.

How to set them up? You can jam a stick through their eyes and hang them that way, you can run a string through the mouth, below the collar and up to your smoking sticks or the rack, or you can just lay them on a rack. Regardless, you'll want to put a little stick in the fish's cavity to prop it open; this allows the smoke to permeate the fish better. I use rosemary twigs, but any twigs will work.

What wood? Something mild. I prefer alder, but maple or fruitwood are good choices, as is oak. But honestly, if you're in love with mesquite or something heavier, go ahead and use it—you won't be smoking your fish very long, anyway.

I like to get a slow ramp-up in temperature for whole smoked fish. I put the fish in cold in a cold smoker set on a low heat. If you want things to move even slower, set a tray of ice in the smoker. You never want the temperature to get beyond 200°F, because at that point, you're barbecuing fish, which is nice but not what we're after here. I like the temperature to be somewhere between 175°F and 200°F. How long to smoke? At least an hour, and to me, ninety minutes to two hours is ideal. I would not go more than four hours with small whole fish. You want decent smoke time, but you don't want trout jerky.

You can eat your smoked trout warm right out of the smoker or chilled. They will keep a little more than a week in the fridge, and they freeze nicely. If you're freezing some, stuff paper towels in the fish's cavity to keep out air, which can cause freezer burn over time.

½ cup kosher salt

½ cup brown sugar

4 whole fish, gutted and gilled

Mix the salt and sugar with a gallon of water and stir to dissolve the salt and sugar. Submerge the trout in this brine and put in the fridge, covered, for at least 2 hours and up to overnight.

Remove the trout from the brine (discard the brine), pat dry with paper towels, and set on a rack over a baking sheet in the fridge for at least a few hours, and up to overnight. You can also set the fish to dry in a cool, breezy place for a few hours.

Put the fish in the smoker, hanging or on the grates, and get a nice cool smoke going. Slowly let the temperature rise to 200°F and hold it between 175°F and 200°F for at least an hour, and up to 4 hours; I prefer 2 hours. If you are having trouble keeping the temperature down, set a tray of ice in the smoker.

When your trout are smoked, you can eat them warm or chilled.

"The fishermen know that the sea is dangerous and the storm terrible, but they have never found these dangers sufficient reason for remaining ashore."

VINCENT VAN GOGH

SALMON JERKY

PREP TIME: 20 MINUTES | **COOK TIME: 5 HOURS** | **SERVES 12**

Salmon jerky is the logical extension of both regular smoked salmon and salmon candy. I do all three in more or less in the same way. Only the cure, cut, and times are different. Let me walk you through it. First, there's my standard smoked salmon recipe (page 292). Then there's salmon candy, which is a half-step toward salmon jerky. Instead of a brine, I salt (and sugar) relatively thick strips of salmon, then smoke them and baste them until they're a bit sturdier than my smoked salmon. This allows them to be carried along on day trips, and they'll keep a long while in cool conditions.

But salmon candy will still go bad at room temperature after a few days. That's where salmon jerky comes in. It's the same basic cure as salmon candy but cured longer, the cuts are thinner, and the smoke time is longer. The most important thing to know about making salmon jerky is to slice it around half an inch thick, from the tail to the head. This is important. If you do cross cuts—from top to bottom of the fish—the jerky will fall apart. I also would not slice thinner than about a quarter inch, or you risk the jerky drying too much and turning brittle.

You'll also notice that I left the skin on. It's perfectly edible, and it helps keep the jerky together. If you don't like it, peel the skin off before you eat it. When done right, the finished product is chewy, a bit salty, and a bit sweet.

I like it a lot as a trail snack or as road-trip food or to eat while catching more salmon. You can play with things a bit, too. The initial amount of sugar in the cure is mostly to remove water from the fish, the same way salt does. Sugar mitigates the harshness of pure salt. But if you can't have sugar at all in your diet, you can replace the sugar with more salt.

If by chance you forget about things and leave the fish in the cure too long, you can dunk them in a bowl of ice water to remove excess cure. In this case, it's better to err on more time in the cure than less, because you're shooting for preservation.

As for the flavoring, I still like my maple or birch syrup baste. But you can go with black pepper pressed into the fish after it cures and before it's smoked, or chile powder or garlic or really whatever makes you happy. Or do a variety.

Wood choice is up to you too, but I recommend alder, maple, or fruitwood.

Let your salmon jerky cool on a rack after it has been smoked until it hits room temperature, then put it in a container in the fridge.

---

1 cup kosher salt

1 cup brown sugar

4 pounds salmon or other fatty fish, cut in strips

½ cup maple syrup, honey, or birch syrup

Mix the salt and sugar together. Sprinkle a thin layer of this over the bottom of a lidded container. Arrange the strips of fish in the container in one layer. Cover with the remaining cure. If you need to do this in more than one layer, heavily dust the first layer with the cure before adding more fish.

Cover the container and let this cure in the fridge for 12 hours. If you can, turn the container upside down once during this time or mix the fish pieces around, so you get a more even cure.

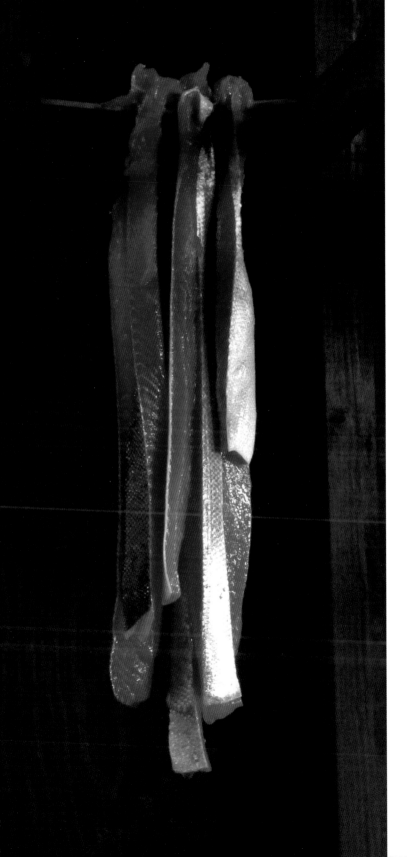

Remove your fish from the cure and quickly dunk it in a large bowl of ice water to rinse off excess cure. Pat the fish dry with paper towels and set on a rack over a baking sheet in the fridge overnight if possible, or in front of a fan or in a cool, shaded, breezy place for at least 1 hour. You want the surface of the fish to get sticky-tacky, which will help smoke adhere to it.

Fire up your smoker. I shoot for an internal temperature of about 200°F. See the headnotes for your wood choices. Smoke your fish for at least 3 hours, and as long as it takes to get dried, but still chewy. It normally takes me 5 hours. If you're using maple syrup, paint it on the fish every 30 minutes or so after 1 hour has elapsed.

Once you have fish jerky, put it back on the cooling rack to return to room temperature. It will keep in cool room temperature—60°F or below—for a long while, but I keep my jerky in small, vacuum-sealed packets in the fridge until I need it. It should last like this for months.

◀ Strips of salmon smoke slowly in Cake, Alaska.

COLD-SMOKED FISH

PREP TIME: 48 HOURS (SEE BELOW) | **COOK TIME: 12 HOURS**

Ah, cold-smoking. This is a hard one. It's the process that gives you those shelf-stable, vacuum-sealed slabs of Scottish or Alaskan salmon you see at holiday time. This is the smoked salmon of Nova; lox is not smoked. Delicate, lightly smoked, a little salty, easy to slice thin. How do they do it?

Cold-smoking, at its core, is salt-curing with an added smoke step. I'll get into salt-curing in a bit, but this will get you started. You salt down a piece of fish until it gets firm, firm enough to slice thin. Many times, you stop there and call it lox or gravlax or whatever. But if you then subject this fish to gentle smoke, often over several days, you'll get a nicer result.

The salt does most of the preservation here, not the smoke, although day after day of gentle smoke does help things.

What do I mean by gentle? Cooler than 80°F, and often much cooler than that. Cold-smoked fish is not cooked.

Achieving all this can be tricky. Salt-curing is pretty easy, as you can do this in your fridge. It's getting smoke that cold that's the issue. Some people have homemade cold smokers, which is ingenious, but for the rest of us, we need to improvise.

Here's what I do. I have an old Bradley smoker, a brand of smoker notorious for not holding a high temperature. In this case, that's a good thing. I will pull it out in our Sacramento winters, on a day below 50°F, and then I'll load the drip pan with ice. This can keep the smoker below the critical 80°F for hours. Doing this before dawn or after dusk helps, and remember that most cold-smoking is done in waves, not constantly. So when something has been cold-smoked say, 10 days, which is a lot, that doesn't mean there was smoke going all 10 days. It means there was smoke on each one of the ten days.

Keep your cold-smoked fish simple. I urge you. It takes time, and it's a wonderful product that you'll want to use in many ways, so loading it up with specific spices or herbs can limit you. Ideally, you've cured in salt and sugar only and then smoked it cleanly with alder or fruitwood. That gives you the maximum flexibility.

But if you must add things, keep them versatile, like black pepper. Many fish like dill or anise flavors, too. Paprika is a nice touch on certain fish, although I don't like it on salmonids.

Once you have your cold-smoked fish, you'll want to slice it as thin as you can with a long, thin knife that is as sharp as lightning. You want a long knife because you can cut most cleanly by slicing with one motion toward you, not by sawing.

It should keep for several weeks tightly wrapped in the fridge, and it can be frozen.

Boneless fillets of salmon or other fatty fish, skin on

Kosher salt

Brown sugar

You'll notice no measurements here. This is because you'll be doing an equalization cure. Weigh your fish in grams. Now weigh out 2.5 percent of that weight in salt, and then 1.5 percent of that weight in brown sugar. Mix the salt and the sugar.

Generously coat the fish in the cure, and if you have a vacuum sealer, vacuum-seal it, tossing in any extra cure. To be clear, if you have multiple fillets, you measure per fillet, so if you have two 1,000-gram fillets of salmon, you measure out 25 grams of salt and 15 grams of sugar, mix them, and coat one fillet with that. Then you repeat the process for the other fillet.

Cover your fish tightly and allow this to cure in the fridge for 48 hours. This will give you a salty, firm product. Slice a thin piece off and taste it; cook it if you want, but I never do. It should be salty, but not unpleasantly so. Remember, you serve cold-smoked fish in thin slices that are cold, both of which mitigate saltiness.

Rinse the fish in cold water then blot dry with paper towels. Allow to sit in the fridge, uncovered, at least 4 hours; overnight is better.

Now smoke your fish. Slick the skin with some oil so it doesn't stick to the grates, then lay the fish in the smoker. You want to smoke below 80°F for as long as you can stand it, at least 6 hours and 12 is better. I've heard of some people going to 24 hours of constant smoke and that is a bit much, but you can try some after 12 hours and keep going if you want.

Allow the fish to cool completely before refrigerating. It will keep for a week or two, tightly wrapped, in the fridge, and can be frozen.

"When I fish, I stop thinking about anything else. But truth be told, if you want to declare victories, I can tell you the fish have won a lot more than I have. It's interesting that something with a brain the size of a fish's can outsmart us humans, who think we are *el supremo*."

NORMAN SCHWARZKOPF

GRAVLAX OR LOX

PREP TIME: 72 HOURS | **MAKES 10 SERVINGS**

Again with the salmon! Sure, salmon is the quintessential fish for all the techniques in this chapter, but I'll reiterate that any fatty fish will work here. This is salt-cured fish for eating, as opposed to salted fish for storing, which is the next recipe.

Gravlax is Scandinavian and usually has lots of seasonings. Lox ("belly lox" is its full name) is Jewish and traditionally has nothing but salt. The technique is elastic. You could absolutely go with chiles, Mexican oregano, tequila, and lime zest on, say, tuna belly or wahoo or king mackerel and make a Mexican "gravlax." Or curry on jack crevalle for an Indian take, or herbes de Provence on mackerel for a French touch. You get the point.

You'll follow what's called an equalization cure for this recipe, only no smoking in this case. You will also want to compress the fish by putting a weight on it. Because of this, most people use blocks of fish, not whole fillets. You put the fish together meat side to meat side, skin out, while you are curing it.

Like cold-smoked salmon, this will be served cold in thin slices. Keep in mind that the weight of the salt and sugar and fish is an exact ratio to follow—so do the math depending on the actual weight of your fish. The other ingredients need not be so precise, but they give you an idea of amounts.

25 grams kosher salt

15 grams brown sugar

2 tablespoons chopped fresh dill

2 tablespoons chopped rosemary, or fresh pine, fir, or spruce needles (optional)

1 tablespoon freshly cracked black pepper

½ teaspoon allspice powder

1,000 grams salmon or other fatty fish, in neat blocks, skin on

1 shot of akavit or vodka

Mix all the dry ingredients together. Match the blocks of fish so you have even pieces that can face each other nicely. Mix the dry ingredients with the blocks of fish, taking care to especially coat the meat sides. Put them all in vacuum bags or one large bag. Before you seal, divide the shot of akavit or vodka between bags. Seal and set in a container in the fridge. Set a brick or other large weight on each bag, compressing the fish. Let this sit there for 3 days, flipping the bags every 12 hours or so.

Remove the fish from the bags. Scrape all the dry ingredients off the skin side and sides of the fish, leaving them on the meat side. Slice thin and serve.

NOTE As I mention above, the ratio of salt and sugar to fish is important, the rest of the ingredients less so. And feel free to play with it to your taste. If you're looking for classic lox, add nothing other than the salt and sugar.

SALT FISH

PREP TIME: 2 DAYS FOR CURING, LONGER FOR DRYING

This one's easy. You're basically salting the hell out of fish for long storage. Unlike everything in the smoking section, in this case, lean fish work best, since their fat will not go rancid over time. Cod, haddock, and pollock are the classics here, but I've salted down pretty much any lean white fish you can imagine, and they all work well. Striped bass is especially good.

The end result is a board-like, hard-as-a-rock slab of fish that will keep until the Second Coming. Great for camping or backcountry trips. This is the baccala famous all over Europe and is the signature ingredient in the Salt Cod Fritters on page 208.

Of course, you must rehydrate your salt fish in several changes of water, keeping the fish cool and changing the water every six to ten hours or so. It normally takes at least thirty-six hours, but really old, heavily salted fish can take two full days.

How to use your salt cod? Other than the fritters, you'll want it in stews and soups or in saucy dishes, of which there are a great many in this book. You can also use it, mashed and flaked, in Salmon Rillettes (page 269) or Smoked Bluefish Pâté (page 270).

Fish

Salt

Again, no measurements here. It's impossible to use too much salt, but a general rule is a cup of kosher salt per pound of fish. You're looking to heavily salt the fish, and you want no pieces touching, so every side of each piece is in contact with salt.

Put the fish and salt in a container and let it sit for 2 days or more. When you're ready to dry it, scrape off excess salt and pat the pieces dry with paper towels. What I do is hang the pieces in a spare fridge by punching a hole in the skin near the tail then tying them to a rack with string. You can put the pieces on a rack, too. Regardless, they will need to be in a cool, dry place for a week at least, and maybe more. The fish isn't ready until it's hard as a board. If you get wet spots during the drying process, add some more salt.

This is a very forgiving process if you don't skimp on the salt. Over months of long storage, you might see some yellowing in the flesh of white-meat fish. This is normal.

I keep mine in the spare fridge, but once it's hard as a board, you can store your fish in warmer places. Even so, I would not store it warmer than about 50°F. Also, they will smell fishy, no doubt about it. So you might want to keep your fish wrapped up or in a container.

How long will your salted fish keep? At least a year, and I've rehydrated three-year-old salted Pacific rockfish that was fine. Rehydrating it took four days, though.

BOTTARGA

PREP TIME: 24 HOURS

Bottarga is a pressed, salted fish roe sac. Sounds gnarly, eh? Admittedly, it can be strong tasting (read: fishy), but the combination of salt and fat—roe is loaded with fat—is wonderful grated fine over pasta or risotto. The Greeks use it in a dip called taramosalata. Bottarga is normally made from the roe of mullet, tuna, or carp, but I prefer using shad roe. Shad are plentiful here in Sacramento, and if you fish for them, you'll end up with more roe than you can handle. Salting a few is a good way not to waste it.

What other fish can you use? Pretty much anything except roe from gar and cabezon, as those are actually poisonous. In general, you want roe sacs with small eggs, so no salmon. That said, you want ripe roe where you can see the eggs. Even overripe roe works, although it takes longer to cure.

It's more or less the same process as making salt fish in the recipe above. You clean the roe well, removing any bloody bits gently but as best as you can (they will be extra fishy later), salt the hell out of them, rinse, dry, and hang.

Roe sacs	Clean your roe sacs well, trying your best to remove the blood lines. Bury them in fine kosher or sea salt for 24 hours in the fridge.
Salt	

Rinse this off, carefully pat the roes dry, then dry them out fully. You can do this in the fridge on a rack for a few days, or you can sometimes hang a pair of roe sacs from a string in the fridge. You can also hang them in a cheesecloth bag. They're ready when hard enough to grate.

Once made, bottarga keeps for a year.

FISH SAUCE

At its core, fish sauce is salty liquid extruded from a mass of ground or chopped fermenting fish. It's not nasty at all, and it's actually quite simple to make.

See, what happens when you get the salt content right is a controlled fermentation that liquifies much of the fish matter into a clear, amber liquid that is as packed with savory umami as soy sauce. It's an essential ingredient in Southeast Asian cuisine and finds its way into West African cuisine, too, as an easy substitute for the various fermented, dried fish used in that part of the world. Under the name garum, fish sauce was a key ingredient in Roman cuisine 2,000 years ago.

Is it fishy? It can be, but long-aged fish sauce, with the right salt content, mellows into something enticing, albeit a bit funky. I typically make mine with bait anchovies we use to fish California halibut in May, let it ferment in my hot garage all summer, and strain it in fall, about four to six months.

Why make your own? First, because you can. Second, you can make good use of scraps of fish or unwanted fish you happen to catch. Third, in my experience, homemade fish sauce is less stinky and more savory than most, but not all, store-bought brands.

What fish to use? Small oily ones are traditional. I use anchovies or small sardines. Mackerel, jacks, and herring are also natural choices. Beyond that, anything goes. If I lived inland, I'd seek out landlocked salmon, trout, gizzard shad, freshwater drum, smelt, and alewives. All are oily enough to be flavorful. That said, my friend Christian has made excellent fish sauce from perch, so it need not be an oily fish.

The process is messy, but easy.

Coarsely chop your fish, or if you're using tiny fish, leave them whole. Put everything in a blender and purée, more or less. Yep, for those of us of a certain age, this is the time to teach the younger generation about the Bass-o-Matic skit from *Saturday Night Live* back in the 1970s. "Mmmm, that's some good bass!" (Google it.)

Find a glass container with a lid, like a Mason or Ball jar, ideally bigger than a quart. After all, this process takes months, so you want to make a year's worth at a time. I use a half-gallon container with a rubber gasket. Weigh this container in grams.

Put the mess into a glass container. You want it to fill the container about halfway. Fill the rest with water, leaving about an inch to two inches of headspace. Weigh the container with the contents, then subtract the weight of the container. This remainder weight will tell you how much salt to add. You want 18 percent by weight of the fish plus water. This matters. A lot. Under-salt the mixture and it will stink worse than pretty much anything. Over-salt it and you won't get the full fermentation you need to ultimately break down any fat that's in the mix.

Mix the salt in well until it dissolves, then wipe the inside of the container so you don't have debris on the rim or edge. Seal the container and put it in a hot, shady place. My garage is perfect. It will hit 120°F on really hot days and will almost always touch 100°F at some point in a summer's day. Does yours need to be this hot? Nope, but you need it hotter than room temperature. Remember, the traditional way to make fish sauce is in ceramic pots outside in Vietnam and Thailand. It gets real hot there.

Ultimately, the solids will settle to the bottom of the container and the liquid will turn a pretty amber. I've never heard of anyone making fish sauce in less than a couple months, so leave it at least three months; four is better. It will keep forever, so err on the side of more time, not less.

When you're ready to decant your sauce, my advice is to very carefully move the container to the kitchen. Have another clean glass container handy. Carefully ladle or spoon off the fish sauce

»

from the top, trying very hard not to disturb the solids, which will have a wispy layer that wants to cloud your pretty sauce. It happens, and it's unavoidable, but you can minimize it.

When you can't go any farther, set a large coffee filter in a strainer over a bowl and pour out the rest into it. Note that cheesecloth isn't good enough.

You need something finer. Now you wait. It can take a day for clear fish sauce to percolate through, but be patient and you'll have clear fish sauce.

Once you've had enough of waiting, toss the solids and bottle your sauce. It will keep at room temperature for years.

SUSHI-STYLE MACKEREL

PREP TIME: 3 HOURS | SERVES 4

There are two "tells" when you try a new sushi restaurant: the tamagoyaki (egg omelet) and the saba, or mackerel. Both are indicators of the chef's skill. If either is subpar, stick with the ramen. In the case of the mackerel, it should be strong but not smelly-fishy. The way they go about this is with a quick cure.

I include this cure in this book because it's very useful for all mackerel's relatives, including the jacks, other mackerels, small tuna, and bonito. The process firms up the fish, removes some strong odors and a little of the oil, and seasons it. In Japan, it was once believed to kill parasites, but this is questionable.

Since you're going to be eating these fish raw, do it at your own risk. Mackerel does not freeze well unless you have a blast freezer, which most people don't. So personally, I roll the dice. You don't have to. Small tuna like skipjack and false albacore and bonito freeze fairly well, at least for the week or so you need to be sure parasites are dead, so this is a safer option. It also works on sardines and herring.

I could have put this recipe in the raw chapter (chapter 17), but since it is technically cured, it's here. But you still eat it as sashimi or on rice as sushi.

---

4 mackerel fillets (or similar fish)

Fine sea salt or kosher salt

Seasoned rice vinegar

Blot away any stray bits of blood on your fish fillets. Generously dust the fillets with the salt. Set them in the fridge for 1 hour, covered.

Remove the fish and rinse gently under cold water, then pat dry with paper towels. Submerge completely in the rice vinegar for 2 hours. Remove and pat dry.

This is as far as I normally go, although I will do my best to remove the pin bones in the fillets at this point; it's easier now than before curing. But if you want the true Japanese experience, you will want to peel the transparent layer of skin off the fish before slicing. Starting at the nape, the part of the fillet that's right behind the head of the fish on the dorsal side, use your fingers to nip up the transparent layer of skin. Once you get it, it will peel off like a sticker. Doing this will give you cleaner slices.

Slice thin and eat with ponzu sauce (page 232) or with shredded daikon radish, maybe some shiso (perilla, or beefsteak) or shungiku (edible chrysanthemum) leaves, or with just wasabi and soy sauce.

BOQUERONES

PREP TIME: 20 MINUTES | SERVES 10

Anchovies are a polarizing ingredient, and here in the United States, the battle lines are typically drawn over their presence or absence atop a pizza. Occasionally, skirmishes will also break out over whether anchovies belong in a Caesar salad; apparently not, at least in its original incarnation.

But these fights are over traditionally cured anchovies, which are a warm, lovely brick color when properly cured. These anchovies come in cans, soaked in olive or soy oil, or are sometimes packaged in little jars, encrusted with salt.

They are, alas, the only sort of anchovies most North Americans ever see. And while they can be good—really good in some cases—a far more delicate delight is the fresh-cured anchovy, known in Spain as boquerones, in Greece as gavros, and often as "white anchovies" here in the United States.

I was an adult when I first encountered boquerones, lined up like little sardines in a tub in the deli section of a glitzy market called Agata & Valentina on the Upper East Side of Manhattan back around 1995. They were labeled "fresh white anchovies," but they sure looked cured. I asked the woman behind the counter if I could taste one. Miraculously, she said yes—there's a tradition in the New York metro area of people "sampling" their way through places like these, essentially eating their lunch for free.

The fish was certainly not fresh. Eating one, I got a big hit of lemon and vinegar, then salt, then garlic, then herbs. The anchovy itself was indeed white, "cooked" like a ceviche, firm and shockingly un-fishy. I mean yeah, you know you're eating a fish, but regular anchovies can be so fishy-salty they're off-putting. Not these. I bought a half pound, and my girlfriend and I ate them in one sitting, on crackers with some white wine.

Since then, I eat them whenever I see them, and I have made boquerones (bo-keh-RONE-es), the name I see most often, at home many times. It is an easy process—if you can get fresh anchovies. There's the rub. Anchovies spoil faster than any other fish I know of. Faster than herring, faster even than sardines. So getting fresh ones is a task and is the biggest impediment to making boquerones at home. I have seen them in fish markets, sometimes at Whole Foods, sometimes at really good local markets, and sometimes at Asian markets. But honestly, the best way to get fresh anchovies is to find a bait shop near the Atlantic or Pacific Ocean. There's one in San Francisco that supplies the fishing fleet in the Bay Area.

If you have to buy anchovies in a market, look at their bellies; sardines, anchovies, and related fish get what's called belly burn rapidly after being caught. The enzymes in their guts start to dissolve the fish itself. This first manifests itself in broken bellies. The fish can still be OK to eat at this point, but they will not have much time left.

To make boquerones, you must clean your anchovies. This is a bit of a pain. You pinch off the head and pull it down and back toward the vent, which should take the innards with it. You then use your fingernail to scrape the cavity and rinse. It will take about forty-five minutes to clean a couple of pounds of anchovies.

Once cleaned, you salt down the anchovies for a few hours, then rinse and soak in lemon juice (Greeks seem to do this most often) or vinegar (the Spanish way). The salt draws out some moisture from the fish and firms them up, while the acid "cooks" the anchovies like a ceviche.

»

To store, you layer them in a lidded container with garlic, chiles, and herbs and cover them with olive oil. Kept in the fridge, they will keep for more than a month.

I have access to fresh anchovies, so I use them. You could, however, try this with sardines or pilchards or sprats or maybe even herring or smelt.

2 pounds anchovies, cleaned

¾ pound kosher salt (roughly)

1 cup red wine vinegar or lemon juice, or sherry or white wine vinegar

½ cup olive oil

6 cloves garlic, minced

3 tablespoons parsley, minced

1 to 5 small hot chiles, thinly sliced (optional)

Keep the cleaned anchovies whole for now. You can pull the two little fillets apart when you're ready to serve your boquerones. Lay down the salt in a wide, lidded, non-reactive container; I use Tupperware. Lay down a layer of anchovies, then sprinkle salt over them. Repeat until you have all the anchovies in the container. Finish with the rest of the salt. Jiggle the container a bit to let things settle, then cover it and put it in the fridge for 3 hours.

Remove the anchovies and rinse them quickly under cold water. Set them in another container like your first one. When they're all nicely rinsed, cover the fish with the vinegar or lemon juice. They need to be fully submerged, so use as much as you need. Cover and refrigerate overnight.

The next morning, remove the anchovies from the vinegar. Toss the vinegar. Now find a final resting place for your anchovies, some lidded container that you can keep in the fridge for a few weeks. Pour a little olive oil into it, then line the container with a layer of anchovies. Sprinkle a little of your seasonings over that layer and repeat until you're done. The anchovies need to be completely covered in olive oil or they'll spoil. You can eat them after a few hours, but they are better after a few days or even weeks. Mine have lasted 6 weeks before getting a little janky.

GLASSBLOWER'S HERRING

PREP TIME: 30 MINUTES | **MAKES 12 SERVINGS**

Herring spoils so fast it's almost always eaten salted, pickled, or smoked. I've eaten (and made) herring in all these forms, but there's something special that makes pickled herring so popular, especially in Northern Europe. I think it's because the acidic twang of the vinegar and lemon counteract the rich fattiness of the herring fillets—these fish are among the foods highest in healthy omega-3 fatty acids. The addition of spices, sugar, and onion add a personal touch.

This particular recipe is for Swedish gläsmastarsill, or glassblower's herring. Why it is called that I have no idea. Best I can tell is because this pickle is always put up in glass jars, with the silvery skin of the herring facing outward. For a pickled little bony fish, this is as pretty as it gets.

Most pickled herring recipes start with pre-salted herring—the kind that come in cans. If you use these, skip the salt in the initial brine and soak the fish in fresh water overnight. They'll still be plenty salty. Having some salt in the fish is important. I once made this recipe with fresh herring that I failed to brine, and they turned to mush within two weeks. A disaster. You need the salt to extract extra moisture from the fish and keep them firm.

I like these just as a snack, with pumpernickel or rye bread, potatoes of any kind, hard-boiled eggs—or just on a cracker.

---

5 cups water, divided

¼ cup kosher salt

1 pound herring fillets

2 cups distilled or
  white wine vinegar

¼ cup sugar

1 teaspoon mustard seed

2 teaspoons whole allspice

2 teaspoons black peppercorns

3 bay leaves

3 cloves

1 lemon, thinly sliced

1 medium red onion, thinly sliced

Fill a pot with 4 cups of water, add the salt, and heat the water just enough to completely dissolve the salt. Let this brine cool to room temperature. When it does, submerge the herring fillets in the brine and refrigerate overnight, or up to 24 hours. Meanwhile, bring the vinegar, sugar, the remaining cup of water, and all the spices to a boil. Simmer 5 minutes, then turn off the heat and let this steep until cool.

When the herring have brined, layer them in a glass jar with the sliced lemon and red onion. Divide the spices between your containers if you are using more than one. Pour over the cooled pickling liquid and seal the jars. Wait at least a day before eating. Store in the fridge for up to 1 month.

PICKLED PIKE

PREP TIME: 30 MINUTES | **COOK TIME: 5 MINUTES** | **SERVES 10**

Every so often, I have the good fortune to fly up to Canada in search of lake trout, rainbow trout, and northern pike. And while I admire the beauty and grace of the trout and its cousins as much as anyone, pike get my blood racing. Trout are a symphony, or perhaps John Coltrane. Northern pike are more like GWAR or Megadeath. Aggressive, arrogant, utterly indifferent to your catching and releasing them, slough sharks are insanely fun to catch.

Pickled pike was the first way I ever ate this awesome fish, back in Minnesota two decades ago. Pickling is perfect for smaller fish—you just fillet them like any other fish, skin them, and cut the meat into bite-sized pieces, right through the bones. The beauty of pickled pike is that the vinegar softens the bones so much you don't even notice them. (This won't work on a pike much larger than about six pounds, which is about twenty-eight inches.)

Pickled pike is basically a Scandinavian/Eastern European version of ceviche. Really, really good on crackers as a snack or as an appetizer. I like it with beer—kolsch, pilsner, or a pale ale are my favorites here—but I hear the Swedes wash their pickled pike down with akavit. *Skål!*

Northern pike is traditional for this Scandinavian-style pickle, but you can use any firm white fish. If it's a fish you can eat raw, like albacore or mahi mahi, you don't need to freeze the fish first. All other fish—including pike—you need to freeze before you can make this. This will kill any potential parasites in the meat; freshwater fish like pike can carry tapeworms, which you absolutely do not want, even if they are a great weight-loss strategy.

5 cups water, divided

1 cup kosher salt

1 pound pike, cut into ½-inch
 pieces

2 cups cider or white wine vinegar

⅓ cup sugar

1 teaspoon mustard seed

2 teaspoons whole allspice

2 teaspoons black peppercorns

2 leaves bay

Peel of 1 lemon, sliced and white
 pith removed

1 medium red onion, thinly sliced

Fill a pot with 4 cups of water, add the salt, and heat the water just enough to completely dissolve the salt. Let this brine cool to at least room temperature, preferably colder. When it's cold enough, submerge the pike pieces in the brine and refrigerate overnight. Meanwhile, bring the cider, sugar, the remaining cup of water, and all the spices to a boil. Simmer 5 minutes, then turn off the heat and let this steep until cool.

When the pike has brined, layer it in a glass jar with the sliced lemon peel, bay leaves, and red onion. Pour over the cooled pickling liquid with all the spice and seal the jars. Wait at least a day before eating; I find it best after about a week to 10 days.

Stored in the coldest part of your fridge, your pickled fish will keep for a solid month or even 6 weeks. Your nose will be your guide when it turns. Trust me.

LOWCOUNTRY PICKLED SHRIMP

PREP TIME: 25 MINUTES | **COOK TIME: 5 MINUTES** | **MAKES 3 PINTS**

Pickled shrimp is a common southern appetizer, especially in Lowcountry, and various versions of it exist from Texas through the Gulf, around Florida up into South Carolina, where it is a Charleston classic. My version is a bit like Mexican escabeche, with pickled onions and jalapeños, but it isn't so spicy that you can't eat lots of it.

This recipe is best made with medium shrimp. It's a nibble, an appetizer, something to eat at a cocktail party or with crackers or on a salad. It excels as a salad topping, where the pickling liquid, which includes some olive oil, becomes the salad dressing.

If you don't love every ingredient in my recipe, you can change things to suit yourself. Onions are traditional, as is mustard seed and bay leaf. Peppers of some sort make an appearance a lot—I use jalapeños, but bell peppers are probably more common.

Unlike a ceviche, pickled shrimp are actually cooked before pickling. Some cooks just toss a bunch of bay leaves in the salty boiling water, but I prefer either some Old Bay seasoning or Zatarain's crab boil. It adds one more layer of flavor. Be sure to add a little bit of the cooking liquid into your pickle, maybe a couple tablespoons.

How long will your pickled shrimp last? A good while in the fridge. I'd say at least two weeks. But this is not intended as a true preservation pickle, so I'd eat them all up within a month.

10 ounces pearl onions

2 tablespoons Old Bay seasoning

1 pound shrimp, peeled

3 jalapeño peppers, sliced

2 tablespoons capers, with a little
    of their brine

1 teaspoon dried thyme

1 teaspoon mustard seeds

7 ounces lemon juice

¼ cup olive oil

Distilled vinegar (see below)

Bring a couple of quarts of water to a boil and boil the pearl onions for 3 minutes. Remove the onions but keep the water. Rinse the onions under cold water so you can handle them, then slice off the root end. Use your fingers to pop out a cleaned onion, leaving the peel in your hand. Compost the peels. Set the onions aside.

Add the Old Bay to the onion water and bring it back to a boil. Add the peeled shrimp and turn off the heat. Pull the shrimp out after a couple minutes, when they are just cooked through.

Divide the onions, sliced jalapeños, and shrimp between three pint jars. Mix together the capers, a little of their brine, the thyme, mustard seeds, lemon juice, and olive oil. Pour this evenly into the jars. Add a few spoonfulls of the cooking water.

The shrimp need to be completely submerged, so top up with some vinegar if you need to. Hand-seal the jars and keep in the refrigerator. They can be eaten 24 hours after they're made.

HOMEMADE CAVIAR

PREP TIME: 15 MINUTES | **MAKES 1 PINT**

Caviar has always had a hold on me. It's a mysterious ingredient, almost otherworldly; the individual eggs look like jewels from an alien planet. Caviar tastes briny and vaguely floral, and the textural surprise of the pop in your mouth has led more than one writer to liken it to Pop Rocks for adults.

I've eaten all sorts of caviar, from spendy osetra sturgeon caviar to our own California white sturgeon eggs, to Paddlefish roe to salmon roe ikura, to the wonderful little eggs from flying fish (tobiko), capelin, and whitefish, which is a golden yellow. I've also eaten caviar from trout and char. Steelhead roe is a particular favorite, as is king salmon roe.

I'd read about a general method of making caviar in a book called *The Philosopher Fish*, by Richard Carey, that involves gently removing the eggs from the skein—the membrane holding them together—rinsing them, salting them, and drying them. It seemed pretty easy, which alarmed me. How could something so mysterious be so easy to create? It didn't seem fair. I delved into some more research, and it is indeed that easy. The art comes in the details. How do you get the eggs out of the skein? How much salt? How long to brine or rub the eggs? What temperature do you store them at?

Homemade caviar keeps for two weeks in the fridge, but I think it gets fishy after about a week. You can eke out an extra day or two by keeping your freshly made caviar in a container surrounded by ice in the fridge, replenishing the ice as it melts.

I prefer my caviar straight, served in a special spoon, so you can linger over the qualities of this caviar versus that one; this is what the Russians do when they serve the three classic sturgeon caviars: beluga, sevruga, and osetra. I'm particularly fond of osetra, which is close to our caviar made from California white sturgeon.

The tobiko and masago you see in sushi restaurants is caviar from the flying fish and the capelin, a kind of herring. It really is like Pop Rocks. Whitefish caviar is even better and is a beautiful canary color. Lumpfish is like a larger sturgeon caviar, but trout and salmon caviar is its own thing: large, luxurious, and slightly fatty—I saw thousands of minute fat droplets floating on the top of the brine when I made it.

When combined with a larger dish, caviar can become an accent that makes a good dish great.

½ cup kosher salt

1 full skein of steelhead, trout, or
   salmon roe

Mix the salt and 1 quart ice-cold water until the salt is all dissolved.

Make sure the roe skeins are split, so you have an opening that the eggs can come out. Set up a cooling rack or something else with a wide mesh (chicken wire works, too) over a bowl. Take a roe skein and, with the membrane facing up, work the eggs out through the rack. Perfectly ripe eggs will come off easily, unripe ones will require some force. Either way, you will pop some eggs in the process.

ALTERNATE METHOD Get the faucet running with warm water (105°F to 115°F) or heat cool tap water to this temperature—some people fear that hot tap water can add harsh minerals to their food. Either way works. Fill a metal or glass bowl with the warm water. Dunk a few skeins of roe at a time in the warm water. Gently massage the eggs out of the skeins with your fingers under the surface of the warm water. They will float away and sink. Discard the skeins.

Have a fine-meshed sieve ready. Pour the strained eggs into the strainer to rinse them well with cold water. Pick out clumps or stray bits of membrane.

Dunk the eggs in the brine for 5 minutes. Taste them, and if they are salty enough for you, drain them again. You can brine for up to 30 minutes, but they will be very salty. My preferred brine time is 10 minutes. Spoon carefully into a clean glass jar and refrigerate.

CRISPY FISH SKIN CHICHARRONES

If you've ever heard of pork rinds, known in Mexican cuisine as chicharrones, you *know*. I mean, really. Crispy, light as air, dusted with salt and whatever other flavors you have in mind. Vaguely porky and oddly non-greasy. Properly made, they are so addictive they really ought to be illegal. You can do the same thing with fish skin. And it's every bit as good. Same as pork chicharrones, but with an oh-so-slight briny thing going on. You know it's fish, but it is in no way fishy in a bad way.

I'd heard of fish chicharrones before but never really quite knew how to make them. Then, years ago, I cooked in a big Sacramento food festival called Have an Offal Day—yes, we all cooked nasty bits—and at this event, Sacramento's greatest sushi chef, Billy Ngo, made sturgeon skin chicharrones; there are a lot of sturgeon farms around our area, so we use sturgeon a lot here. Billy told me how to make the chicharrones, and I was immediately obsessed.

It soon occurred to me that sturgeon has a thick, largely scaleless skin, and besides, not many people have access to it. So I began working on other fish skins to see if it would work. It does. Oh yes, folks. It does. I am happy to report that I've now made chicharrones from the skins of sturgeon, small sharks, walleyes, Pacific rockfish, white bass, amberjack, tripletail, red snapper, and salmon. Having done this, I'm pretty sure you can make chicharrones from any skin you can slice off a fillet, meaning that only the ultra-thin skin like that on a mackerel might not work.

Let me walk you through the process. Start by scaling your fish if they have scales; sturgeon, eels, and sharks don't, so you're good to go there. Scale when the fish is whole, by the way. It's a pain to scale fish once you've filleted them.

Slice the skin from the meat off the fillet. You'll notice that you still have some meat and fat attached to the skin. That needs to go. You also need to tenderize the skins of thick-skinned fish like sturgeon, sharks, salmon, and triggerfish. You do this by boiling in salty water; the salt helps season the skins.

Here's what I've found with certain skins:

▶ Sturgeon and leopard shark should be boiled for about five minutes.

▶ Salmon I'd boil for one or two minutes, but you can scrape the skin even without cooking.

▶ Most bass-like fish—walleyes, rockfish, bass, and perch—you will only need to boil for a minute or two. They're tender already.

Now you need to carefully remove all the meat and fat from the skins. Gently lift the skins out of the boiling water and lay them meat-side up on a cutting board. Now, using a butter knife, carefully lift and remove all the meat and fat. This is fairly tricky, and if you have oven-mitt hands, you'll tear the skin. Take your time until you get the hang of it.

Once you have all the meat removed, you need to dry the skins. I do this in a dehydrator at 120°F until the skin dries, which isn't too long—about two to four hours depending on the species of fish.

ODDITIES AND FUN STUFF

I've also greased a baking sheet and laid the skins down (meat-side up) and dried them in an oven set to 170°F. You will need to flip the skins at least once if you do this option. When the skins are dried you can save them in the freezer indefinitely.

Frying is easy. Heat about one inch of high smoke point oil—I prefer rice bran or grapeseed oil, but canola or other vegetable oil works, too—to between 350°F and 360°F. Get your seasonings nearby, as you will have only seconds to season before the skins' surface dries. Salt is a must, but I've used Cajun seasoning, smoked paprika, and even lemon pepper.

Drop a couple of skins into the hot oil and watch the magic; they'll puff up immediately in an amazing and miraculous way. They'll be ready in less than a minute. Watch for the sizzling to die down dramatically. Move them to paper towels with a slotted spoon and season immediately. Once fried, they'll stay crispy for a few hours, depending on the humidity.

All I can say if you are on the fence about fish skin chicharrones is try them. You will never look at the skin on fish in the same way again. Trust me.

NAVIGATING A FISH HEAD

I'm talking to anglers here, but I do see fish noggins for sale in better markets. My advice: use them when you have them. They're a treasure.

At the very least, use them to make fish stock. They're so rich in collagen that your stock will gel up in the fridge, and when hot, they will give your broth a silky body you will remember. Next level up is to make fish-head soups or curries, and while they are normally eaten whole in Asia—picking meat from a fish head is far easier with chopsticks than a fork—I prefer to make a broth with the head and then pick off all the meat.

For the most part, all fishes' heads possess the same structure. First are the cheeks, so sought after that even otherwise head-averse anglers will keep them. Anatomically, they are where you think they'd be, and they require a small, sharp knife to remove them if you don't cook them with the head. Cheeks are generally the only part of a head eaten separately from the rest, although cod throats are a thing.

OK, you're staring at a cooked fish head. Now what?

Slip out the cheeks first. Above the cheeks is another pocket of meat behind the eye. Get that, too. Now pull off the lower jar. Tucked behind the jaws will be two flat muscles, easy to slip out of the grooves they live in. Behind the head will be lots of meat where the spine meets the skull. Pull this off in the direction the tail once was and you will leave most or all of the bones on the spine. You'll then notice two parallel pockets of meat jammed into the skull next to where you pulled off the neck meat. You might need to stick a chopstick or toothpick to get at them. Now, under the top jaw will be two rectangular blocks of meat, not terribly big, but very tasty.

That's mostly it for the head itself, but if you have the pelvic fins, which are usually attached to a head after you've filleted off the sides, you have a series of muscles at their base that look very much like the "oyster" in a turkey; this is where a bird's thigh meets the body. These are arguably the best bits of meat on the whole fish. There are generally about five different muscles there, but you may not notice this unless you are dealing with a fish over fifteen pounds.

Is it worth it? You bet. It's fun to scare your squeamish friends by picking through a fish head, and from an eater's perspective, the meat you get is far superior to fillets. It's denser, silkier, and fattier than the side meat, and it's why you hear stories about Americans freaking out when traveling to fish-centric countries: they've been offered the head as an honor, but they had no idea what they were missing. Now you do.

FISH TERRINE

PREP TIME: 45 MINUTES | **SERVES 6**

Normally, I will use collars and heads and skeletons to make broth or some variation on the debris soup on page 173. But sometimes, I'll be inspired to use them to make this terrine. I'd known about fish and seafood terrines for decades—they're an element in classical French cuisine—but I finally decided to start making them after reading the excellent book *The Whole Fish Cookbook* by Josh Niland. This terrine is inspired by his.

The key is to start with broth you made a day or so ago, as it is what you cook the heads in. Fish heads have the collagen you need to set the terrine. Fish heads also have all sorts of delectable meaty bits on them (see the sidebar on page 323) So in a way, this would be fish head cheese. But since that sounds revolting, I'll continue to call it a fish terrine.

Now, a terrine needs to be in a terrine pan. I happen to have one, but you can make this recipe without one. You do need a bread loaf pan, big ramekins, or even just quite a lot of plastic wrap—rolling the terrine up like a log in plastic wrap makes a nifty round terrine.

Niland's terrine is pretty basic, with white fish, standard herbs, and a little mustard. It's good. But you can play with things quite a lot here. I like to add an alternative protein, like salmon or some other fish with a different color. Bits of smoked salmon are nice, or little shrimp, or crabmeat, or small, shucked clams or mussels.

This is a place to personalize your version depending on the cuisine you cook. Scandinavian? Lovage or angelica, thyme, and a horseradishy mustard. Italian? Basil, oregano, maybe diced peeled San Marzano tomatoes. Vietnamese? Rau ram or cilantro, garlic chives, and be sure to add star anise, ginger, and lemongrass to the broth. Mexican? Mexican oregano, cilantro, roasted green chiles. See how you can play with things?

---

5 quarts or more fish stock

6 pounds fish heads

½ cup chives, minced

½ cup parsley, minced

¼ cup dill, minced

½ cup shallots, minced

¼ cup small capers

½ cup pickles, minced
   (I like spicy dills)

2 teaspoons prepared mustard

Salt and black pepper

Pour off about 2 cups of the broth and simmer it down by a little more than half. If you want to get specific, go from 500 ml to 200 ml.

Bring the rest of the stock to a boil, drop in as many heads as will fit, turn off the heat, cover the pot, and let this steep for 15 minutes. Fish out the heads and pick off all the meat as soon as they're cool enough to handle; you want to do this while they're still warm. Repeat with the remaining heads if you have to do this in batches.

When you have all the meat picked off the heads, break up the big pieces, which will be hard to slice through later. Mix all the other ingredients, including the cooked-down stock, in with the meat and pack this into a terrine pan or bread loaf pan that is lined with plastic wrap. Really pack it tight. Cover and refrigerate overnight before turning it out to slice and serve with pickles and mustard.

ALTERNATE METHOD You can lay out several large sheets of plastic wrap and position the mixture on it like a log. Roll it up, leaving long ends on it like a candy wrapper, and roll this tightly into a log shape. If you can, tie the ends to each other. If you can't, tie them off tightly or use twist ties to do so. Then set in the refrigerator overnight before serving.

FRIED FISH SKELETONS

PREP TIME: 10 MINUTES | **COOK TIME: 20 MINUTES** | **SERVES 6**

This is exactly what you think it is. Little skeletons, dusted in some sort of starch or flour, fried crispy enough that you can eat them without fear. Hard-frying small fish bones renders them edible and crispy. Most people have encountered this with grilled fish tails; the ends of a fish tail, fried or grilled hard and crispy, tastes more or less like a potato chip. Skeletons are similar.

Which skeleton you use matters a lot. I generally fry skeletons only from fish smaller than about eighteen inches, but some species, like Pacific pomfret, will fry up nicely even when they're larger. Bass-like fish tend not to be great; they have heavy bones that aren't easily rendered safe to eat. That said, very small bass-like fish—bluegills or teeny largemouth bass or smallish yellow perch—all will work. The ideal skeletons are from mackerel. Small trout and kokanee are fantastic, too. These fish have softer bones that break down more easily, and so you will be able to eat more of it.

The best way to make these is with raw skeletons that you've just cut fillets off of. Oh, and I don't keep the heads on, because they are so much rounder than the bones that they throw off the frying process.

Why bother? Because not only do you get to make use of a part of a fish that you'd normally throw out, but you get a big calcium boost in the bargain. And of course—and most importantly—it tastes wonderful, like a meaty, crispy potato chip.

Skeletons from 6 smallish trout
  or mackerel
Salt and brown sugar
Oil for frying
Cornstarch or flour (any kind)

Sprinkle the skeletons with salt and brown sugar. Let them sit for 20 minutes before proceeding.

Get your oil hot, about 350°F, in a large pan. You will want enough to fully fry the skeletons without turning, about ½ inch deep.

Dust your skeletons in cornstarch or whatever sort of flour you plan on using. Shake off the excess and fry until crispy. You will want to err on frying them a little longer than you might think. You want the bones to break down under the hot oil. You can turn them if you want, but you definitely want them to be at least mostly submerged while frying.

Once they're crispy, lay the fried skeletons out on paper towels to drain, then serve with a dipping sauce.

FISH SAUSAGE

PREP TIME: 90 MINUTES | COOK TIME: 10 MINUTES | SERVES 6

Over the decades, I've played with the concept of fish sausage many times. I find that they primarily fall into two categories: a mousse stuffed into a casing, or a combination of finely ground fish with hand-cut fish. This recipe is the latter. The mousse-style sausages are OK, but other than a salmon "hot dog" I made once, they've all underwhelmed me.

This sausage has a lot more going on. It has good texture, and it grills or fries up well. A word on the casings. You want casings as thin as you can get them, and while thin hog casings work, sheep casings are better. The issue is that the sausage itself is delicate, so biting into a link made with a hefty hog casing will mar the experience; you need to put so much pressure on the casing when you bite it that the filling spooges out. This doesn't happen with sheep casings.

Another factor in making fish sausage is that you must work colder than you would with pork. Fish fat is far less saturated than pork fat, and to properly emulsify it, you need to whip it when it's practically frozen. A good hack is to add a little crushed ice when you whip it.

You'll notice precise measurements here. Precision matters. If you want to make decent sausage of any kind, you need a scale. There are no two ways about it.

Sheep casings

45 grams unsalted butter,
    about 3 tablespoons

325 grams minced white or
    yellow onion, about 3 cups

500 grams diced fatty fish, like
    salmon or tuna belly or trout

500 grams lean white fish,
    cut into ¼-inch cubes

21 grams salt, about 2 tablespoons

4 grams white pepper, about
    1 teaspoon

4 grams ground anise seed or
    fennel seed, about 1 teaspoon

6 grams whole anise or fennel
    seed, about 2 teaspoons

4 tablespoons chopped chives

4 tablespoons chopped parsley
    or lovage

Soak the sheep casings in warm water to rehydrate.

Heat the butter in a pan over medium heat and sauté the minced onion until soft and translucent, but without browning it, about 8 minutes. Turn off the heat and let this cool, then refrigerate the onions. You want them cold before proceeding.

Put the salmon or other fatty fish into a food processor, along with a handful of crushed ice. Process into a fluffy purée, about 1 minute or so. Move this to a large bowl.

Add all the remaining ingredients, along with the cooled onions and any butter you can scrape from the bowl, and mix well with your (very clean) hands until it all comes together in one big ball. This should take about 90 seconds to 2 minutes of kneading and mixing.

Put this mixture into a sausage stuffer and thread the sheep casings onto the funnel. Fill the casings, erring on a little looser than tighter, as sheep casings are fragile. If you break one, move the fish mixture away from the break so you can tie it off, then continue with a new coil. It happens.

When you have the mixture all stuffed, you'll want to pinch off links. I like links in sheep casings about four to five inches long. To do this, you can tie them off with string or pinch down with your fingers to make two links—the end link and the one between your fingers. Spin the link between your fingers away from you to tighten the link. You

may see air pockets forming underneath the casing; we'll deal with them in a bit. Now move down the coil and pinch off another two links. This time you spin the link toward you. Repeat this process, away from you, then toward you, all the way down the coils.

When you're done, gently compress the fish mixture in a link at the end, then tie off that link. Do the same on the other end. Now get a needle or a sausage pricker and set the point in a burner until it glows; you are sterilizing it. Use this to prick every air pocket you can find in the links. When you get them all from a link, rotate it in the direction it was made (toward or away from you) to compress the meat into the link and seal up any air pockets.

Put your links in the fridge, uncovered, for up to a day. This tightens them and allows the links to bloom a bit. They'll keep for a few days in the fridge and freeze well. I generally grill or pan-fry them and serve with a seasonal salad.

BASQUE COD PIL PIL

PREP TIME: 10 MINUTES | **COOK TIME: 15 MINUTES** | **SERVES 4**

It sounds exotic, and while it is from Basque Country, the only thing mystical about Cod al pil pil (sounds like "al PEEL-PEEL") is how the sauce comes together in the pan. Normally done with reconstituted salt cod or bacalao (page 305), this dish is one of those simple masterpieces: fish, olive oil, lots of garlic, a few chiles, maybe some parsley or dried oregano. Why serve fish this way? It's rich, garlicky, and slightly spicy from the chile, although some people omit the chile. And it comes together very quickly. You can use any white fish to do this. I used cod throats or collars because I happen to like them.

If you're using salt cod, you need to freshen it up for twenty-four to forty-eight hours before you make this recipe. You do that by soaking the block of salted fish in cold water, changing the water every eight hours or thereabouts. It's just as good with fresh fish, though.

Serve this with potatoes or rice or crusty bread. You want something to sop up that sauce with.

A word on the sauce. It's an emulsion of olive oil, garlic, and the juices from the fish that, when taken all the way, actually makes a bright yellow mayonnaise-looking thing. We took our pictures before I stirred the pot a bit more to get that consistency, which is traditional in Spain. I personally like it a bit thinner, as you see in the photo.

One other tip: I used the codfish collars because they have a lot of collagen in them, which helps emulsify the sauce. Cooks in Basque Country will often leave the skin on their salt cod for the same reason. Then, you can choose to eat it or leave it on the plate when dinner is ready.

---

2 pounds cod or other white fish, skin on if possible

Salt

1 cup olive oil

6 to 8 cloves garlic, thinly sliced

1 to 3 small hot, dried chiles, crushed (optional)

1 teaspoon dried oregano or parsley, or 1 tablespoon chopped fresh parsley

Salt the fish well and set aside for 10 to 20 minutes. Heat the olive oil over medium heat in a large, wide pan that can hold all the pieces of fish.

Sauté the garlic slices for a minute or two, until they just start turning golden. Remove them as best you can. It's OK if a few escape you.

Put the fish, skin-side down, in the pan and cook gently over medium-low heat for a minute or two. Turn the fish and cook for another 2 to 4 minutes, or until the fish is mostly cooked. Turn the heat off and remove the fish for now.

Start swirling the pan. You want to gently agitate the olive oil and juices from the fish into an emulsion. This should take about 5 minutes and no more than 10 minutes. One way to help this along is to whisk it with a strainer. As the emulsion comes together, add back the garlic along with the crushed chiles, if using. It will eventually look like a salad dressing, and if you keep stirring it while the whole thing cools, it will set up into a mayonnaise-like sauce. It's up to you if you want it this way.

When you're ready, pour the sauce over the fish, sprinkle on some dried herbs, and serve.

ACKNOWLEDGMENTS

I've been fishing since the 1970s and cooking fish since the 1980s. And on almost every trip, every time I heat up a pan or fire up the grill, I learn something. I learn from experience, yes, but also from those around me—deckhands, friends, random strangers fishing next to me on boats, fellow chefs, and talented cooks in practically every country, state, and province I've been to. It is impossible to name all those who helped me create this book that you hold right now. They are a multitude.

I am thrilled that your support over the years as readers of Hunter Angler Gardener Cook (*honest-food.net*), my other books, and my social media feeds has allowed me to make this book a family affair, much as my previous two have been. My partner in adventures, Holly A. Heyser, has, as usual, taken all the prettiest photos in this book. My sister Laura designed it, and my brother-in-law Richard served as master editor. The folks at Versa Press in Illinois and Publishers Shipping and Storage in Michigan have been steady and true partners and have allowed this book to be 100 percent American made. That matters to me.

A few folks I do want to call out by name. First, to Lloyd Ballou, who came up with the title: told ya I'd put you in the book! Second, to Tyson Fick of the *F/V Heather Anne*: thanks for giving this old salty dog another crack on deck. Thanks go to Jay and Silent Kevin on the *Right Hook*, to R. J. on the *Sundance*, and to everyone on the *Sea Wolf* and *Laura Lee* and *Norma K III*; to Chris Niskanen, who taught me to love freshwater fish; and to Joe Baya, who has shown me—and I hope will continue to show me—the glories of the Gulf.

Finally, thanks to all the readers of this book. May your lines be tight and your oil hot!

INDEX

*Page references in **bold** indicate recipe photographs.*

A

Aguachile, 284, **285**
Aioli, Saffron, **209**, 210
Anchovies
    Boquerones, 310–12, **311**
Avocados
    Aguachile, 284, **285**
    California Christmas Crab Salad, 262, **263**
    Poke, 280, **281**

B

Bacon
    Baja Grilled Clams, 236, **237**
    Cornmeal-Crusted Speckled Trout, 126, **127**
    Fish and Grits, 252–53
    Lowcountry Perloo, **247**, 247–48
Baja Grilled Clams, 236, **237**
Baking and pan-roasting
    Deviled Crab, **84**, 85
    English Fisherman's Pie, 78–79
    Shrimp Mac and Cheese, 80, **81**
    Snapper Veracruz, 76, **77**
    Stuffed Clams, 82–83, **83**
    tips and tricks, 74–75
Barbecued Fish, 228, **229**
Basque Cod Pil Pil, 328, **329**
Basting brush, 291
Beans. *See also* Black-eyed peas
    Pan de Cazon, 266–68, **267**
    Simple Spanish Fish Soup, 174, **175**
Beer-Battered Fish, 113–15, **114**
Bisque, Crawfish, 184–86, **185**
Black Bean Lobster Stir-Fry, 110, **111**
Black-eyed peas
    Cornmeal-Crusted Speckled Trout, 126, **127**
    Gulf Fish Stew, 187–88
Bloodlines, removing, 48
Bluefish
    flavor pairings, 67
    Smoked, Pâté, 270–71, **271**

Bonito flakes
    Japanese Dashi, 172
Boquerones, 310–12, **311**
Bottarga, 306, **306**
Bowfin, skinning and filleting, 51–52
Brining, 289–90
Broiling
    Broiled Trout, 73, **73**
    tips and tricks, 71–72
Butter
    Butter-Poached Fish, 90, **91**
    Butter-poached seafood, tips and tricks, 92
    Ethiopian Spiced, 90

C

Cajun Seasoning, 230
Cakes
    Clam, 212, **213**
    Crab, 203
    Fish, with Wild Rice, 206, **207**
California Christmas Crab Salad, 262, **263**
Capers
    Crudo, 282, **283**
    Halibut Puttanesca, 98, **99**
    Salmon Piccata, 100–101, **101**
    Snapper Veracruz, 76, **77**
Carrots
    Fish or Seafood Escabeche, 272–73, **273**
    Vietnamese Smoked Fish Salad, 260, **261**
Catfish
    Courtbouillon, 136–38, **137**
    skinning and filleting, 51
    Vietnamese Claypot, 194, **195**
Catfish pliers, 40
Caviar
    Bottarga, 306, **306**
    Homemade, 318–19, **319**
Ceviche, 278, **279**
Cheese
    Baja Grilled Clams, 236, **237**
    English Fisherman's Pie, 78–79
    Fish and Grits, 252–53

    Shrimp Mac and, 80, **81**
    Tacos Gobernador, 164–65, **165**
Chicharrones, Crispy Fish Skin, 321–22, **322**
Chiles
    Aguachile, 284, **285**
    Basque Cod Pil Pil, 328, **329**
    Chinese Steamed Fish with, 145
    Chinese Sweet and Sour Fish, 106–8, **107**
    Conch Fritters, 211, **211**
    Crab Curry, 196, **197**
    Kung Pao Shrimp, 109
    Seafood Tamales, 150–51
    Simple Sautéed Shrimp, 96, **96**
    Tacos Gobernador, 164–65, **165**
    Thai Fish Curry, **198**, 198–99
    Warm Crab Salad, 105
Chinese Salt and Pepper Fish, **117**, 117–18
Chinese Steamed Fish with Chiles, 145
Chinese Sweet and Sour Fish, 106–8, **107**
Chowder
    Clam, Maine, 178, **179**
    compared to soups, 176
    Perch, Lake Erie, 180, **181**
    Salmon, 182–83
Cilantro
    Aguachile, 284, **285**
    Vietnamese Crispy Fish with, 104
    Vietnamese Smoked Fish Salad, 260, **261**
Clam(s)
    Baja Grilled, 236, **237**
    buying, 22–23
    Cakes, 212, **213**
    and Chorizo, Spanish, **148**, 148–49
    Chowder, Maine, 178, **179**
    Dumplings, 254, **255**
    flavor pairings, 66
    Fried, New England Style, 128–29, **129**
    home-canning, 61
    keeping alive, 29

Clam(s), *continued*
    purging sand from, 29–31
    Sauce, White, Classic Linguine
        and, 240
    shucking, 56–57
    steaming times, 144
    Stuffed, 82–83, **83**
Cocktail Sauce, 276
Cod
    Pil Pil, Basque, 328, **329**
    Salt, Fritters, 208–10, **209**
Cold-Smoked Fish, 302–3
Conch Fritters, 211, **211**
Corn
    Ceviche, 278, **279**
    Gulf Fish Stew, 187–88
    Salmon Chowder, 182–83
Cornmeal-Crusted Speckled Trout,
    126, **127**
Courtbouillon, Catfish, 136–38, **137**
Crab(s)
    Cakes, 203
    cleaning, 56
    Curry, 196, **197**
    Deviled, **84**, 85
    flavor pairings, 66–67
    Fried Rice with Pineapple, 246
    home-canning, 61
    keeping alive, 29
    raw, parasites in, 18
    Rolls, 156, **157**
    Salad, California Christmas,
        262, **263**
    Salad, Warm, 105
    Sauce, Spaghetti with, 241–43,
        242
    steaming times, 144
Crawfish (crayfish)
    Bisque, 184–86, **185**
    buying, 23
    keeping alive, 29
    Pies, 158–59
    raw, parasites in, 18
    steaming times, 144
Crayfish. *See* Crawfish
Crudo, 282, **283**
Cucumbers
    Aguachile, 284, **285**
    Butter-Poached Fish, 90, **91**
Curing and pickling
    Boquerones, 310–12, **311**
    Bottarga, 306, **306**

Fish Sauce, 307–8, **308**
    Glassblower's Herring, 313
    Gravlax or Lox, 304
    Homemade Caviar, 318–19, **319**
    Lowcountry Pickled Shrimp,
        316, **317**
    Pickled Pike, 314, **315**
    Salt Fish, 305
    Sushi-Style Mackerel, 309
Curries
    Crab, 196, **197**
    Thai Fish, **198**, 198–99
Cutting board, 40

D

Dashi, Japanese, 172
Deviled Crab, **84**, 85
Dry-salting, 289
Dumplings
    Clam, 254, **255**
    Pike Quenelles, **217**, 217–18

E

East African Fish Stew, **192**, 192–93
Eels, skinning and filleting, 51
Eggs
    Crab Fried Rice with Pineapple,
        246
English Fisherman's Pie, 78–79
Equipment, 39–40, 291
Escabeche, Fish or Seafood, 272–
    73, **273**
Ethiopian Spiced Butter, 90

F

Fennel
    Fennel-Watercress Salad, 204, **205**
    Sicilian Tuna Meatballs, 214
    Spaghetti with Crab Sauce,
        241–43, **242**
Fillet knives, 39
Fish (general information). *See also*
    Fish (recipes); *specific fish types*
    allergies to, 18
    American-caught, 15
    American farmed, 15
    baking and pan-roasting, about,
        74–75
    bleeding, 26–28
    bloodlines, 48
    breading, 119
    broiling, about, 71–72

butterflying (kiting), 53–55
    buying, 21–23
    catching your own, 15
    categories and characteristics,
        36–38
    fillets, buying, 22
    flavor pairings, 65–66
    food safety considerations,
        17–19, 275
    freestyling recipes, 68–69
    freezing, 32–33
    fresh-caught, field care for,
        23–33
    freshwater, types of, 36
    frying, about, 113
    grilling, about, 220–21
    gutting, 41–42
    handling, 28–29
    heads, removing meat from, 323
    heads and fins, for soup, 173
    health benefits, 14
    home-canning, 60–61
    hot smoking, about, 289–91
    how to fillet, 42–52
    killing, 26, 27
    live, buying, 22
    poaching, about, 87
    pressure-bleeding, 27–28
    raw, preparing and serving,
        275–76
    rigor mortis, 28–29
    saltwater, types of, 35–36
    scaling, 40–41
    searing and sautéing, about,
        94–95
    skin, removing, 48
    small, cleaning, 42
    smoking, best varieties for, 290
    steaks, cutting, 227
    steaming, about, 141–44
    stinky smell on, 31
    stir-frying, about, 106
    storing, 31–32
    sustainability of, 14–15
    thawing, 33
    vacuum-sealed, 22
    whole, buying, 22
    whole, serving, 75
Fish (recipes). *See also specific*
    fish types
    Barbecued, 228, **229**
    Beer-Battered, 113–15, **114**

Butter-Poached, 90, **91**
Cakes with Wild Rice, 206, **207**
Ceviche, 278, **279**
Chinese Salt and Pepper,
    117, 117–18
Chinese Steamed, with Chiles,
    145
Chinese Sweet and Sour,
    106–8, **107**
Cold-Smoked Fish, 302–3
Collars, Grilled, 232, **233**
Crudo, 282, **283**
Curry, Thai, **198**, 198–99
English Fisherman's Pie, 78–79
and Grits, 252–53
on the Half Shell, 230
Hmong Crispy, 132–33, **133**
Honeyed, with Ouzo, 97
Meatballs, German, **215**, 215–16
Mexican Fried, 124, **125**
My Tunafish Sandwich,
    257–59, **258**
Risotto, 249–51, **250**
Salt, 305
Sandwich, A Simple, 153–54, **155**
Sauce, 307–8, **308**
Sausage, 326–27, **327**
Seafood Escabeche, 272–73, **273**
Seafood Gumbo, 189–91, **190**
Skeletons, Fried, 325
Skin Chicharrones, Crispy,
    321–22, **322**
Smoked, Salad, Vietnamese, 260,
    261
Soup, Simple Spanish, 174, **175**
Stew, East African, **192**, 192–93
Stew, Gulf, 187–88
Stock, **169**, 169–70
"Tamales," or Mextlapiques,
    146–47, **147**
Terrine, 324
Vietnamese Crispy, with
    Cilantro, 104
Whole, Grilled, 222–24, **223**
Whole, Smoked, 298–99
Fish roe
    Bottarga, 306, **306**
    Homemade Caviar, 318–19, **319**
Fish scaler, 40
Fish Skeletons
    Fried, 325
    uses for, 44

Fish spatula, 39
Flounder, Fried, 119–21, **120**
Food safety considerations,
    17–19, 275
Fried, then sauced recipes
    Catfish Courtbouillon, 136–38,
        137
    Shark with Pine Nuts and
        Tomatoes, 139
Fritters
    Conch, 211, **211**
    Salt Cod, 208–10, **209**
Frying
    Beer-Battered Fish, 113–15, **114**
    Chinese Salt and Pepper Fish,
        117, 117–18
    Cornmeal-Crusted Speckled
        Trout, 126, **127**
    Fried Clams, New England Style,
        128–29, **129**
    Fried Flounder, 119–21, **120**
    Fried Smelt or Whitebait, 130
    Hmong Crispy Fish, 132–33, **133**
    Japanese Tempura, 116
    Mexican Fried Fish, 124, **125**
    Pan-Fried Trout with Peas, 131,
        131
    Snapper Bites, 122–23, **123**
    Thai Fried Pomfret, 134, **135**
    tips and tricks, 113

G
Gaper clams, cleaning, 58–60
Garfish, skinning and filleting, 51
Garlic
    Basque Cod Pil Pil, 328, **329**
    Boquerones, 310–12, **311**
    Saffron Aioli, **209**, 210
    Simple Sautéed Shrimp, 96, **96**
Geoducks, cleaning, 58–60
German Fish Meatballs, **215**,
    215–16
Glassblower's Herring, 313
Grapefruit
    Ceviche, 278, **279**
Gravlax or Lox, 304
Grilling
    Baja Grilled Clams, 236, **237**
    Barbecued Fish, 228, **229**
    Fish on the Half Shell, 230
    Grilled Fish Collars, 232, **233**
    Grilled Fish Steaks, 225–27, **226**

Grilled Lobster Tails, 234, **235**
Grilled Octopus, 231
Grilled Whole Fish, 222–24, **223**
tips and tricks, 220–21
Grits
    buying, 239
    Fish and, 252–53
Grundens overalls, 40
Gulf Fish Stew, 187–88
Gumbo, Seafood, 189–91, **190**

H
Halibut Puttanesca, 98, **99**
Herbs. *See also specific herbs*
    Fish Terrine, 324
    German Fish Meatballs, **215**,
        215–16
    Grilled Octopus, 231
Herring
    flavor pairings, 67
    Glassblower's, 313
Hmong Crispy Fish, 132–33, **133**
Honeyed Fish with Ouzo, 97
Horseradish
    Cocktail Sauce, 276
    Cream, 203
    Salmon Tartare, **286**, 287
Hot smoking
    overview of, 289–91
    Salmon Jerky, 300–301
    Smoked Oysters or Mussels,
        295–96, **296**
    Smoked Sablefish, 297
    Smoked Salmon, 292–94, **293**
    Smoked Whole Fish, 298–99

I
Ice, for fresh-caught fish, 24
Ikejime, 27

J
Japanese Dashi, 172
Japanese Tempura, 116
Jerky, Salmon, 300–301

K
Kitchen shears, 39
Knife sharpener, 39
Knives, 39
Kombu
    Japanese Dashi, 172

L

Lake Erie Perch Chowder, 180, **181**
Lime
  Ceviche, 278, **279**
Lobster
  Black Bean, Stir-Fry, 110, **111**
  cleaning, 56
  flavor pairings, 67
  keeping alive, 29
  steaming times, 144
  Tacos, 161–63, **162**
  Tails, Grilled, 234, **235**
Long spatula, 39
Lowcountry Perloo, **247**, 247–48
Lowcountry Pickled Shrimp, 316,
  317
Lox or Gravlax, 304

M

Macadamia nuts
  Poke, 280, **281**
Mackerel
  flavor pairings, 67
  Sushi-Style, 309
Mahi mahi, skinning and
  filleting, 52
Maine Clam Chowder, 178, **179**
Meatballs
  German Fish, **215**, 215–16
  Sicilian Tuna, 214
Mercury toxicity, 18–19
Mexican Fried Fish, 124, **125**
Mextlapiques, or "Fish Tamales,"
  146–47, **147**
Mignonette, 276
Miso
  Salmon Head Soup, 200, **201**
Monkfish, skinning and filleting,
  52
Mullet, skinning and filleting, 52
Mushrooms
  Fish and Grits, 252–53
  Pike Quenelles, **217**, 217–18
Mussels
  buying, 22–23
  home-canning, 61
  prepping, 57
  Smoked, 295–96, **296**
  steaming times, 144

N

New Orleans BBQ Shrimp, **102**,
  102–3

New Orleans Remoulade, 123, **123**
Noodles
  Salmon Head Soup, 200, **201**

O

Octopus
  cleaning, 56
  Grilled, 231
  Spanish, with Paprika (Pulpo a la
    Gallega), 264, **265**
Olives
  Halibut Puttanesca, 98, **99**
  Sicilian Salad, **226**, 227
  Snapper Veracruz, 76, **77**
Ouzo
  Honeyed Fish with, 97
  Sicilian Tuna Meatballs, 214
  Spaghetti with Crab Sauce,
    241–43, **242**
Oysters
  buying, 22–23
  Fish or Seafood Escabeche,
    272–73, **273**
  home-canning, 61
  shucking, 56–57
  Smoked, 295–96, **296**
  steaming times, 144

P

Pan de Cazon, 266–68, **267**
Pan-roasting. See Baking and
  pan-roasting
Paprika, Spanish Octopus with
  (Pulpo a la Gallega), 264, **265**
Parasites, 17–18, 275
Pasta
  Classic Linguine and White
    Clam Sauce, 240
  for recipes, 239
  Shrimp Mac and Cheese, 80, **81**
  Smoked Salmon, 244, **245**
  Spaghetti with Crab Sauce,
    241–43, **242**
Pâté, Smoked Bluefish, 270–71, **271**
Patties, Salmon, 204, **205**
Peanuts
  Kung Pao Shrimp, 109
  Vietnamese Smoked Fish Salad,
    260, **261**
Peas. See also Black-eyed peas
  Pan-Fried Trout with, 131, **131**
  Thai Fish Curry, **198**, 198–99
Pellicle, 290

Pepper and Salt Fish, Chinese, **117**,
  117–18
Peppers. See also Chiles
  Catfish Courtbouillon, 136–38, **137**
  East African Fish Stew, **192**,
    192–93
  Sicilian Salad, **226**, 227
  Warm Crab Salad, 105
Perch Chowder, Lake Erie, 180, **181**
Perloo, Lowcountry, **247**, 247–48
Persimmon
  California Christmas Crab Salad,
    262, **263**
Pies
  Crawfish, 158–59
  English Fisherman's, 78–79
  Samosas, 160
Pike
  Pickled, 314, **315**
  Quenelles, **217**, 217–18
Pil Pil, Basque Cod, 328, **329**
Pin-bone pliers, 39–40
Pineapple, Crab Fried Rice with,
  246
Pine Nuts and Tomatoes, Shark
  with, 139
Plastic containers, 291
Pliers, 39–40
Poaching
  Butter-Poached Fish, 90, **91**
  Sake-Poached Sablefish, 88, **89**
  tips and tricks, 87, 92
Poke, 280, **281**
Pollution, 19
Pomfret, Thai Fried, 134, **135**
Pork. See also Bacon; Sausages
  Clam Dumplings, 254, **255**
Potatoes
  East African Fish Stew, **192**, 192–93
  English Fisherman's Pie, 78–79
  Lake Erie Perch Chowder, 180,
    181
  Maine Clam Chowder, 178, **179**
  Salmon Chowder, 182–83
  Salt Cod Fritters, 208–10, **209**
Pufferfish, skinning and filleting,
  52
Pulpo a la Gallega (Spanish
  Octopus with Paprika), 264,
  265

Q

Quenelles, Pike, **217**, 217–18

R

Racks. *See* Skeletons
Ray, skinning and filleting, 52
Remoulade, New Orleans, 123,
    123
Rice
    Crab Fried, with Pineapple, 246
    Fish Risotto, 249–51, **250**
    Lowcountry Perloo, **247**, 247–48
    for recipes, 239
    Wild, Fish Cakes with, 206, **207**
Rillettes, Salmon, 269
Risotto, Fish, 249–51, **250**
Rockfish, how to fillet, 42–44
Roe
    Bottarga, 306, **306**
    Homemade Caviar, 318–19, **319**

S

Sablefish
    Sake-Poached, 88, **89**
    Smoked, 297
Saffron Aioli, **209**, 210
Sake-Poached Sablefish, 88, **89**
Salads
    Crab, California Christmas, 262,
        263
    Fennel-Watercress, 204, **205**
    Pulpo a la Gallega (Spanish
        Octopus with Paprika), 264,
        265
    Sicilian, **226**, 227
    Smoked Fish, Vietnamese, 260,
        261
    Warm Crab, 105
Salmon
    Chowder, 182–83
    Cold-Smoked Fish, 302–3
    flavor pairings, 67
    Gravlax or Lox, 304
    Head Soup, 200, **201**
    Jerky, 300–301
    Patties, 204, **205**
    Piccata, 100–101, **101**
    Rillettes, 269
    skin, making crispy chips with,
        286, 287
    Smoked, 292–94, **293**
    Smoked, Pasta, 244, **245**
    Tartare, **286**, 287
Salt
    for brining and salting, 289–90
    Fish, 305

and Pepper Fish, Chinese, **117**,
    117–18
    for smoking fish, 291
Salt Cod Fritters, 208–10, **209**
Samosas, 160
Sandwiches
    Crab Rolls, 156, **157**
    Fish, A Simple, 153–54, **155**
    My Tunafish, 257–59, **258**
Sashimi, note about, 276
Sauces
    Cocktail, 276
    Fish, 307–8, **308**
    Mignonette, 276
    New Orleans Remoulade, 123,
        123
    Saffron Aioli, **209**, 210
    Tartar, **120**, 121
Sausage, Fish, 326–27, **327**
Sausages
    Gulf Fish Stew, 187–88
    Lake Erie Perch Chowder, 180,
        181
    Spanish Clams and Chorizo, **148**,
        148–49
Scallops, buying, 23
Seafood. *See* Fish; Shellfish; *specific*
    seafood types
Searing and sautéing. *See also* Stir-
    frying
    Halibut Puttanesca, 98, **99**
    Honeyed Fish with Ouzo, 97
    New Orleans BBQ Shrimp, **102**,
        102–3
    Salmon Piccata, 100–101, **101**
    Simple Sautéed Shrimp, 96, **96**
    tips and tricks, 94–95
    Vietnamese Crispy Fish with
        Cilantro, 104
    Warm Crab Salad, 105
Seasoning, Cajun, 230
Shad, flavor pairings, 67
Shark
    Pan de Cazon, 266–68, **267**
    with Pine Nuts and Tomatoes,
        139
Shellfish. *See also specific shellfish*
    types
    allergies to, 18
    American-caught, buying, 15
    American farmed, about, 15
    baking and pan-roasting, about,
        74–75

breading, 119
broiling, about, 71–72
buying, notes about, 22–23
buying from the store, 21–23
English Fisherman's Pie, 78–79
flavor pairings, 65–66
food safety considerations,
    17–19, 275
freestyling recipes, 68–69
freezing, 32
frying, about, 113
grilling, about, 220–21
health benefits, 14
home-canning, 61
hot smoking, about, 289–91
keeping alive, 29
poaching, about, 87, 92
poisoning from, 19
Seafood Stock, 171
searing and sautéing, about,
    94–95
steaming, about, 141–44
stir-frying, about, 106
sustainability of, 14–15
vacuum-sealed, 22
Shrimp
    buying, 23
    East African Fish Stew, **192**, 192–93
    flavor pairings, 67
    Japanese Tempura, 116
    Kung Pao, 109
    Lowcountry Perloo, **247**, 247–48
    Lowcountry Pickled, 316, **317**
    Mac and Cheese, 80, **81**
    New Orleans BBQ, **102**, 102–3
    raw, parasites in, 18
    Samosas, 160
    Seafood Gumbo, 189–91, **190**
    Seafood Tamales, 150–51
    shelling and deveining, 55–56
    Simple Sautéed, 96, **96**
    steaming times, 144
    Tacos Gobernador, 164–65, **165**
Sicilian Salad, **226**, 227
Sicilian Tuna Meatballs, 214
Skate, skinning and filleting, 52
Skeletons, Fish
    Fried, 325
    uses for, 44
Smelt, Fried, 130
Smokers, 291
Smoking. *See also* Hot smoking
    Cold-Smoked Fish, 302–3

Snails
    keeping alive, 29
    small, prepping, 57–58
Snapper
    Bites, 122–23, **123**
    Veracruz, 76, **77**
Soups. *See also* Chowder
    Crawfish Bisque, 184–86, **185**
    Fish, Simple Spanish, 174, **175**
    Salmon Head, 200, **201**
    tips and tricks, 173
    Spanish Clams and Chorizo, **148**,
        148–49
    Spanish Fish Soup, Simple, 174, **175**
    Spanish Octopus with Paprika
        (Pulpo a la Gallega), 264, **265**
Spatulas, 39
Squash
    Butter-Poached Fish, 90, **91**
Squid, cleaning, 56
Steaming
    Chinese Steamed Fish with
        Chiles, 145
    Mextlapiques, or "Fish Tamales,"
        146–47, **147**
    Seafood Tamales, 150–51
    Spanish Clams and Chorizo, **148**,
        148–49
    tips and tricks, 141–44
Stews
    Crab Curry, 196, **197**
    Fish, East African, **192**, 192–93
    Fish, Gulf, 187–88
    Seafood Gumbo, 189–91, **190**
    Thai Fish Curry, **198**, 198–99
    Vietnamese Claypot Catfish,
        194, **195**
Stir-frying
    Black Bean Lobster Stir-Fry, 110,
        111
    Chinese Sweet and Sour Fish,
        106–8, **107**
    Kung Pao Shrimp, 109
    tips and tricks, 106
Stocks
    Fish, **169**, 169–70
    Japanese Dashi, 172
    Seafood, 171
    storing and freezing, 168
    thawing, 168
    tips and tricks, 167–68
Stuffed Clams, 82–83, **83**

Sushi, note about, 276
Sushi-Style Mackerel, 309
Sweeteners, for smoking fish, 291

T
Tacos
    Gobernador, 164–65, **165**
    Lobster, 161–63, **162**
Tamales, Seafood, 150–51
"Tamales, Fish," or Mextlapiques,
    146–47, **147**
Tartare
    preparing, 286
    Salmon, **286**, 287
Tartar Sauce, **120**, 121
Tempura, Japanese, 116
Terrine, Fish, 324
Thai Fish Curry, **198**, 198–99
Thai Fried Pomfret, 134, **135**
Thermometer, 40
Tomato(es)
    Catfish Courtbouillon, 136–38,
        137
    Ceviche, 278, **279**
    Crawfish Bisque, 184–86, **185**
    East African Fish Stew, **192**,
        192–93
    Fish and Grits, 252–53
    Gulf Fish Stew, 187–88
    Halibut Puttanesca, 98, **99**
    Lobster Tacos, 161–63, **162**
    Lowcountry Perloo, **247**, 247–48
    Mextlapiques, or "Fish Tamales,"
        146–47, **147**
    Pan de Cazon, 266–68, **267**
    and Pine Nuts, Shark with, 139
    Sicilian Salad, **226**, 227
    Sicilian Tuna Meatballs, 214
    Simple Spanish Fish Soup, 174,
        175
    Snapper Veracruz, 76, **77**
    Spaghetti with Crab Sauce,
        241–43, **242**
    Tacos Gobernador, 164–65, **165**
    Vietnamese Smoked Fish Salad,
        260, **261**
Tortillas
    Lobster Tacos, 161–63, **162**
    Pan de Cazon, 266–68, **267**
    Tacos Gobernador, 164–65, **165**
Trout
    Broiled, 73, **73**

    flavor pairings, 67
    Pan-Fried, with Peas, 131, **131**
    Speckled, Cornmeal-Crusted,
        126, **127**
Tuna
    flavor pairings, 67–68
    Grilled Fish Steaks, 225–27, **226**
    Meatballs, Sicilian, 214
    Poke, 280, **281**
    Sandwich, My, 257–59, **258**
    skinning and filleting, 52

V
Vietnamese Claypot Catfish, 194,
    195
Vietnamese Crispy Fish with
    Cilantro, 104
Vinegar
    Boquerones, 310–12, **311**
    Fish or Seafood Escabeche,
        272–73, **273**
    Glassblower's Herring, 313
    Mignonette, 276
    Pickled Pike, 314, **315**
    Sushi-Style Mackerel, 309

W
Watercress-Fennel Salad, 204, **205**
Whitebait, Fried, 130
Wild Rice, Fish Cakes with, 206,
    207
Wire racks, 291
Wood, for smoking fish, 290, 291

Y
Yellowtail
    Aguachile, 284, **285**
    Grilled Fish Collars, 232, **233**